3-19-63 (62-182/6)

17-11-63

MINERVA SERIES OF STUDENTS HANDBOOKS

NO. 7

General Editor
BRIAN CHAPMAN

British Foreign Policy

In the same series

British Foreign Policy

THE PROCESS OF READJUSTMENT
1945–1961

BY

F. S. NORTHEDGE

FREDERICK A. PRAEGER, *Publisher*

New York

BOOKS THAT MATTER

Published in the United States of America in 1962
by Frederick A. Praeger, Inc., Publisher
64 University Place, New York 3, N.Y.

Library of Congress Catalog Card Number: 62–18270

PRINTED IN GREAT BRITAIN

PREFACE

The aim of this book is to provide an account of British foreign policy from the end of the Second World War until the opening of negotiations in October 1961 on the conditions of Britain's entry into the European Economic Community. There is a certain completeness about these sixteen years in that they mark the transition of the country from membership of the inner circle of Powers which shaped the world at the end of the war to what may become the status of an essentially European community. If Britain enters the movement towards integration in western Europe, this period may be the last in which she could be described as having an independent foreign policy. The emphasis in this book is on this process of change and readjustment. For this reason, and also in order to keep the account within reasonable limits of space, certain aspects of British external affairs are treated only incidentally. For example, defence policy and the British role in the United Nations Organization are dealt with in this way and colonial and Commonwealth affairs are discussed only in their bearing on foreign policy.

Any account of international policy written so shortly after the events with which it deals must to some extent lack historical perspective and the advantage of access to official papers. The former drawback, however, is partially offset by the better appreciation of the mental climate of the times which is available to the contemporary writer. It is also doubtful whether the traditional methods of diplomatic history, with their heavy reliance upon archival material, are as relevant to the twentieth century as they were, for instance, to the nineteenth. Most of the centrally important facts with which the British Government had to deal in the years covered in this book are sufficiently accessible in published sources for the student to understand the general considerations which led to the decisions taken. The method adopted here is therefore that of describing the successive external situations confronting the Government and the significant factors which they were bound to take into account. The sources used are accordingly as far as possible official documents and statements by Government critics, rather than second-hand accounts.

At the same time it is not pretended that foreign policy decisions by British Governments in the postwar period have always been rational. Where errors of judgment appear to the writer to have been committed, on the evidence at present available, he has not hesitated to say so. In each case, however, reference has been made to the

21071

existing external situation, the prevailing political and economic climate within the country and other such elements which may help to explain such misjudgments. The proper understanding of foreign policy demands compassion. But it also requires the appreciation of conditions and forces at work outside the Cabinet room which are often by no means what the responsible authorities would wish. Especially is this true for a country which, like Britain, has had to accommodate itself within the brief space of sixteen years to the momentous changes described in this book.

December 1961.

CONTENTS

CONTENTS

MAPS

CHAPTER ONE

The Postwar Setting

The dominant feature of Britain's position when first Nazi Germany and then Japan surrendered unconditionally in 1945 was her reduced status in the world scale of power. Of all the belligerents, Germany included, Britain was the only one who fought from beginning to end. The war itself, however, had in its course been transformed from a European into a world conflict. At its close it was two extra-European Powers, the United States and the Soviet Union, continental in extent, gigantic in population and resources, which sealed the Allied victory and then confronted each other as the chief states of the day. After the fall of western Europe in May 1940 Britain had been Hitler's sole active opponent; but after the entry of the United States into the conflict in December 1941, she increasingly yielded precedence to that country as the foremost spokesman of the West. That fact was at once a condition of British foreign policy in the postwar years and the source of some of its main problems.

This decline in British power was aggravated by the Second World War, but it had begun some sixty or seventy years before. Once the German Empire had been founded by Bismarck in 1871, it was no longer open to Britain to act as a mediator in European politics, though it was many years before this was recognized. For a short period the role of fulcrum in the European balance passed to Bismarck himself, as at the Berlin Congress in 1878, but almost immediately after the Chancellor's dismissal in 1890 there followed the swift formation of the two European camps which fought the First World War. After 1918 many British diplomats believed it was possible to resume a balancing role between France and Germany; this was to some extent confirmed by the Locarno agreements signed on October 16, 1925, by which Britain guaranteed the Franco-German frontier. But with the remilitarization of Germany under Hitler and the German reoccupation of the Rhineland on March 7, 1936, it became clear, not only that a mediating role between France and Germany was out of the question for Britain, but that Britain and France together were no match for Germany without the assistance of Russia. The refusal of the two Western Powers to pay

Russia her price for this assistance in terms of military access into eastern Europe, coupled with British and French unpreparedness for war in 1939, persuaded Stalin to join Hitler in the partitioning of Poland in the Nazi-Soviet Pact of August 23, 1939. The collapse of France in 1940 left Britain no alternative, should war break out between Germany and Russia, but to accept Stalin's terms for eastern Europe, unless the United States entered the war and imposed on Russia conditions more consistent with Western ideas. The United States did enter the war but was unwilling to try to force Stalin to disgorge his gains.

The reduction in British power which the closing stages of the war revealed was part of the general decline of Europe in world affairs. As late as the 1930s Europe was still the hub of diplomacy. At the Munich conference in September 1938 the four Powers, Britain, France, Germany and Italy, decided the frontiers of a central European state, Czechoslovakia, which was the gateway to Eastern Europe, without thinking it necessary to consult Russia. But Munich was the last purely European congress. Europe, which up to 1939 had been a centre of decisions with extra-European consequences, became, from the fall of Hitler Germany, an area which felt the effects of decisions reached outside it. This change in the status of Europe, like that in the status of Britain, had origins preceding the Second World War by many years. In 1902 Britain for the first time contracted an alliance with a non-European Power, Japan, for the purpose of dealing with a rival in Europe, Russia. When she wound up that alliance in 1921 she did so under pressure from another non-European Power, the United States. The retirement of the United States from European diplomacy in 1920, after having helped the Entente to re-establish the balance of power in Europe, did not mean her retirement from European affairs. The economic recovery of Europe in the 1920s was largely under the impulse of American funds; similarly, the Great Depression of 1931–33, which set the menacing political tone of the 1930s, was touched off by a collapse of the American stock market and the withdrawal of American money from Europe. When the war ended in 1945 it was therefore clear that Western Europe was almost wholly dependent upon the United States for military security and economic recovery. For the time being Europe had become a pensioner of the United States, and Britain with it.

The tendency of the war to transcend Europe was further underlined by the way in which the struggle against Hitler Germany was increasingly merged with the struggle against Japan in the Far East.

On September 18, 1931, the first great challenge to the League system came with the Japanese attack on Manchuria. But East Asia was then still so remote that this event was never regarded in European capitals as opening the road to the Second World War. By the time the Sino-Japanese War proper began in July 1937 Britain and France were fully occupied with problems presented by revisionist Germany and Italy. Russia herself entered into a Pact of Neutrality with Japan on April 13, 1941, in order to have her hands free to deal with Germany should she turn eastwards. The war of 1939 therefore had its real origins in Hitler's challenge to a European settlement, the Treaty of Versailles. After Hitler's invasion of Russia in June 1941 a moment came when it looked as if Germany and Japan might join hands over a devastated Soviet Union and a Middle East from which all Anglo-American forces had been expelled. That danger was averted by the halting of German forces at Stalingrad and the victory of El Alamain in November 1942. But the defeat of Hitler Germany still left the formidable problem of Japan; this task, though the British made their contribution in south-east Asia, was mainly an American responsibility after war in Europe had ended. General Marshall, the American Chief of Staff, estimated that an assault on the Japanese home islands would cost at least half a million American lives. The ending of the Japanese war, before the power of the atomic bomb was known, therefore required Soviet assistance and the price for this was British and American acquiescence in Stalin's policy for eastern Europe, Manchuria and the North-west Pacific. In the agreement reached between President Roosevelt and Marshal Stalin settling this price Britain, now primarily a European Power, was virtually a spectator.

But the immediate cause of the decline of Europe as a factor in world politics was the total collapse of Germany in 1945, occurring against a background of physical devastation and political chaos in almost every part of Europe. The Nazi destruction of every element of free political life in Germany left the Allies no alternative but to assume sovereignty over the country themselves when German military power was broken; this brought Russian power to the Elbe and made the security of western Europe entirely dependent upon the United States presence in Germany west of the Elbe. Whatever the criticism of the unconditional surrender policy decided by President Roosevelt and Winston Churchill at the Casablanca conference in January 1943, the Nazis destroyed every coherent political force with which negotiations could be held. In Churchill's words, a headless Germany had fallen into the hands of the conquerors. Both he and his Cabinet colleagues had misgivings about the unconditional surrender policy, as encouraging resistance in Germany and leaving a power vacuum in the heart of Europe. But the view of the United States was that the basis of peace in the postwar world must be great Power co-operation, and this implied disarming Soviet suspicions of an Anglo-American separate peace with Germany. Churchill fell back, in the last months of Nazi Germany, on the proposal that Anglo-American forces should strike at Trieste and through to Vienna in order to prevent the spread of Soviet influence in south-east Europe.[1] Again, after the crossing of the Rhine he advised that British and American forces should race as far ahead as possible, so as to hamper Soviet entrance into the German power vacuum and secure pledges for Stalin's fulfilment of the obligations in eastern Europe which he had assumed at the Yalta conference.[2] But this was of no avail; such proposals would have reduced American forces for the assault against Japan and, in American eyes, would have given still further grounds for Soviet suspicions. Once the division of Germany between East and West had been stabilized, however, it became all the more necessary to build up the strength of western Europe lest it fall, like the Soviet occupied zone of Germany, under Communist control.

The qualifications of western Europe in 1945 for playing any further role in world affairs were highly discouraging. Over extensive areas there was unrelieved chaos. Transport had in many places come to a standstill; farm products were hoarded in the countryside through mistrust of unstable currencies; raw material stocks for industry had run down; shortages of food and clothing kept workers at home. The sheer problem of dealing with refugees and displaced persons caused organized life to hang by a thread. In August 1945, Field-Marshal Montgomery was reporting to the new British Foreign Secretary, Ernest Bevin: 'so far nearly 1,100,000 displaced persons have been evacuated from the British zone. Over 300,000 were west-bound. Over 600,000 Russians have been transported from our zone to the east and the movement of 200,000 to the south has begun. One and a quarter million displaced persons are still housed in camps in our zone and perhaps another 500,000 are still at large.'[3] Italy was convalescing from a war which had passed like a scythe from one end of the peninsula to the other. France was under the unpredictable regime of General de Gaulle, who seemed more con-

[1] Winston S. Churchill, *The Second World War*, Vol. VI, *Triumph and Tragedy*, London, 1954, p. 133.
[2] Churchill, *op. cit.*, p. 407.   [3] 413 H.C. Deb. 5s. Col. 285. (August 20th).

cerned to restore her ancient glories than to set the country on its feet. It was doubtful whether western Europe was viable at all with the impermeable line now shutting it off from middle and east Europe. The only conclusion for Britain was that everything must be done to rouse western Europe from its shock and depression if the shape of the postwar world was not to be wholly determined in Moscow or Washington. Primarily that implied the restoration of France. Churchill told the House of Commons in September 1944: 'I have repeatedly stated that it is the aim, policy and interest of His Majesty's Government, of this country of Great Britain, and of the Commonwealth and Empire to see erected once more, at the earliest moment, a strong, independent and friendly France.'[1] Thus, despite bitter conflicts with de Gaulle over the independence of Syria and Lebanon, Britain was the chief advocate of France's restoration to the rank of a Great Power. All the more was this so since President Roosevelt had told the British at the conference at Yalta in the Crimea in February 1945 that American forces would remain in Europe only two years after VE day. It was on British insistence at Yalta that France was given an occupation zone in Germany, to be formed out of the British and United States zones, a seat on the Allied Control Council for Germany and on the Reparations Commission in Moscow and, subsequently, at the San Francisco conference for drafting the United Nations Charter, on the United Nations Security Council as a permanent member.

There were two other elements in Britain's relative weakness in 1945. One was the effect of technical changes in warfare. The First World War, by introducing the submarine and the bombing aircraft, had struck at Britain's traditional means of national security, sea power. The Second World War and the political tensions following it placed a premium on states which enjoyed either vast potential economic strength or capacity to hold down living standards in order to meet the defence bill. Britain was not well placed in either respect. Moreover, the resort to flying bombs and missiles by Germany at the close of the war seriously jeopardized a small island, a score of miles from Europe and with populous cities near the coast. By the end of the war Britain had begun to design her own guided missiles and founded a permanent organization for that purpose. But all this was dwarfed by the application of nuclear energy to warfare, news of which reached the leaders of the three Powers from the United States at Potsdam in July. Just as Japan found it impossible to continue to fight against an enemy possessing

[1] 403 H.C. Deb 5s. Col. 495 (September 28th).

B

nuclear weapons, the similar geographical position of Britain gave her an even greater interest in the maintenance of peace than before. For a short period that interest was belied when Churchill urged the Americans to take greater risks with the atomic weapon than they were willing to take; his view was that it should be used as a threat to force the Russians to accept Anglo-American conceptions of the peace. But the opportunity was short-lived. Once it had passed, British interest in cooling international tempers returned.

The other major disability confronting British foreign policy when the war ended was the economic plight of the country. In the 1930s Britain was already drawing slightly on foreign holdings in order to pay her way with the rest of the world. By 1941 the bulk of British assets in the New World was exhausted. At the end of the conflict more than a half of total foreign investments had been sold and an external debt of some £3,000 million had been contracted, to be repaid out of unrequited exports after the war. After 1945 Britain did escape the mass unemployment from which she suffered almost from the moment peace was signed with Germany in 1919, but the heavy claims on the British economy during reconversion from war to peace were a diplomatic liability. On becoming Foreign Secretary at the end of July 1945, Ernest Bevin discovered that what he chiefly needed was coal.

Britain and the giant Powers

Britain thus found herself in 1945 one of the undoubted leaders of the coalition against the Axis, but nevertheless a junior partner compared with the two senior leaders, the United States and the Soviet Union. Towards both countries British public opinion at large was almost equally sympathetic, although much Conservative mistrust of Russia remained. The totalitarian character of the Soviet regime tended to be overlooked during the war; great admiration was felt for Russian patriotism and the achievements of the Red Army under Stalin's leadership. Critics of social inequality in pre-war Britain saw in Russia an advanced community from which much could be learned about social services and economic planning. The Left in Britain, and many on the Right as well, also believed that Soviet foreign policy had been far more realistic than that of the western democracies in the 1930s. On the other hand, while British opinion feared a return to isolation in the United States, it was felt that the leadership of President Roosevelt was much more subtle and realistic than that of his predecessor in 1919, Woodrow Wilson, and that he had done far more than Wilson to guide American opinion towards participation

in a world organization. No one doubted that in the harmony between these two great states lay the main hope for peace, in itself the
basic condition of British security and welfare. As for the other
major partner, China, a not dissimilar attitude existed as in relation
to Russia, namely that although the Nationalist regime might fall
short of democratic standards as understood in the West, the war
itself had given China an impulse towards democratic government,
which would be reflected in representative organs after the country
was on its feet again. It was thought that these four Powers, together
with France, would stand together in destroying the remnants of
militarism in Germany, Italy and Japan and in safeguarding the
world against a return to Fascism.

At the official level the closest co-operation undoubtedly existed
with the United States of all the allies. Besides the obvious racial and
ideological reasons for this, President Roosevelt's early recognition
of the nature of the Fascist threat to peace in Europe, his efforts in
the 1930s to educate the American people in the international facts
of life and his various definitions of the principles to inspire international relations after the war, together with the intimacy established between the President and Churchill as early as September
1939 ensured that relations between Britain and the United States
should always be close. Anglo-American co-operation in all the
issues of war, whether supply problems, research, military planning,
or tactical operations, had reached a point in 1945 where the two
countries were often regarded as all but federated. Nevertheless,
Anglo-American affairs were rarely without their strains. Many of
these arose from the clash between traditional American idealism
and the more pragmatic outlook of the British. Before America's
entry into the war the President had met Churchill in Placentia Bay,
Newfoundland, in August 1941 and proposed the declaration of
common principles which later became known as the Atlantic
Charter. For Churchill the significance of the Charter was psychological and he saw it in the whole context of world forces; for the
President of the neutral United States to meet the British Prime
Minister and put his name to a document which referred to the 'final
destruction of Nazi tyranny' must, he thought, depress Germany's
morale, while the intimation in the final paragraph that the United
States would remain armed along with Britain after the war was an
immense reassurance. He told the Deputy Prime Minister, Clement
Attlee, to give the Charter the widest publicity; 'let this soak in on
its own merits on friend and foe'.[1] The reference in the Charter to

[1] Churchill, *The Second World War*, Vol. III, London 1950, p. 398.

the freedom of people to choose the form of government under which they would live applied, he argued, to territories liberated from the Axis; it could not be used to prise open the British Empire.[1] President Roosevelt was in sharp disagreement and attempted to get the British leader to revise this statement. He tended to regard the British Empire as a species of that imperialism which it was an object of the war to end. There was therefore a fear, which President Roosevelt's warm attitude towards Stalin at Yalta served to confirm, that the United States might act against Britain's imperial position rather than support it. Already in December 1944 there had been sharp criticism in America of British intervention in the civil war in Greece. At the Yalta conference the President sided with Marshal Stalin in a move to create voluntary trusteeships under the United Nations, to which Churchill's reply was 'never, never, never'.[2]

At the same time, American idealism clashed with British strategical notions in a different way. The Prime Minister would have liked to see a territorial understanding reached with Stalin as early as possible, before Soviet forces had entered Europe. This was the course he urged on Roosevelt in March 1942.[3] But the President objected and the Anglo-Soviet Treaty was signed in London on May 26 without reference to territorial changes after the war. Churchill recognized that Stalin would demand the Baltic States, the 'Curzon line' as the future Soviet-Polish frontier, half of East Prussia, Bessarabia, frontier adjustments with Finland and Hungary and a predominant position in Bulgaria and Rumania. These claims Stalin had revealed to the British wartime Foreign Secretary, Anthony Eden, in talks in Moscow in December 1941.[4] Churchill himself reached an agreement with Marshal Stalin in Moscow in October 1944 under which Bulgaria and Rumania were recognized as areas of Soviet predominance, while Britain was accorded predominance in Greece.[5] His assumption was that Soviet territorial demands occupied pride of place in Stalin's thought and that it was wise to reach some understanding about them while Britain and the United States were still fully under arms. Against this President Roosevelt firmly set his face. To all intents he believed that when Stalin signed the Declaration on Liberated Areas at Yalta, guaranteeing fundamental

[1] 374 H.C. Deb. 5s. Col. 69 (September 9, 1941).
[2] Edward R. Stettinius, *Roosevelt and the Russians*, London, 1950, p. 212.
[3] Herbert Feis, *Churchill, Roosevelt, Stalin*, Princeton, New Jersey, 1957, p. 60.
[4] Redvers Opie and others, *The Search for Peace Settlements*, Washington, 1951, pp. 32–33.
[5] Churchill, *The Second World War*, London, 1954, Vol. VI, p. 198.

rights and freedoms for eastern Europe, and when he agreed that the predominantly Communist committee created by the Soviet authorities at Lublin in Poland should be broadened by the inclusion of Poles from London and from inside Poland, he was accepting democratic observances as understood in the West. If there was any doubt about this, President Roosevelt appeared to think that this was a small price to pay for Soviet agreement to enter into a world organization.

When Roosevelt died suddenly at Warm Springs, Georgia, on April 12, 1945, there was immediate uncertainty as to whether his successor, Harry S. Truman, could adjust to his immense tasks quickly enough to hold his own with Stalin. This was what Churchill called 'the deadly hiatus'. But the main lines of Roosevelt's policy of great Power co-operation continued. Truman determined to avoid every sign of 'ganging up' with Britain against Russia. He led the way in accepting the slight reconstitution of the Lublin regime before recognizing it as the provisional Government of Poland in July and, while chiding Russia with infringing the Yalta agreement in regard to Rumania and Bulgaria, was as anxious as his predecessor not to alienate Stalin before the defeat of Japan. Although the new President did not take long to inform himself about Soviet intentions, the British attitude towards the United States could not be other than one of anxious watchfulness.

Towards his Soviet colleague the Prime Minister entertained much the same feelings as Stalin appeared to have towards him. Churchill conceived Russia as regarding her ties with the West as a convenience unmixed with either gratitude or trust, which would last only as long as it served Russia's purposes. Friendship between leaders of states (and Stalin regarded Churchill as a fundamentally honest man) was confused by neither statesman with the long-term interests and aims of their respective communities. As in his broadcast on the evening following Hitler's attack on Russia, Churchill kept ideology and foreign policy apart; there was no reason, he felt, why Russia's claims on her eastern and western borders should not be frankly recognized for what they were, the rewards of military power, without any obligation to endorse her internal political or social principles. The question was: where was the opposing military strength to limit those claims? On his side, Stalin was unhesitating in defining his claims with scarcely a veil of moral justification. He told the United States that in Poland he must have a regime which was definitely friendly towards Russia; that was far more important than Polish independence.[1] If an independent Poland was anti-Russian

[1] Harry S. Truman, *Year of Decisions, 1945*, London, 1955, p. 174.

(and the Polish government in exile was undoubtedly that) then it must subordinate itself to Russia's security needs. For Churchill, on the other hand, Polish independence was more important than Polish frontiers, for the British guarantee to Poland in March 1939 did not apply to Poland's pre-war shape.[1] A strong and independent Poland, however, as Clemenceau had seen in 1919, might insulate Europe against Communism. For this very reason even this had to give way before Russian military power on the spot.

Britain was aware of Russia's weakness at the end of the war. Russia had mobilized twelve million men, against Germany's eighteen million, and had lost five million. The British Government sympathized with Stalin's feeling of shock at the abrupt scaling down of Lend-Lease the moment the war in Europe ended; President Truman subsequently amended this decision, on the advice of Harry Hopkins, the President's special envoy to Moscow, although by then much of the damage had been done. But it was not known until many years later how damaging the effects of the war on Russia had been. Many of Russia's acts in 1945, which widened the breach between the two giant Powers, had an understandable basis in the Soviet Government's fear of an attack from the two Western democracies while Russia was still struggling to her feet. It was not forgotten in Moscow that in 1919 Winston Churchill had been an advocate of the use of the defeated German army for an attack on the Soviets. It was firmly believed that Neville Chamberlain's policy towards Hitler was inspired by anti-Soviet motives and it was suspected that throughout the war Britain and the United States had conspired together, either to let Russia defeat Hitler alone while husbanding their strength for a later attack on her or to make a separate peace with Nazism preparatory to a joint incursion into Russia from the West. At Yalta Stalin frankly admitted his fears of what might happen ten years later, when the then Western leaders had gone and a new mood had come over the West. Hence Russia's weakness in 1945 bred fear; fear stimulated hostility and the ideologically tinged decision to ensure future security while the going was good.

In the intervening period between the Yalta conference in February 1945 and the meeting of the three heads of government at Potsdam, Berlin, in July harmony between the three followed a downward course. This may have been due to a stiffening in the Soviet position after criticism of the Yalta agreements in governing circles in Moscow.[2] The Yalta decisions, however, were in themselves open to

[1] Mr Eden confirmed this in the House of Commons on July 30, 1941; H.C. Deb. 5s. Col. 1504.   [2] Edward R. Stettinius, *op. cit.*, p. 272.

differences in interpretation by nations with political outlooks as divergent as those of Russia on one side and Britain and the United States on the other. First, there was dispute over reparations from Germany. Russia's attitude was brutal and uncomplicated; she wanted as much as possible as soon as possible. The two Western Powers, with memories of the reparation fiasco after the First World War, sensed the folly of financing Germany out of their own pockets in order to pay reparations to Russia; they, and especially Britain, could not profit from a plundered and starving Germany. Owing to these fundamental differences the Reparations Commission in Moscow never really got down to work. Secondly, Stalin was little interested in the conception of the United Nations Organization as the Americans understood it, that is, as a symbol of good works and focus of world opinion. He had to be persuaded to send his Foreign Minister, Molotov, to the San Francisco conference on the United Nations in April–June when Britain and the United States refused to let the Lublin regime in Poland participate in the conference. He wanted the General Assembly of the new organization to have the minimum of authority, and for long insisted that the principle of unanimity between the five permanent members of the Security Council should apply, not merely to decisions involving action, but even to the initiation of discussions. Thirdly, there was in February a striking example of Soviet indifference towards the Western Powers, when Andrei Vyshinsky, on Stalin's behalf, arrived in Rumania and imposed the National Democratic Government, led by Petru-Groza and formed from the Communist Party, upon King Michael. On March 6th a Soviet-nominated administration took over in Bucharest. This *coup* was followed on April 21st by a treaty of alliance between Russia and the Polish Lublin regime, now recognized by Moscow as the Provisional Government, and the arrest of sixteen Polish resistance leaders for 'diversionary activities' against the Red Army; fifteen of these had been invited to Moscow under promise of safe conduct to discuss the broadening of the Lublin regime. Britain and the United States were at length obliged on July 5th to recognize a new Polish government, predominately based on the Lublin group, for it was now clear the Russia meant to have her way in Poland and and could only be deterred by force.

This was the melancholy context in which Mr Churchill wrote his historic letter to Stalin on April 29th: 'There is not much comfort,' he wrote, 'in looking into a future where you and the countries you dominate plus the Communist parties in many other states are all drawn up on one side and those who rallied to the English-speaking nations and their associates are on the other. It is quite obvious that their quarrel would tear the world to pieces and all of us leading men on either side who had anything to do with that would be shamed before history.'[1] Such an appeal, however, presupposed that Russia's fears and suspicions could be relieved by assurances. When the Potsdam conference of the three Powers assembled in July it was clear that the climax of inter-Allied unity had passed for ever. It was hopefully agreed that a Council of the Foreign Ministers of the three states, together with those of China and France, should meet 'to do the necessary preparatory work for the peace settlements', including the drawing up of peace treaties with the five smaller ex-enemy states, Bulgaria, Finland, Hungary, Italy and Rumania. Only those states which had signed the terms of surrender accepted by these countries, however, would be represented on the Council in its negotiations on the treaties. The same gesture was made as at Yalta to the principles of democratic rights and freedoms in the former enemy states, while it was tacitly recognized that the interpretation to be given to the word 'democratic' would in practice vary with the local facts of power. The city of Königsberg, in East Prussia, was awarded in principle to Russia, while the conference 'examined', without having power to approve or disapprove, Russia's proposal to annex the northern half of East Prussia 'pending the final determination of territorial questions at the peace settlement'. This same qualification was to apply to the decision of the conference to hand over to Polish administration all German territory east of a line drawn from the Baltic due west of Swinemünde, along the Oder and western Neisse rivers and down to the Czech frontier; this agreement was based on the assumption, first, that Poland was now a properly constituted state and secondly that her territory east of the 'Curzon line', including Lvov, had definitely passed to Russia.

But the centre-piece of the Potsdam meeting was the German problem.[2] Difficulties had already arisen in carrying out the plan for dividing Germany into three, later four, zones of occupation which the three-Power European Advisory Commission in London had drawn up the previous autumn. The Commission was therefore dissolved. Supreme authority in Germany, pending a peace treaty, was now to be exercised by the Commanders-in-Chief of Britain, France, the United States and the Soviet Union, each in his own zone of occupation and jointly, in matters affecting Germany as a whole, as members of the Control Council in Berlin. There was to be a

[1] Churchill, *The Second World War*, Vol. VI, p. 433.
[2] The German question is treated in detail in Chapter III.

uniform political treatment of Germany; she was to be disarmed, demilitarized, de-nazified and re-educated. The aim was 'to prepare for the eventual reconstruction of German political life on a democratic basis and for eventual peaceful co-operation in international life by Germany'. The economic objective was to convert Germany into a non-military, economically decentralized state, with primary emphasis on agriculture and peaceful domestic industry but with sufficient resources to subsist without external assistance. An economic balance in Germany as a whole was to be aimed at. As for reparations, Soviet and Polish claims were to be met from the Soviet zone of occupation and all other claims from the three Western zones. A quarter of all 'usable and complete' industrial equipment in the Western zones which was not required for Germany's peacetime economy was to be removed and handed to Russia: she was to pay for two-fifths of this equipment by exports of such products as food, coal and petrol from the Soviet zone. Finally, it was agreed that, as to the proposed trial of major German war criminals, a list should be compiled by September 1st. This last provision echoed the Soviet-American accord at Yalta on the subject, while Britain was alone in urging that, instead of the dubious legality of a trial, Germany's highest leaders should be summarily shot.[1]

The Potsdam conference was the end of one phase in relations between Russia and the West and the beginning of another. At Yalta the British Government were balancing between doubt and hope about the achievement of democratic conditions in the areas of Europe now decisively under Soviet control. At Potsdam not only did doubt on this issue turn into resignation to the inevitable, but the agreements reached on the central problem of Germany, the key to war and peace in Europe, contained in almost every word possibilities of later conflict. The question was not so much whether the Potsdam accords would be kept, for there was no agreement, on substantive questions, on what they meant, but whether the tendency for Russia and the West to go their separate ways in Germany would not, sooner or later, place Britain in an intolerable position.

Old principles: new requirements
The new context of British foreign policy, as its outlines appeared in 1945, called for the re-thinking of traditional methods and principles. Many of these had already undergone revision. One of the earliest axioms of British policy, the maintenance of naval supremacy, had

[1] The text of the Potsdam agreements is given in *Protocol of the Proceedings of the Berlin Conference*, Cmd. 7087 of 1945.

been virtually abandoned by the end of the nineteenth century. It was not possible for Britain to face naval rivalry in the Mediterranean and Persian Gulf from Tsarist Russia, to say nothing of the potential hostility of Germany, without the neutrality of Japan, which was secured by the Anglo-Japanese alliance in 1902. By an arrangement reached with France before 1914 Britain was allowed to concentrate her fleet in home waters and the western approaches to the home islands. After the First World War, although Germany was for the time being out of the running as a naval competitor and Russia had withdrawn from all armaments rivalry, Britain was obliged to recognize parity with the United States in capital vessels in the Pacific at the Washington conference in 1922. The ensuing strategic interdependence between Britain and the United States was forcefully acknowledged by the then Prime Minister, Stanley Baldwin, in a speech in Glasgow in November 1934, when he said that as long as he had any responsibility for governing the country he would never sanction the use of the British navy for a naval blockade until he knew what the United States was going to do.[1]

At the end of the war in 1945 there were two further threats to British maritime security. On the one hand, the Soviet Union had revived older Russian pretensions as a naval Power. By the Yalta agreements, in return for a promise to enter the war against Japan three months after VE day, she had re-established her naval position in the Pacific to what it was before her defeat by Japan in 1904–5. The promise of the southern half of Sakhalin, the Kuriles islands and a lease of Port Arthur gave her a footing from which to dominate the waters surrounding Japan. The United States countered by succeeding Japan as the administrator of the widely scattered mandate islands in the Pacific, the Marshalls, Marianas and Carolines; subsequently her lease of the naval and air base of Okinawa gave her command of the Chinese coasts. The change in the strategic picture in the Pacific was strikingly symbolized by the Anzus Pact, concluded in 1951, by which the United States inherited Britain's former role in the defence of Australia and New Zealand. Russia's behaviour in eastern Europe determined President Truman to give Stalin no real share in the control of Japan after her surrender and hence, blocked in the Far East, Russia's naval ambitions turned to the Mediterranean. At the San Francisco conference Molotov asked for a share in United Nations trusteeships, with the Italian colonies in Africa in mind. Later, at the Potsdam meeting, Stalin pressed for a Soviet base in the Straits connecting the Black Sea with the Aegean

[1] *The Times*, November 24, 1934.

or at least a revision of the Montreux Convention of 1936, to allow Russia a more secure access into the Mediterranean. This demand was to turn into a virtual war of nerves against Turkey in the following year. These moves were frustrated, but so long as relations between Stalin and Marshal Tito remained friendly, Russian influence was felt in the Adriatic. At the same time the pressure which the Soviet Union was able to exert on Greece, through Greece's two Communist neighbours in the north, Rumania and Bulgaria, added further uncertainties to British communications through the Mediterranean.

The second factor affecting Britain's naval position was the disturbed political state of the lands lying athwart some of her traditional sea routes. At the western end of the Mediterranean, where Gibraltar marked Britain's only land frontier in Europe, British diplomacy had contributed towards keeping Spain neutral during the war; but the powerful movement at the end of the war, which Russia led, for ostracizing General Franco placed Britain in a dilemma, for, whatever the sins of his regime, Franco's occasional mutterings against Gibraltar were not to be taken seriously. The most harmful event that could happen, from the British angle, was a renewal of the Spanish civil war; this was what Churchill, with his eye on Russia's other encroachments into the Mediterranean, mostly feared.[1] At the other end of the Mediterranean Egyptian nationalists' demands in 1946 for revision of the Anglo-Egyptian Treaty of Alliance of 1936, which afforded Britain her military base in the Suez Canal zone, brought into question Britain's naval position at this nodal point of Commonwealth communications. There were other factors of uncertainty: the dangerous situation in the British mandated territory of Palestine, which, if Jewish refugees from Europe continued to flood into the country, threatened to turn the whole Middle East into a scene of chaos; the possibility of a Soviet move to subvert Persia, the northern part of which Russia had occupied by agreement with Britain in 1941, a design which, had it succeeded, would have imperilled British oil supplies and realized the permanent nightmare of Victorian statesmen, a Russian fleet in the Persian Gulf; and the unsettled state of the Indian sub-continent throughout the war, which left uncertain the future naval situation in the Indian Ocean.

The second principle of policy, the maintenance of a balance of power in Europe yet without Britain herself being permanently bound to one side or the other, had been abandoned in 1942, when

[1] Truman, *op. cit.*, p. 284.

Britain committed herself for twenty years by the Anglo-Soviet Treaty. The significance of this was that, in the event of another war with Germany, Russia would have acted as the stone of attrition enabling Britain to muster her forces and attack Germany in the West. This was the role Russia had played in 1914 and 1941 and in 1812 in the war against France. France herself had played that part in 1914–18. But now, with the alienation of the Soviet Union from the West in 1945 and with the political weakness in central Europe, there was no longer a balance in Europe, but a void. The heart of that void lay in Europe west of Bohemia; eastern Europe beyond the void was being rapidly and purposefully filled by the incursion of Soviet power, with Berlin left as an island of inter-Allied occupation in the midst of it. In the 1930s Baldwin had recognized that Britain's frontier lay on the Rhine,[1] though that was not widely understood when Hitler remilitarized the left bank of the river in March 1936. Now, with Germany west of the Elbe inert and dependent, Britain's frontier had moved over 200 miles further east into Europe. For a short period after the war many on both Right and Left wings of British politics toyed with the idea of Britain joining with the countries of western Europe to form a prosperous and strong, but uncommitted Third Force mediating between the two giant Powers. To this there were at least two objections. Western Europe could neither revive nor defend itself without United States assistance; it was therefore drawn into the American orbit. Moreover, although neutralism might conceivably have been open to France, the Low Countries, Italy or west Germany (when an independent government was formed there), though only on the assumption that Russia had reached the limits of her power in the east, neutralism was not practicable for Britain, with her wide international connections and still extensive Empire. She was now bound to western Europe as long as there was no firm balance against Russia without her; but neither this policy nor the maintenance of the British position in the world outside Europe was possible without a solid relationship with the United States. The days of a flexible European balance, formed as between European countries alone and with an uncommitted Britain in the wings, were over.

There were, however, two former British principles of foreign policy which had not been invalidated; the post-1945 scene seemed rather to have heightened their relevance. The first was the British interest in pacification and stability abroad and in the employment of international organizations for reconciliation and co-operation

[1] 292 H.c. Deb. 5s. Col. 2339 (July 30, 1934).

rather than for enforcement. This had provided the basis for the crucial difference between the European policies of Britain and France after 1918, the French wishing to see the League of Nations primarily as a pillar of security against Germany, while Britain wanted Germany to be restored as soon as possible to a co-operative relationship with other nations. Towards the end of the Second World War British opinion tended to side with the American view that the League had been too weak, and hence that the new world organization should be based in the first instance on the united military strength of the great Powers. But this view lasted only as long as great Power unity was credible. With the onset of the Cold War British influence was thrown on the side of moderating East-West tensions where possible and of preventing the United Nations from being used solely to organize world opinion against the East. As Clement Attlee put it in describing the British position at the San Francisco conference on the United Nations Charter:

> In the discussion of the powers of the Security Council the British delegation took a foremost part in seeking to make the Security Council something more than a policeman who is called in only when there is already a danger of a breach of the peace. We sought, and sought successfully, to make it a place where the policies of the states, and especially the greater states, could be discussed and reconsidered, especially when they showed signs of such divergences as to threaten the harmony of international relations. Collective Security is not merely a promise to act when an emergency occurs, but it is active co-operation to prevent emergencies occurring.[1]

That conception was inherent in Britain's international position, as a Power with hostages to fortune all the world over in the event that war should come.

Secondly, British foreign policy after the First World War had always to measure the effects of decisions taken in London on a Commonwealth and Empire a fundamental axiom of which was that its constitutent parts should enjoy self-determination at the earliest practicable moment. In August 1914 it had been for Britain alone to decide whether or not she should enter the war against the Central Powers. But throughout the inter-war period the question was whether Britain should assume commitments or embark on courses which might not in the end be supported by the Dominions, which effectively acquired independence in foreign policy at the Paris Peace

[1] 413 H.C. Deb. 5s. Col. 665 (August 22, 1945)

Conference in 1919, formally at the Imperial Conference in 1926 and legally by the Statute of Westminster, an Act of the British Parliament, in 1931. It is true that the Dominions were not parties to the Locarno treaties of 1925, by which the United Kingdom for the first time undertook to guarantee territory in mainland Europe. But the inability of Britain in the 1920s to assume general obligations as a guarantor under the League Covenant and the nervousness of the Chamberlain Government about challenging the Dictators on issues on which the Dominions might not, in the event, stand unitedly by Britain's side, showed the interdependence between British policy and the Commonwealth. This was no less the position after the Second World War. Consultation with the Commonwealth had been a first rule of British policy before 1939; it remained a first rule after 1945. But in one vital respect the position was different. Self-determination was now being pressed in the non-Europeanized parts of the Empire, especially in India, Ceylon and Burma. These countries might still wish to remain in the Commonwealth after independence, but it could not be assumed that they would approach international questions with the same mental outlook as the older Dominions. This meant some decline in the number of issues on which Britain could take a stand in opposition to other countries knowing that Commonwealth countries would be disposed to respect her point of view even if they did not join her.

To these four principles a fifth had to be added in the changed circumstances of 1945; that of reconsidering from time to time the sum of British international commitments to see whether they could not be reduced in the light of the country's diminished strength. This question was one of the main subjects of controversy in the country immediately after the end of the war. On the side of maintaining the full range of British interests abroad stood Churchill, supported by the Conservative Party; he had not been made Prime Minister, he said in 1942, to preside over the liquidation of the British Empire. He appealed to the pride of a country which had stood alone against Hitler, as well as to its lack of complete confidence either in the United States, as a relative newcomer to world affairs, or in the Soviet Union, with its dubious ideology and patent creed of *Realpolitik*. On the other side was the old Radical tradition of Little England, joined with the demand for better living conditions at home and the longing for a more rationally ordered world, this having now been strengthened by alliance with two super-Powers which, in their different ways, renounced the older brand of imperialism. For the moment this Radical tradition was the stronger of the two. Britain in 1945 showed none of the thirst for territorial acquisitions at the expense of the defeated which had been in evidence in 1918. The resignation to the United States of primacy in the negotiations with Russia in 1945 was not widely resented in Britain. The British people, as their attitude towards the Palestine mandate in 1947–49 proved, had caught something of the mood of withdrawal from active participation in world politics, with all its costs and sacrifices, which was affecting their neighbours in Europe. The presence of this feeling, however, imposed on the Government an even greater obligation to see that any cession of British authority abroad was not such as to endanger really vital national interests.

Labour in office
The problem was all the greater in that Churchill, the champion of maintaining the full scale of British interests, fell from power in the General Election on July 5th and was succeeded by the first secure Labour Government in British history. The new Prime Minister, Clement Attlee, had an overall majority of 247 seats in the House of Commons; he was assured by constitutional practice of full authority to decide and implement any foreign policy of his choice. He had himself written a book in the 1930s in which he argued that a Socialist foreign policy would be wholly different from that of Conservatives.[1] Many Labour voters agreed with Sir Stafford Cripps' statement in the election campaign that the 1939 war had been caused by the failure of the National Government to support the League of Nations, and that a Labour Government was better qualified than the Conservatives for co-operation with Russia.[2] In the event, however, Labour's accession to office made scarcely any difference to the main lines of foreign policy which the Coalition Government had already decided.

This is less surprising when it is remembered how party conflict, especially in matters of foreign policy, tends to exaggerate the actual extent of differences between responsible party leaders. To which must be added the fact that in 1945 there were circumstances which especially softened the effect on external relations of a change of government. In the first place, the Labour Party's chief men had a share in the wartime Coalition Government from its formation in May 1940. They had been privy to the whole course of diplomacy during the war. Owing to their support several widely unpopular acts

[1] *The Labour Party in Perspective*, London, 1937, p. 226.
[2] R. B. McCallum and Alison Readman, *The British General Election of 1945*, London, 1947, p. 138.

of the Government, as for instance the intervention in Greece in December 1944, had been made acceptable to the country. In the first debate in the Commons after the formation of the Labour Government Anthony Eden said that there have never been a serious difference of opinion on foreign affairs between Labour and Conservative Ministers in the wartime Cabinet, and Labour's Foreign Secretary, Bevin, confirmed this.[1] This was in sharpest contrast with experience in the First World War, in which a Labour leader entered the wartime Cabinet only in December 1916, after most of the secret agreements of the war had been made. Hence the change-over in 1945 was smoothly effected in July at the Potsdam conference, at which Churchill led the British delegation at the beginning and Attlee at the end. Moreover, experience of office in the War Cabinet had communicated to Labour leaders a much more realistic grasp of foreign policy than was general among the Opposition before the war. The fact that Attlee and Bevin were men of severely practical bent, whose reformism was centred rather on home affairs, ensured that British policy would follow largely traditional courses. This did not mean, however, that the Labour Movement as a whole would be satisfied with this result.

But the most important reason for continuity was the absence of practical alternatives to the principles laid down by the Coalition; namely co-operation as far as possible with the two giant Powers, close accord with the United States, the utmost possible contribution to European recovery and support for the new United Nations Organization. This limitation of choices was partly due to the reduced power of Britain at the end of the war, partly to the sudden and alarming breach occurring between the allies. But it was also due to the fact that the policy generally agreed between the two parties at the General Election was no more than an outline the details of which would have to be filled in as the situation developed. If Russia and the United States overcame the frictions arising from the Yalta accords and remained friends, Britain stood to gain from the ensuing prospects for the development of the United Nations. But if their rivalry intensified, Britain might use the United Nations to moderate the conflict while strengthening her ties with the United States, western Europe and the Commonwealth in order to shield herself against its consequences. On the razor's edge between these two prospects Britain and the world in 1945 stood poised.

---

[1] 413 H.C. Deb. 5s. Col. 312 (August 20, 1945).

CHAPTER TWO

Diplomacy on a Shoe-string

When in 1945 Britain voted into power a Labour Government intent on improving the ordinary person's lot the country was financially insolvent for the first time in its modern history. This fact was not always in the focus of discussion on foreign policy but it influenced almost every act of British diplomacy in every part of the world. The war effort was estimated to have cost about a quarter of the country's national wealth, or some £7,300 million. Physical destruction on land accounted for some £1,500 million of this, the loss of shipping and cargoes for £700 million. Internal disinvestment, through failure to replace plant and machinery, totalled some £900 million. But the most serious inroad into financial strength was the sale of foreign assets, valued at £4,200 million, as payment for essential imports and military supplies from abroad during the war.[1] The task of making good this loss in earning capacity was increased by pent-up demand within the country, intensified by demobilization and the state of full employment, which attracted resources away from the re-establishment of the country's external position. Four million houses alone had been either destroyed or damaged by enemy action; the domestic cupboard was bare, the population down-at-heel and much industrial property superannuated.

The effects in terms of the external economic situation were two. First, an increase in exports of between 50 and 75 per cent above the pre-war level was assumed to be necessary to pay merely for the pre-war scale of imports; it would probably take from three to five years to achieve this. Visible and invisible exports which had financed purchases of food and raw materials before the war had been pared to the bone. In the export industries the labour force had been reduced from 1·3 million in 1939 to 400,000 in 1945, so as to provide men for the Services and war industries. The merchant marine, earning Britain an eighth of her pre-war imports, was in a severely mauled condition, with less than three-quarters of its 1939 tonnage in use despite wartime building. Above all, the drastic liquidation of foreign

[1] *Statistical Material presented during the Washington negotiations*, Cmd. 6707 of 1945, Appendix VIII.

C

securities reduced income from this source to one-half of what it had been in 1939.[1] The result of these losses was that when the Labour Government was formed British income from abroad sufficed to pay for scarcely a half of current purchases. Imports of food and raw materials were running at the rate of £2,000 million a year. Visible exports contributed no more than £350 million towards this figure, while income from United States and British Commonwealth spending in Britain and her possessions added a further £450 million. It is true that in 1945 the world constituted a seller's market, but other countries would first have to restore their economies in order to make their demands effective. Hence, as Attlee said in August, 'the initial deficit with which we start the task of re-establishing our own economy and of contracting our overseas commitments is immense'.[2]

Secondly, there was, as at the end of the First World War, the burden of debt to other countries. Enormous cash outlays in local currencies had been necessary in India, the Middle East, North Africa and elsewhere to pay for the upkeep of troops, the construction of airfields, harbours and supply bases, the use of local labour and the purchase of local supplies. Even after hostilities had ceased payments continued for the maintenance of British forces beyond their peacetime strength. Only to a limited extent had all this expenditure been covered by Lend-Lease, British earnings abroad or the sale of foreign investments. The balance was entered up on the debit side. The result was that British external liabilities, which totalled £476 million in August 1939, had swollen to the huge figure of £3,355 million by June 1945. By far the greatest proportion of these liabilities was held by Sterling Area countries, that is, the British Commonwealth, excluding Canada and Newfoundland, together with certain Middle Eastern countries; this sterling indebtedness totalled £2,723 million. These liabilities did not have to be, nor could they be, met at once; but their very existence constituted a distinct weakness in the British diplomatic situation.

No sooner had Attlee's Government settled down to digest these unwelcome statistics than a crippling blow was struck in the form of the ending of Lend-Lease and the cancellation of outstanding contracts by a stroke of President Truman's pen on August 21, 1945. Warning had already been given in May, when this 'most unsordid act in history' had been sharply contracted on Germany's surrender. At the Potsdam conference Churchill had proposed talks with the

[1] Cmd. 6707, Appendices I–VII.
[2] 413 H.C. Deb. 5s. Col. 956 (August 24th).

United States Government on postwar finance and accordingly Assistant Secretary of State Clayton had been sent over by the White House to prepare the ground. Now, not only was the lifeline cut, but Britain, the recipient of over two-thirds of all Lend-Lease, was called on to assume liability for supplies in transit or in British hands or waiting to be delivered under existing contracts. The shock of this decision, effected without consultation with the British Government, was such that Churchill, now leader of the Opposition, said he could not believe it was the last word of the United States on the subject.[1] Lord Halifax, the British Ambassador in Washington, at that time at home on leave, was asked to return at once and with him went a strong delegation which included Lord Keynes, Mr Brand, the Treasury representative in America, and Sir Percival Liesching of the Board of Trade. In their talks in Washington, which began on September 11th, their task was to set the economic facts about Britain's plight before the American officials and to try to reach some arrangement about further dollar aid. Without further dollar assistance there was a distinct possibility of widespread unemployment in Britain and even scarcity of the basic necessities.

There was a pardonable suspicion in Britain that the United States, with its faith in individual enterprise, had terminated Lend-Lease by way of comment on the verdict Britain had just given in the general election. The lack in the United States of much public enthusiasm for the British Empire, now applying for a subsidy, was also felt to have played its part. Legally, however, the President was bound by the terms of the Lend-Lease Act of March 11, 1941, not to prolong the operation into peacetime.[2] Britain herself in signing the Mutual Aid Agreement with the United States in February 1942 had placed it in the President's hands to determine the date of the end of the emergency and with it the end of the Agreement.[3] Moreover, American opinion was at this time far from alarmed about affairs in Europe and saw no reason for subsidies to allies as though in wartime. James Byrnes, the new Secretary of State, was advocating a twenty-five year four-Power security pact in Europe, one object of which seemed to be to create conditions for a withdrawal of American forces. Churchill's speech at Fulton, Missouri, in March 1946, pleading for recognition of the dangers facing the western democracies, drew no fervent response. Recollections of Europe's failure to settle its debts after the First World War were more frequent visitors

[1] 413 H.C. Deb. 5s. Col. 957 (August 24, 1945).
[2] Harry S. Truman, *Year of Decisions, 1945*, p. 410.
[3] Cmd. 6341 of 1942.

to the American mind. Hence the determination to place relations with Europe on a 'business' footing at the earliest moment, unaffected by sentiment or political considerations.

The American loan

This American mood was reflected in tough bargaining in Washington on the terms of dollar assistance. Extending over three months, the talks came more than once within an ace of collapse. Their eventual success was purchased at the cost of the disappointment of most of the hopes of the British side, which had, however, not improved their case by somewhat overstating the severity of the country's position. 'The true financial status of our chief Ally was never agreed upon,' President Truman observed, 'although it was obviously serious.'[1] The British delegates had expected either a grant-in-aid or an interest-free loan. They were offered instead a line of credit at the modest annual rate of 2 per cent or rather 1·62 per cent when account was taken of the fact that repayments would not commence until December 1951. The credit was fixed at $3,750 million (£930 million), to be drawn upon before the end of 1951, to which was added a further $672 million (£167 million) to cover outstanding British liabilities on Lend-Lease account and the sale by the United States of certain surplus war properties and installations in Britain. Repayment was to extend over fifty years, each annual instalment being fixed at $31 million (£8 million) for each $1,000 million of the line of credit which had been drawn at the terminal date for encashing it. In any one year the element of interest in the sum due for repayment might be waived at the request of the British Government provided the International Monetary Fund certified that the British balance of payments warranted it.[2] Since the proportion of interest to principal would be greater in the early years of repayment, this meant that the burden of reimbursing the loan would be heaviest in the years of immediate postwar recovery.[3]

But the American loan was more than a loan. By the Loan Agreement, which was signed in Washington on December 6th, Britain accepted three conditions extending beyond the normal scope of creditor-debtor relations. She undertook to make sterling freely convertible into other currencies not later than twelve months after the Loan Agreement came into force; that meant the end of the

[1] Truman, *op. cit.*, p. 414.
[2] The Fund is referred to below, pp. 37–8.
[3] Financial Agreement between the Governments of the United States and the United Kingdom, dated December 6, 1945, Cmd. 6708 of 1945.

Sterling Area dollar pool which limited the freedom of Sterling Area countries to spend dollars earned by their exports. She also agreed not to apply quantitative restrictions discriminatingly against dollar goods, which implied that any British restrictions on purchases from the United States, applied in order to conserve dollars, would have to extend to imports from every part of the world. Thirdly, Britain consented to enter into negotiations with countries holding British sterling liabilities with a view either to scaling them down or refunding them; from the American point of view this would have the effect of diverting to the dollar market the import demands of countries holding sterling balances which they might otherwise liquidate by purchases in Britain. In addition Britain accepted as a basis for discussion at a future world conference the American proposals for an international trade organization,[1] and agreed to ratify the agreements concluded at Bretton Woods, New Hampshire, in July 1944 for the creation of an International Monetary Fund and an International Bank for Reconstruction and Development.[2]

These conditions were steeped in the American philosophy of multilateral world trade unembarrassed by political obstacles or intervention. They were not wholly disadvantageous to Britain as a trading nation. The Monetary Fund, for example, designed to guard against competitive exchange depreciation by providing limited amounts of scarce foreign exchange to countries in debt, promised some easement in cases of temporary shortages of foreign currency, while avoiding the harsh impact on the level of internal demand of the Gold Standard. It allowed depreciation of a member's currency up to 10 per cent of par value without consultation with the Fund authorities and a further 10 per cent with the Fund's consent. The only question was whether the initial value of sterling proposed (4·03 dollars in the £) was realistic in the circumstances. The World Bank also held out advantages for a country with Britain's interest in economic reconstruction abroad; unfortunately only one-fifth of the Bank's capital was to be paid up at the outset, and this was to prevent it from meeting more than a small fraction of postwar needs. Even the American aspiration for a world trade charter embodying the gospel of free trade could hardly jeopardize British interests provided it emphasized, as the British delegation insisted, the precedence of full employment at home over the stability of world trade as a

---

[1] Proposals for consideration by an International Conference on Trade and Employment, Cmd. 6709 of 1945.
[2] United Nations Monetary and Financial Conference, Bretton Woods, New Hampshire, USA, July 1 to July 22, 1944, Final Act, Cmd. 6546 of 1945.

whole and provided also that any reduction in Imperial Preference was conditional on a real expansion of Commonwealth trade with dollar countries. But the most hazardous of the Washington undertakings were the promises to make sterling convertible after only one year's readjustment and to remove discrimination against dollar goods. If it was assumed that British balance of payments difficulties were merely an aftermath of war these promises were not unreasonable. But in the presence of a long-standing lack of balance between the dollar and the pound the attempt to make the British economy freely competitive with the American was positively quixotic. The agreement for an International Monetary Fund by contrast provided for a transitional period of five years before the free exchange of currencies became operative.[1] The United States argued that in view of the support afforded to Britain by the dollar credit these five years could be safely reduced to one. It was on this point that the British delegation most strongly dissented.

In support of their arguments the American officials insisted that Britain was already bound to abandon restrictive commercial practices by the Mutual Aid Agreement signed on February 23, 1942, which provided for the final liquidation of Lend-Lease. Article VII of the Agreement read:

> In the final determination of the benefits to be provided to the United States by the Government of the United Kingdom in return for aid furnished under the Act of Congress of March 11, 1941, the terms and conditions shall include provisions for agreed action by the United States and the United Kingdom, open to participation by all other countries of like mind, directed to the expansion, by appropriate international and domestic measures, of production, employment and the exchange and consumption of goods, which are the material foundation of the liberty and welfare of all peoples; to the elimination of all forms of discriminatory treatment in international commerce and to the reduction of tariffs and other trade barriers; and in general to the attainment of all the economic objectives set forth in the Joint Declaration made on August 12, 1941, by the President of the United States and the Prime Minister of the United Kingdom.[2]

The American administration, well aware of the allergy of Congress to the very sound of the words 'Imperial Preference', insisted on making the implementation of this clause a condition of the line of

[1] Cmd. 6546. Article XIV.
[2] Cmd. 6431 of 1943.

credit. The British reply was that when the Joint Declaration, in other words the Atlantic Charter, was drawn up, the Prime Minister had taken care to see that the reference to freedom of trade should include the phrase 'with due respect to their existing obligations'. In any case, the British delegation argued, any contraction in Imperial Preference would have to be matched with reductions in the American tariff. It was no good, they said, demanding of Britain that she stand on her feet commercially while forbidding her to make trading arrangments with friendly countries to balance the impermeability of the American market. But these protests were without avail.

The Loan Agreement had a cold reception in Britain. The Foreign Secretary, Bevin, pointed out that it was never agreeable to come away from a money-lender's office and reckon up the cost.[1] The terms were hard enough. The haste with which the United States demanded ratification of the Agreement, together with that of the Bretton Woods agreements, allowing only until December 31st, when the Agreement itself was not signed until December 6th, seemed indecent to many. The greatest doubt, however, was whether sterling could stand the strain of convertibility after so brief an acclimatization. The leader of the Opposition, Churchill, described it as a proposition so doubtful and perilous that the best hope was that in practice it would defeat itself.[2] The hope was fulfilled. In the event it was only two years to a day from the ending of Lend-Lease that the experiment in convertibility had to be terminated on August 21, 1947, only a month after sterling had been freed. The reason for this was the rush of foreign holders of sterling proceeds from sales to Britain to convert their balances into scarce dollars in order to buy more readily available American goods. British gold and dollar reserves ran down some $300 million in the first nine months of 1947, the year in which convertibility was tried and failed. But these unfavourable aspects of the Loan Agreement did not shake the view of responsible people that the bargain was the best obtainable in the circumstances. 'I for my part,' said a former Chancellor of the Exchequer, Sir John Anderson, 'do not doubt that His Majesty's Government have secured the best terms that were open to them.'[3] The feelings aroused by the Agreement, however, were such that ninety-eight MPs voted against it, including many Conservatives who refused to follow their leader's recommendation to abstain in order to avoid any appearance of hostility towards the United States.

[1] 417 H.C. Deb. 5s. Col. 725 (December 13, 1945).
[2] Ibid., Col. 714 (December 13, 1945).
[3] Ibid., Col. 445 (December 12, 1945).

The dollar gap and Marshall aid

The Anglo-American Loan Agreement was based on the assumption that the lack of balance between the economies of the Old World and the New was largely an after-effect of the war. Britain needed dollar support, the Chancellor of the Exchequer, Hugh Dalton, explained, 'because our national economy has been distorted and violently twisted out of shape for the sake of our common war effort'.[1] But events were to show that the postwar disequilibrium was merely the climax to trends which had their beginnings long before.

Even in the 1930s a deficit had existed on the British side in commercial dealings with the Western Hemisphere. Its true extent was concealed by three factors: exports to the New World in the form of raw materials from British oversea possessions such as Malaya; favourable terms of trade in pre-1939 times, which enabled Britain to buy a given volume of imports with only two-thirds of the exports she had had to sell before 1914; and the earnings in the United States of the primary-producing colonies of Britain's neighbours in Europe, providing a supply of dollars to which Britain had access through her own sales to Europe. All three factors had almost entirely disappeared by 1945. Exports from colonial areas such as south-east Asia had temporarily dried up; there was a sharp decline in the output of primary products owing to the dislocations of war and the rice famine in the Far East, thus turning the terms of trade against the industrial countries; and many oversea possessions of Europe were in process of gaining their independence. Moreover, before the war there had been an average import of $1,400 million (£290 million) in gold into the United States every year, largely owing to capital movements into that country. So that by 1945 the United Kingdom and the rest of Europe had not only to face the standing problem of an excess of imports in trade with the dollar area, but were denuded of gold and other reserves to tide over the period before a more balanced state of payments had been reached.[2] In their combined effect these factors provided the United States with a surplus on trading account of something like $10,000 million (£2,500 million) a year shortly after the war ended. Dollars to cover this surplus were distributed through many American schemes of public and private assistance to a less fortunate world outside. But these would not last indefinitely. Only in one or other of two ways could this huge deficit

[1] 417 H.C. Deb. 5s. Col. 423 (December 12, 1945).
[2] E. A. G. Robinson, 'The United Kingdom's Economic Problems', in *United Kingdom Policy*, The Royal Institute of International Affairs, London, 1950, pp. 63–67.

be met. Either the United States would have to supply the missing dollars as a formal act of policy or Europe must cut its imports from the Western Hemisphere, with disastrous effects on European recovery, American export business and all the hopes for a revival of international trade.

A third possibility, that Europe should finance its purchases by its own sales in dollar markets, was ruled out by the prevailing state of the European economy. Production in western Europe was undergoing temporary paralysis caused by physical devastation (though this turned out to be not nearly as severe as was at first thought), the German collapse, the habits of sabotage and disloyalty which had been acquired during the war in the occupied countries, the chaotic state of the transport system and the segregation from western Europe of the principal food and timber-producing areas in the east. Almost every country was affected by monetary disturbance, the by-product of a long war, with its freezing effect on trade and production. Food and industrial raw materials previously obtained from extra-European dependent territories were in short supply. Nevertheless, the population which consumed this diminished production had not decreased; certain areas, such as the western occupation zones of Germany, had experienced abnormal increases owing to the influx of refugees from former German territories in the east now occupied by Russia, Poland or Czechoslovakia.[1] As a crowning misfortune, the exceptionally severe winter of 1946-47, when wood was burned on a large scale owing to the dearth of coal, depleted timber supplies for building and the manufacture of pit props. This was preceded and followed by the exceptionally dry springs of 1946 and 1947.

To a limited extent this sorry state of Europe was alleviated in the months immediately after the war by the United Nations Relief and Rehabilitation Administration (UNRRA), created in 1944. The United States naturally made the largest financial contribution to this agency, which came to be regarded in that country as little more than a department of state. It was therefore exposed to the moody self-criticism which sometimes follows on the heels of American acts of generosity. The feeling in Congress that UNRRA was being used to sustain regimes unfriendly towards the United States, together with the American taxpayer's wish to employ relief with more discrimination, therefore served to bring the agency's work to a close at the end of 1946. UNRRA had in truth been far more active in eastern Europe

[1] Committee of European Economic Co-operation, Vol. 1, General Report, HMSO, 1947, p. 4.

than in the west, which gave some point to Congressional complaints. But this was due, not to any ideological bias in its officials, but to the reluctance of west European governments to accept what were in effect doles from a relief organization. UNRRA's demise accordingly left unaffected the conclusion reached by the British Government in the closing months of 1946 that Europe's dollar needs would have to be satisfied, and that soon, or paralysis of unlimited extent and duration would ensue.

The initiative came from the United States in the form of one of those massive conceptions which are the natural offspring of the American mind. A hint had been thrown out by Dean Acheson, the Under-Secretary of State, in a speech at Cleveland, Mississippi, on May 8, 1947, when he told a meeting of cotton growers that 'the United States is going to have to undertake further emergency financing of foreign purchases if foreign countries are to continue to buy in 1948 and 1949 the commodities which they need to sustain life and at the same time rebuild their economies'.[1] This was the curtain-raiser to the historic speech by the Secretary of State, George Marshall, at Harvard University on June 5th, when he stated the implications of the economic plight of Europe in the following terms :

Europe's requirements for the next three or four years of foreign food and other essential products—principally from America— are so much greater than her present ability to pay that she must have substantial additional help or face economic, social and political deterioration of a very grave character. Before, however, the United States can proceed much further in its efforts to alleviate the situation and help start the European world on its way to recovery, there must be some agreement among the countries of Europe as to the requirements of the situation and the part these countries themselves will take in order to give proper effect to whatever action might be undertaken by this Government.

'The programme,' Mr Marshall concluded, 'must be a joint one, agreed to by a number of, if not all, European nations.'[2] A week later the Secretary of State answered the obvious question raised by the speech by saying that he had in mind the entire continent of Europe west of Asia and meant to include both Britain and the Soviet Union. In view of the estrangement already evident in Russo-American affairs it was open to doubt whether the reference to the Soviet Union was serious. The State Department had announced in

[1] Department of State, *Bulletin*, May 18, 1947, pp. 991–4.
[2] Department of State, *Bulletin*, June 15, 1947, pp. 1159–60.

the previous October the suspension of the remaining four-fifths of a $50 million credit to Czechoslovakia and had asked the United States Export-Import Bank to hold up negotiations for a further $50 million rehabilitation loan on the grounds that certain Czech newspapers had echoed Soviet allegations of American 'dollar diplomacy'. It was even more doubtful whether Congress would sanction financial help without demanding the kind of concessions which the Soviet authorities were unlikely to accept. Marshall himself had said in his Harvard speech that 'governments, political parties or groups which seek to perpetuate human misery in order to profit therefrom politically or otherwise will encounter the opposition of the United States'. In the event the question was never put because the Soviet Government, after sending the Foreign Minister, Molotov, to a three-Power meeting on the Marshall offer in Paris at the end of June, refused to join Britain and France in their invitation to the European states to collaborate in a temporary organization to study their economic requirements. Subsequently the Soviet Union ensured that the east European countries, including Czechoslovakia, should follow her example and boycott the Anglo-French invitation, or change their minds if they had already accepted it.

The Soviet Union's reasons for dissociating herself from the Marshall offer remain obscure, although it is fairly certain that the objection made public at the three-Power meeting in Paris in June, namely that a recovery programme in any other form than that of a mere shopping-list of requirements 'would inevitably result in the imposition of the will of the stronger European Powers upon other European countries', was not genuine.[1] The Soviet authorities may have feared too close an involvement with the United States economy, which Marxist Holy Writ represented as being on the verge of collapse. They may have thought that they had more to gain from economic paralysis in western Europe, following upon the anticipated American recession, than from American aid, even if this was given without strings. They may also have concluded that a common European programme, such as appeared to be a condition of American assistance, would probably weaken Russia's grip on the east European countries and draw them into the richer, if moribund, capitalist orbit. The Communist and semi-Communist countries which the Red Army had joined together were not meant to be put asunder by American dollars.

[1] French Yellow Book. Documents of the Conference of Foreign Ministers of France, the United Kingdom and the USSR held in Paris from June 27 to July 3, 1947. Proposal submitted by the Soviet delegate at the Third Meeting, p. 49.

The Soviet withdrawal was not regretted by the British Government. After the negotiations on the peace treaties with the five ex-enemy states the principal fear in London was that the state of Europe, grave almost to the point of despair, would only be lost to sight in further bouts of sterile wrangling which characterized the Council of Foreign Ministers. The United States had already shown herself to be a hard bargainer in the matter of the Loan Agreement; it was possible that she might drop the Marshall offer in a huff if there was too much trouble with the Russians. On the eve of the Paris talks on the offer Bevin told the House of Commons: 'the guiding principle that I shall follow in any talks on this matter will be speed. I spent six weeks in Moscow trying to get a settlement. I shall not be a party to holding up the economic recovery of Europe by the finesse of procedure or terms of reference or all the paraphernalia which may go with it. There is too much involved.'[1] While it may be inaccurate to accuse the Foreign Secretary of having intrigued to keep Russia out, he leapt at the Marshall speech and hastened to hold talks with the French Foreign Minister, Georges Bidault, in Paris on June 17th and 18th, in order to arrange a common Anglo-French position on the terms of an approach to Russia. When the two Ministers met Molotov in Paris from June 27th to July 3rd, and the anticipated dispute did spring up as to the composition and terms of reference of a steering committee for the proposed organ for European recovery, Bevin must have breathed a sigh of relief to hear that Stalin could not go along with the two western Powers.

The Anglo-French invitation led to a conference in Paris which met under Bevin's chairmanship on July 12 to draw up the joint plan for European reconstruction which the US Secretary of State had asked for. The conference appointed the Committee for European Economic Co-operation to which was entrusted the task of surveying Europe's economic needs, the form of co-operation required to fulfil them and the nature of external assistance necessary to complete the plan. In addition to the sponsoring states, Britain and France, the following fourteen countries were represented on the Committee: Austria, Belgium, Denmark, Greece, Iceland, Ireland, Italy, Luxemburg, the Netherlands, Norway, Portugal, Sweden, Switzerland and Turkey. Britain and France assumed responsibility for western Germany's participation in the plan.[2] The Committee adopted a report on the general situation in September which was then forwarded to

[1] 438 H.C. Deb. 5s. Col. 2239 (June 19, 1947).
[2] See below, p. 79.

the United States. By a convention concluded on April 16, 1948, the Committee became the Organization for European Economic Co-operation (OEEC) for the distribution of the funds appropriated by the United State Congress and for the fulfilment of the four-year recovery programme. While this was happening on one side of the Atlantic, the United States on the other was adopting the necessary legislation in the form of the Economic Co-operation Act, which Congress passed in April 1948. As was to be expected, Congress reduced the total appropriation proposed by the administration for the four-year term and consented only to annual appropriations in preference to sanctioning funds for the whole period of the plan. During the entire programme of the European Recovery Programme (ERP) only one-fifth of the funds provided by the United States took the form of loans, the rest being grants carrying no obligation to repay.

The countries participating in ERP had two features in common. They lay outside the Soviet sphere of interest in eastern Europe and they agreed in regarding the Marshall offer as leading to economic integration of a more permanent kind between themselves, though Britain did not accept the French thesis that it was the starting point for European union in a federal sense. The former ensured that ERP should be the first formal stage in the postwar division of Europe into two camps, one having its policy choices increasingly determined in Moscow, the other looking towards the United States as its champion. The Soviet retort to the formation of OEEC was to call a conference of the seven dominant Communist parties of East Europe and Russia, together with Communist delegates from France and Italy, which met on September 22 and 23, 1947, at Wiliza Gora in Silesia and founded the Cominform. The object of this body, which recalled with some differences the old Comintern disbanded by Stalin in the interests of Allied unity in 1943, was at once to aid and succour Communist groups in western Europe in their efforts to impede the recovery programme and to co-ordinate from Moscow the general policies of the Communist-controlled countries. The most striking immediate outcome of the founding of Cominform was the expulsion of the heretical Tito, the President of Yugoslavia, from the Communist camp owing to his failure, in Stalin's eyes, to make the firm choice presented to all Communists by the issue of the Marshall plan. The second characteristic of the ERP countries, their agreement to make a more perfect economic union, was indispensable to the receipt of large-scale dollar aid in that American public opinion was willing to endorse it only if it seemed to expedite European union.

The west European countries had reasons of their own for closer integration, but Marshall aid provided a further stimulus along with the means for translating their plans into reality.

Certain movements towards European union had already begun. The Benelux union, creating a limited economic federation between Belgium, the Netherlands and Luxemburg, had been initiated in London on September 5, 1944; its tariff union came into force on New Year's Day 1948. The Scandinavian countries followed with negotiations in August 1947 on a customs union, to be called 'Danosve', while similar talks commenced early in 1948 between France and Italy. Britain had a clear economic interest in these movements; besides, her prestige in western Europe at the end of the war was such that it rested with her to influence the general direction they should take. As Bevin put it in January 1948, 'Britain cannot stand outside Europe and regard her problems as quite separate from those of her European neighbours'.[1] On March 4, 1947, the British Government had entered into the Treaty of Dunkirk with France; this was a purely defensive arrangement pledging either country for a period of fifty years to give the other all the military and other support in its power in the event of Britain or France becoming again involved in hostilities with Germany.[2] With the incorporation of the western zones of Germany into ERP the Dunkirk Treaty lost much of its significance, but it remained an assurance to France as west Germany was absorbed step by step into western security arrangements. On January 22, 1948, when it had become clear, first, that Russia intended to try to wreck the European recovery programme and, second, that four-Power agreement on Germany had failed to materialize at the meetings of the Council of Foreign Ministers in Moscow in March–April 1947, Mr Bevin came out with the Government's proposals for west European union. 'All these developments,' he said, 'point to the conclusion that the free countries of west Europe must draw closely together. . . . I believe the time is ripe for a consolidation of Western Europe. First in this context we think of the people of France . . . we are not now preparing a formal political union with France . . . but we shall maintain the closest possible contact. . . . The time has come to find ways and means of developing our relations with the Benelux countries. . . . I hope that treaties will be signed with our near neighbours, the

[1] 446 H.C. Deb. 5s. Col. 397 (January 22, 1948).
[2] Treaty of Alliance and Mutual Assistance between His Majesty in respect of the United Kingdom of Great Britain and Northern Ireland and the President of the French Republic, Cmd. 7217 of 1947.

Benelux countries, making our treaty with France an important nucleus in western Europe. We have then to go beyond the circle of our immediate neighbours . . . (to) Italy.'[1]

The enthusiasts for closer British relations with Europe, and especially those who supported the unofficial United Europe Movement of which Churchill had assumed the leadership, heard these words with dismay. They did seem to rule out a common political framework for western Europe with Britain forming a distinct element. What Bevin evidently had in mind was a number of bilateral defensive pacts with the west European countries severally, on the model of the Dunkirk Treaty, rather than a single political and economic complex. The form eventually taken by the Foreign Secretary's gropings, the Treaty of Economic, Social and Cultural Collaboration and Collective Self-Defence, signed at Brussels on March 17, 1948, actually turned out to be a multilateral arrangement uniting Britain with Belgium, France, Luxemburg and the Netherlands in economic, social and cultural co-operation as well as defence; it provided for a permanent structure consisting of a Consultative Council of the Foreign Ministers of the five signatories, to meet at least once every three months in the various capitals in turn for continuous consultation on the questions covered by the treaty, and a committee formed from the five Defence Ministers, together with a Permanent Military Committee in London and a nucleus Land, Air and Naval Command.[2] But none of this modified the impression that the Brussels Treaty was essentially a provision for mutual aid in the event of an armed attack in Europe, rather than a step towards federal Europe. The British Government remained firmly opposed to the idea of closer constitutional integration. In the view of Christopher Mayhew, the Under-Secretary of State for Foreign Affairs, 'it would be wrong to support a scheme such as this well-known scheme for the United States of Europe merely because it aims at the elimination of sovereignty'. The Cabinet's position from the outset was that 'at present these schemes are premature and more likely to lead to disunity than to unity in Europe'.[3] The Foreign Secretary had sounded the same note a week after Mr Marshall's Harvard speech, when the tide of pan-European feeling was rising. The emphasis in European recovery, he said, should be

[1] 446 H.C. Deb. 5s. Col. 395 (January 22, 1948).
[2] Treaty of Economic, Social and Cultural Collaboration and Collective Self-Defence, Brussels, March 17, 1948, Cmd. 7599 of 1948. Collective Defence under the Brussels and North Atlantic Treaties, Cmd. 7883 of 1950.
[3] 433 H.C. Deb. 5s. Col. 2400 (February 27, 1947).

on severely functional co-operation in food production, coal mining and transport. He repeated that Britain was not solely a European Power. Echoing a standard British theme he continued: 'while the first and most urgent problem is to get Europe right, there must be a wider and more comprehensive plan which will bring greater productivity and an even flow of trade and exchange throughout the world'.[1]

This attitude towards European union was based upon three major considerations. First, it was assumed that west Europe was indefensible against a Soviet military attack and incapable of rising to its feet economically unless a permanent link with the United States was forged. That link, the Government believed, could neither be created nor kept in repair without the exercise in Washington of an independent British influence, derived from the long diplomatic experience of the United Kingdom and its world-wide status, symbolized, though not exclusively, by the Commonwealth. Secondly, there was concern in Labour Party circles lest the postwar mood in western Europe of revolt against national sovereignty should sweep Britain into supranationalist arrangements at the moment when the main levers of her economy were being brought, for the first time in peace, under state control at home. Thirdly, the hope still flickered that, despite Communist hostility towards the Marshall plan, European recovery would not have the effect of dividing the continent for all time. It could never be wholly consistent with traditional British assumptions, or serviceable to British interests, to agree too readily with the gloomy diagnostics of Zdanov at the inaugural meeting of the Cominform, by which the world was pronounced to be irrevocably split into two camps.

The diplomatic consequences

In the period between the Potsdam conference, the last of the wartime 'summit' meetings with Russia, and the launching of ERP in 1948 the strain of insolvency made its impact at every point in British foreign policy. Problems pressing for solution were assisted neither by the hideously narrow financial margins in which the country moved nor by the pressures at home for some relief from austerity. Although Bevin was somewhat given to dwelling on his burdens, his favourite lament, 'all the world is in trouble, I have to deal with all these troubles at once', not unfairly described his predicament. Calumny from the Soviet Union and her allies was

[1] In a speech to the Foreign Press Association, June 13, 1947; *The Times*, June 14, 1947.

continuous, rising to an intensity which in old diplomacy would have signalled the approach of war. At the United Nations Security Council on January 17, 1946, only four days after its first meeting, the Soviet representative, the biting and brilliant Vyshinsky, by way of reply to Western attacks on Soviet policy in Iran accused Britain of attempting to impose a Fascist dictatorship on Greece. Bevin's position was not an easy one. The Greek Government, with British consent, had postponed for a period vaguely described as two or three years the national plebiscite on the constitutional future of the country which had been promised in the Varkiza agreement of February 12, 1945, which ended the civil war with the Greek Communists. Trade union leaders in the country had received rough treatment, and had their champions in the House of Commons. Moreover the United States delegation at the Security Council feared the injurious effects of public wrangling in the United Nations on an American public opinion which had been induced to regard that organ as the main hope for peace. But this did not deter the Foreign Secretary from making some of his typically trenchant speeches, the tone of which alarmed his American colleague almost as much as it surprised the Russians. The speeches secured acceptance of the view that British troops in Greece did not constitute a threat to peace and security as Vyshinsky alleged. The Security Council therefore divested itself of the subject on May 6th.

Simultaneously with the Greek question British policy in Indonesia came under attack at the Security Council from the Soviet side. Agreement had been reached with the United States Command in the Pacific in 1945 that, as soon as the Imperial Government in Tokyo capitulated, British troops should disembark in the Dutch East Indies in order to accept the surrender of Japanese forces there and to release British and Dutch internees. By a chapter of accidents their arrival was delayed until September. Meanwhile local nationalist forces aiming at the expulsion of European rule had taken advantage of the interregnum to establish control. On August 19th, a month before the British landed in Java, they created an Indonesian Republic under the presidency of Dr Soekarno. The British commander, General Christison, while genuinely reluctant to intervene in political issues, had no alternative but to try to disarm the nationalists if he was to carry out his instructions to restore order. In doing so he somewhat unwisely made use of Japanese troops and this action, when denounced at the Security Council by the Ukrainian delegate, Dimitri Manuilsky, with the support of Vyshinsky, aroused all the anti-colonialist sentiments which were becoming perhaps the strong-

D

est single force in the United Nations. The position was hardly made easier for Britain by Bevin's refusal to accept the Soviet proposal to send a mission of inquiry to Indonesia. For this seemed to throw doubt on the British contention that the rebels did not represent a genuine nationalist movement; it also served to endorse Soviet tactics of forbidding international commissions of inquiry in areas under Soviet control. The situation was saved by British pressure on the Dutch behind the scenes, which secured an announcement from The Hague that negotiations would shortly begin on the basis of the right of the Indonesian people to determine their own destiny within the framework of the Kingdom of the Netherlands. Only the Soviet Union and Poland, then a non-permanent member of the Security Council, supported the Ukrainian resolution in favour of keeping the question on the agenda and accordingly it passed out of the Council's purview. The sequel to the talks between the Netherlands Government and the Indonesian nationalist leaders was the Linggadjati Agreement of November 15, 1946, which gave *de facto* recognition to an independent United States of Indonesia, which was to form part of a Netherlands-Indonesian Union together with the Netherlands, Surinam and Curaçao.

Likewise, in the wearisome negotiations to draw up peace treaties with the five ex-enemy states, Bulgaria, Finland, Hungary, Italy and Rumania, the hard-pressed position of Britain, and the East-West schism which was an integral part of it, came forcefully to light. While Bevin was protesting from the Treasury bench at Westminster that power-politics and spheres of influence were things of the past, the main function of the negotiations, extending from the first meeting of the four-Power Council of Foreign Ministers on September 11, 1945, to the signing of the treaties on February 10, 1947, was to reaffirm the division between the Soviet-dominated Balkan states on one side and western-oriented Italy on the other, with Finland occupying an indeterminate middle ground between. The first two stages of work on the treaties comprised, respectively, the Foreign Ministers' meetings in London in September-October 1945 and in Moscow between December 16 and 27, 1945, and the drafting of the peace treaties at the Foreign Ministers' meeting in Paris from April to June 1946 on the basis of preparations made by their deputies working in London. It was clear in these two phases that the three western Powers were exploring the prospects of relaxing Russia's grip on the Balkan states, while Molotov played a contrary tune in his attempts to weaken Italy, the public opinion of which the western Powers were now endeavouring to win to their own side. At the third stage of the negotiations, represented by the Peace Conference in Paris of the four major Powers together with China and sixteen other countries, which was in continuous session from July 29 to October 15, 1946, the ostensible aim was to allow the smaller members of the United Nations coalition to have their say on the labours of the Council of Foreign Ministers. In reality the conference took the form of a struggle for influence over these minor countries between the United States and the Soviet Union. In this struggle the United States Secretary of State, James Byrnes, learning the new role of spokesman for the western nations, enjoyed on the whole the greater success. Of one hundred recommendations sent forward by the Paris Conference to the Council of Foreign Ministers at their final session on the treaties in New York in November and December 1946 the great majority were endorsements of the British and American positions. The treaties were eventually signed in Paris by representatives of the twenty-one nations and the five ex-enemy states on February 10, 1947.[1]

Three leading British preoccupations were distinguishable in these negotiations. First, while there was no mistaking Russia's determination to have the dominant voice in the politics of the Balkan states north of Greece, it was hoped to secure terms of peace which might still leave the Danube basin open to influence from the west. In the event this was achieved only in one minor respect, and that a temporary one. From the outset Soviet delegates insisted that control of the Danube was a matter for the riparian states alone, of which Russia, after her acquisition of Bessarabia from Rumania, was one. In doing so they ignored the British argument that the river had been a matter of general international concern since the Peace of Paris in 1856. At the Foreign Ministers' meeting in New York in December 1946, however, Molotov suddenly agreed to join in a declaration by the four Powers to convene, within six months of the treaties coming into force, a conference to establish a new regime for the Danube based on the freedom of trade and navigation assured by the peace treaties with the three Balkan states. The conference duly met in Belgrade on July 30, 1948, but the three Western Powers failed to prevent a convention being signed by the riparian states on August 18th which placed in their own hands the supervision of the river as far as the Hungarian frontier with Austria. In effect this meant control by Russia.[2]

---

[1] Commentary on the Treaties of Peace with Italy, Rumania, Bulgaria, Hungary and Finland, Cmd. 7026 of 1947, pp. 3–4.
[2] Peter Calvocoressi, *Survey of International Affairs 1947–48*, London, 1952, pp. 172–3.

But the most serious failure of the West to moderate Soviet pressure on the Balkan states was the total ineffectiveness of the obligations to maintain human rights to which Bulgaria, Hungary and Rumania were bound by the peace treaties.[1] These legalisms could do nothing to check the drift to one-party rule by identical stages in the three states. When the peace treaty negotiations opened in September 1945 Britain was still refusing to recognize the governments of these countries; in Bevin's words 'wartime totalitarianism had been succeeded by peacetime totalitarianism'.[2] But by the time Britain ratified the treaties on April 29, 1947, recognition of the Bulgarian, Hungarian and Rumanian regimes could no longer be withheld. The utmost that the western Powers could do was to veto for a brief period their application for admission to the United Nations on the ground that human rights were not assured to their peoples. Nevertheless, the persecution of the Peasant Parties and the Social Democrats continued. In Bulgaria the leader of the Agrarian Party, Petkov, was arrested on July 24, 1947, and indicted on a charge of treason. In September he was executed. After general elections in Bulgaria, which in the opinion of the British Government were corrupt, twenty-three Opposition deputies who had been allowed to sit in Parliament were expelled. The same process was taking place in Rumania. The general elections there, in the British Government's view, had been marked by wholesale falsification of the results by the authorities.[3] Maniu, the leader of the Rumanian National Peasant Party, was sentenced to life imprisonment in July 1947 and the Social Democratic and Communist parties were forcibly united in February 1948. But the most serious turn of events occurred in Hungary, where the Secretary-General of the ruling party, the Smallholders, was arrested by the Soviet military authorities on February 26, 1947, on a charge of espionage against the Red Army. All British and American efforts to obtain information about his fate were unsuccessful. The final blow was the dismissal of Prime Minister Nagy, the leader of the Smallholders' Party on May 29th. Further protests by Britain and the United States only had the effect of tightening Communist control.

A circumstance which helped the Communists in these three

---

[1] Treaty Series No. 55 (1948), Treaty of Peace with Rumania, Cmd. 7486, Part II, Sect. I, Article 3. Treaty Series No. 52 (1938), Treaty of Peace with Bulgaria, Cmd. 7483, Part II, Sect. I, Article 2. Treaty Series No. 54 (1948), Treaty of Peace with Hungary, Cmd. 7485, Part II, Sect. I, Article 2.

[2] 413 H.C. Deb. 5s. Col. 291 (August 20, 1945).

[3] 438 H.C. Deb. 5s. Col. 2232–4 (June 19, 1947).

countries, apart from the geographical proximity of the USSR, was the refusal of Russia to discuss a peace treaty with Austria at the Council of Foreign Ministers. For so long as there was no progress on the Austrian question the Soviet Union retained the right by the peace treaties with Hungary and Rumania to keep forces in those countries in order to protect lines of communication with her occupation zone in Austria. Even Austria, although she had, unlike Germany, retained an independent government, was not immune from Communist pressure. While the consolidation of Communist power in east Europe was going forward the leader of the Austrian Communist Party, Herr Fischer, was bullying the Chancellor, Dr Figl, to admit more Communists into his Cabinet, even though the Communists, after elections supervised by a Four-Power commission, held only four out of the 165 seats in the Austrian Chamber. When a peace treaty was finally signed with Austria in May 1955, however, she was still a non-Communist state. The peace treaties therefore, so far from shaking Soviet dominance in east Europe, to all appearances had placed the final seal upon it. Moreover, what was happening in the three Balkan states had its parallels in other parts of Europe accessible to Soviet influence. In Poland contrived elections in January 1947 secured the mastery over the country of the Democratic Bloc, consisting mainly of the Communists and their allies. In the course of 1947 the Polish Peasant Party and the Social Democrats were gradually reduced to impotence. There followed in February 1948 a textbook Communist *coup* in Czechoslovakia which drew the only western-oriented state in east Europe behind the Iron Curtain.

The second British object in the peace treaty negotiations had been to establish an economically viable Italy, which would be neither a burden to its conquerors nor a victim of excessive reparation obligations, and if possible with its face turned towards the west. 'Our own policy towards Italy,' said Bevin in June 1946, 'is first to enable her to repay what has been supplied as relief; secondly, to help her restore her economy on a peacetime basis and thereafter to remove any surplus war machinery and equipment which is not needed for peacetime economy.'[1] He therefore sought to frustrate the more fantastic reparation claims entered up against Italy by the smaller countries at the Paris Peace Conference and, while endeavouring to limit Russia's claim, tried to compensate her in kind, as for instance, by handing over Italian passenger liners. These efforts were successful in reducing the final reparation obligation in the Italian treaty to

[1] 423 H.C. Deb. 5s. Col. 1838 (June 4th).

$360 million. Of this Russia was to receive $100 million, the two western Powers agreeing to waive their reparation claims. This reparation bill, though certain items in the treaty were left for further specification, was well within Italy's capacity to pay. Although the country had suffered extensive damage to its agricultural areas in the south, the industrial north had come through the war relatively unscathed and Italy's industrious working population, now without heavy armaments or unproductive colonies to maintain, was greater than before the war. But Bevin did not succeed in his demand that no reparations should be paid out of current production, although a qualified two-year moratorium was introduced into the clauses of the treaty referring to payments from this source. The effect of this was that the occupying Powers, Britain and the United States, stood very little chance of receiving back any of the $1,000 million of relief which they had poured into the country after its unconditional surrender until the whole reparation bill had been met.[1]

As to the Italian frontiers, the British desire to keep Italy in much the same physical shape as before the war, with adjustments in the east to correct the excessive territorial gains of 1919, was largely fulfilled. Four minor rectifications in the west, involving less than 5,000 people, were made in France's favour. In the north the frontier with Austria at the Brenner Pass remained unchanged, thus leaving the 300,000 Austrians in the Alto Adige still in Italy. This decision was sharply criticized in the House of Commons as reminiscent of Axis diplomacy, and it was clearly inconsistent with the decision of the Foreign Ministers at their first meeting in September 1945, when they determined to apply the ethnic principle to Italy's frontiers. In the prevailing balance of power, overshadowing more generous considerations, Italian goodwill was deemed to be more important to the western Powers than Austrian national rights. On Italy's eastern borders, however, the Soviet proposal that the whole of Venezia Giulia, which had been awarded to Italy in 1915 as her price for joining the Entente, should be ceded to Yugoslavia was defeated; it would have meant putting the Italian port and city of Trieste into Slav hands and transferring half a million Italians to foreign rule. The three western Powers adopted the French compromise proposal, the most unfavourable to Italy of the western suggestions, that the new frontier should run from the Austrian border at a point somewhat to the east of Tarvisio, then west of the Izonzo river as far as Gorizia, at which point the boundary would sweep eastwards

[1] Council on Foreign Relations, *The United States in World Affairs 1945–47*, New York, 1947, p. 53.

across the river, leaving Trieste on the Italian side and meeting the sea at Cittanova on the Gulf of Venice.

From the ethnic point of view this proposal was the most acceptable of all those considered by the Foreign Ministers; it was estimated to leave only 60,000 Slavs and 100,000 Italians divided from their countrymen. Opposition naturally came from Belgrade, which gave way only when it became clear that Russia was willing to accept the French line on the tacit understanding that her own ideas should have priority in the settlement with the Balkan states. This bargain was finally made possible through the introduction of the conception of a Free Territory of Trieste, to be placed under the protection of the United Nations Security Council. This was to extend from Duino in the North to Cittanova in the south and represented a reconciliation of Italian sovereignty over Trieste with the interests of the Balkan states in the port. The idea was consistent with the British desire to keep Trieste open as a possible avenue for future western economic communications with the rapidly closing Balkans. It was vital, however, Mr Bevin said, that the responsibilities of the Security Council should begin from the moment the Italian treaty came into force and that the Governor of the Free Territory should possess adequate power to carry out the Council's responsibilities on the spot. Otherwise the Free Territory ran the risk of being subverted from the Balkan side.[1] But the Trieste compromise, which endured until 1954, when the territory was divided between Italy and Yugoslavia, ensured that, whatever Communist pressures might be exerted lower down the Dalmatian coast, the outlet of Trieste would not be available as a Communist foothold in the Adriatic.

The third British preoccupation was to place obstacles in the way of any attempted Soviet penetration into the Mediterranean; that, in the Foreign Secretary's words, would be a 'thrust across our throat'. It was achieved by keeping the three ex-Italian colonies in Africa, Italian Somaliland, Eritrea and Libya, temporarily in British hands. Agreement was reached to cede the fourth group, the Dodecanese islands, to Greece after the strongest Soviet opposition in the Council of Foreign Ministers. Thus Molotov's insistent demand for either a Soviet trusteeship or a Soviet share in a joint trusteeship over Tripolitania was fobbed off to the last. Britain herself claimed that she had no interest in any trusteeship over the former Italian colonies, although she would have accepted one for Cyrenaica, the eastern portion of Libya, in order to fulfil the promise given by Eden to the Senussi tribes in 1942 that they would never be returned

[1] 427 H.C. Deb. 5s. Col. 1504. (October 22, 1946).

to Italian rule. The British Government also proposed a British trusteeship to be formed out of British, French and Italian Somaliland, together with the Somali parts of Kenya and a portion of Ethiopia (which would be otherwise compensated) in order to provide common grazing grounds for the nomadic peoples of these areas. This suggestion was denounced as blatant imperialism by the Soviet Foreign Minister and it was dropped. It remained essential, however, that whichever of the many proposals were finally adopted, no trusteeship should be granted to Russia or any ally of Russia. The different possibilities were discussed at length but no agreement could be reached for insertion into the Italian treaty. The problem was therefore referred back to the Foreign Ministers for a further year's discussion. It was agreed that if the Foreign Ministers were still unable to decide the General Assembly of the United Nations should be left to determine the future of the colonies. In the meantime they continued under British administration.[1]

The restraint of Soviet pressure: from Germany to Japan

The two features of the postwar scene which had been evident during the interchanges on the peace treaties, that is, the division of forces between East and West and the economic stresses facing Britain, characterized other problems with which London had to deal in this period. It was noted, however, that, as these problems extended outwards from Europe, the effects of the East-West schism tended to be somewhat less marked. But the inclination of the policies of the west European nations, including Britain, to be interfused with that of the United States grew.

The central point of East-West tensions was Germany.[2] It was widely felt that peace had been made too quickly with Germany in 1919 for the more remote consequences to be weighed. Neither Russia or the western Powers were in a hurry to see peace concluded with a central German Government until more was known of the kind of political forces likely to come to the surface in that country. For Britain the immediate problem was to resuscitate a controlled political life in the zone assigned to her by holding elections first at the local, then at the provincial level, while attempting at all price to make the zone self-supporting. The cost of maintaining the zone, £80 million a year and rising to an estimated £130 million in 1947, most of which had to be paid in dollars, was an unwelcome strain on

[1] Treaties of Peace with Italy, Rumania, Bulgaria, Hungary and Finland, Cmd. 7022 of 1947, pp. 15, 65.
[2] See Chapter III.

the British balance of payments. Germany, contrary to the Potsdam agreement, was not being treated by the four Powers as an economic unit; in particular the food producing areas of the east, now under Soviet occupation, were not furnishing the industrial western regions with the imports necessary to maintain life. But neither were these areas, especially the British-occupied Ruhr, with its traditional dense concentration of population and heavy industry, in a position to purchase food imports on world markets. Their inability to do so was partly due to the Four-Power Level of Industry Agreement, which in the opinion of the British Government was too low, partly to the facts that the Ruhr shared the general economic paralysis of western Europe and the future ownership of Germany's heavy industry was still unsettled.

On the last of these issues the views of France could not be ignored. These were that the Saar should be brought under French adminis-tration, though not necessarily French sovereignty, and that the Ruhr and the whole west bank of the Rhine should be detached from Germany and formed into some kind of independent state. The British Government were ready to agree to the French claim as con-cerned the Saar but saw no reason to revise the objections raised in 1919 to further dismemberment of Germany. A federal German system was about as far as they would travel along that road. This left unsolved the question of the Ruhr industries. Bevin's Labour supporters were indignant at any suggestion that this power-house of western Europe should be restored to the magnates who had 'paid Hitler'. Nevertheless the economic strain of the British zone was making itself felt and it was clear that if the United States was to help with the zonal deficit that country's opinion was bound to influence the disposal of the Ruhr industries. On December 2, 1946, an agreement was reached in New York between the United States and Britain by which the zones these two countries occupied in Germany were fused to form a single economic unit.[1] Although the burden on Britain was not directly lightened by the agreement, its effects were expected to relieve her of further financial liability in Germany in 1949, by which date a start could be made on repaying the costs of occupation. The result in terms of the Government's attitude towards the ownership of the Ruhr industries was striking. On October 22nd, before the agreement to create Bizonia, Bevin told the Commons that 'our intention is that those industries should be owned and controlled in future by the public'.[2] When he spoke on

[1] Cmd. 6984 of 1946.
[2] 427 H.C. Deb. 5s. Col. 1516,

the subject again in the House on May 15, 1947, after the Bizone agreement had come into effect on January 1st he was more circumspect. The rights of the allies, he said, must be safeguarded and German opinion had to be taken into account.[1] This foreshadowed the later Anglo-American agreement that the question should be left to the decision of a freely elected German government.

A comparable assimilation of British commitments with American took place in the Near East. British military forces had been in Greece since the outbreak of the civil war in December 1944 in order to prevent an unconstitutional Communist seizure of power. The position was invidious for a Labour Government, all the more so since Greek leaders followed the Balkan custom of allowing opponents to think out the problems of the day in a quiet cell. Throughout 1946 Bevin was under pressure from his back benches, which condemned the use of British bayonets to support a Greek military dictatorship. The Foreign Secretary's defence was that the Greek elections held in March 1946 had been supervised by British, French and American commissioners and were the fairest in Greek history. The threat to democracy in Greece, he said, came, not from the Government but from the EAM (Communist) faction and from armed incursions across Greece's northern frontiers. To deal with these raids he tried and failed at the Council of Foreign Ministers to secure a frontier readjustment in Greece's favour at the expense of Bulgaria. However, by Article XII of the peace treaty certain demilitarization measures were imposed on Bulgaria along her borders with Greece. But it was neither criticism from home nor calumny from abroad which compelled Britain to withdraw from Greece; it was the financial crisis. It was this which forced the Government to notify both the Greek and United States Governments that further British assistance to Greece would not be forthcoming after March 31, 1947. The result was that on March 3rd the Greek Prime Minister and Foreign Minister, Maximos and Tsaldaris, set out in a letter to the American President the expected plight of the country after the British withdrawal. At the same time Britain was obliged to terminate the assistance she was giving to Turkey, the victim of menacing Soviet pressures throughout 1946. In notes to the western allies and Turkey the Soviet Union demanded a new regime of the Straits to which only Black Sea Powers would be parties; she also argued that responsibility for defence of the Straits should not be Turkey's alone, as under the existing Montreux Convention of 1936 on the Straits, but should be shared with Russia. Britain was fully behind

[1] 437 H.C. Deb. 5s. Col. 1737.

Ankara in its refusal to entertain either demand, although Bevin was agreeable to a conference for revising the now out-of-date Montreux Convention.[1] But with the British Government actively contracting their commitments there was a distinct possibility that Turkey, though economically strong, might find it impossible to withstand Soviet demands.

The answer came from the United States in a revolutionary message to Congress of President Truman on March 12, 1947. The so-called 'Truman Doctrine' which the message expressed differed from the Monroe Doctrine of 1823 in having no defined geographical application. In language which was criticized for its disturbing vagueness it described United States policy as one of support for 'free peoples who are resisting attempted subjugation by armed minorities and by outside pressure'. Although the President did ask for a specific sum, $400 million, for a year's assistance to Greece and Turkey, together with the despatch of civil and military officials to advise on the use of the funds, he ended the message by saying that he would not hesitate to come before Congress again for help if required.[2] It was clearly intended that the Doctrine should not necessarily be restricted to the two states whose appeals had evoked it. It was in fact largely to restrict this implication, as well as to amalgamate a number of separate requests for help, that the Marshall offer was put forward in June. For Britain, however, the significance of the Truman Doctrine lay in the fact that it represented, in the clearest possible manner, the abandonment of historic commitments on the southern fringe of Europe. It remained to be seen whether these commitments could be resumed after the economic crisis had passed.

In a sharp dispute between the Soviet Union and Iran which assumed critical proportions during 1946, thus forming a further example of Russia's pressure across her southern borders, it was again the United States which took the lead in upholding Iran's right to be heard at the Security Council and in resisting Soviet designs on the country's northern provinces. This was all the more striking in that the United States had had no share in the treaty signed in 1942 by which Iran consented to an Anglo-Russian military occupation as a wartime measure. At the Council of Foreign Ministers in London in September 1945 Molotov had given an undertaking that Soviet forces would be withdrawn from northern Iran by the following March 2nd. The first threat to this undertaking came in

[1] 427 H.C. Deb. 5s. Col. 1495 (October 22, 1946).
[2] Department of State, *Bulletin*, March 23, 1947, pp. 534–7.

November, when the Iranian province under Soviet occupation, Azerbaijan, proclaimed its autonomy at the instance of the left-wing Democratic Party and Russia refused to allow two battalions sent by the Government in Teheran to enter the province to restore their authority. When the four Foreign Ministers met in Moscow in December Bevin proposed the despatch of a commission representing the four Powers to report on the facts. Molotov dissented.[1] Iran therefore decided to take the case to the newly formed United Nations Security Council.

There then intervened one of the twists of Persian politics by which the country traditionally accommodated itself to pressures from the great Powers. A new regime came to power, led by the pro-Soviet Ahmad Ghavam es Saltaneh, and agreed to suspend the appeal to world opinion pending direct negotiations with Moscow. The Soviet Government, thinking they had the situation in hand, formulated their demands; they included the right to keep troops in Iran *sine die*, the recognition by Iran of an autonomous Azerbaijan and a Soviet share in the northern oilfields of Iran. Not even the pliant Iranian Premier could satisfy such demands and March 2nd came and went without the withdrawal of Soviet forces. The only outcome of the Soviet-Iranian talks was a powerful movement of opinion in the United States towards Iran's side. Despite Russian efforts to prevent the Security Council from discussing the question, including a decision, at that time sufficiently novel to be alarming, by the Soviet representative, Gromyko, to boycott the Council's meeting, the Council continued its hearings, largely owing to the calm insistence of the American Secretary of State, James Byrnes. On March 24th an agreement was reached between Moscow and the Iranian Government by which Soviet troops were to withdraw within six weeks, provided the autonomy of Azerbaijan was recognised and the joint Soviet-Iranian companies to exploit the northern oil wells agreed to. Accordingly, the Soviet military evacuation was completed on May 9th and on May 21st the Iranian Government informed the Security Council that Soviet troops had left the country. It testified to the difficulties faced even by a great Power in forcing a Middle Eastern country to dance to its own tune that, by the end of the year, the Soviet-sponsored regime in Azarbaijan had fallen and the future of the joint oil companies was in doubt. The incident showed that Iran was one of the points where Soviet pressure could be contained, given firmness. It also showed that at Iran's side stood a United States which had so completely inherited Britain's role of policing

[1] James Byrnes, *Speaking Frankly*, London, 1947, pp. 120–1.

the southern margins of Russia that, whereas at the beginning of the crisis American opinion tended to regard Iran as under almost equal threat from Britain as from Russia, by May 1946 it was loudly applauding Byrnes for his defence of Iran against her northern neighbour.

At the furthest remove from Europe the United States established at an early stage its primacy in the occupation of Japan. The American administration's Initial Post-Surrender Policy statement of September 6, 1945, provided that, in the event of differences between the allies over policy in Japan, 'the policy of the United States shall govern'. The instrument of this policy, the Olympian General MacArthur, had already embarked upon reforming Japanese life and purging the militarist elements before Washington seriously took up the question of consultation with the allies. Britain joined Russia in voicing resentment at this attitude, especially when Secretary of State Byrnes refused to create an allied control council in Tokyo during the Foreign Ministers' meeting in London in October 1945.[1] Particular indignation came from Australia, with its bitter recollections of the struggle against Japan; the Australian Prime Minister, Dr Evatt, acidly reflected on what he called American preferences for theoretical rather than practical international co-operation. In deference to such criticisms Byrnes relented at the Foreign Ministers' conference in Washington in December and consented to an eleven-Power Far Eastern Commission to sit in that city, on which Britain and Russia would be represented, and a Four-Power Control Council to sit in Tokyo, representing the United States, the British Commonwealth, China and the Soviet Union. The Commission was supposed to formulate general principles for the Occupation and review directives issued to the Supreme Commander by his own government, while the Council was authorized to consult with him on the fulfilment of these directives. On basic issues, such as that of the new Japanese constitution, General MacArthur was required to delay his orders, if the Council insisted, until the Far Eastern Commission had given its decision on differences between the General and the Council.[2] In addition, token Commonwealth forces were to take their place in the hitherto wholly American machinery of Occupation.

This machinery of inter-Allied consultation was for all material purposes without effect. The Occupation remained, as it had begun, an American affair. The British Commonwealth representative on the Control Council in Tokyo, Professor MacMahon Ball, an Aus-

[1] Byrnes, *op. cit.*, p. 102.
[2] W. MacMahon Ball, *Japan, Enemy or Ally?* London, 1948, pp. 27–29.

tralian, untiringly wrestled with his United States colleague, Ambassador George Atcheson, jnr., objecting not so much to the Supreme Commander's policy as to his patent contempt for the consultative machinery. In reply General MacArthur had his spokesman on the Council say that all major directives to Japan had been issued by January 1946, before the Council met, and that therefore the duties of the Council were superfluous.[1] The United States thus appeared to be adopting in Japan the same principle Britain followed in the ex-Italian colonies in Africa, namely that conquest confers the right to determine the future of the conquered. But Washington also realized that to introduce genuine quadripartite control into Japan meant to open the door to the same failure in international co-operation which was taking place in Germany. Japan itself was not the question; the situation in Japan was merely a function of the state of Russo-American relations.

The camps take shape

In explaining the British Government's approach to the problems of these stressful years Ernest Bevin was never at loss for the misty generality. He abjured 'power politics, spheres of influence and all that kind of approach to world affairs'. He pleaded with other countries to 'put their cards on the table face upwards', in the massive confidence that no aces would be found up Britain's sleeve.[2] He was willing to join with anybody to form a world federation, but said we must be sensible and look upon the United Nations as the 'prelude to further development'.[3] These open-handed gestures were no doubt intended for the benefit of the Labour Party's rank-and-file, disturbed to see their own Minister treading the paths of traditional diplomacy. But Bevin was himself disposed to live on two planes, that of guileless sonority—as though the world would be all sweetness and light if only foreign statesmen were as sincere as himself— and the plane of tough defence of British interests. As for the latter, there were few tricks which the Foreign Secretary missed during these years. British insolvency made itself felt at every point in the hand he could play. Nevertheless the Government continued their efforts to keep the lines open to Russia, refusing to accept the inference from postwar dealings with Moscow that the world was irremediably split.

In December 1945 Bevin saw Marshal Stalin in Moscow and pro-

[1] W. MacMahon Ball, *Japan, Enemy or Ally?*
[2] 415 H.C. Deb. 5s. Col. 1337 (November 7, 1945).
[3] *Ibid.*, 416 Col. 786 (November 23, 1945).

posed an extension of the Anglo-Soviet Treaty of May 1942 from twenty to fifty years. 'I had at the back of mind,' he said, 'the creation of some permanent link between the two countries which would avoid misunderstanding.'[1] It was not, however, until March 29, 1947, that talks actually began in Moscow between the British Ambassador and Vyshinsky and then only to peter out in May. In June 1946 the Prime Minister was firmly rejecting the notion of crystallized blocs, with Britain's position frozen in the Western bloc. 'We do not want in any any way,' Attlee said, 'to get an exclusive friendship . . . I say that it would be a fatal thing to accentuate, in any way, this line of division between east and west Europe, because we have to try to get across the barrier and get a real understanding . . . we have equally to try to understand the Russian mind and Russian history to understand why they take the line they do.'[2] For the United States, still mentally remote from European affairs, the idea of a divided world might seem little more than an extension of the frontiers of American isolation. For Britain, whose policy had since 1918 been that of reconciliation between the Powers, division could only be the conclusion of despair. The facts which rendered the acceptance of division unavoidable, as stated by Churchill, were bleak: 'it is better to have a world united than a world divided, but it is better to have a world divided than a world destroyed'. What the Marshall plan, the Truman Doctrine and the fusion of the two western zones of Germany had done was to pose the question whether the 'all-inclusive friendship' was at all feasible. The descent into doubt was swift.

[1] 423 H.C. Deb. 5s. Col. 1828 (June 4, 1946).
[2] *Ibid.*, 423 Cols. 2037–8 (June 5th).

CHAPTER THREE

The Partition of Germany

For Britain the German problem in 1945 was in some ways similar to what it had been in 1918. After both wars public opinion was convinced of the importance of inter-Allied unity to prevent Germany ever again becoming a menace to peace; the disarray of the anti-Nazi forces in Europe in the 1930s had at last driven this lesson home. Few people objected to the exaction of retribution from Germany's war leaders, despite the failure of war trials after the First World War. Moreover, there was in 1945, as in 1918, one country among the Allies who wished to extract reparations from Germany at whatever cost to Europe as a whole, and who was ready to go to any lengths to render Germany incapable of further aggression. France had played that role in 1918; now it was assumed by Russia. But whereas France had tried to impose guarantees for the fulfilment of the Versailles Treaty on the weak Weimar regime in Germany, Russia sought a strong central government in Germany, which she hoped would be Communist and hence serve her own purposes. From these policies Britain dissented, exactly as she had done after 1918; she desired a disciplined but solvent Germany, which would be no financial burden to its conquerors, and which would be ruled eventually by liberal forces in the western sense. Britain had discovered in the 1920s the folly of exacting reparations from Germany to the general ruin of Europe; she also looked to Four-Power co-operation for keeping Germany disarmed, rather than to the rigid control of internal German politics.

The essential difference, however, between the German problem of the 1920s and that of 1945 was that on June 28, 1919, a German delegation, representing a central German government, had signed a peace treaty laying down in some detail the terms of future relations between the Allies and Germany; whereas in 1945 the Allies themselves had to take over the machinery of government in the country they had defeated. This was partly because the Allies had pledged themselves to an Unconditional Surrender policy, but more importantly because Hitler's regime had left in Germany no successor capable of executing any conditions of the Allies. The Allies in 1945 were therefore not required to agree between themselves on peace terms to be presented to a German government, and hence the differences in their approaches to the German problem were never moderated, as in 1919, by the fear that either Germany would refuse to sign their terms or would try to play off one of its conquerors against the others. On the contrary, the Allies were masters of Germany in law and fact; their problem was the far more difficult one of determining how they would rule Germany together. The machinery through which this joint government was to function was the military occupation of the country. There had been a military occupation in Germany after 1919. But then it was partial, being confined to the west bank of the Rhine and the main bridgeheads of the river; it was limited to fifteen years, was reduced by five-year periods and its purpose was to ensure that the terms of the treaty were carried out. In 1945 the occupation covered the whole country, was unlimited in time and was meant, not to force a German government to do the Allies' will, but to provide a framework in which the Allies could carry out their separate wills in German territory.

The machinery of Allied occupation was determined before agreement was reached, or seriously attempted, on any Four-Power policy for governing Germany within the framework of the occupation. The only notable effort to frame a policy for postwar Germany was the so-called Morgenthau Plan, named after the then United States Secretary for the Treasury, which was provisionally adopted by the President and Mr Churchill at their Quebec meeting in September 1944.[1] This envisaged the extraordinary picture of a Germany reduced to a pastoralized state, with no power to maintain a modern standard of living, much less to make war. The plan was no sooner adopted than it was pigeon-holed. The Prime Minister said he had not had time to consider it in detail. The President remarked six weeks after initialling the plan that he disliked making plans for a country they did not yet occupy.[2] By contrast with this absence of agreement on policy, the occupation machinery was drawn up long before Hitler fell. At the Moscow meeting of the Foreign Ministers of the three Powers in October 1943 a European Advisory Commission had been created to consider, among other matters, the terms of surrender. The Commission was charged by the Teheran conference of the three heads of government in November-December 1943 to consider postwar policy in general towards Germany. This proved to be

[1] Winston S. Churchill, *The Second World War*, Vol. VI, London, 1954, pp. 138–9.
[2] Robert E. Sherwood, *The White House Papers of Harry L. Hopkins*, Vol. II, London, 1949, p. 810.

E

beyond the Commission's powers and the only important agreement it was able to reach, concluded in September 1944, defined the zones of occupation and provided for a Greater Berlin under joint inter-Allied control. Since Berlin lay some 80 to 100 miles within the projected Soviet occupation zone, provision had to be made for its division into three sectors. In each of these the Commander-in-Chief of one of the occupying Powers would be the ultimate authority, while a Four-Power body, with the Russian name of Kommandatura, consisting of officers appointed by the Commanders-in-Chief, would decide matters affecting Berlin as a whole.

After the liberation of Paris in August 1944 the agreement was modified to make room for French participation; later France was given a sector of her own in Berlin. In May 1945 the four Governments issued a statement summarizing the control agreements. This said that

> ... supreme authority in Germany will be exercised on instructions from their Governments by the British, United States, Soviet and French Commanders-in-Chief, each in his own zone of occupation, and also jointly in matters affecting Germany as a whole. The four Commanders-in-Chief will together constitute the Control Council.
>
> 2. The Control Council, whose decisions shall be unanimous, will ensure approximate uniformity of action by the Commanders-in-Chief in their respective zones of occupation and will reach agreed decisions on the chief questions affecting Germany as a whole.[1]

This control machinery was reaffirmed at the Potsdam conference in August 1945.[2]

The zones of occupation of Germany were therefore drawn up in anticipation of the ceasefire. They by no means reflected the extent of penetration into Germany from east and west since Anglo-American forces had to retire considerable distances to the agreed occupation boundaries after the surrender. Churchill once said that this retirement was in some places up to 150 miles on a 500-mile front.[3] The effect was to leave Russia with the former German capital deep within her zone; she spared no effort to convince its inhabitants that she considered Berlin as her own prize. On July 3rd, when British and American forces were at length allowed to enter

[1] Germany No. 1 (1945), Cmd. 6648.
[2] Miscellaneous No. 6 (1947), Cmd. 7087. See above, Chapter I, pp. 24–25.
[3] In a speech in the House of Commons on June 30, 1948; 452 H.C. Deb. 5s. Col. 2228.

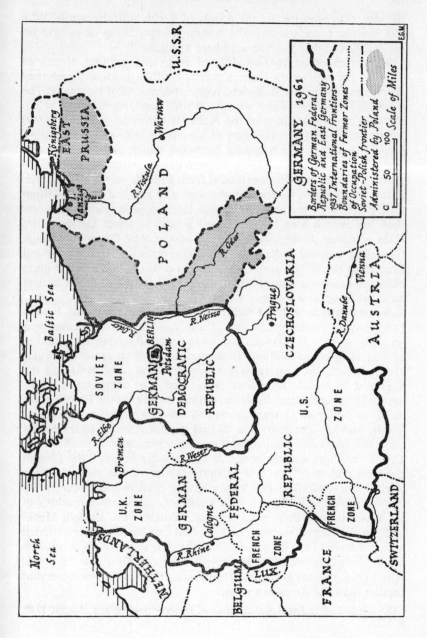

the city, they were met by the people of Berlin with the words 'Why did you not come sooner? The Russians kept telling us to take no notice of you since you are only here as guests.'[1]

The zones of occupation differed from one another almost as much as the policies the Powers pursued within them, although they corresponded to no well-marked regional divisions of Germany. The most highly industrialized was the British zone, including as it did the coal and steel centre of the Ruhr. It consisted of some 36,900 square miles with a population of almost 19 million. The territory formed that part of north-west Germany which had been brought under Prussian control, largely through British influence, at the Congress of Vienna in 1815. It extended from Lübeck on the Baltic to the Dutch and Belgian frontiers in the west and reached as far as Bonn on the Rhine in the south. The American zone was slightly larger than the British area but contained a million fewer Germans. Its main components were Bavaria and west central Germany though there was a small enclave of American-occupied territory round Bremen in the British zone. The zone as a whole had a much more balanced economy than that entrusted to Britain and might almost have subsisted as a separate state.

By comparison with the British and American zones, the French zone, having been formed out of the two western territories, was small, being only 21,000 square miles in area and having a population of less than seven million. It comprised two separate triangular areas: Baden and western Württemberg in the south-west and the Saar and the middle Rhineland in the west. The comparative smallness of the French zone, however, did not mean that the French voice in Allied policy on German questions was insignificant. General de Gaulle and his successors saw to that. Coming finally to the Soviet zone, this was more compact and more economically diversified than any of the three western zones. It lay broadly between the Elbe in the west and the Oder and western Neisse in the east (German territory beyond these two rivers having been placed under Polish administration at Potsdam), with a south-western corner reaching to the Weser beyond Erfurt and Weimar. With most of Eastern Mecklenburg, Western Pomerania and the Mark of Brandenburg included in it, the Soviet zone disposed of rich farming country while possessing the industrial wealth of Saxony, Anhalt and Thuringia. In population ($16\frac{1}{2}$ million) and area (41,300 square miles) it was somewhat smaller than the American zone.

[1] *The World Today*, The Royal Institute of International Affairs, August 1948, p. 322.

In the absence of agreed principles of any specific character, the occupation policies of the Powers tended to follow separate lines dictated by their own national needs, their traditional attitudes to the German problem and such larger ideological tenets as they had. Britain, having few clear preconceptions, soon went in for reconstructing the political and economic life of her zone with little in the way of a distinct idea of the kind of Germany she wished to see emerging. In practice the distaste of British administrators for deliberate wrecking of machinery and the agencies of orderly living disposed them to get the wheels running again, industry working, houses built, schools and hospitals repaired and staffed. Nearest to the British in their methods were the Americans. They placed much greater emphasis on purging German politics (which they did with almost Germanic system) and teaching the ordinary German the ABC of western-type democracy; they did not share British indifference towards the imputed evils of German industrial combines; they suspected any attempt to favour progressive or Left-wing elements on the assumption that these were the natural antidotes to Nazism. Much of this American didacticism soon gave way, however, before the natural friendliness of the American soldier and the belief of the American administrator that the common man, left to himself, strikes out in the right way in the end.[1]

While British and American occupation policies assumed a minimum interference in German life and the creation of a peaceful and democratic Germany on roughly the same lines as before 1933, both France and Russia aimed at fundamental inroads into the shape and spirit of Germany. France was determined to bring the Saar into her own territory, an object she had pursued without success in 1919. In May 1947, when elections were held in the French zone, tacit assent was given by voters in the Saar to its economic annexation to France and the first step was taken forthwith by France by the establishment of a customs barrier between the Saar and the rest of the French zone. During 1946 France was also intensely active on behalf of the separation of the entire Rhineland from Germany and some form of internationalization of the Ruhr.[2] It was, moreover, entirely in accord with France's traditional dread of German militarism and her sense of cultural mission that her social and educa-

[1] US Department of State, *Germany 1947–49*, Washington, US Government Printing Office, 1950, p. 22 ff., giving the text of the basic US occupation policy directive, J.C.S. 1067.
[2] France, Government, *Documents français relatifs à l'Allemagne*, Paris, 1947, p. 24.

tional policy should have aimed at stamping on the German mind her own faith and principles. With equally clear, though different, ideals to serve, the Soviet authorities left no doubt that they proposed to interpret political freedom for Germans as excluding elements hostile to their own creed. Almost from the inception of the occupation there occurred a Sovietization of almost every aspect of life in the Russian zone. This culminated in the involuntary fusion of the Social Democrats with the Communists to form the Socialist Unity Party in April 1946. In elections held in October 1946 the Party won majorities, though not all absolute ones, in all the provinces of the Soviet zone. In Berlin, however, it suffered a miserable defeat.

Underlying this policy of co-ordination under Communist leadership was not merely Russian belief that elements other than the extreme Left would be unreliable instruments of Soviet rule, but the abiding hatred of everything that Russia stood for among the Germans, leading the Soviet authorities to place their faith only in attested Communists. The latter were not always party members of standing; one of the curious features of Russia's policy in Germany was her willingness to entrust authority to almost anybody, provided he joined the party and gave evidence of being a reliable worker for Socialism as the Russians understood it. This policy was accompanied, as in the French zone, by indifference as to how much of Germany was amputated in the process. East Prussia had been divided at Potsdam into a northern and southern area, the former to be administered by Russia and the latter by Poland. As far as Russia was concerned, the rich industrial area of Germany east of the Oder-Neisse line had been permanently absorbed into Poland at the Potsdam conference. Nevertheless, while French and Soviet policies thus agreed in the emphasis they laid on indoctrination and control, the question of German unity sharply divided them. France was the strongest opponent to the formation of a central German Government among all four Powers. Russia, at least in the early years of Four-Power control, was the leading advocate of centralization.

Economic disunity and the British zone

Although it had been expected that the major difference between the Western Powers and Russia in Germany would concern the nature of the political forces to be encouraged there, it was in fact economic issues which presented the first threat to Four-Power unity and eventually forced East and West to go their separate ways in Germany. In these issues it was the British Government which at first played the leading role, largely owing to the industrial character of the zone in Germany which had fallen to them. For the latter part of 1945 and during the whole of 1946 the zone constituted a drain, and a heavy drain, on British resources which, as we have already seen, were insufficient to provide a tolerable standard of living for the British people at home. The nineteen million Germans in the British zone, swollen by considerable proportions of the German population which had been expelled from territories now incorporated into Poland or Czechoslovakia or had fled from Soviet rule, were a dead weight of dependence. They were unable to provide fully for themselves, either because of their exhausted state at the end of the war or because of the lack of food, clothing, housing and fuel to serve as work incentives or because of the destruction of industrial plant, permanent way or other capital equipment. Even before the war the British zone had produced only slightly more than half its food supplies. The excess food required in the conditions of 1945 could not, however, be purchased from abroad by the sale of exports from the zone. In the first place the inter-Allied Level of Industry agreement of March 28, 1946, based on an estimate of what was required to keep German living standards below those of her neighbours, placed formidable restrictions on industrial output.[1] In the British zone in 1946 actual industrial production fell far below even the Level of Industry standards owing to shortages of food, accommodation and fuel; the zone produced only 10 per cent of pre-war output. Secondly, the demands for reparations from capital equipment and current production stripped the economic sinews of the zone bare. During 1946 a fifth of the meagre supply of Ruhr coal went to France as reparations and, from the moment of the assumption of British responsibilities in Germany, plant and machinery, by the Potsdam agreement, had to be torn up and shipped to Russia, in all amounting to a quarter of the zone's industrial equipment not deemed to be necessary to Germany's peacetime economy. This Luddite practice was continued until October 1946.

The total effects of these handicaps to the recovery of the British zone were that the zone, so far from making any contribution to the hard-pressed economy of western Europe, was a heavy liability to Britain, who, unlike the other three Powers, had borne the strain of war from beginning to end. During 1946 and 1947, in the midst of the dollar crisis described in the previous chapter, Britain was contributing some £100 million, mostly for supplies of food, to the zone; one-third of this had to be paid for in dollars. There was a small

[1] The text of the agreement is found in US Department of State, *US Economic Policy Towards Germany*, Washington, 1948, p. 133.

compensation for this in the form of proceeds from exports from the zone, stocks of goods purchased by Britain from German agencies and the acquisition by British manufacturers of German patents and industrial designs.[1]

The British Government argued that this had come about because the Soviet Union, while continuing to demand plant from the western zones under the heading of reparations, had sealed off her own zone from the west, thus preventing the western industrial areas from meeting their food needs in the east. Despite the Control Council's having approved the establishment of a common import-export programme, in fulfilment of the Potsdam agreement, the Soviet delegate on the Council, General Dratvin, made quite clear in April 1946 that each zone should be responsible for its own trade. A month later he refused to allow the fact that the British zone was a deficit area to influence the Soviet policy of drawing reparations from stocks and current production in the eastern zone.[2] In reply the British referred to the principles laid down in the Potsdam agreement to govern the treatment of Germany in the initial control period. In Article 14 of that section of the agreement it was determined that during the occupation 'Germany shall be treated as a single economic unit. To this end common economic policies shall be established in regard to . . . import and export programmes for Germany as a whole.' In the following article it was laid down that 'Allied economic controls should be imposed . . . to ensure in the manner determined by the Control Council the equitable distribution of essential commodities between the several zones so as to produce a balanced economy throughout Germany and reduce the need for imports'. But the article chiefly appealed to by Britain in the argument with Russia came at the end of the section of the Potsdam agreement dealing with the initial control period. This said that:

> Payment of reparations should leave enough resources to enable the German people to subsist without external assistance. In working out the economic balance of Germany the necessary means must be provided to pay for imports approved by the Control Council in Germany. The proceeds of exports from current production and stocks shall be available in the first place for payment for such imports.[3]

[1] Eighth Report from the Select Committee on Estimates, Session 1946–47. British Expenditure in Germany.
[2] Germany No. 2 (1948). Cmd. 7534, p. 10.
[3] Miscellaneous No. 6 (1947). Cmd. 7087, p. 7.

So long as these principles were not applied, British subsidies to West Germany were compared to the hard-earned food supplied by a farmer to his cow while somebody else milked it at the other end.

During this phase of the argument Russia did little good to her case by refusing to give the economic statistics relating to her zone and by failing to state exactly what her difficulties were. She would not disclose, when asked by Western delegates, what the total Mark circulation in her zone was. At meetings of the Council of Foreign Ministers in December 1946 and December 1947 Mr Molotov would not state the total value of reparations Russia had taken from her zone unless the Western Powers agreed to the figure of $10,000 million for Russian reparations from Germany as a whole, which had been provisionally entered into the Yalta agreements as a basis for discussion. The Western Powers were therefore left to form their own estimates of Russia's reparation takings from Germany. At the London meeting of the four Foreign Ministers in December 1947 Mr Bevin put forward the view that by that date Russia had extracted some $7,000 million from Germany.[1] The United States Secretary of State, George Marshall, estimated at the same meeting that the Soviet Union was drawing some $500 million a year from the current output of East Germany while Britain and the United States were importing food alone to the value of $700 million into West Germany. Not merely did the Russians fail to produce estimates of their own to set against these figures, but they were never able to give the western governments the reasons for their German policy. This policy nevertheless has its rational basis. The Russian standard of living was in 1945, and always had been, much lower than that to which Germany and western Europe had been accustomed. The Soviet authorities saw no reason why they should help Germany return to living standards higher than those their own people enjoyed when they had been the victims of German aggression. Moreover, it did not take the Russians long to realize that there was little sense in dismantling plants in Germany and transferring them to Russia to repair the ravages of war; it was far better to set up joint Soviet-German concerns to run the plants in the Soviet zone and draw off the goods as they were produced. This output was needed, not merely to make good war damage, but to supply the consumer's empty shelves and give at long last the promise of better days to come. A loan from the United States for this purpose might at one time have been thought possible, but in the opinion of the Soviet

[1] See Bevin's speech in the Commons on June 30, 1948: 452 H.C. Deb. 5s. Col. 2222.

authorities this could never have been arranged except on terms incompatible with Russia's sovereignty. However, since any explanation on these lines would have been a strain on Russia's strong national pride, it was not given. In its place went abuse of the West and stale charges against Britain and the United States of breaking 'the historic decisions of Potsdam'.

The Moscow and London conferences

Throughout 1947 attempts were made to secure Four-Power agreement on the German question through the Council of Foreign Ministers created at Potsdam. When the London meeting of the Council at length adjourned indefinitely on December 15th, it was clear that they had decisively failed and that the way was now open to the organization of East and West Germany virtually as independent states under the auspices and protection of the respective occupying Powers. Before these negotiations began the British Government clarified the stand they took in a series of statements. On June 5, 1946, for instance, the Prime Minister, Mr Attlee, said in the House of Commons:

> We desire that Germany should be treated as an economic whole. We have been placed in a terribly difficult position . . . in having an area which was always a deficit area from the point of view of food and, as I see it, in changing what were intended merely to be lines of occupation into rigid divisions of Germany, into zones with separate systems of administration. Our endeavour is that Germany should be treated as an economic whole.

As for the political future of Germany, the Government adopted a federal approach, 'to get rid of that uniformity and over-centralization which characterized not only the Nazis but also the preceding regime'.[1]

The trouble about the Potsdam agreement, Mr Bevin said in a speech in the House in October, was that only parts of it which were unfavourable to Britain were being carried out. The basic principle of the agreement that Germany should be treated as an economic unit was being evaded so long as Russia's demand for reparations from current production continued. 'There must be no reparations from current production,' Bevin said, 'so long as there is a balance

[1] 423 H.C. Deb. 5s. Col. 2036. The British Government did not take this view of the Weimar regime in the 1920s. Mr Lloyd George, for instance, often argued that the German government's authority over such provinces as Bavaria must not be weakened even further by excessive Allied demands.

of payments deficit in any one zone.' He said he had made clear at the Foreign Ministers' talks in July that Britain could not carry on paying large sums to keep economic life in her zone going; the zone must be put on a sound economic basis so as to prevent the cost falling on the British taxpayer. Hence the favourable British reaction to the American offer, made at the Foreign Ministers' meeting in New York the previous December, to fuse the American zone with the British and thus implement at least part of the Potsdam requirement of German economic unity.[1] But if the eastern and western zones were to remain as watertight compartments, the Level of Industry agreement was called into question. The Armistice and Postwar Committee set up by the British wartime Government had proposed a level of industrial production for Germany based on an annual steel production of eleven million tons. The interim Four-Power agreement of March 1946 had laid down the unduly low level of seven and a half million tons. 'We agree, if Germany was treated as an economic unit,' Bevin said. 'As this has not been done we have the right to revise the plan.' Germany must become self-supporting as soon as possible, while production of war materials in the broadest sense must be absolutely prohibited.

To achieve this (he went on) more coal must be produced and retained in Germany. Thereafter German industry should be free to expand, subject to a measure of international control whose form is to be determined. We should give active support to the plan for the socialization of their basic industries.

When he came to deal with Germany's territorial future, Mr Bevin explained that the Government opposed the French proposal for separating the Rhineland and the Ruhr from Germany, though they approved the incorporation of the Saar in France. They also refused to recognize the cession to Poland of German territory beyond the Oder-Neisse line without some guarantee that free elections in Poland had been carried out.[2]

When the Council of Foreign Ministers met in Moscow on March 10, 1947, to consider the German question it was already apparent that Russia and the West were fundamentally divided. The Foreign Ministers' deputies had been meeting in London in January and February to try to clear the ground for the preparation of a peace treaty with Germany, but had been able to do little more than discuss how far other states than the Four should share in the negotiations,

[1] See above, Chapter II, pp. 57–58.
[2] 427 H.C. Deb. 5s. Cols. 1513–17 (October 22, 1946).

on which they heard the views of some of the smaller countries. In these hearings it became clear that the minor Western Powers shared the British and American preference for a federal German constitution, while the east European states followed the Soviet view that Germany should be centralized. Oddly, in view of her experiences of Germany, Norway also associated herself with the Communist position on this. Moreover, the British-United States agreement to fuse their zones had come into effect on January 1st and there was enough experience of the difficulties of even this operation to cast doubt on the feasibility of treating the four widely different zones on uniform lines, as Britain wished. Above all, the tension in East-West relations had now grown to a point at which the greater part of the Moscow conference was spent in angry recriminations thrown across the table in the full glare of publicity. Of those intimate exchanges which are supposed to oil the diplomatic wheels there was none. Bevin had only one talk with Premier Stalin during a conference lasting from March 10th until April 24th, and his Western colleagues, Mr Marshall and M. Bidault, had no more. Instead of discussing with the Russians such questions as German imports, reparations and frontiers, the British Foreign Secretary found that much of his time was taken up answering charges that prominent Nazis were being harboured in the British zone, and that Britain was conspiring with Wall Street financiers to carve up Germany and farm it out to private capitalists. No one knew whether the Soviet rulers really entertained these fantastic notions or believed that East and West could not be bridged and needed some explanation for their public why this should be so.

The basic conflict lay between the Soviet determination to derive the maximum profit from current production in the eastern zone and the Western demand that East Germany should help meet the deficit in the west, while West German production should be allowed to rise in order to lift the burden on the Western Powers. Britain and the United States could not accept Molotov's insistence that the Yalta agreement to refer Russia's claim for $10,000 million in reparations to the Reparation Commission as a basis for discussion constituted an endorsement of that figure on their part. Nor could they discuss the reparation question as a whole unless Russia gave an account of what she had already taken from her zone, and this she refused to do. The effect of Russia's attitude was to nullify the second, and most important, of Bevin's 'supplementary principles to govern the treatment of Germany' which he submitted to the Council as a memorandum on March 31st. The aim of this principle was:

To establish economic conditions which will enable Germany to become self-supporting and to repay the expenditure incurred on her behalf by the occupying Powers; which will enable her to make good the damage done by the war; and will further enable Germans and the world outside Germany to benefit from German industry and resources without re-establishing the economic foundations of an aggressive policy.[1]

It was unfortunate, but not wholly illogical, that Russia could not warm to these sentiments. She had no interest in making West Germany economically stable or self-supporting. As her doctrine taught that the Western Powers must soon suffer an economic collapse, there was no harm in seeing this accelerated by the burden of West German deficits. And since she held that the economic foundations of Nazi aggression lay in the nature of the capitalist system itself, she could not take seriously Western pretensions to deal with German militarism by reviving a free economy.

The failure to agree on the economic issues was repeated in the discussions on Germany's political future. Apart from a decision to accept the Control Council's recommendation that the state of Prussia should be abolished (its territory had already been dismembered) the Soviet policy of a centralized Germany and the British and American wish for a federal solution remained in conflict. Bevin sought to mediate between the Soviet extreme of centralization and the French extreme of separatism by a proposal that federal powers be listed in the future German constitution while residual powers were left to the Länder, or provinces. But this proved fruitless.

Nor was progress possible at Moscow on issues peripheral to the main theme of Germany. Molotov attached unacceptable conditions to any Soviet agreement to the Four-Power European Security treaty to last twenty-five years, on which Byrnes, the American Secretary of State, had set such hopes. He wanted it made conditional, for instance, on Western consent to the $10,000 million Soviet reparation claim.[2] Although Bevin told the Commons on May 15th that there was still a prospect for the treaty, American hopes of a general European settlement had received a setback. Nor was progress possible at Moscow on a peace treaty with Austria, which Bevin considered to be a minor issue capable of being despatched in a few weeks. The stumbling block was the definition of German assets in Austria which it was agreed at Potsdam should be appropriated as repara-

[1] Cmd. 7534, p. 8.
[2] James F. Byrnes, *Speaking Frankly*, London, 1947, pp. 173–6.

tions; those in western Austria were to fall to the Western Powers and those in the eastern part of the country to Russia. The Soviet argument was that the assets should be deemed to include properties which were legally German after the Nazis took over the country in March 1938. Bevin contended that this was unfair to Austria as it would sanctify the forcible seizure of Austrian properties by the Germans. Since Russia was permitted to retain troops in Bulgaria and Rumania in order to safeguard communications with her occupation forces in Austria, it was suspected that what Russia was really seeking through raising difficulties over Austria was the consolidation of her grip on those countries.

There were two further stages in the widening gulf between East and West Germany before the four Foreign Ministers met again, this time in London in December 1947. In May, shortly after the breakdown of the Moscow conference, Britain and the United States created a central economic administration at Frankfurt in the American zone. The object of this was partly to increase the efficiency of the bi-zonal economic organization and partly to draw the Germans into the ordering of their own affairs on Bevin's principle that they must increasingly look to themselves for their own recovery. The Economic Council created by this decision was formed from Germans nominated by the various political parties represented in the elected Land Diets. At the same time an Executive Committee composed of heads of the Land governments was created to look after the interests of the Länder and to supervise the German executive departments. As the Foreign Secretary explained in the Commons in January 1948, the Economic Council was regarded as an interim expedient pending the formation of a West German government should agreement with Russia on Germany prove unattainable.[1] Nevertheless this step marked a decisive move towards a separate political destiny for Germany west of the Elbe. The British and American military governors in Germany in announcing the decision repeated the invitation to other occupying Powers to join them which had been issued when the bi-zone was formed; but it was evident that this had become little more than a gesture to Four-Power co-operation. As it happened, it was not until February 1948 that the French agreed to co-ordinate their zone with the bi-zone and not until April 1949 that they agreed to fuse it. Along with the creation of the Economic Council went a renewed drive to raise industrial production and exports in the bi-zone. In August, over French protests, the Level of Industry agreement was bilaterally

[1] 446 H.C. Deb. 5s. Col. 404 (January 22, 1948).

revised by the two Western Powers, their explanation being that they were now free to take this step in view of Russia's refusal to have Germany treated as an economic unit. The revised targets in the bi-zone were set to bring industrial production back to the 1936 level although the population was eight million greater than it had been in the 1930s.[1]

An additional circumstance adversely affecting Four-Power relations on Germany was the offer of Marshall Aid in June 1947. The fact that, with the failure of Russia and eastern Europe to participate in the European recovery programme, economic rehabilitation in western Europe was now launched, not merely without the Communists but in the teeth of declared Communist hostility, could not but deepen the void in Germany. The western zones of Germany were not included among the countries qualifying for Marshall Aid by the Committee for European Economic Co-operation, but in a statement accompanying the Committee's first report the countries which had been at war with Germany adopted in effect what had now become the Anglo-American view on the German question. While avoiding the issues in dispute with Russia, the report said that

> . . . If European co-operation is to be effective the German economy must be fitted into the European economy so that it may contribute to a general improvement in the standard of living. In particular, the output of the Ruhr coalfield . . . must contribute to the rehabilitation and economic stability of the whole of Europe, including Germany herself. An increased production and export of Ruhr coal is in fact essential for European recovery. . . . The machinery, raw materials, food and other supplies which are required to increase Ruhr coal production deserve high priority in any programme of imports either into Germany or into Europe as a whole.[2]

These statements in the report, issued in September 1947, plainly intimated the absorption of the three western zones into the Marshall programme as soon as the final break with Russia had come.

That event occurred after meetings of the Council of Foreign Ministers at Lancaster House, London, which lasted from November 25 to December 15, 1947. Here was witnessed a repeat performance of the Moscow fiasco, the atmosphere of suspicion and the propaganda accompaniment remaining unchanged. The Ministers did

[1] US Department of State, *Germany 1947–49*, p. 358.
[2] Committee of European Economic Co-operation, July–September 1947, Vol. I, General Report, HMSO, 1947, p. 39.

succeed in adopting an agenda, which was by no means always the case in discussions with Russia, but they got no further than the third item. The first item, the Austrian treaty, which Britain wished to dispose of before coming to Germany, was in fact dealt with after the failure on Germany had become apparent; it foundered on the same disagreement on the definition of German assets as had blocked progress at Moscow in the spring. No greater success was registered with the second item, 'preparation of the German peace treaty (frontiers and procedure)'. Molotov withheld consent from a British proposal to create a commission to examine the question of Germany's frontiers on the ground that it implied reopening the issue of the Oder-Neisse line assigned to Poland. He could not see eye to eye with the West on the character and time of formation of a central German government. Russia adhered to her view that authority must be handed to a central government before economic principles for Germany had been settled, and that the Government must be unitary, not federal. Britain and the United States wished to settle the economic issues first and were determined, as at Moscow, that the federal pattern must be followed in any future German regime. It was, however, on the third item, economic principles, that the London conference met with its most abject, though unsurprising failure. All four Ministers accepted the general principles of economic unity in Germany and the abolition of zonal barriers, but the breach on their application was such that the principles were no more than words. Russia remained insistent that East Germany must serve exclusively the needs of her own shattered economy and returned to the demand for $10,000 million reparations as a first charge on Germany's current production. The two Western Powers were no less adamant that they would not shoulder the burden of their occupation zones while Germany's productive capacity was not allowed to meet the bill for food and raw materials imported from the outside world. After an icy prepared statement had been read by Molotov the United States Secretary of State, George Marshall, proposed the adjournment of the Council. It was not to meet again for eighteen months.[1]

Behind these different national interests of Russia and the West in Germany there loomed, as the preliminary talks on the Marshall plan had shown, the much larger antagonisms of East and West in Europe, with Germany as the glittering prize. Each side feared, and with reason, the precipitation of a chain of events in Germany which might bring the whole of that fateful country into the other camp.

[1] Lucius D. Clay, *Decision in Germany*, London, 1950, p. 348.

This fear was particularly evident on the Ruhr question. Britain wished to resuscitate the Ruhr either under some form of international control or on a basis of public ownership, thus ensuring its exploitation for peaceful purposes only. But she thought it intolerable to have to listen to repeated Russian demands for a share in the administration of the Ruhr, especially when Germany's other great industrial centre, Silesia, was under exclusive Communist control.[1] The Soviet Union on her side, given her belief in the built-in aggressiveness of the capitalist world, looked with dread on the addition of the Ruhr to the existing resources of Britain and the United States.

The parting of the ways

In his report on the London talks Bevin expressed his disappointment at the failure to agree about Austria. 'What was thought to be a generous act,' he said, referring to the Four-Power agreement to waive reparations from Austria, 'has been used to get a grip on the whole Austrian economy.' The vilification Soviet and Cominform sources had directed against the Western Powers throughout the three weeks of the London meetings alarmed and angered him. But the main point was that the parting of the ways in Germany had been reached.

> We cannot go on as we have been going on (Bevin said). We have hoped against hope that Four-Power collaboration would work. Most of the world Powers can find a basis of agreement; they cannot all be wrong. We shall close no doors. We shall maintain all the contacts we can and we shall do our best to find a way out. . . .[2]

In the following January, while talks were proceeding in the Western capitals on the conclusions to be drawn from the Moscow and London failures, the Foreign Secretary was more decisive in saying that 'we have to face a new situation. . . . All these developments . . . point to the conclusion that the free countries of western Europe must now draw closely together'.[3] He admitted that he had resisted pressures, presumably from Washington, to create a German parliamentary instrument to control the Economic Council of the bi-zone, but his insistence that the Germans could not expect others to solve

---

[1] Mr Bevin in the Commons: 452 H.C. Deb. 5s. Col. 2224 (June 30, 1948).
[2] 445 H.C. Deb. 5s. Col. 1875 (December 18, 1947).
[3] 446 H.C. Deb. 5s. Col. 395 (January 22, 1948).

F

their problems for them implied that before long they would have to govern themselves.

I must say once again that if the German people are going to rely on us or act as if we are to feed them all the time, they must be suffering from a delusion. Germany must work and produce like other countries.[1]

These words at once foreshadowed the creation of a separate west German government within a general scheme of European economic recovery and collective defence.

None of this was achieved, however, without immense difficulty. First, the growing burden of occupation, which Britain could no longer hope to lighten by Four-Power agreement, necessitated further arrangements with Washington for dollar assistance. By an agreement signed with Britain on December 17, 1947, the American government assumed the whole of the dollar burden in the bi-zone, which had previously been on a fifty-fifty basis. This raised the cost of the bi-zone to the United States Treasury to some $400 million a year, while the British contribution, now to be paid in sterling only, was variously estimated at between £17·5 million and £21·75 million annually, exclusive of the cost of occupation forces. This represented a fall in the proportion of the external subsidy paid by Britain to the bi-zone from one-half to one-quarter. At the same time the British voice in commercial and economic policy in West Germany was reduced.[2] Secondly, it was evident throughout the series of discussions in London on the constitutional reform of West Germany during 1948 that the position of France would be hard if not impossible to reconcile with those of the Anglo-Saxon Powers. This was not merely owing to French touchiness with respect to her status in relation to the Powers which were largely responsible for her liberation in 1944. Eight years after 1940 were not long in which the French could rid themselves from security fears with regard to Germany from which Britain and the United States, with their now largely symbolic detachment from the continent, were still predominantly free.

France's difficulties were fully revealed in the two series of conferences on Germany which were held at ambassadorial level in London from February 23 to March 6, 1948, and from April 20th to June 1st respectively. The Benelux countries were invited to join these talks, the principal subjects of which were the future of the

[1] 446 H.C. Deb. 5s. Col. 405.
[2] The text of the agreement was published in Cmd. 7301 of 1947.

Ruhr, German provincial boundaries and the calling of a constituent assembly to represent the western zones now that the political future of Germany as a united state was obscure. In the discussion on the Ruhr the French gained their point that an international authority should be created before a German constitution came into operation. The Americans would have preferred the Ruhr to remain under the control of the military governors. But the French demand that the Ruhr authority should own, and not merely control, the resources of the Ruhr was more successfully resisted by the United States, who also ensured that the Ruhr should not be separated from the rest of Germany, as the French wished, and that the Ruhr authority should represent all six Powers and Germany; this made it possible for France to be outvoted in the authority's decisions on the allocation of Ruhr products as between Germany and the Allies. On the issue of provincial boundaries in West Germany, France, with American support, had her way in the decision to restore the old boundaries, in opposition to Britain's view that changes should be made in the interests of administrative efficiency. The French believed that to strengthen provincial loyalties in Germany was one more way of avoiding a strong central government. France was also successful at the London meetings in preventing the direct election of German delegates to a constituent assembly which it was decided to summon on September 1st. Contrary to British and American opinion and in deference to France, the assembly was to consist of sixty-five delegates chosen by the Länder Diets on the basis of one delegate for every 750,000 inhabitants.

Nevertheless the swift movement towards the making of a West German state could not fail to cause alarm in France. In Britain the London agreements[1] were principally attacked by Labour MPs who deplored the lack of any provision for public ownership of the Ruhr industries. In France both Gaullistes and communists united against them. General de Gaulle feared that the Ruhr authority would work against French interests and that rivalry would develop between the proposed west German state and any state which Russia might form out of her own occupation zone. The French communists had their own reasons for denouncing the agreements. On March 20th the Soviet representative, Marshal Sokolovsky, walked out of the Allied Control Council for Germany on the grounds that the London talks of the Western Powers implicitly broke the agreement on which the

---

[1] For the text of the London agreements see 'Memorandum on the Measures Agreed by the UK, US and French Foreign Ministers on the Programme for Germany'. Cmd. 7677 of 1949.

Council was based. This was a signal to all European communists that the London agreements were their enemy. But socialists in France were also fearful. Leon Blum and André Philip urged that further approaches should be made to Russia, who should be asked to hold free elections in her zone, before irrevocable steps were taken. In replying to these criticisms the Foreign Minister, M. Bidault, found little sympathy for his reminder that the Ruhr authority would continue after the end of occupation; that the Allies would retain key points in Germany after their occupation troops had left; and that there would be no Allied withdrawal without consultation. The final Assembly resolution approving the agreements was loaded with reservations. Many French politicians felt that their misgivings had been justified by November, when, on the eve of a Three-Power conference on the Ruhr, Generals Clay and Robertson, the American and British commanders in Germany, promulgated laws for the reorganization of the German coal and steel industries which provided for the ownership of the Ruhr mines to be vested for the time being in German trustees pending a decision on their future by a German government. It was suspected, though wrongly, that this news had taken the French government unawares.

French discontent, however, was not much greater than the resentment felt in West Germany when it was learned that the Ruhr would remain under foreign control even after the occupation had ended. Moreover, many West German politicians were unwilling to be a party to moves towards a separate West German state which might postpone indefinitely the hope of a united Germany. Consequently, the Minister-Presidents of the West German Länder governments, who had talks on the proposed constituent assembly with the three Western military governors during July, decided at a three-day conference of their own at Coblenz in early August not to proceed for the moment with the drafting of a definitive West German constitution. They preferred to create the somewhat more provisional instrument of a Basic Law (*Grundgesetz*) for the administration of West Germany.[1] This task was entrusted to a Parliamentary Council, instead of the constituent assembly proposed by the Western Powers, which met at Bonn on September 1st on a basis of representation of the Land Diets. Before the Federal German Government envisaged in the Basic Law could be proclaimed at Bonn in May 1949 still further differences remained to be ironed out between the Christian Democrats (CDU) and the Social Democrats (SPD) on the constitutional issue. The former preferred a loose federal body and were

[1] Clay, *op. cit.*, pp. 409–411.

supported by the United States and France, while the SPD preferred a more centralized regime and were believed to have the backing of Britain. Meanwhile the question of the status and authority to be retained by the Western Powers in the West German state required protracted inter-Allied discussions, in which France continued to hold out against going as fast or as far as her two partners in handing over self-government to the Germans.

These movements in West Germany had their parallels in the east, where the occupying Power, Russia, drew a similar conclusion to that of the Western Powers, namely that in the absence of Four-Power agreement on all-German questions the consolidation of her own zone must go forwards. There were, however, certain differences between the processes of reorganization in East and West Germany. In the east there were no apparent disagreements between allies to overcome at each stage. At a meeting in Warsaw on June 23 and 24, 1948, of eight Foreign and Defence Ministers from central and east Europe and Russia the well-known Soviet positions on Four-Power control of the Ruhr, reparations and the 'historic decisions' of Potsdam were reaffirmed with seemingly little dissent from Russia's neighbours.[1] In the second place it was the Western Powers who set the pace towards the two Germanies after the failure of the Council of Foreign Ministers, while Stalin still appeared to hanker after Four-Power agreement. Hence the Economic Council created at Frankfurt by Britain and the United States in May 1947 was followed shortly after by a Russian-sponsored German Economic Council representing five provincial governments, five German departments and two workers' organizations. The negotiations in the west for a German constituent assembly were likewise matched by the drafting of a constitution for a People's Republic in the east, which a People's Council for Unity and a Just Peace, dominated by the Socialist United Party (SED), considered in the summer of 1948. The constitution was approved in March 1949 and the German Democratic Republic based on this constitution came into being in October of that year.[2]

The third important difference between developments in East and West Germany was that the Soviet Union went to much greater lengths to appeal to an all-German opinion and to mobilize approval over the whole of Germany for the political structure she was creating

[1] *Declaration of Warsaw Conference of Foreign Ministers adopted on June 24, 1948* (London, *Soviet News*, 1948).
[2] *Documents on Germany Under Occupation 1945–54*, Selected and edited by Beate Ruhm von Oppen, R.I.I.A., London, 1955, pp. 412–22.

in her own zone. The People's Council, for example, which was to approve the constitution for a German Democratic Republic, was established in March 1948 by a People's Congress which was reported to contain over 500 delegates from West Germany, as well as over 1,000 from the Soviet zone. Moreover, the 'plebiscite on questions of unity and a just peace', which the Congress resolved to hold from May 23 to June 13, 1948, was ostensibly an expression of all-German opinion. In the event the American and French authorities refused to allow voting to take place in their zone, while the British disapproved but allowed the voting. There was little doubt that this essay in democracy by acclamation was intended to secure a certain effect rather than test opinion. It did, however, show the Soviet Government's concern to reduce the prestige of the Western Powers over both parts of Germany, and not merely to consolidate their own zone of Germany. Britain, France and the United States, on the other hand, while announcing that nothing that they were doing precluded German reunification under Four-Power sponsorship, had no alternative but to write off East Germany after the failure of the four Foreign Ministers in London in November-December 1947.

The Berlin Blockade

The most serious Soviet retort to the Western reforms in Germany, however, was not to form an East German state but to attempt to prise the Western Powers out of Berlin. The basic fact in the Berlin crisis of 1948 was the anomalous situation of the former capital some 100 miles deep within the Soviet zone. So long as hope existed that a central German government might be formed Russia had no interest in disturbing Four-Power control in Berlin. When at the end of 1947 that hope had petered out and when Russia followed the West in shaping her zone into a separate state, it was of great moral importance to the future East German Republic to capture Berlin. As long as the western sectors of the city provided a model of free political life, nourished by substantial economic help from the West, Communist power in East Germany could never be wholly secure, nor could the pretension of East Germany to speak for all Germany be serious. The issue was complicated by the wish of all four occupying Powers to reform the currency in their own zones; while the money in circulation inspired no confidence it was impossible to eliminate the black market and provide incentives to work. Currency reform was introduced into the western zones by decrees issued on June 18th, 21st and 27th, after attempts to agree on a single currency for all Germany had failed. As General Robertson explained to the

Soviet military governor, Marshal Sokolovsky, on June 18th, it was not intended, owing to the special position of Berlin, to introduce the new Deutsche Marks into the western sectors of the city.[1] Nevertheless the Soviet Union affected to believe that the economy of the eastern zone would be disturbed by the new currency system in the west. Hence, two days after Robertson's letter, the Soviet representative on the Four-Power Committee of Financial and Economic Advisers in Berlin announced that the could be no currency in the city different from that of the surrounding zone. When the meeting was over the Soviet authorities made known a currency reform to cover Greater Berlin as well as their own zone in Germany. The Western Powers were not unwilling to accept the Ostmark of the eastern zone into their sectors of Berlin, provided that its emission and circulation were under quadripartite control.[2] As this was refused by Russia, the Western Powers forthwith introduced the new Mark into West Berlin overstamped with a 'B'. To all these Soviet considerations had to be added the desire to use Berlin for bringing pressure to bear on the West to defer or arrest the steps being taken to form a separate state in West Germany. This remained a persistent Soviet theme in the months of negotiation which followed.

Russia's method of raising these questions was simply to interrupt communications with the western sectors of Berlin. She was able to do this since, from the moment Anglo-American troops first entered Berlin in July 1945 in fulfilment of the European Advisory Commission's agreement on the zoning of the city, the Soviet authorities instituted an inspection of transit documents. The Western Powers had unmistakable rights to get to and from Berlin; they had practically no documentary title to do so without their movements being checked. As Bevin told MPs in April 1948, 'there is a clear Four-Power agreement for the occupation of Berlin, of the validity of which there can be no doubt . . . the regulations for travel to and from Berlin are not so clearly specified. When the arrangements were made a good deal was taken on trust between the Allies.'[3]

The first interference with access to Berlin came on January 6th, when Soviet inspectors boarded an American military train running between Frankfurt and Berlin and demanded to check papers carried by German passengers. British communications underwent the first

[1] Cmd. 7534, p. 17.
[2] See Bevin's statement in the Commons on June 30, 1948; 452 H.C. Deb. 5s. Col. 2231.
[3] 449 H.C. Deb. 5s. Cols. 34–5 (April 6, 1948).

restriction on January 24th, two days after Bevin's speech in the Commons on the uniting of the West; the Berlin to Bielefeld night train carrying British officials and 120 Germans was detained for eleven hours. From then onwards Soviet interference mounted until on June 23rd all railroad passenger and freight traffic on the Berlin-Helmstedt line was suspended. Barge traffic was partially stopped until, on July 10th, with the Soviet announcement that the lock at Rathenow was under repair, all communications by water ceased. By that date the blockade of Berlin by road, rail and canal was complete. At first these restrictions were said to be due to technical difficulties. But this pretext was almost at once discarded. In their reply to a British note of July 6th protesting against these infringements of Allied rights (identical notes were sent by the French and United States Governments) the Soviet authorities made clear that their actions were intended as retorts to alleged Western contraventions of Four-Power agreements on Germany, especially the Western currency reform.[1]

There now remained only one loophole through which contact with West Berlin could be carried on: the air. Although the Soviet authorities repeatedly complained that 'air discipline' over Berlin and in the air lanes to the city from West Germany was unsatisfactory, and on April 5th a Russian fighter collided in suspicious circumstances with a British passenger plane near Gatow airfield, no attempt was made to seal this passage to Berlin. To do so would have meant throwing down a challenge to the Western Powers which they could not escape taking up short of total surrender. The Russians no doubt believed that the two and a quarter million West Berliners could never be kept supplied by airlift alone when their coal and light had been cut off, and that the Western Powers would either be forced to abandon Berlin or would make some concession over the larger German issues.[2] That these Powers did neither was due to the remarkable success of the airlift operation. During the ten and a half months until the blockade was lifted on May 12, 1949, more than a million and a half tons of supplies were taken into the city in almost 200,000 flights by British and American planes. The British share of the effort was estimated at 40 per cent and the American 60 per cent.[3] It was the unforeseen success of the airlift, combined with the effects of the counter-blockade on the Soviet

[1] Cmd. 7534, Annex IIIA, pp. 50–2.
[2] Considerable doubt about the practicability of the airlift was also expressed in the British Press. See *Berlin Air Lift*, HMSO, 1949.
[3] Bevin in the Commons, September 22, 1948; 456 H.C. Deb. 5s. Col. 903.

zone and the morale of the West Berliners, which ultimately provided the West with a diplomatic victory.

During talks on the situation in Moscow between the three Western representatives and Molotov and Vyshinsky, and in two discussions with Stalin, British policy, like that of the United States and France, was actuated by four main requirements. First, there could be no concession in the matter of Britain's right to a military position in Berlin. This right was denied by Stalin at his first meeting with Western delegates on August 2nd. In the Soviet draft agreement presented by Molotov on August 9th reference was made to the 'present agreement' as the legal basis of communications with West Berlin. To accept any such formula would have been to nullify the wartime agreements on Berlin and agree with the Soviet contention that the West was no longer in Berlin by right but only by Russia's leave. Molotov did not press the point, however, and in his revised draft of August 16th freedom of access to Berlin appeared to be absolute.[1] Secondly, Britain, in common with her two Western partners, refused to abandon her position in relation to West Germany or go back on the London agreements of June. At the start of the discussions in Moscow, Molotov demanded that the formation of a West German government should not be proceeded with until further Four-Power discussions on Germany or Berlin had taken place either at the Foreign Ministers' Council or elsewhere. This demand was withdrawn on Western insistence, but Stalin at a second meeting with Western representatives on August 23rd asked that the communiqué on the talks should mention that the London agreements had been discussed in Moscow. The British Government refused to agree unless it was clearly stated that the West could not accept any deferment of the London decisions, which did not however exclude an eventual Four-Power solution for Germany. As a result of forceful arguments by Frank Roberts, the British representative, Molotov agreed that the matter should not be pursued further until the four military governors in Berlin had carried out the directive for producing a currency agreement which was to be drafted in the Moscow talks.[2]

But it was on the two other requirements of Britain and her partners that breakdown came in talks between the four military governors in Berlin, which began on August 31st to work out a formula for lifting the restrictions based on the directive agreed to in Moscow on August 30th after such long and hard bargaining. In

[1] Cmd. 7534, p. 32.
[2] *Ibid.*, p. 40.

the first place the Western Powers insisted on the unequivocal removal of all restrictions on communications and transport. This seemed to have been secured in the agreement reached in Moscow on August 30th.[1] But, when the talks began in Berlin, Marshal Sokolovsky at first insisted that only restrictions imposed after June 18th, the date of the currency reform, were meant. At length he gave way on this point but continued to make the lifting of the restrictions conditional on the acceptance of still further restrictions, this time on air traffic. The Western Powers read no such meaning into the understanding of August 30th. Marshal Sokolovsky then refused to accede to the fourth requirement of the Western Powers, namely that if the Soviet Mark was to be accepted as the currency for the whole of Berlin there must be adequate arrangements for quadripartite control of its issue and continued use. This seemed to have been attained in the directive to the governors, for it proposed the creation of a financial commission representing the governors 'to control the practical implementation of the financial arrangements indicated above, involved in the introduction and continued circulation of a single currency in Berlin'.[2] Marshal Sokolovsky, however, argued that the commission was intended to deal only with subsidiary matters and that a paragraph in the directive referring to the regulation of currency circulation in Berlin by the German bank of emission in the Soviet zone expressly excluded international control. He also claimed for Russia the exclusive right to control the trade of Berlin with the western zones of Germany and with other countries.[3]

Such interpretations were puzzling. They were, however, upheld by the Soviet Foreign Minister in his exchanges of notes and talks with the Western representatives in Moscow towards the end of September. It was evident that on the three points at issue, the raising of the restrictions, the control of the Soviet Mark in Berlin and the control of Berlin's trade, the Soviet military governor was merely echoing his master's voice. Either Stalin had now come to regret any concessions he had made in the shaping of the directive of August 30th or (and this was perhaps more likely) he was dragging out the negotiations in the hope that the onset of winter would make the airlift impossible. The Western Powers did not therefore wait for further talks. On September 27th they referred the dispute to the United Nations Security Council while reserving the right to take the

---

[1] The text of the agreement, forming the directive to the military governors, is given as Annex VI to Cmd. 7534, p. 56.
[2] *Ibid.*, final paragraph.
[3] Cmd. 7534, pp. 41–2.

necessary measures to maintain their position in Berlin. Meanwhile the blockade and airlift continued.

The positions of both sides in the dispute received a public airing during the opening debate at the Security Council on the Council's competence to consider the question. The Western delegates claimed that they had exhausted ordinary diplomatic channels in seeking to get the agreed directive of August 30th carried out; now they had no recourse but to the Security Council. Vyshinsky, for the Soviet Union, retorted that Berlin was an aspect of German affairs and by Article 107 of the Charter should come before the Council of Foreign Ministers and not the United Nations. The Council voted on October 5th by a 9 to 2 majority to consider the matter.[1] But since the Western Powers and Russia formed four out of the eleven members of the Council and had got nowhere between themselves, all they could do was to listen to mediatory proposals from the neutral members of the Council. Under the leadership of Dr Bramuglia of Argentina, and later of M. van Langenhove of Belgium, these suggested first one formula then another without satisfying both sides in the dispute at the same time. Russia vetoed a resolution proposing that the blockade be lifted simultaneously with the resumption of talks on currency questions.[2] When the neutral members then sought a formula which included reference to further discussions on all-German questions, the Western Powers professed to see little point in going over the same ground again after such conclusive failure at the Foreign Ministers' Council. They refused to talk at all about Germany until all restrictions on access to and from Berlin were lifted. The last phase in the efforts of the neutral members to effect a settlement came in February 1949, when an expert committee proposed by Dr Bramuglia to study the currency problem admitted failure to reach agreement.

By this time it had become clear to both sides that the blockade and counter-blockade were doing more harm than any good they did in the way of changing the mind of the other side. Russia had failed to starve out West Berlin; she had failed to impose her currency unilaterally on Berlin. The Western Powers on their side, seeing that they had argued that the building of a West German state did not preclude Four-Power agreement on Germany, could hardly refuse Stalin's persistent wish to have the German question thrashed out again at the Council of Foreign Ministers. Whether Stalin still hoped for agreement on the German question or whether he wanted further

[1] Security Council, Official Records, Third Year, No. 114, p. 21.
[2] *Ibid.*, No. 120, October 25, 1948, pp. 5–9. M. Vyshinsky's statement.

use of the Council as a platform for Russia's voice in Germany, it was unnecessary to inquire. For the Western Powers, provided the currency question did not have to be settled in Russia's favour as a price for lifting the blockade, another round of Foreign Ministers' talks was not a bad exchange for an airlift which was costing Britain alone £6,000 a day. Hope appeared in Stalin's answers to an American journalist's questions on January 27th, when, amongst egregious replies to egregious inquiries as to Russia's desire for peace, the Premier said he was willing to lift the blockade, if the counter-blockade ended at the same time, provided the establishment of a West German government was postponed pending a further meeting of the Council of Foreign Ministers. The remarkable thing about this statement was its complete silence about the currency question which had caused almost all the trouble.

Stalin having made a concession, the Western Powers had no difficulty in making one themselves, though not the one he asked for. After informal exchanges in March and April, representatives of the three Western Powers and Russia met in New York on May 4th and on the following day agreed that the blockade and counter-blockade would be lifted in the first minute of May 12th. This was conditional on an agreement that the four Foreign Ministers should meet in Paris on May 23rd for another assault on German questions. Russia's abandonment of the blockade had been foreshadowed at the beginning of March by the replacement of Molotov at the Foreign Ministry by Vyshinsky and the substitution of General Chuikov for Marshal Sokolovsky as Soviet military governor in Berlin. But the truth of the matter was that both Russia and the West had suffered a defeat, though the former's was by far the greater; Russia had not forced her currency on West Berlin as a step towards controlling its life and the Western Powers had for the moment given up the consolidating of West Germany without reference to Russia. The Foreign Ministers duly met in Paris in May, but when they disbanded on June 20th, although the atmosphere was less tense, there was no agreement to do more than facilitate trade between East and West Germany and to hold further discussions on Germany at the next session of the United Nations General Assembly. There was an undertaking, however, to maintain the normal functioning of road, rail and water communications in Germany.[1]

The settlement of the Berlin dispute, contrary to Stalin's wish, had not delayed the handing over of political responsibilities to the West Germans. By a coincidence the lifting of the blockade was

[1] Cmd. 7729 of 1949, p. 18.

timed for the very day on which the military governors approved the revised draft Basic Law on which the Parliamentary Council in Bonn had been at work since February. Difficulties had arisen because the military governors of the Western Powers wanted stronger Länder governments than the Bonn constitutional draughtsmen; they believed, for example, that the Länder should put forward their own electoral laws as a safeguard against domination from the centre. After some protest from the Social Democratic Party, the Parliamentary Council revised the draft and, after approval by the military governors and the Länder, it was finally signed at Bonn on May 23rd. The military governors, however, had less success with their efforts to draw up an Occupation Statute to define the position of the three Western Powers in the new West German regime. They finally gave up the attempt in December 1948 owing to the insistence of the French representative on leaving less power to the Germans under the Statute than either Britain or the United States thought to be workable.[1] This difference was at length resolved by the Foreign Ministers of the three Powers in Washington on April 8th. By the Occupation Statute which the Ministers then signed full legislative, executive and judicial power was to be exercised by German central and provincial organs in accordance with the Basic Law, although nine reserved fields of government were left under the contingent control of the occupying Powers. They could resume this control in any one of three conditions: if it was essential to security; if it was required to maintain democratic government; and if it was necessary for the fulfilment of the international obligations of the occupying Powers.[2] As Germany was still a disarmed state and had not yet proved its capacity for democratic government, the first two stipulations were called for. The third seemed to leave the door open to some future agreement with Russia on a united Germany.

The Occupation Statute was finally promulgated, along with the Basic Law, in May. The first free general elections since 1933 were held in August in what were formerly the three Western zones and the Federal German Republic was inaugurated in September, the Allied military regime being replaced by an Allied High Commission in Bonn.[3] The Western Powers decided to end the state of war with Germany in September 1950 and in March 1951 the Federal Republic was authorized to establish its own Foreign Ministry and maintain direct

[1] Clay, *op. cit.*, pp. 413–8.
[2] Cmd. 7677. Memorandum on the Measures agreed by the UK, US and French Foreign Ministers, Washington, April 6–8, 1949.
[3] Cmd. 7729 of 1949.

diplomatic representation abroad.[1] The road from Potsdam had ended.

For Britain the significance of the Berlin dispute was that it showed how she had, through the failure of quadripartite rule in Germany, come to assume commitments entirely contrary to precedent. Very rarely in recent times (and the Polish example in 1939 was a doubtful one) had Britain taken on obligations for which she was prepared to fight as far east in Europe as Berlin. That she would fight in defence of these obligations Bevin left no room for doubt. At the beginning of the Berlin crisis he told Parliament: 'we cannot abandon those stout-hearted Berlin democrats who are refusing to bow to Soviet pressure.'[2] When, in the autumn, the crisis was at its height he said at the Labour Party's annual conference: 'we intend, whatever the provocation may be, to stay in Berlin.'[3] He was able to hold to this position because he knew that it was fully endorsed by the United States, with that country's immense resources and unmatched atomic striking power. The greatest achievement of British diplomacy during the Berlin crisis was indeed, not its firmness against Stalin's pressure, but its securing of American endorsement of the Brussels Treaty, out of which, with the addition of Canada and five more European states, emerged the North Atlantic Pact. The fact that, by mid-1948, American opinion had moved of its own accord towards underwriting the Brussels Powers did not lessen this achievement.

The formation of the Atlantic pact

The close interest which the United States was now taking in the defence arrangements of western Europe was made clear in several pronouncements. On the occasion of the signing of the Brussels Treaty on March 17, 1948, President Truman said in a message to Congress: 'I am confident that the United States will, by appropriate means, extend to the free nations the support which the situation requires . . . the determination of the free countries of Europe to protect themselves will be matched by great determination on our part to help them to do so.' This was followed on April 29th by another voice from the New World, that of Mr Saint Laurent, the then Canadian Minister for External Affairs, who not only endorsed the Brussels Treaty in a notable speech in Parliament, but forecast a closer association for collective defence of all free nations under

[1] Department of State *Bulletin*, October 2, 1950, p. 530; Cmd. 8252 of 1951, *Revision of the Occupation Controls in Germany*, p. 12.
[2] 452 H.C. Deb. 5s. (June 30, 1948), Col. 2232.
[3] The Labour Party. Report of the 47th Annual Conference, p. 195.

the United Nations Charter.[1] But the most striking symbol of the end of American isolation was the resolution moved by Senator Vandenberg, Chairman of the Foreign Relations Committee, in the United States Senate on June 11th. This proposed, as the three axioms of American foreign policy, the encouragement of collective security arrangements within the terms of the Charter, the association of the United States with such arrangements when based on the fullest possible self-help and mutual aid by the signatories, and the pledge that any attack on a peaceloving nation would be met by American forces acting in self-defence.[2] The Vandenberg resolution was carried by a vote of 64 to 4. Its importance was, first, that it showed how a former leading isolationist, converted by the Second World War into a supporter of the United Nations, could recognize that the organization was no longer adequate, owing to the veto, to deal with the danger of a Soviet attack; and secondly it demonstrated the Senate's new conviction that American partnership in defence of the North Atlantic area was not altruism, but prudent concern for national security in a world in which the traditional defence, distance, was no longer relevant.

The Senate's resolution was a great encouragement to the Brussels Treaty Powers now that they were exploring the prospects for a wider security system to embrace the whole of the North Atlantic. These discussions were carried on partly in the Permanent Commission set up by the Brussels Treaty, which began work in London in April, and partly at the Consultative Council of the five Foreign Ministers, which sat at The Hague in July. On July 6th talks began in Washington between the Ambassadors of the Brussels Powers and Canada with the United States Under-Secretary of State, Mr Lovett, and continued throughout the summer. After further discussion in the Permanent Commission in London and at a Consultative Council meeting in Paris in October, the talks were then moved back to Washington on December 10th. Here it was decided to invite the Governments of Denmark, Iceland, Italy, Norway and Portugal to sign the proposed North Atlantic collective defence treaty along with the seven core Powers. Despite considerable Soviet pressure to the contrary, they accepted the invitation and signed the treaty with the others in the presence of President Truman in Washington on April 4th. The treaty came into force on August 24, 1949.

The signature of the Atlantic Pact was, for the United States, a

[1] Miscellaneous No. 9 (1949). Cmd. 7692, p. 3.
[2] *The Private Papers of Senator Vandenberg*, ed. by Arthur H. Vandenberg, jnr., London, 1953, pp. 407–11.

revolutionary act of diplomacy, running counter to all the hallowed maxims of American thought. In the Senate debate on the treaty Robert Taft attempted to recruit these sentiments in his fight against ratification: the fear of embroilment in European quarrels; the reluctance, even after the collapse of Four-Power rule in Germany, to admit the existence of a divided world; the suspicion of a British 'divide and rule' policy. Taft found only twelve senators ready to stand with him in this last ditch, but the fact that hearings on the treaty occupied sixteen days in the Senate Foreign Relations Committee and the ratification debate in the Senate took twelve days showed the extent of the mental revolution in America that the pact symbolized.

In Britain the Government's attitude to the treaty was much more pragmatic. Four-Power co-operation had clearly failed both to solve such pressing problems of the day as Germany and to provide security against war. The United Nations was out of action for the time being as a producer of security. No one could be sure what Stalin's object really was, whether merely security for Russia against a German military revival encouraged by the Western Powers, or the spread of Communism across the globe by force, if not by peaceful means. But there was no doubt, after the Czech *coup*, that weak countries had no assurance that they would not be swallowed up into the Communist camp. For west Europe's defence against this threat three things were needed: co-operation among the west European countries for collective defence—that was the object of the Brussels Treaty; the economic sinews of defence—that was provided by ERP and Marshall Aid; and the underwriting of their efforts by the United States, with its resources and atomic strength—this was ensured by the Atlantic Pact. For Britain, then, the treaty was by no means a revolution, but a practical way of dealing with a practical question. Hence the Minister for Commonwealth Relations, Mr Noel-Baker, described the treaty in the one-day debate on the subject in the House of Commons on May 12th, as a 'stop-gap and a stop-gap only'. 'We want a world security system as soon as ever we can,' he said, 'but we do believe that if we are having a collective pact at all it should be as strong as possible in order that its restraining effect on the mind of the aggressor may be as great as possible.'[1]

This conception of the North Atlantic Treaty as an unfortunate makeshift made necessary by Soviet obstructiveness was underlined in its spirit and phrasing. The preamble indentified the pact with the aims and methods of the United Nations. The parties were com-

[1] 464 H.C. Deb. 5s. Col. 2127.

mitted to settle their disputes peacefully and not to use force in any way inconsistent with United Nations principles (Article 1). There was a heavy emphasis on international co-operation for economic stability and better understanding of the signatories' free institutions (Article 2). The pact was said not to affect the rights and obligations of the parties under the Charter or the primary responsibility of the Security Council for maintaining peace and security (Article 7). Above all, the key Article (5), under which the signatories pledged themselves to assist each other, by armed force if necessary, against any armed attack occurring in Europe or North America drew its authority from Article 51 of the United Nations Charter, which authorizes member-States to use force in self-defence, whether individually or collectively, in cases where the Security Council is unable to defend them against armed attack. United Nations members, such as the Atlantic Powers, are enjoined to look for security to the organization, but the Charter allows (if it does not exhort) them to develop their collective power to resist attack against the day when the Security Council may be stultified by the veto. This authority the Atlantic Powers availed themselves of.[1]

The British Government's arguments on behalf of the treaty, and of the lead they had taken in getting it launched, were not criticized by the Opposition. Military pacts never held fears for Conservatives, and the fact that the pact was itself something of an adverse judgment on Russia rather commended it to the Right. All Mr Churchill asked for was that steps should be taken to mend relations with Spain, a possible future member of the pact.[2] Two forceful criticisms which the Foreign Secretary had to face from his own backbenches were that the pact helped consolidate the division of the world, from which it was alleged that only Washington and Moscow, if anyone, stood to gain, and that the pact represented a repudiation of the United Nations. On the former of these arguments, Mr Warbey said in the Commons that 'if we build up a polarization, a power bloc around Washington, then we are encouraging similar polarization in the other part of the world', while Mr Zilliacus put the United Nations case against the pact in the words: 'we can have either power politics or the rule of law, a balance of power or the United Nations. But we cannot have both.'[3] Mr Bevin's reply was that the absence of a pact like the Atlantic treaty had not prevented war in 1939, or in 1914,

[1] The text of the North Atlantic Treaty is printed in Cmd. 7883 of 1950, Collective Defence under the Brussels and North Atlantic Treaties.
[2] 464 H.C. Deb. 5s. Col. 2028 (May 12, 1949).
[3] *Ibid.*, Cols. 2040, 2079.

G

and that war could only be avoided by making clear to an aggressor what he would have to face if he began one. As for the United Nations argument, he denied that there was any inconsistency between the Charter and the pact; the Charter admitted in Article 51 that it might not work, and recognized that if action were not taken by the United Nations other agencies must be ready to fill the gap.[1] At the vote after the debate only six MPs opposed the treaty.

Critics of the pact on the Left in Britain represented the schism in Germany, and the accompanying Cold War which led to the treaty, as largely due to the refusal of ruling forces in the West to accept the Communist Revolution in Russia, which, it was alleged, they had tried to strangle in 1919. The pact's defenders, and Mr Bevin in particular, denied any personal hostility towards Russia. The Cold War, they said, had arisen from Russia's own suspicions and her determination to extend her power by insult, subversion and force against the West. Had Russia been willing to co-operate in Germany, they said, the whole dismal tale of deadlock, mutual invective and now pact against pact would never have been written. Both arguments, by placing the blame on the hostility or ambition of one side or other in the Cold War, missed perhaps the most important element in the story. This was that both sides feared to lose Germany to the other, which both genuinely thought to be bad for themselves and bad for the world. This fear they might have exorcised by united efforts to build a regime in Germany which would have neither wish nor opportunity for aggression. But Russia and the West did not agree on what made for a peaceful Germany. The West held that a freely elected German government could hardly be aggressive. Yet history did not offer much support for the argument that an independent Germany would continue to enjoy a free elected government. Russia believed that only the extermination of forces in Germany other than the extreme Left could keep her peaceful. But any such regime must either be a pawn of Russia (and therefore unacceptable to the West) or beyond the control of either East or West (as the Russians themselves may have suspected). To this conflict of view other factors were added: the Western tendency to allow a situation to grow up out of day-by-day expedients, and Soviet pressures to stamp their ideas all over Europe. But the basic dilemma remained.

[1] 464 H.C. Deb. 5s. Cols. 2015–7.

CHAPTER FOUR

Rearguard Action in the Middle East

Britain has had an interest in the area comprising south-west Asia and the Nile lands, now known as the Middle East, since the eighteenth century. At first this interest was primarily naval and commercial: to preserve the region as a bridge to British possessions in the Far East and a highway for British trade, especially after the opening of the Suez Canal in 1869. With the coming of air power the Middle East began to lose its importance for naval communications and during the Second World War the Mediterranean, the sea approach to the area from the west, was closed to Allied shipping from 1940 until 1943. Nevertheless, the maintenance of British power in Egypt, the Persian Gulf and at the Aden colony continued to be thought essential to defend the region against hostile Powers.

This strategic significance of the region was rivalled in the twentieth century by its growing importance as a source of oil supplies for western Europe. This factor was one of the principal reasons for the desire of Britain and France for supervisory powers over the Arab states which freed themselves from Ottoman rule in 1918. But it was not to be realized to its full extent until after the Second World War. In 1938 the total output of crude oil and natural gas from the Middle East was 335,000 barrels daily, a poor fourth in the world's table. This figure rose to 865,000 barrels daily in 1947 and to 3,480,000 in 1956, when the Middle East was second only to North America in oil production.[1] Although the oil wells themselves were irregularly distributed over the region, the most important producing states being Iran, Iraq, Saudi Arabia and the Gulf States, a sizeable fraction of the output was carried by pipeline across the Arab states of the hinterland to Mediterranean ports. This meant that stability in the area as a whole was essential to the continued supply of oil to Britain and Europe, both as a raw material to be used in home industries and as an export.

While these two interests prescribed for Britain a policy aimed at keeping the region peaceful and friendly towards herself, conditions

[1] The Royal Institute of International Affairs, *The Middle East: a Political and Economic Survey*, 3rd edition, London, 1958, p. 541.

at the close of the Second World War were unfavourable to the implementation of such a policy. Apart from Soviet hostility and the new, competitive interests acquired in the area by the United States, Arab nationalism, expressed in the Arabs' desire to expel all foreign influence and master their own affairs, was able to profit from Britain's declining power. Culturally Arab nationalism represented a cross-fertilization of Western education with an Islamic revival occurring in the second half of the nineteenth century. Politically it had embraced the self-determination ideals of the Allies in the First World War. When General Allenby entered Damascus on November 7, 1918, after the rout of Turkish forces in Palestine, he pledged Britain and France to the creation of national Arab governments based upon popular consent. Instead of this, however, which the Arabs considered was already their right under the Husein-Mac-Mahon correspondence of 1915, they found themselves after the war under British and French rule in the thinly disguised form of League of Nations mandates. The resulting Arab sense of betrayal was accessible to nursing by the government of any state in conflict with Britain or France during the inter-war years. Bolshevik Russia repeatedly summoned the Arabs against the capitalist West, but was too close to be regarded as disinterested and too Godless to be thought respectable. Germany and Italy, the dissident states of the 1930s, were better placed to exploit Arab discontents, with the result that the Middle East, including Iran, was so penetrated with Axis propaganda and intrigue that it was virtually brought under close Allied control during the Second World War in order to protect communications between Russia and the West. The Allied victory in 1945 was in fact founded upon the suppression of Arab nationalism. This meant that, after the removal of the German threat to the Middle East by 1944 and the revival of tensions between Russia and the West in 1945, Arab nationalism had a free field in which to express itself.

The campaign against the West was a factor in Arab unity; at the same time the unstable and highly xenophobic spirit of Arab politics was due to local factors. Whereas European nationalism was traditionally steeped in democratic protest against arbitrary government, Arab nationalism was in the first instance a protest against the foreigner voiced by a middle-class intelligentsia which often considered local governments as the mere puppets of foreign states. Moreover, the fact that in 1919 no united Arab state had been formed, but the Arab lands were parcelled out among leaders most of whom had been appointed by the West, with frontiers decided by bargaining between London and Paris, meant that Arab nationalism was based, not so much on loyalty to a country, but on the abstract ideal of a united Arab state, failure to attain which was laid at the West's door. The will to form an Arab nation tended to be left with only two real affinities from which to draw its strength: the Arab language and hatred of the foreign imperialist. The former has been described as the least suitable in the world to orderly and rational politics; the latter was the one persistent theme in Arab relations with the West.

Britain might have stood a better chance of coming to terms with this phenomenon on one or other of two conditions: had she disposed of sufficient power to demonstrate the will to maintain her interests whatever the challenge of Arab nationalism, or had other Powers with interests in the Middle East been willing to co-operate. In the circumstances of 1945 neither condition existed. We have seen how economic pressures, together with the widespread feeling in Britain that the country had done its part during the war and now deserved some relaxation, limited the possibilities before a British Foreign Secretary. The Arab mind is said to respect great power; the spectacle of Britain peering into an empty purse at the end of the war was certainly no invitation to Arab quiescence. Nor did other Powers with a stake in the area make it easy for Britain to maintain something of her former position. Germany and Italy had departed but the Soviet Union made up for their absence. As early as 1940, in discussions with its ally, Nazi Germany, Moscow sought to have the area south of Batum and Baku in the general direction of the Persian Gulf recognized 'as the centre of the aspiration of the Soviet Union'.[1] These dreams were not realized but at the end of the war Russia, seen from London and Washington, seemed poised for acts of incursion in the Middle East. Though she was in no want of oil, the protection of her own oilfields in the Caucasus justified advances by the standards of traditional diplomacy, especially now that Britain was much weaker. After his early threats against Turkey and Iran, however, Stalin paused and it was not until two years after his death in 1953 that active Soviet policy in the area was resumed. But this did not mean that Russia did not stand to gain from stirring up the Arabs against Britain from a distance by every means in her power. The mere fact that Britain was locally present and Russia was not gave the latter an added appeal to the Arab nationalist.

The other dominant Power of the day, the United States, saw no

[1] US Department of State, *Nazi-Soviet Relations, 1939–41*, Washington, 1948, p. 250.

particular reason for underwriting British authority in the area and was only reluctantly persuaded to defend Iran against Russia in 1946. Provided Britain's case took the form of defending free peoples against Soviet threats, as in Greece and Turkey, America was generous with aid; but the essence of Middle East affairs after 1946 was that Russia had to all intents retired and American distaste for great Power interference with small nations was apt to re-focus on Britain. Moreover, heavy contributions were made to the campaign funds of the ruling Democratic Party by American sources interested in a Jewish Palestine; the Democratic Senator McGrath was convinced that Truman would lose New York State, Pennsylvania and California in the 1948 elections unless he went along with the Zionists.[1] This, however, is to exaggerate the unity of official American opinion. By 1945 the United States had acquired substantial local interests in the Middle East of its own, especially the oil and air base facilities of Saudi Arabia, which conflicted with the electoral considerations of the administration. Some of these interests competed with those of Britain. The result was that for at least a decade after the war American policy appeared in London to be vacillating, at war with itself and more disposed to edge British authority out of the Middle East than support it. If so, it found an ally in the estranged mood of France. After the French liberation in 1944 it was fully in accord with General de Gaulle's notions that France should return to Syria and Lebanon, which she had acquired as League mandates in 1920 and Britain had occupied after 1939 to prevent them falling into German hands. When this led to a French bombardment of Damascus in May 1945 it was Britain who forced the French out of Syria and who ensured Syrian and Lebanese independence a year later. French opinion was left to conclude that, while Britain wished to meet Arab grievances if possible, she preferred to do so at an ally's expense.

Britain's policy of insulating the Middle East against hostile influences from the outside had generally been expressed through friendly overlordship over the Arab states relieved by subsidies and occasional doses of independence. Iraq was freed in 1930 from British-imposed restrictions and concurrently entered into a treaty relationship affording Britain the use of airfields and communications. Transjordan became independent in 1946, with British subsidies and military assistance to its ruling Hashimite family. Egypt, which Britain had declared an independent state in 1922 while reserving certain powers, became fully sovereign by a treaty of friendship in 1936, when British forces were confined to the Suez

[1] *The Forrestal Diaries*, ed. by Walter Millis, NY, 1951, p. 363.

Canal zone. The Gulf states remained British clients under their feudal rulers, while the friendly, isolated kingdom of Saudi Arabia was separated from the other Arab states in the north by the desert and fringed by British protectorates on its Indian Ocean side. The tempo of independence could hardly be expected to satisfy Arab nationalists excited by the heady pronouncements of both belligerent sides in the Second World War, but so long as Britain was the principal source of funds, of officers to staff the armies of Arab rulers, of arms, oil and oil-transit royalties, Arab impatience could perhaps be controlled. When at the end of the war the Arab states found themselves, not the pensioners of Britain, but the owners of sterling balances resulting from British spending in the Middle East during the war, which Britain was in no position to repay, a new relationship seemed required. One possibility was an organic association of the Arab states; this was espoused by the wartime Foreign Secretary, Anthony Eden, in a speech in the Commons in May 1941 and culminated in the formation, with British encouragement, of the Arab League, the pact of which was signed by seven states on March 22, 1945.[1] The Arab League might have proved an efficient means for maintaining a friendly alignment between the Arabs and Britain, even though the financial reserves of the latter had now been depleted by the war. That it failed to do so was partly due to the bitter rivalries dividing Arab leaders, such as the clash between the courts of Transjordan and Egypt; the League itself resulted from the failure of a plan for a Fertile Crescent federation sponsored by the Iraqi statesman, Nuri As-Said, and represented a temporary victory for Egypt in the struggle for power. But equally important in frustrating the Arab League as a link with Britain was the Palestine question. So long as Britain held to the Palestine mandate, either as a champion of the Jewish National Home or merely as an umpire between Jews and Arabs, British policy requirements and Arab discontents could find no point of mutual reconciliation. So long as the Jews were not driven out of Palestine the sole link of real substance in the Arab League was opposition to the National Home, of which Britain was the sponsor. But when the Arabs at length attacked the Jews the League broke in their hands.

The Palestine problem
The obligations assumed by the British Government in November 1917 to support on certain conditions the creation of a home for the

[1] The signatories were: Saudi Arabia, Syria, Lebanon, Transjordan, Iraq, Egypt and the Yemen.

Jews in Palestine, embodied after the war in a League of Nations mandate entrusted to Britain, was in the first instance a wartime measure to meet a wartime need. Its object was partly to rivet American opinion to the Entente cause, partly to dissuade the Bolsheviks, many of whom were Jews, from throwing in their lot with Germany, partly to forestall an adoption of the Jewish dream by Germany, and partly to seize from the collapsing Ottoman Empire a naval foothold on the eastern shore of the Mediterranean. On its romantic side, the Jewish National Home was part of the traditional practice of protecting European minorities in the East by means of capitulations and unequal treaties. As such, it was out of tune with the twentieth century since nationalist ideas of the postwar period ruled out reservations to the principle of nationally homogeneous states. Moreover, the brutal policies of the German Nazis forced European Jewry to seek refuge in Palestine in numbers far exceeding the anticipations of 1917. By the reciprocal action peculiar to nationalism, Germany's attitude forced the Jews to demand a national state of their own in Palestine which their leader, Weizmann, had not appeared to be seeking in the First World War. The same nationalism filled the Arabs with fear and hatred of a Jewish National Home which might become an alien state in their midst. In 1918 the Arab spokesman Feisal had consented to the National Home in an agreement with Weizmann. But he made this conditional on the Arabs receiving full independence elsewhere. When the Arabs concluded that they had been cheated by the Entente promise of independence, they regarded this agreement as a scrap of paper.

By the 1930s the mandate had become unworkable. The Jews were not content to remain a minority and the Arabs refused to allow them to be more than a minority. When the Palestinian Arabs rose in revolt in April 1936 and both Jews and Arabs refused to accept the recommendation of the Peel Commission appointed by the British Government, that this tiny country, no larger than Wales, should be split between them, Britain decided in May 1939 to put the National Home into cold storage, hoping that it might freeze to death. Jewish immigration was limited to 75,000 during the five years from April 1939, after which no more Jews would enter the country without Arab consent. The sale of land in Palestine to Jewish settlers was also restricted. The White Paper announcing this decision was rejected by a majority of one by the Mandates Commission of the League of Nations. It did not prevent Jewish efforts to smuggle immigrants into Palestine during the war. But the Jews saw no reason to give Britain trouble during her conflict with Nazism. Like the Arabs, who however welcomed rather than feared a German victory, they prepared to resume the struggle for Palestine when peace came.

The Zionists viewed the accession to office of a Labour Government in Britain in 1945 with joy equal to the misgivings of the Arabs. At its congress in the United States in 1942 the Zionist Organization had adopted the Biltmore programme envisaging a definite Jewish state after the war. This had been officially urged on the British administration in Palestine in May 1945, before Attlee's Cabinet was formed, and Churchill adhered to his position that the issue must await discussion between the allies.[1] Now, with Labour's victory, the road seemed clear. The strong connections of the European Left with Jewish life were well known; in its statement on reconstruction after the war, issued in April 1944, the national executive committee of the British Labour Party had called on the Arabs 'to move out as the Jews move in'. This was more than the Zionists themselves had ever asked for, since they had never sought to make Palestine exclusively Jewish.[2] In addition to this Labour sympathy and the general moral strength of the Zionist cause in view of the appalling tragedy of the Jews in Europe, the Biltmore programme had the approval of the Government of the United States, with its five million Jews. At the Potsdam Conference President Truman passed on to the British the Jewish demand for permission for 100,000 Jewish refugees in Western Germany to enter Palestine, while extending little hope of American military help in dealing with the consequences in terms of Arab reactions. At the same time the Zionist Organization was making its own approach. Only ten days after the Labour Government was formed the Colonial Secretary, George Hall, received a Zionist delegation led by Ben-Gurion which asked for immigration certificates for the 100,000. Behind this cabalistic number loomed the massive proportions of the Biltmore programme.

The negative reaction of the Labour Cabinet to these demands, and their coldness to Zionist aspirations as a whole, except on the impossible condition that the Arabs freely accepted them, have received many interpretations, most of them biased. Some focused on the personality of Bevin, the Foreign Secretary. That he was a mild anti-Semite is possible, if to be anti-Semite is to accept the image of the Arabs as courteous, leisurely, contemplative folk which

[1] 408 H.C. Deb. 5s. Col. 1289 (February 27th).
[2] Chaim Weizmann, *Trial and Error*, London, 1949, p. 535.

T. E. Lawrence and others have injected into British political mytho-
logy. It was on this ground that Bevin was criticized for failing to
punish subordinates who expressed anti-Semitic statements, such as
Lieutenant-General Sir Evelyn Barker, the British commander in
Palestine, who issued a non-fraternization order after the King
David Hotel tragedy in July 1946. That Bevin came under the spell
of Arab-biased advisers in the Foreign Office and Colonial Office is
also possible; this may have led him to over-estimate the military
strength the Arab States would oppose to further Jewish immigration. But such explanations are unnecessary to account for the
dilemma facing British policy-makers at the end of the war. They
could neither suppress Jewish resistance to the White Paper policy
nor could they yield to its demands.

The Labour Government denied that the 1939 White Paper was
still valid and pointed to the policy of admitting 1,500 Jews a month
as evidence for this. But when the Jewish authorities dismissed this
scale of immigration with contempt, refusing even to accept the
immigration certificates, and when they ran unseaworthy ships
crowded with pathetic refugees into the country, the British were
powerless to deal with the situation. After twelve months of mounting Jewish violence, the administration finally took action at the end
of June 1946, when widespread arrests were made, including four
members of the executive of the Jewish Agency. But the Jewish
resistance, the military form of which was the 70,000-strong Haganah,
the Jewish defence force, and its mobile striking force, the 5,000-
strong Palmach, with the two terrorist organizations, the Irgun Svai
Leumi and the Stern Gang, was in fact not that of a handful of
terrorists; it was the resistance of a nation. The Nazis in Europe had
found that where resistance movements are backed by the local
population, only war against every man, woman and child is effective. Bevin and the Cabinet affected to be shocked that the Jewish
Agency should connive with the military resistance against Britain
while verbally dissociating itself. But the Jews had never been discouraged by Britain from handing out violence to Germans during
the war; they had in fact been armed and instructed in the use of
effective violence in the name of freedom. Their freedom to build
Israel they now regarded as no less precious. Hence the British purge
in June 1946 had its inevitable outcome in the blowing up of the King
David Hotel in Jerusalem in July by way of reprisal. Eighty-four
British, Arabs and Jews were killed, forty-six maimed and twenty-
two unaccounted for. The Jews seemed to calculate that the policy of
blood against blood would not be tolerated for long by British public

opinion. In this they calculated rightly since the creation of Lidices in Palestine could not be acceptable in Britain.

To capitulate to Jewish demands, however, was equally impossible. The Arab Bureau, which had been set up in London in 1945 by the newly formed Arab League, warned the British Government that to allow 100,000 Jews to enter Palestine would ruin Anglo-Arab relations.[1] This was no idle threat. During the Arab uprising of 1936–39 some 4,000 people were killed and two divisions of British troops, along with several squadrons of the RAF, had to be employed to deal with the revolt, which took almost two years to suppress.[2] With the strong anti-British feeling prevalent in the Arab world at the end of the war, with the existing United States and Soviet attitudes on the Middle East, and with Britain's diminished military and economic strength in 1945, such an operation could not be seriously contemplated. Moreover, the British policy of support for the Arab League and the special British relation with Transjordan ruled such a policy out. In February 1946 Abdullah, the ruler of Transjordan, was invited to London, to be given the title of King of a fully independent state as a reward for his war services. On March 22nd a treaty of alliance was signed with Transjordan providing for the garrisoning of British troops and mutual assistance in case of armed attack on Britain or Transjordan.[3] The subsidy Britain paid Abdullah was increased to £2 million and eventually to £12 million. Above all, the future of the British military base in the Suez Canal zone was uncertain in view of Egyptian demands for revision of the 1936 treaty.[4] These considerations excluded British support for the full Zionist demands, or even for further Jewish immigration on any scale appropriate to the needs of the Jewish displaced persons in their camps in Europe. Had agreement between Jewish and Arab authorities been possible, the outlook would have been different. But Jews and Arabs had never agreed, since the mandate began, even on a joint legislative council. Agreement was inconceivable in the mid-1940s when Jews wanted an immediate Jewish state and Arabs an independent Palestine based on their existing 2 to 1 majority over the Jews.

The Anglo-American inquiry
The British Government insisted that the problems of European

---

[1] J. C. Hurewitz, *The Struggle for Palestine*, NY, 1950, p. 229.
[2] Palestine. Termination of the Mandate, May 15, 1948, London, HMSO, 1948, p. 6.
[3] Cmd. 6916 of 1946.
[4] The Egyptian negotiations are dealt with in Chapter VII.

Jewry and the Palestine issue should be kept apart. The plight of European Jewry, they said, was on the conscience of the whole world; it was unfair to ask the Arabs, who had never consented to the mandate, to shoulder it alone. Other countries, with far greater absorptive capacity than Palestine, showed no great haste to admit the Jews. Despite the presence in Europe at the end of the war of some one and a half million surviving Jews, the US Displaced Persons Act provided for the entry into the United States of only 202,000 Jews in excess of the regular quota, and did not become law until June 1948, by which time the Palestine issue was within an ace of being violently settled.[1] The British Government therefore argued that, if the Zionist demand for 100,000 immigration certificates was to receive serious consideration, the United States should share some of the responsibility for the implications. This led President Truman, who was keeping up the pressure on Britain on the Jewish refugee question, to agree to a joint Anglo-American inquiry into the problem of European Jewry and the question of further immigration into Palestine. The inquiry was announced by Bevin in the House of Commons on November 13, 1945.[2] The committee of inquiry, to consist of six Americans and six British appointed by their respective governments, was to make interim recommendations pending a permanent solution of the Palestine issue to be submitted in due course to the United Nations. Although the committee's terms of reference began with conditions in Palestine, as bearing on the immigration question, and then went on to the question of how many Jews could remain in Europe without fear of further persecution, the committee decided to investigate the conditions of the Jews in Europe before proceeding to Palestine. This meant that they arrived in the Middle East with a mental background of the refugee camps, and this may have weighed with them more than the sullen political deadlock in Palestine. In the event they deprecated Jewish violence, proposed the immediate issue of 100,000 Jewish immigration certificates and, while rejecting partition, recommended that the mandate be continued pending the negotiation of a trusteeship agreement. Less than a week after the publication of the committee's report in April 1946 a Jewish terrorist attack on a car park in Tel Aviv resulted in the death of seven British soldiers. In this setting the British Government heard that President Truman, without consulting Britain, and almost without reference to the rest of the report,

[1] The Royal Institute of International Affairs, *The Middle East, 1945–50*, 1954, p. 189.
[2] 415 H.C. Deb. 5s. Cols. 1927 ff.

endorsed the committee's appeal for the 100,000 immigration visas.

The Government in London replied by extracting that part of the report which suited them, namely the condemnation of Jewish terrorism. The Prime Minister made clear immediately on the publication of the report that there could be no question of admitting so large a number of Jews as 100,000 so long as Jewish private armies refused to surrender their weapons.[1] Since there was no immediate prospect of this, and as Bevin considered that the attempt to force the 100,000 Jews on the Arabs would cost Britain as much as £200 million, as well as the quartering of another army division in Palestine, the only alternative was to try to put the committee of inquiry's recommendations into effect as a whole. The question of the interim regime to be set up in Palestine, which the committe had not defined, was therefore entrusted to a group of British and American officials working on the basis of the committee's report. At first the US Government refused to allow their officials to discuss anything but the implementation of the immigration proposal and only in mid-July did an American Cabinet committee of three arrive in London to discuss the recommendations as a whole. The outcome of the talks, which was unanimously agreed, took a twofold form: first, that all countries concerned should do their utmost to settle the displaced persons, either in their own territories or elsewhere through a projected International Refugee Organization; and secondly, that neither a Jewish nor an Arab nor any kind of unitary state was desirable in Palestine, but that there should be a regime of provincial autonomy to last for several years, thus leaving the way open either to partition or federalism in the more distant future.

The provincial autonomy plan and the London talks

A provincial autonomy plan, in the drawing up of which the Americans had no part, was in fact outlined in the Commons by Herbert Morrison on July 31, 1946.[2] It provided for an Arab and a Jewish province, the boundaries of which could only be altered with the consent of the other parties. The Jewish province was intended to include land already settled by Jews together with certain additional areas round and between the settlements. The Arab province was to extend over the rest of Palestine, except for the desert triangle of the Negeb in southern Palestine and the district of Jerusalem, including Bethlehem. The two provinces would be governed by Councils of Ministers, appointed by Britain in the person of the High Com-

[1] 422 H.C. Deb. 5s. Col. 197 (May 1, 1946).
[2] 426 H.C. Deb. 5s. Cols. 957 ff.

missioner from elected legislative chambers, and would be virtually autonomous in matters of provincial concern. The High Commissioner, assisted by a nominated executive council, would however retain full authority in defence, foreign affairs, customs and excise and, for a short period, law and order. Jerusalem was to be ruled by a separate municipal council and for the time being the Negeb would be directly under the High Commissioner. The 100,000 displaced Jews were to be admitted during the following twelve months after the initiation of the plan, provided that the financial burden of resettlement was borne by the United States, the Jewish organizations themselves and German reparations. Further immigration was to be authorized by the Central Government on the recommendation of each provincial authority in respect to its own territory, but the 'economic absorptive capacity' of either province was not to be exceeded. There were also provisions for external economic aid to Palestine; these relied heavily on United States co-operation. When the plan had been agreed by the parties concerned it was to form the basis of a trusteeship agreement submitted on behalf of Britain to the United Nations.

It was no weakness of the autonomy plan that it had been taken out of a drawer in the Colonial Office where it had long been held in readiness should partition prove unworkable.[1] Nor was the provisional character of the plan a reason for not exploring Arab and Jewish reactions to it, though some suggestion as to the probable duration of the plan might well have been inserted. The fact was, as Morrison emphasized, that the plan was conditional on American support and President Truman, after declining to comment on the plan until he had talked with the American officials on their return from London, dissociated himself from it.[2] In this decision the approaching mid-term Congressional elections in November no doubt played a part. Truman's withdrawal did not prevent the British Government calling a conference in London on September 10th to consider the implementation of the plan. But the executive of the Jewish Agency, which had already rejected the plan in August on the cue from Washington, refused to attend except to discuss its plan of partition and with a delegation nominated by itself. The same decision was made by the High Executive of the Palestinian Arabs, since the Executive could not accept the British proposal to appoint Arab delegates from outside that body. The Government therefore

---

[1] Oliver Stanley, the wartime Colonial Secretary, disclosed this fact during the Commons debate on the plan; 426 H.C. Deb. 5s. Col. 979 (July 31, 1946).
[2] Palestine. Termination of the Mandate, p. 9.

found only envoys of the Arab states to discuss the plan with at the conference. These produced a plan on September 30th for a Provisional Government to consist of seven Palestinian Arabs and three Jews and to hold elections for a Constituent Assembly of sixty members to draw up a constitution. Since Jews could not exceed one-third of the membership of the Constituent Assembly, the constitution was bound to consolidate the two-thirds majority of the Arabs in Palestine. To bolt the door against any change in that majority, further immigration, together with amendments of the existing land transfer regulations, would require the consent of a majority of the Arabs in the Legislative Assembly of the eventual unitary state.[1]

It was clear by now that the British attitude was toughening and that the Government did not intend to give up its control of Palestine without a struggle. The new factor in the situation was the Bevin-Sidki agreement signed in London in October on a withdrawal of British forces from the Suez base with provision for the base to be reactivated by Britain in emergencies; in the event Egypt did not ratify the agreement, but so long as the reactivation formula was under consideration Britain would require a foothold in some part of Palestine from which the necessary military operations could be carried on. On the other hand, the Colonial Secretary, George Hall, was replaced on October 4th by Creech Jones, a former pro-Zionist who had come to regard partition as inevitable. The Cabinet's legal advisers considered that partition was in principle inconsistent with the Mandate, but it was clear that during the three months' recess of the London conference, announced shortly before the change at the Colonial Office, British policy would be swayed by conflicting pressures. The moment thus seemed ripe for the President of the Zionist Congress, Chaim Weizmann, to attempt a dilution of the Biltmore programme and to canvass support for the principle of a 'viable Jewish state in an adequate area of Palestine'. This proposal was defeated, however, at the twenty-second Zionist Congress held in Basle in December 1946 and Weizmann paid the price of his revisionist tactics by losing the Presidency. By a tiny majority the Congress decided against attending the London conference when it resumed on January 27th.[2]

Informal talks were held in London in January, outside the resumed conference, between Bevin and Creech Jones on one side and members of the executive of the Jewish Agency on the other; but the

[1] Palestine No. 1 (1947). Proposals for the Future of Palestine. Cmd. 7044, pp. 9–11.
[2] Chaim Weizmann, *Trial and Error*, London, 1949, p. 544.

minimum demands of the latter never fell short of immediate partition and the creation of a Jewish state in an adequate area of the country. When the British Ministers left the Jews and met representatives of the Arab states, now accompanied by Palestinian Arab spokesmen, at the conference, Arab claims for an independent Palestine with a permanent Arab majority had not materially altered. A compromise, proposed by Bevin to both parties on February 7th, clearly demonstrated the British desire, while the strategic outlook in Egypt and Iraq remained uncertain, to maintain the *status quo* in Palestine in the hope that within five years or so something might have turned up. The compromise amounted to an abandonment of the autonomy plan. Instead a system of locally self-governing Arab and Jewish cantons was to be organized, Britain under a new trusteeship agreement continuing her general responsibilities under the Mandate. Immigration was to be at the rate of 4,000 Jews a month during the first two years of the trusteeship; thereafter it was to be dependent on the old criterion of economic absorptive capacity. As if to underline the Government's unwillingness at this stage to contemplate any form of Palestinian independence, with or without partition, the calling of a Constituent Assembly was postponed until the fifth year of the trusteeship, and in the likely event of Arab and Jewish members of the Assembly being unable to agree the problem was to be referred to the United Nations Trusteeship Council. Many years of disputing were plainly foreseen. Not surprisingly the Bevin compromise was at once unconditionally rejected by both Palestinian factions and their various supporters. A week later the Government announced their intention to refer the problem to the United Nations.

The United Nations debate: Israel and the Arab defeat
In reporting on the London talks to the House of Commons on February 18, 1947, Bevin defined the positions of the two groups in Palestine as follows:

> For the Jews the essential point of principle is the creation of a sovereign Jewish state. For the Arabs the essential point of principle is to resist to the last the establishment of Jewish sovereignty in any part of Palestine. The discussions of the last month have quite clearly shown that there is no prospect of resolving this conflict by any settlement negotiated between the parties.[1]

Britain, the Foreign Secretary went on, had no authority under the
[1] 433 H.C. Deb. 5s. Col. 988.

mandate to award the country either to Jews or Arabs, nor to partition it. But it was noted that, in explaining the reference of the problem to the United Nations, as the legal successor to the League of Nations, he did not include partition among the alternatives between which he was inviting the United Nations to choose. While proposing no British solution, Bevin defined three possibilities:

First, should the claim of the Jews be admitted that Palestine was to be a Jewish State, or, secondly, should the claim of the Arabs be admitted that it was to be an Arab State, with safeguards for the Jews under the decision for a National Home, or, thirdly, should there be a Palestinian State in which the interests of both communities were as closely protected as possible?

Since each of these alternatives had already been rejected by one party or the other, or by both, and therefore neither was likely to command a two-thirds majority in the United Nations General Assembly, the effect of a debate in the Assembly, the Government seems to have hoped, would be merely to advertise the deadlock and leave the situation much as it was. That the Government were in no hurry for active intervention by the United Nations seemed implicit in their initial proposals to wait for the next ordinary session of the General Assembly in September. Opposition pressure, however, combined with the deteriorating situation in Palestine, forced the Cabinet to ask for a special session of the General Assembly.

When the special session of the Assembly met in April Sir Alexander Cadogan, the British delegate, said that Britain could not act alone. 'We shall not have the sole responsibility,' he said, 'for enforcing a solution which is not accepted by both parties and which we cannot reconcile with our consciences.'[1] This seemed not to rule out British participation in any collective enforcement of a United Nations solution. But when it became clear that, contrary to expectations, the United Nations would arrive at an agreed solution, the tone changed. The Special Committee on Palestine which the General Assembly appointed in May failed to agree on a unanimous formula for the Palestine issue, but seven members produced a report which came before the Assembly's ordinary session in September.[2] The essence

---

[1] UN First Special Session of the General Assembly, Official Records, Vol. III, p. 184.
[2] Canada, Czechoslovakia, Guatemala, the Netherlands, Peru, Sweden, Uruguay. A minority plan supported by three other members of the Special Committee, India, Persia, Yugoslavia, favoured a federal Palestine with Jerusalem as the capital. The representative of Australia, the eleventh member of the Special Committee, did not vote for either plan.

H

of this was the proposal to create an Arab and a Jewish state, each in three segments, and an international City of Jerusalem. The two States were to be fully independent after a period of two years from September 1, 1947; Britain in the meantime continuing as the administering authority under the United Nations. Jewish immigration was to be fixed at 150,000 over the two years and at 60,000 a year afterwards if the transition period should last longer than two years. The Negeb was awarded to the proposed Jewish state. When discussion of the plan began in an *ad hoc* committee created by the General Assembly, Creech Jones at once said that Britain could not support any solution which did not command the assent of both sides. On September 26th he said:

> The United Kingdom Government was not prepared to undertake the task of imposing a policy in Palestine by force of arms. In considering any proposal that it should participate in the execution of a settlement, it would have to take into account both the inherent justice of the settlement and the extent to which force would be required to give effect to it.

To which was added the threat that, in the absence of a settlement agreed among the parties, Britain would have to plan for an early withdrawal of British forces and the administration from Palestine.

At each stage of the tense discussions in New York Britain applied pressure on friendly delegations to vote against the partition plan, while issuing repeated warnings in public that she would not co-operate in the plan if adopted. When both the Soviet Union and the United States gave their support to the plan in the *ad hoc* committee Creech Jones said that Britain could accept no responsibility 'either alone or in a major role'. Since Britain was the *de jure* ruling power in Palestine, she could hardly act in a minor role if she was going to assist in implementing the plan at all. When on November 10th a Soviet-United States compromise proposed bringing the Mandate to an end on May 1, 1948, and the establishment of the Arab and Jewish states on July 1st, Cadogan repeated that Britain would take no part in imposing the plan on either Jews or Arabs. She would instead hand over to the Commission of Five to be appointed by the United Nations to supervise the implementation of the plan and use her forces in Palestine only for the maintenance of law and order. When the General Assembly at length debated the *ad hoc* committee's report in favour of the partition plan in November, Cadogan once more declared that British troops and administrators would not be available to enforce a plan which was not acceptable to both sides.

In effect this meant that Britain would never again use force against the Arabs in Palestine. Nevertheless, after intensive lobbying and log-rolling by all parties, the partition plan in slightly revised form was adopted by the General Assembly on November 29th by a vote of 33 to 13 with 10 absentions. The most serious modification of the plan was that the proposed Jewish state was reduced from 6,000 to 5,500 square miles in area; it would constitute some 55 per cent of the total land area of Palestine. The majority for the plan, which had only numbered twenty-five in the *ad hoc* committee, reached the required two-thirds in the General Assembly since six states (France, Haiti, Liberia, Luxemburg, the Netherlands and New Zealand) which abstained in the committee now voted with the majority, and two, Paraguay and the Philippines, which had been absent during the committee's vote, now supported the plan. No Middle East or Asian delegation voted for the plan. Britain and as many friends as she could muster abstained.

In view of her delegate's statements at the United Nations Britain could hardly do other than take her leave of Palestine with the least delay. The British Ministers responsible, Bevin and Creech Jones, told the House of Commons that the Mandate would be terminated on May 15, 1948, and the military withdrawal completed by August 1st. In effecting these operations they have been charged with collusion with the Arabs to sabotage the United Nations partition plan. The British authorities in Palestine certainly prevented the United Nations Commission, the 'Five Lonely Pilgrims',[1] from entering the country until May 1st, though they allowed a small advance party to see conditions for themselves, on the grounds that the Commission's presence would inflame Arab feeling and make the maintenance of order more difficult during the last days of the Mandate.[2] Arab irregular forces, however, were permitted to cross the Syrian border to attack Jewish settlements in Palestine, while Jewish forces were still prevented from arming themselves and Palestinian ports were denied to Jewish immigrants. But this is not conclusive evidence that Britain was conspiring with the Arabs to destroy the plan and Zionist dreams with it. For if Britain was unable to suppress Jewish terrorist violence under the Mandate, when she had a perfect legal right to do so, she could hardly hope to undermine the emerging Jewish State promised in the General Assembly's resolution when her troops were packing up to leave. Moreover, had the Arab States received definite

[1] The states represented on the Commission were Bolivia, Czechoslovakia, Denmark, Panama and the Philippines.
[2] Palestine. The Termination of the Mandate, p. 11.

The Middle East

The U.N. Palestine
Commission Plan

offers of clandestine British assistance against the Assembly plan, it is surprising that they did not enter the Palestine war with more enthusiasm. When the Arab League Council met in Cairo on December 8th it issued a statement saying that 'previous plans' would be carried out, but until British forces left Palestine the Arab States confined themselves to sending irregular bands over the frontier rather than putting their own armies into the country.

The more probable explanation of Britain's sullen attitude during and immediately following the United Nations debates is that the Government, and even more so public opinion, were sick of a sterile and costly argument into which the high idealism of the Balfour Declaration had sunk, and wished to unburden themselves of the conflict, all the more since the United Nations had adopted a solution they had themselves rejected time and again. Since 1945, 338 British subjects had been killed in Palestine. The upkeep of troops in Palestine had cost the taxpayer £100 million. By the time the Assembly plan was voted the country was in effect a British police state. Over 80,000 British troops, one-tenth of the total strength of the British army at that time, were unable to maintain order in the face of rising Jewish resistance.[1] The impossible task of insulating the two warring factions from one another was dramatically symbolized in February 1947, when the families of all British civilians and non-essential officials in Palestine had to be evacuated. The remaining non-military British were herded together in security zones from which Jewish families had been evicted. To assist in implementing the partition plan in conditions in which the Arabs plainly meant to fight was to increase still further the military burden of this unhappy country while utterly destroying such elements of British influence as still remained in the Arab countries. The British view, Weizmann concluded, after seeing Creech Jones in New York when the General Assembly had voted its plan, was therefore that the Jews and Arabs should be left to themselves for an unavoidable period of blood-letting.[2] On the common assumption in British military circles that the Arab invasion of Palestine after the end of the Mandate would succeed at least in reducing the area allotted to the Jews in the United Nations' plan and in particular in robbing the Jews of the Negeb awarded to them by the plan, Britain would be able to come to some arrangement with the Arabs when the fighting was over without having compromised herself by attempting to enforce a pro-Jewish partition scheme against them.

[1] Palestine. Termination of the Mandate, p. 10.
[2] Weizmann, *Trial and Error*, p. 580.

These calculations were based on the accurate assumption that the United Nations would not be able to enforce the plan and hence that the issue would remain to be fought out between Jews and Arabs, and on the false assumption that the Arabs would get the better of the fighting. Considering that the Arab states number some thirty million people, as against the 600,000 Jews, and that the Jordanian, Iraqi and Egyptian forces were armed and in some cases officered by the British, the latter assumption did not seem as wild as it proved. That the Jews were in the event so successful that by February-April 1949, when armistices were signed with the surrounding Arab states, they had virtually brought the whole of Palestine, except for Samaria and Judaea, under their control was due to many factors: their superior military equipment, much of it purchased in Iron Curtain countries with funds collected in the United States; their better generalship and far greater zest to win the struggle; and the purely accidental fact that the crossing into Palestine of irregular Arab forces from Syria as soon as the General Assembly voted the partition plan gave the Jews a pretext to occupy the continuous line of the mountains facing west from Jerusalem, thus cutting the Arabs off from the sea.[1] The effect of the Arab military defeat, however, was not merely to create the new state of Israel consisting of the whole of Mandate Palestine, with the exception of the Gaza strip along the coast, and having on its eastern flank an Arab salient, assigned to Transjordan to form the new state of Jordan, which was, from the Arab standpoint, a point of entry into Israel and, from the Jewish, a territory some day to be absorbed. It was to deepen the tensions between Britain, the official author of the National Home from which Israel had sprung, and the Arab States. The latter, now venting their disillusionment in strife between themselves, found a convenient scapegoat for their defeat in Britain.

But the British assumption that the United Nations would be unable to enforce its plan was confirmed when attention in New York moved to the question of implementation. The Soviet Union had voted for the partition plan on condition that the Security Council, if it found that a threat to peace existed by virtue of the Palestine situation, took the necessary measures to enforce the plan and authorized the Commission to carry out its functions. Britain herself had tacitly underlined the need for enforcement by her warnings of the likelihood of Arab resistance. But in the event it was unnecessary for Britain to do more in the Security Council than sit and wait for the United States to withdraw support from enforce-

[1] Sir John Glubb, *Britain and the Arabs*, London, 1959, p. 288.

ment and thus set herself against the Soviet Union. This reversal of the American position occurred on March 19, 1948, when the United States representative at the Security Council, Warren Austin, rejected the partition plan and made the astonishing proposal of a temporary trusteeship for Palestine, leaving the way open for a possible solution through partition at a later date. It was apparent that strategical and economic considerations in United States policy had triumphed over Zionist influence. For some months American oil concessions in the Arab states had been under threat and this was no time to make their position more difficult. Above all, the possibility that a United Nations force in Palestine might include Russian contingents was now recognized as a threat to the policy of resistance to Soviet advances in the Near and Middle East which was embodied in the Truman Doctrine of the previous year. Already Jewish forces were receiving help from East Europe in making their military preparations. One of the countries represented on the Commission of Five for the implementation of the plan, Czechoslovakia, had fallen into the Soviet orbit after the Communist *coup* in Prague in February 1948. These wider considerations had the effect of making the United States as much a target for Jewish venom as Britain when the American plan for a trusteeship in Palestine came before a special session of the General Assembly which met on April 16, 1948. But by this time no other outcome was possible except for a trial of strength between Jewish and Arab forces. The United Nations, once enforcement proposals had broken down, was compelled to stand in the sidelines, despatching its mediator, only to be murdered, calling for and negotiating truces, and compelled to confess that affairs must be left to a military solution on the spot.

The United States Government sought to improve their position with the Jews after the volte-face of March 19th by granting *de facto* recognition sixteen minutes after the proclamation of the State of Israel on May 15th. This was not followed by Britain until January 29, 1949, a month before the first armistice in the Palestinian conflict, that between Israel and Egypt, signed at Rhodes on February 24th. *De jure* recognition was granted by the United States to Israel and the reorganized state of Jordan on January 31st. A deep chagrin and disappointment with the outcome of the war in Palestine had held up British recognition, which was forced on the Government only by the revulsion of feeling in Britain caused by the events of January 18th, when five RAF aircraft over the Israeli-Egyptian border were shot down by Israeli defence forces. This incident marked the end of British efforts to embarrass the establishment of the Jewish state. As though to mark the close of a chapter the Foreign Secretary gave news in the House of Commons of the release of Jewish immigrants of military age from detention in Cyprus.[1]

The Palestinian war showed that the Arab states would be unable to deal with an aggressive state of any power which invaded the Middle East from outside. The more was this so since the immediate aftermath of the Arab defeat in Palestine was a series of military *coups* and assassinations as the discredited regimes paid the penalty for the mismanaged effort to destroy Israel. In Syria in March 1949 the Deputy Chief of Staff, Colonel Shishakli, executed a seizure of power, which he consolidated two years later by dismissing Parliament and suspending the constitution. In Jordan King Abdullah was assassinated by nationalists in July 1951 and a year later Farouk, the ruler of Egypt, was forced to abdicate by a young officers' rising led by Colonel Neguib. In these circumstances British policy sought to strengthen the Arab states against Israel on the assumption that Israel would retain a definite preponderance of military strength. Hence, after the Security Council lifted the embargo on the supply of arms to the Middle East in August 1949 British supplies of arms in limited quantities were resumed under existing treaty commitments to Egypt, Iraq and Jordan. The United States and France, however, besides being highly suspicious of alleged British designs for assisting Iraq and Jordan in their efforts to bring Syria into a united Fertile Crescent, were unwilling to see an arms race develop in which Israel might turn to Russia through fear of being outpaced by the Arabs. The formula which was devised to relate these positions of Britain, on one side, and her two allies, on the other, was the Tripartite Declaration issued in the name of the three Powers on May 25, 1950. This statement deprecated an arms race between Israel and the Arabs and laid down the principle that applications for arms should be considered only 'in the light of legitimate self-defence and . . . defence of the area as a whole'. The Declaration then went on to pledge the three Powers to take action both within and outside the United Nations should they discover that preparations were being made to violate the agreed armistice lines.[2]

The Tripartite Declaration, though it introduced the only element of stability into the unsettled Arab-Israeli conflict, did nothing to conciliate the governments of the Arab states. They remained doubtful whether the three Powers would ever really use force to restrain Israel should she seek to expand her frontiers by aggression, which

[1] 460 H.C. Deb. 5s. Col. 36 (January 18, 1949).
[2] *The Times*, May 26, 1950.

they regarded as inevitable. At the same time they denounced the Declaration as an attempt to sanctify armistice lines which Israel had in their view won by breaking the United Nations truce with the acquiescence of the United States, one of the signatories of the Declaration.

This reaction of the Arab states to the Tripartite Declaration and their persistent refusal to acknowledge the *fait accompli* of the Israeli state were basic factors in the failure of British and American efforts to organize a collective defence pact for the Middle East after the Palestinian war on the model of the North Atlantic Treaty. The military weakness of the Arabs showed that such an organization was essential to fill the power vacuum created by the gradual retirement of British strength. But every Arab state knew that to join such a pact meant to betray the anti-Israel cause and hence to incur the hatred of its Arab brothers. As an aftermath to the war in Palestine the Arab States had themselves formed a defence pact, but this was without substance and remained to all intents a dead letter; in any case it excluded outside Powers and would almost certainly be unable to contain any Communist incursion from the north. This was the Inter-Arab Joint Defence Alliance and Economic Pact adopted by a majority of the Council of the Arab League on April 13, 1950. A permanent military commission representing the General Staffs of the signatory states was created, together with a Joint Defence Council consisting of Foreign and Defence Ministers, both organs being under the control of the Arab League Council. The Pact was signed by Egypt, Lebanon, Saudi Arabia, Syria and Yemen. Iraq signed a revised version of the Pact in February 1951 at a meeting of the Arab League Council in Cairo after one more abortive discussion of Arab federation. Jordan did likewise in February 1952 following the assassination of Abdullah in the previous July.

Britain could not seriously consider this arrangement as a substitute for Western plans for an effective Middle East defence organization. These plans, in one form or another, had been urged by British negotiators in the talks with Egypt since 1946 as the price to be paid for a British withdrawal from the Suez base. From the outset Egyptian Ministers, both under the Farouk regime and after the officers' revolution in July 1952, consistently refused to merge the Suez base either in an Anglo-Egyptian defence pact or in any general Middle East security pact which included a Western Power as a member. They regarded all such projects, though they had the support of the United States, France and Turkey, as merely a pretext for continued British occupation of Egyptian soil. Hence, after eight years' negotiation, the agreement providing for Britain's withdrawal from the Suez base, which was signed by the British Minister of War, Anthony Head, in Cairo on July 27, 1954, was coupled, not with any collective defence arrangement, but merely with the grant of permission to Britain to reactivate the base in the event of an armed attack on Egypt or any other member of the Inter-Arab Defence Pact or Turkey.[1] The treaty incorporating these heads of agreement was signed on October 19th and marked the end for the time being of the efforts for a general Middle East defence organization. By this time a new and more dubious defence scheme was taking shape.

The Anglo-Iranian oil dispute

Arab resistance to the programme of a Middle East defence organization was almost certainly increased by the apparent impunity with which the Persian Prime Minister, Dr Moussadig, was able to annex Britain's greatest economic asset in the Middle East, the Anglo-Iranian Oil Company. This he did by a nationalization law promulgated on May 1, 1951. The AIOC had been formed in 1909 to take over a concession granted by the Persian Government to an Australian prospector eight years previously. When the blow fell in 1951 the British Government held 56 per cent of the shares of the company's ordinary stock and enjoyed preponderant voting rights. In that year Persia was the most important oil producer in the Middle East, though rapidly being overtaken by Saudi Arabia. A quarter of British oil requirements was derived from the AIOC's refinery at Abadan, the largest in the world, the costly installations of which formed a bizarre contrast with the semi-feudal conditions in the rest of the country.

Owing to Persian dissatisfaction with their share of the industry's profits, a so-called supplemental oil agreement had been initialled in July 1949 which raised Persian royalties and gave Persia a share in the company's reserves. The lower house of the Persian Parliament, the Majlis, acting on the recommendation of its Oil Committee, on which Moussadig was the dominant figure, failed to ratify this agreement, and after the assassination of the then Prime Minister, General Razmara, in March 1951 the road was clear for the nationalization of the industry and a three-year virtual dictatorship by Dr Moussadig. Ostensibly Moussadig's quarrel with the AIOC was that it paid more to the British than to the Persian Treasury, that there was no check on the amount of oil leaving the country, and that the British Admiralty received oil from the company at cut rates.

[1] For a fuller account of Anglo-Egyptian relations since the war see Chapter VII.

But in a more real sense the AIOC was perfectly fitted for the role of scapegoat for the nationalist demagogue, of whom Dr Moussadig was the supreme example. Much the same desire to exploit the country's resources from within and prevent the drain of wealth, generally much inflated in the nationalist's mind, to the foreigner, and much the same confidence in native capacity to manage complex enterprises motivated Moussadig and those on whom he cast his spell as moved Egyptian nationalists in the matter of the Suez base.

Whatever Persia's motives, nationalization of the AIOC meant to Britain the loss of a great industry paying huge annual amounts in taxation. It meant a threat to British oil supplies in peace and war; although it was true that Saudi Arabia, Iraq and Kuwait could probably make good the Persian loss within a few years, there was no refinery in the Middle East capable of replacing the Abadan plant. Moreover, the political forces behind the Persian Prime Minister, especially the left-wing Tudeh party, and the violent and arbitrary character of his methods suggested that what Russia had not achieved in Persia by force in 1946 she might now achieve by making Moussadig her puppet. It was this aspect which made the United States an anxious observer of the crisis. Generally speaking American sympathies were more deeply committed on Persia's side than on Egypt's during the differences between these two countries and Britain. Where Farouk's dissolute Court offended American puritanism, the hypochondriacal Moussadig, seen by millions of Americans on television when he visited the United States in October 1953 to attend the Security Council debates, appeared to symbolize a weak but highly cultured nation under the heel of British imperialism. Where British arguments on the importance of the Suez base for Middle East defence had an obvious appeal to the United States and turned it against Egypt, British oil interests in Persia were competitive with American companies in Saudi Arabia. Above all, the Persian oil crisis was enacted in the midst of the Korean war and President Truman feared a Soviet *coup* in Persia while America's hands were fully occupied in the Far East. For these reasons the United States was a central figure in Anglo-Persian negotiations from the outset of the crisis, seeking to bring both sides towards a peaceful settlement. The Persian Government, unlike the Egyptian in their negotiations with Britain on the Suez base, did not object to this intervention. In fact Dr Moussadig made a desperate appeal to Truman's successor, President Eisenhower, in May 1953, shortly before his fall from power. The Prime Minister's object was to try to fill the emptying Persian Treasury, as the Abadan refinery moved to a standstill, by economic aid from the United States and the World Bank. These efforts were without effect so long as a settlement with Britain had not been reached. The American Government made quite clear to the Persians that Congress would never sanction the use of the taxpayer's money to bolster Moussadig's regime while the country's oil wealth remained idle through his intransigence.

American interest in the Persian oil crisis in effect ruled out the use of force by Britain to secure her rights under the oil agreement signed with Riza Shah Pahlavi in 1932, which was still valid and had until 1993 to run. There was a show of force in June 1951, when a British parachute brigade was moved to Cyprus, but the Government relied on patient willingness to negotiate, coupled with reference of the dispute to the International Court of Justice and economic pressure. In the meantime they considered that, while nationalization could not be undone, action in the courts could prevent Persia from profiting from it so long as the ownership of the oil was in doubt. In many cases courts in various parts of the world did uphold the AIOC's claim to ownership of oil shipped by the newly created Persian national company, although in one striking case in October 1954 a Rome court gave judgment against the British company in the matter of oil carried by the tanker *Miriella*. A further disincentive to armed action was the warning given by the Persian Foreign Minister, Dr Makki, that any landing by British troops would be regarded as a signal for the Persians to blow up the refinery. It was also doubtful whether armed action, save in defence of the lives of British technicians at Abadan, would have been approved by public opinion in Britain.

In the House of Commons the Opposition, under Mr Churchill's leadership, accused Labour Ministers of 'scuttle', but this applied, not to the refusal to try to reverse the nationalization decree by force, but to the Cabinet's order, given on October 1, 1951, for the withdrawal of the remaining British technical staff after Ministers had appeared to promise in August that they would not issue such an order.[1] During the British General Election campaign in October 1951, which gave the Conservatives an overall majority of eighteen seats when votes were cast, neither Government nor Opposition advocated the use of force to settle the deadlock. Nor did leading Ministers actually accuse Mr Churchill of proposing to use force, though this was not true of some of their followers. This British restraint, coupled with the successful termination of the Suez base negotiations with Egypt in 1954, at length had its reward. Twelve

[1] D. E. Butler, *The British General Election of 1951*, London, 1952, p. 113.

months after Dr Moussadig's fall from power in August 1953 a satisfactory agreement was reached with his successor, General Zahedi. This was ratified by the Majlis on October 21st and by the Senate on October 28, 1954.

The agreement provided that the AIOC, shortly afterwards renamed the British Petroleum Company, should receive from Persia £25 million in payment of all compensation claims, this liability to be discharged over ten years. The oil remained nationalized but effective control of the Abadan refinery and Persian oil fields, with some small exceptions, passed to a new international consortium, consisting of four companies; on the boards of directors of two of these, that is, the operating companies, Persia was to nominate two out of the seven members. 40 per cent of the assets of the consortium was to be held by the British company, 40 per cent by five American companies, 14 per cent by Royal Dutch Shell and the remaining 6 per cent by the Compagnie Française des Petroles. The AIOC was to receive £214 million for the sale of the 60 per cent of its rights to the other members of the consortium. Profits from all oil operations in Persia were to be shared equally between the Persian Government and the consortium. The agreement was to run for twenty-five years with provision for three possible five-year extensions.[1]

Thus, in spite of an interruption of the oil industry lasting over three years, the crisis had a not unsatisfactory outcome as far as Britain was concerned. The restraint and subtle pressures exercised by London throughout might well have been remembered during later crises in the Middle East. The compensation ultimately agreed was derisory compared with the value of the installations and that part of the concession which had yet to run. But the AIOC received a good price for the sale of its 60 per cent share; on the London Stock Exchange its £1 shares, which stood at £5 after the evacuation from Abadan, were valued at £18 after the agreement was signed.[2] The British company was now buttressed with the interests of foreign concerns which provided an assurance against further one-sided expropriations, which Persia in any case now had the strongest financial inducement to avoid. Moreover, the rising importance of the newer fields of Kuwait reduced the contribution of Persian oil to British needs, while at the same time it served to remind more level-headed Persians of the price they had paid in terms of a

---

[1] See Benjamin Shwadran, *The Middle East, Oil and the Great Powers*, NY, 1955, p. 184.
[2] The Royal Institute of International Affairs, *Survey of International Affairs, 1954*, London, 1957, p. 225.

dominant position in the world oil market for Dr Moussadig's adventure.

Middle East defence and the Baghdad pact

Meanwhile British thinking on the strategical picture in the Middle East had to take account of rising American interest in filling the gaps in the Asian containment belt around Russia's land mass. After his tour of twelve Arab and Asian countries in May 1953 the United States Secretary of State, John Foster Dulles, had returned convinced that for the time being the Arab states were improbable starters for any Western-backed defence network to cover the Middle East. Reliance would therefore have to be placed on Turkey, with its geographical location on Russia's southern flank, its considerable army and long history of opposition to Russian advances towards the Mediterranean. Turkey, along with Greece, had been admitted to the Atlantic Pact on America's urging in October 1951. Another candidate for the new Asian containment girdle was Pakistan, which had every reason for seeking American economic and military assistance in view of the quarrel with India over Kashmir and which was to join the American-sponsored South East Asia defence organization pact concluded at Manila in April 1954. American policy therefore concentrated on bringing Turkey and Pakistan together, thus linking NATO with the South East Asia defence treaty and in doing so insulating the military vacuum of the Middle East against Russian penetration, even though of that penetration there was yet no sign. In the autumn of 1953 the Governor-General of Pakistan, Mr Ghulam Mohammed, fulfilled an invitation to visit Washington and, although President Eisenhower denied at the end of the visit that military aid and bases had been discussed in detail, it became apparent in the New Year that Pakistan was in fact negotiating a friendship pact with Turkey on American initiative and also a military aid agreement with the United States. It was no surprise when on February 19, 1954, the Turkish and Pakistani governments announced their intention to study methods of collaborating for peace and security. On April 2nd a treaty was signed to cover five years of co-operation and was accompanied by an invitation to other states to join. The striking feature of the pact was its non-committal character: it merely pledged both sides to study methods of co-operation should an unprovoked attack be launched against either. No doubt this moderate obligation was intended to lull Soviet and Indian suspicions, by now thoroughly aroused, and to serve as an inducement to others to join. Meanwhile on February 26th the

Prime Minister of Pakistan had announced the impending receipt of military aid from the United States. An aid agreement was signed on May 19th, after the pact with Turkey had been effected.

While pessimistic about the intentions and strength of the Arab states in general, the American Government hoped that all countries in the Middle East would gradually come to appreciate the example set by Turkey and Pakistan. In particular they regarded Persia and Iraq as hopeful prospects. Both countries, especially after the Persian oil crisis had been settled, had strong inducements to enter defensive agreements against Russia. Persia still had lively memories of the Soviet war of nerves directed against her in 1945–46 and suspected Soviet intrigue during the semi-dictatorship of Moussadig. The very proximity of Russia, however, which gave Persia a natural interest in any strong defensive pact, also acted as a deterrent and it was not until September 1955 that Teheran felt strong enough to join a Middle East defence arrangement. Iraq, the nearest to Russia of all the Arab states, was in a similar position to Persia in that her minority peoples to the north overlapped Russia's southern frontier. Hence Iraq might one day find herself confronted by the same kind of Soviet-sponsored secessionist demand which Moscow had imposed on Persia in 1946, an independent Kurdistan playing the same role in Iraq's case as Soviet Azerbaijan had in Persia's. But a different set of obstacles had to be overcome by Iraq before she could join a collective military pact from those confronting Persia. Iraq was an Arab state, and hence any Iraqi decision to enter a military treaty under the aegis of the Western Powers must appear in the rest of the Arab world as a betrayal of the Arab cause against the West. By the same token it was bound to revive suspicions that Iraq proposed to establish an hegemony over the Arab world with Western help, to which end she was allegedly sacrificing the most sacred of Arab causes, the fight against Israel.

These difficulties in the way of Iraq's participation in any anti-Soviet defence system were fought and temporarily overcome by the Iraqi Prime Minister, the pro-Western statesman Nuri As-Said, who, after his overwhelming victory in the Iraqi elections in September 1954, dominated the politics of his country until his assassination at the hand of nationalists in the July revolution of 1958. Nuri Pasha had little if any of the emotional neutralism of the typical Arab nationalist in his make-up. While neutralism signified to him a barren and negative struggle against the West, he lived rather for the prospect of making his country the leader of the Arab world through a judicious blend of Iraq's own natural wealth and the assistance of the West. This ambition naturally brought him into conflict with Egypt, Iraq's acknowledged rival for predominance in the Arab world, and with Saudi Arabia, with its traditional hostility towards the Hashimite dynasty of Iraq.

At a meeting of the Arab states in Cairo in September 1954 Nuri argued the case for turning the Arab League security pact into a regional defence arrangement with Britain and the United States. This was firmly opposed by Colonel Nasser, who had by now ousted Neguib as leader of the Egyptian revolutionary regime. Thus began the struggle between the two men which reached a crisis after the announcement of January 12, 1955, of an impending treaty of mutual defence between Iraq and Turkey. This news was at once followed by feverish efforts by the two Arab leaders, Nuri and Nasser, to recruit Arab support for and against the proposed pact. Nuri unsuccessfully canvassed Syrian and Lebanese agreement to join with Iraq and Turkey in the pact, which was signed on February 24th and was known as the Baghdad pact. Nasser summoned a meeting of Foreign Ministers of the Arab League to meet in Cairo on January 22nd with the object of arraigning Nuri for desertion of the Arab collective security pact and for consorting with Turkey, with whom the Arabs still had an unsettled quarrel about Alexandretta. Nuri failed to attend the Cairo meeting on a plea of indisposition, but said that he would not regard himself as bound by the Arab League security pact if the League condemned Iraq. Nasser retorted with the threat to leave the Arab League if Iraq signed the pact with Turkey. Neither threat was very seriously intended. Nevertheless the lines were drawn and the battle for and against the pact had begun.

Britain welcomed the Turko-Iraqi pact as a godsend. It seemed a distinct contribution towards filling the military void in the Middle East without involving Britain in efforts to cajole the Arab states into a Western-oriented regional pact, in which she had already failed. At the same time the Baghdad pact seemed to open the way to a solution of the problem of British bases in Iraq. By the Anglo-Iraqi treaty of 1930 the RAF enjoyed the use of the air bases at Habbaniyah and Shaiba and Iraq agreed to place her communications system at Britain's disposal in time of war.[1] This agreement had been replaced by the Treaty of Portsmouth, signed on January 15, 1948, which offered similar facilities to British forces.[2] Violent anti-British demonstrations in Iraq, however, prevented the ratification of the

[1] Treaty Series No. 15 (1931), Cmd. 3797.
[2] Iraq No. 1 (1948). Treaty of Alliance between H.M. in respect of the UK, and H.M. the King of Iraq. Cmd. 7309.

Portsmouth treaty and by 1955 the original treaty of 1930 had only two years to run. The British Government therefore decided to adhere to the Baghdad pact, the adherence being formally completed on April 4, 1955, as a means of concluding new arrangements with Iraq to replace the abortive treaty of 1948. Thus, by supplemental agreements signed by Britain and Iraq on the same day as Britain adhered to the Baghdad pact the two air bases were recognized as under Iraqi sovereignty, but the RAF's right to use them was affirmed in accordance with the mutual defence provisions of Article I of the pact. The British Foreign Secretary, Anthony Eden, emphasized in the Commons, however, that Britain was not a party to the exchange of letters between the Turkish and Iraqi governments at the time of the signing of the pact, which could be construed as committing Turkey to support Iraq in the event of hostilities between the latter and Israel.[1]

It was not long before the welcome given to the Baghdad pact and Britain's adherence to it on both sides of Parliament was recognized as having been premature. No other Western Power followed in Britain's steps. France seemed to fear that to do so would be to compromise herself with Syria, whom she was advising not to join the pact on the grounds that it might turn out to be one more British scheme for uniting the Fertile Crescent against French influence. Nor did the United States join the pact, though she did become a member of its military committee two years later, despite the fact that much of the inspiration behind the pact came from Washington. The reason for American hesitations was thought to be unwillingness to be too much identified with British policies in the eyes of Arab nationalists. It was said that the United States preferred to wait until the dust of Anglo-Egyptian quarrels had settled. Whatever the motives, the effect may well have been to add to Colonel Nasser's deep prejudice against the pact, which he now saw to be without apparent American support and which might even have incurred American dislike. If France and the United States remained aloof, other Powers were free with their condemnation. Russia promulgated her unsurprising warnings, while remaining curiously passive. In India Mr Nehru bitterly attacked the pact both as strengthening Pakistan, India's rival in Kashmir, and on the grounds that it imported external tensions into a Middle East which seemed in 1954 to be settling peacefully most of its angriest problems.

In this latter charge there was much truth. The immediate consequence of the Baghdad pact was to inflame everybody against

[1] 539 H.C. Deb. 5s. Col. 381 (March 30th).

I

everybody. Egyptian hostility against Britain, which had seemingly been allayed by the Suez base and Sudan settlements, was re-awakened. Whereas before the pact was signed Nasser seemed genuinely poised in indecision on the issue of commitment to the West, the pact, by once more kindling suspicion of British intrigue, precipitated him into the neutralism into which he was being induced at the Bandoeng conference of African and Asian states at the very time when Britain adhered to the pact. The Soviet Union was not slow to take advantage of this fact. The British decision was the immediate cause of the offer of military aid by the Soviet bloc to Egypt and Syria in the autumn of 1955. The Arab states' acceptance of this offer was viewed with intense alarm in the Western capitals, though it could be argued that Britain and the United States, by encouraging the formation of the Baghdad pact, had evoked the very Soviet threat which the pact was ostensibly designed to meet. Nor did the pact do anything to improve Arab-Israeli tensions. Israel, who was prevented from joining the pact by Article 5, which excluded from membership any country not recognized by the Arab states, feared that Iraq was being reinforced against her, while Egypt, believing that the pact divided the Arab countries and was therefore to Israel's advantage, began to fear Israel more. The resulting Israeli-Egyptian tensions, which had been taking the form of sporadic frontier raids throughout 1954, culminated in a full-scale clash between the armies of the two countries in the Gaza area on February 28, 1955. Egypt suffered a second heavy defeat. The effect was to reinforce Colonel Nasser's ambition to make the extermination of Israel the primary basis of his claim to the leadership of Arab nationalism.

In Cyprus, too, tensions were heightened by the Baghdad pact since the withdrawal from the Suez base and Iraq forced Britain to make the island its principal fortress for the conduct of operations in fulfilment of the pact's obligations. As though to raise the curtain on the virtual civil war which broke out in Cyprus in May 1955, the Greek Cypriot leader, Archbishop Makarios, expressed the attitude of all Middle East neutralists when he said on returning from the Bandoeng meeting that by its 'international machinations' the British Government was undermining and endangering the peace of the eastern Mediterranean. But the most serious adverse effect of the pact was to align the Arab states into warring factions with Nuri Pasha at the head of one faction and Colonel Nasser at the head of the other. Neither succeeded in entirely winning the support he sought. Nuri was perhaps the less successful; he found that no other

Arab state would join the pact and that in his own country he alone was its sole advocate of eminence. But neither did Nasser drive all the rest of the Arab states into an anti-Nuri stand. In October 1955 bilateral defence pacts were signed between Egypt and Syria and Egypt and Saudi Arabia, and arrangements made for a joint military command. But that was as far as Nasser's success extended. In the midst of the Nuri-Nasser stalemate Jordan remained the focus of rivalry.

Jordan, being to all intents a British client state and being linked to Iraq by dynastic ties, looked a probable member of the pact. When inquiries about the pact came from Amman Sir Gerald Templer, the British Chief of the Imperial General Staff, was sent to Jordan in December 1955 to provide the necessary explanations. But these efforts were frustrated by public demonstrations, in the fomenting of which Nasser almost certainly played a part; but what was probably more important in Amman's rejection of the pact was the influence of refugees from Palestine, who had now come to play a dominant role in Jordanian politics. Jordan therefore marked the outer limit of support for the Baghdad Pact among the Arab states. But it played an even more important part than this. The demonstrations in Amman against the pact showed how far Britain had moved from her historic role as guardian over the Arab states as a whole. Now, by a series of decisions each in itself sensible, she had become involved in an inter-Arab conflict in which she was fighting Egypt in almost every Arab capital. It was not surprising that Colonel Nasser threw down the challenge to Britain in well-chosen circumstances in the following year.

CHAPTER FIVE

Britain and European Unity

We have seen in an earlier chapter how after the end of the war the Labour Government co-operated with Britain's neighbours in western Europe in economic recovery and defence.[1] The expression of this was British participation in the Marshall plan, the formation and work of OEEC and the making of the Brussels treaty, as well as many other inter-governmental organs for specific needs. A British government was bound to view with concern the sight of a depressed and defenceless Europe only twenty miles away, capable of dragging the British economy into the depths if it did not actually fall victim of Communism itself. But equally convinced were British Ministers that co-operation in Europe (or as much of Europe as remained free after Russia had pushed her influence to the Elbe) must not advance to a point at which there was a risk of the loss of British independence. Let it once be suggested that Western Europe might unite and form one body, with one centre of decision, and Britain was quick to withdraw. This impulse to retract was second nature to British politicians whether Labour or Conservative. It never cost them votes. If they ever had to defend it at home they could point to tradition, the Commonwealth connection, the Atlantic community, or national psychology, as occasion required.

Time and again in modern history British governments have shrunk from hard and fast commitments in Europe, preferring the policy of the free hand appropriate to an Imperial Power. When, not without regret, Britain undertook to guarantee the territorial *status quo* in Europe at the Locarno conference in 1925, the pledge was limited to two frontiers, those of Germany with France and Belgium. At Locarno the peace settlement in east Europe, which a British Prime Minister had signed, though reluctantly, was shown to be not a firm British commitment. In May 1930, when Briand, the French Prime Minister, made his revolutionary proposal for European union, it was mainly British opposition which left the scheme in the clouds. The Foreign Office wrote off the Briand proposal as 'vague

[1] Chapter II, pp. 44–8.

and puzzling idealism'.[1] Ten years later, in June 1940, when France was collapsing, the British Government did make an offer of union with France, but the Prime Minister, Churchill, was at first against it and only consented to it as a 'dramatic announcement to keep France going'.[2] The tradition of detachment, described by Victor Hugo as *'des alliances, soit, pas de mariages'*, had a basis in British interests though it tended to harden into an inert habit of the mind.

Contrary to a common suspicion abroad that Britain's European policy has always been in the spirit of divide and rule, British Governments have generally sought to reconcile the European Powers with one another and maintain a concert between them. They insisted on the restoration of France to the concert as soon as possible after 1815 and did the same for Germany after 1918. The assumption was that intra-European feuds were dangerous to peace, which has been a basic interest since the Empire reached its maximum extent at the end of the Napoleonic wars, and that the alignment of Britain with one group of European Powers against another endangered national unity, jeopardized Britain's role as a mediating influence and reduced her power to defend oversea interests. But while good feelings between the European states was a British interest, complete unity was more doubtfully so. Unity might be unity *against* Britain, and in any case the process of attaining unity in Europe would present Britain with the awkward choice between forming a part, and hence endangering her position as a world Power, and standing aside, with the risk of losing her power to influence European affairs to her advantage. The awkwardness of this choice was all the greater after 1945 for two reasons. First, British foreign policy in the inter-war years had been constantly influenced by the need to retain the general sympathy of the now independent Dominions; since their attitude to European affairs was generally isolationist, this meant that every British commitment in Europe placed a strain on the co-ordination of British and Dominion policies. After 1947, with Ceylon, India and Pakistan as independent countries in the Commonwealth, it was even more vital to ensure that Britain was not too tied by European connections to help in the creation of a common outlook on world affairs in the Commonwealth. Secondly, it was becoming clear that the main centre of decision in world politics had shifted from Europe and might well come to be divided between an Asia in which the Soviet Union was dominant and a

[1] *Documents on British Foreign Policy, 1919–1939*, edited by E. L. Woodward and Rohan Butler, Second Series, Vol. I, London, 1947, p. 326.
[2] Winston S. Churchill, *The Second World War*, Vol. II, London, 1949, p. 183.

North America led by the United States. This migration of power encouraged some British politicians, mainly Labour but including some Conservatives as well, to favour British membership of a politically uncommitted west European union, but the main effect was to suggest that a Britain, stripped of its Empire and reduced to a mere unit in a European federation, might be wholly unable to influence those larger forces outside Europe which were coming to shape affairs in the world as a whole. It was thus a British interest that the issue of European union should not be forced, at least until the pattern of the new Commonwealth and the realignment of world power had become clearer.

These factors of tradition and interest were reinforced by the notorious emotional detachment of British people from mainland Europe which was at once a consequence of tradition and an impediment, as time went on, to the proper appreciation of national interest. For British public opinion Europe has tended to appear either as a picturesque holiday playground, which does not need to be taken too seriously, or as a welter of political quarrels, none of them entirely healthy or innocent, which constantly threaten to involve this country. Costly wars which Britain has fought have generally begun in Europe; Britain's allies in these wars have sought to implicate her, so the British think, in the maintenance of vindictive peaces holding the seeds of future conflicts. From the European scene British politicians have been apt to turn with relief to their fortunate island just outside the rim of chaos, have often been deeply ignorant of European affairs and have been able to speak to British audiences as though knowledge of Europe was not an essential part of political *savoir-faire*. Stanley Baldwin, of whom Churchill wrote that he 'knew little of Europe and disliked what he knew', Neville Chamberlain, who referred to Czechoslovakia as a 'faraway country of which we' (it is often forgotten that he did not say or mean 'I') 'know nothing', even Churchill himself who once said it was 'an Englishman's right' to pronounce foreign names just how he liked, have all in their various ways expressed British distaste for too intimate a connection with those people across the Channel. These feelings were not weakened by the Second World War. It is true that the occurrence of two wars within twenty-five years led many British people to think that without the abandonment of sovereignty there would be no lasting peace; that Churchill insisted that European revival and unity were vital in the face of the new Soviet threat; that the shrunken resources of Britain seemed to demand some revision of the traditional image of the country as a lofty mediator. Nevertheless the mere fact that Britain had survived the war with her sovereignty intact heightened rather than diminished the 'Channel complex', as Salvador de Madariaga has called this British insularity.

Here is a paradox. Although European unity has always cast its spell on political visionaries, from Charlemagne to Briand, the presence of some definite threat to European values has generally been required to bring the concept into practical politics. Fear of war and the economic depression were the forces making for the French plan in 1930, the threat of Communism provided whatever voluntary assent there was to the Nazi blueprint for a united Europe, dread of reversion to militarism was the major force behind the European idea in postwar West Germany. The most important corresponding factor in 1945 was the loss of national faith in Western Europe which resulted from the German occupation and the liberation by Anglo-American forces. This fall in national self-confidence, a temporary inner defeatism in people who had been overrun by alien superior force and then freed mainly by alien superior force, sometimes took the form of conversion to Communism, or neutralism, or the time-honoured chauvinism of a Charles de Gaulle. But its most lasting and constructive form was the yearning for a united Europe. It was precisely this aspect which not only had no appeal to Britain but was positively distasteful. Britain had never been occupied since 1066; she had had no collaborationists worth speaking of; for a vital twelve months she had been Hitler's only serious opponent and had played a major part in the destruction of a Europe united by the Nazis. It was therefore natural that, when the crisis of national self-confidence led continental Europeans to call for political unity after the war, Britain should show a somewhat patronizing interest, always provided that the movement for European unity did not go too far. It was hard to believe that Britain's situation was so desperate that it was best for her to commit suicide in order to be born again into a European federation. It was almost as hard to believe that the Europeans, after all their talk and paper constitutions, really had the political ability to make a fundamentally constructive advance. It was considered that Europe, after all, owed its survival to British insularity. How could Europe hope to succeed if its uncle across the Channel, who was always ready to help when things got out of hand, gave up his freedom and married into a bankrupt family which could never keep out of debt?

The fact that Britain had a Labour Government in 1945 did not change these basic attitudes. The British Labour Party has always had a vaguely federalist complexion, which is in fact reflected in its constitution, and some of the strongest British advocates of federal union, whether in Europe or the world as a whole, have belonged to the Left in British politics, if not actually to the Labour Party. Attlee himself had made a powerful attack on national sovereignty in a speech in November 1939, when he uttered the words 'Europe must federate or perish' which were to dog him so much when he became Prime Minister. His Foreign Secretary in the 1945 Government, Ernest Bevin, apart from his close association with the European trade union movement, had been a firm advocate of British membership of a European customs union in the 1920s.[1] But federalism in the British Labour Movement, like socialism, has generally been a flexible creed, splendidly evocative but practically circumspect. British Labour politicians never saw eye to eye with their continental colleagues on the question. Office, too, had its effects. Possibly the strongest basis of mass support behind the Labour Government in 1945 was the result of its undertaking to rid Britain of unemployment and social insecurity. This could only be fulfilled, in the Labour view, by firm control of the national economy through the state machinery. Once in possession of that machinery and seeing the effects of its use in terms of better living standards and welfare services for the worse-off groups in Britain, a natural pride in British social achievements clearly developed in Labour leaders. 'We are determined,' said Hugh Dalton in 1950, 'not to put these gains in peril through allowing vital decisions on great issues of national economic policy to be transferred from the British Parliament at Westminster to some supra-national European assembly. . . . We intend to hold what we have gained here in this island.'[2] This pride in the peaceful victories of the British people did not prevent some Labour critics of Bevin's foreign policy, especially the *Keep Left* group, from supporting west European unity in the immediate postwar years, when it looked as though socialism might spread on the continent, bringing with it the same pattern of controlled use of national resources for public welfare.[3] But when, as from 1948, a definite swing to the moderate Right took place in western Europe and the Christian Democrat parties there became the leading advocates of European union, even this support turned

[1] Alan Bullock, *The Life and Times of Ernest Bevin*, Vol. I, London, 1960, pp. 361, 371, 387–8.
[2] *Report of the 49th Annual Conference of the Labour Party*, Margate, 1950, p. 166.
[3] *Keep Left*, a manifesto proposing 'a more drastic Socialist policy' than that of the Government, was drawn up by a group of Labour MPs led by R. H. S. Crossman, Michael Foot and Ian Mikardo and published in April 1947.

to hostility. In practically all major sections of the Labour Party ideology, national pride and anxiety not to lose control of the planned economy joined hands so as to set British Labour against participation in European union. It was indeed asking a great deal of the Labour Party, when they at last had the opportunity to apply the state machinery to the defeat of the social evils they had fought so long, that they should forthwith agree to hand over these powers to a European federal body largely controlled by forces which, in Labour's view, had not yet learned the lessons of the long years of economic depression.

Moreover, the cause of European union often seemed to draw to its defence allies who were far from being innocent in Labour's eyes. The Labour Party had had some unpleasant experiences over unity in the movement before the war, when Communists sought to use the emotional force of the idea in order to capture the party. Now the idea of unity in Europe was being welcomed in Right-wing circles which often saw in it a means for further dividing the world against Russia. The foremost champion in Britain of European unity, Churchill, was clearly actuated by intense anxiety over Russia's incursions into Europe; his call for European unity at Zurich in September 1946 followed logically after his appeal at Fulton, Missouri, in March for resistance to the Soviet menace by the English-speaking peoples. For all Bevin's bitter experience of dealing with the Russians he remained loathe to resign himself to the conclusion that the world was irremediably divided and continued to hope that patient work would in the end find a way through. Besides, a Labour Government which sought to co-operate with Churchill in the European movement must be reconciled to his being its leader, on account of his prestige and support for European union, going back to the war years. This would have placed the actual British Prime Minister, Attlee, in a difficult position, all the more so because it was never quite clear just where Churchill stood on the European issue and how far he was prepared to go to commit Britain.

Sometimes Churchill spoke, as at Zurich, of European union with Britain outside but acting, along with the United States and possibly Russia, as its 'friend and sponsor'.[1] At other times, as in his speech at the Congress of the European Movement at The Hague in May 1948, Europe and the British Empire were somehow united in his mind. He spoke of the 'gradual assumption of a larger sovereignty' and yet was at all times sure that a definite federation was not within the scope of practical affairs. Such groping was not improper in a

[1] *The Sinews of Peace*, ed. by Randolph S. Churchill, London, 1948, p. 202.

statesman temporarily out of office and chiefly concerned to rally opinion on the continent to the larger perils of the day. But it was not possible for a government which had to decide whether or not to commit the country to engagements for which there was by no means a majority of opinion in Britain. The Government were also irked by the way in which Churchill seemed to use the movement for European unity to throw discredit on themselves as allegedly behind the times. The National Executive Committee of the Labour Party discouraged party members from attending the Hague Congress of the International Committee of the Movement for European Unity in May 1948 on the ground that the Committee was an unofficial body and such a serious question as European union was a matter for governments to decide. Churchill chided Attlee about this in the playful way he had of suggesting, probably without meaning seriously to imply, that the Government were at the beck and call of the Labour Party.[1] None of this made co-operation between the Government and Churchill on the European question easy. It is true that many socialist leaders on the continent were as enthusiastic about unity as the Right; prominent among them were Spaak of Belgium, Guy Mollet and André Philip in France, and Van der Goes Van Naters in Holland. But in meetings held by European socialists after the war national differences proved to be more important than party differences, British socialists standing with their Scandinavian colleagues against continental socialists who had become firm advocates of European union. At the Baarn conference of European socialists in May 1949 this split came into the open and remained a dominant feature of the European international relations of the Left.[2]

The fact that European union, with British membership, was powerfully and persistently pressed for by the United States Government and public opinion was not a recommendation of it to Labour Ministers. The United States gave no enthusiastic welcome to Labour's social programme; it was suspected that the terms of the American loan to Britain were all the harsher because a Labour administration was at the receiving end. America could not want European union for the same reason as Left-wing dissidents in the Labour Party in 1947, namely as a model of social democracy intermediate between communism and capitalism. American sponsorship of United Europe, British Labour MPs tended to conclude, could have no other aim than that of binding Europe together in opposition

[1] Royal Institute of International Affairs, *Documents on International Affairs*, *1947–48*, London, 1952, pp. 235–7.
[2] *The World Today*, October 1950, pp. 415–23.

to Soviet Communism. Such consolidation might be necessary if it should prove beyond doubt that Russia meant to try military conclusions with the West. But it was not proposed to allow the United States to decide the tempo of consolidation. But there was an even stronger reason for not accepting charges by the United States that Britain was 'dragging her feet' and American pressures to merge with Europe. British politicians had long been familiar with the tendency of Americans to be so spellbound with their own history as to wish to press other countries into the same mould. This often made them blind to the idiosyncrasies of national outlook which were real enough on the other side of the Atlantic. To argue that Europe could soon end its quarrels by drafting a federal constitution, with division of powers and a Supreme Court, ignored, and in a way humiliating to Europeans, the long histories of other countries and their many connections with peoples and affairs outside the continent in which they happened to be situated. Americans were free to give their advice on European politics. But when this was accompanied by threats that economic aid would be stopped if European states did not comply there was a natural refusal to be hurried into such serious decisions as the abandonment of national independence at the instance of politicians many of whom were wholly ignorant of the real state of things in Europe.

The United States Government made clear where they stood. In August 1948, when Britain was resisting federal tendencies in the drafting of the statute of the Council of Europe, the State Department declared that the Truman administration 'strongly favours the progressively closer integration of the free nations of western Europe . . . it does not make sense to us to contemplate a democratic Europe attempting economic unity without political agreement, at any rate on broad lines'.[1] In general, however, the American Government refrained from the cruder types of open public pressure. The Marshall offer of June 1947, for instance, was linked with an invitation to the European states to form an association for the collective definition of their requirements, but this was probably more of a recommendation of the offer to American public opinion than a statement of conditions. Nevertheless, European union continued to figure as the aspiration of Congress, as expressed in its resolutions, and Senators made their speeches rebuking Britain for sloth. Little of this was a stimulus to the British Government. It was realized that behind much of this pressure, perhaps at the subconscious level, was an American assumption that if Europe could settle its problems

[1] Quoted in *The Times*, August 28, 1948.

through adopting the federal solution the need for American assistance, in goods, troops and arms, would be less. It was the suspicion that this hope lay behind American support for European union which chiefly determined the British Government not to yield to it.

The aim of British policy was thus to promote European cooperation for practical purposes, short of federation which would present Britain with the impossible choice already referred to, but to do so if possible within the larger framework of the Atlantic community as a whole. No one who remembered Stalingrad or General MacArthur's victories over the Japanese in the Pacific could believe that Europe could still provide for its own security without a permanent relationship with the United States. This was the theme to which Bevin constantly returned. As he said in May 1948:

> The organization of all the West European democracies, excellent and necessary as it is, can hardly be accomplished save within the framework of an even larger entity. I am not content to confine either propaganda or speeches or action to the assumption that Western Europe alone can save itself.[1]

Throughout the inter-war years uncertainty as to how the United States would act in an emergency had bedevilled all British thinking about security. Now that America was committed to Europe, through Marshall aid, the Truman doctrine and the many declarations of her statesmen, the British Government wished to give isolation no pretext to return. Ironically, this end could best be served, so they considered, by frustrating America's policy for Europe.

The Council of Europe

It is not surprising then that the strongest opposition to the first postwar essay in the construction of a common political framework for Europe, the Council of Europe, should have come from Britain, supported in this by the Scandinavian countries which shared to a greater or less extent the British feeling of being in, but not of, Europe. The project for a Council of Europe arose from the acceptance by the French Government of the proposal made by the Congress at The Hague in May 1948 in favour of a political and economic union to be expressed through a Consultative Assembly drawn from the Parliaments of member states. The case for an all-European assembly was put by Bidault, the French Foreign Minister, at the Consultative Council of the Brussels Treaty Powers in July and

[1] 450 H.C. Deb. 5s. Col. 1110 (May 4, 1948).

opposed by Bevin. The Foreign Secretary held that the roof could not be erected before they had the building and argued that Europe still had a long way to go by way of co-operation in defence and in the economic and other fields before representative political organs were created 'to deal with the practical things we have accomplished as governments'.[1] He proposed instead a mere committee of Ministers drawn from member states. When the Consultative Council appointed a sub-committee to consider these proposals, the Government appointed Hugh Dalton, a well-known opponent of federalism, to represent them. Britain did agree to a consultative assembly, provided it was overshadowed by a committee of Ministers in order to ensure governmental control, but a further difference sprang up between Britain and the federalists, represented by France and Belgium, at meetings of the sub-committee in November when the composition of the assembly was considered. Britain wanted delegates to the assembly to be appointed by governments and to vote strictly as national blocs, while France and the Benelux countries preferred election by Parliaments and voting on an individual basis. A compromise was eventually adopted at a meeting of the Foreign Ministers of the Brussels Powers in January 1949; this authorized governments to decide the method of appointing delegates to the assembly for themselves and placed no restrictions on individual voting.

The Statute of the Council of Europe was finally signed in London on May 5 by the five Brussels Powers and five other European countries which had been invited to join them.[2] It bore in every phase the marks of the British resistance to federalism of the previous year, which was fully endorsed by the Scandinavian signatories. The Committee of Ministers, representing the governmental element in the Council, was to meet in private and was simply an intergovernmental conference on the traditional model. The principle of unanimity, in other words the veto, was preserved on all but procedural and administrative questions, and in any case the Committee's resolutions had only recommendatory force when addressed to governments. The Committee clearly dominated the Consultative Assembly, the parliamentary element. The Assembly was to report, not to governments or electorates, but to the Committee and then

---

[1] As explained by Bevin in the Commons on September 15, 1948; 456 H.C. Deb. 5s. Col. 106.
[2] Ireland, Italy, Denmark, Norway and Sweden. Greece and Turkey were admitted to the Council in August 1949. Iceland joined as a full member in 1950 and the German Federal Republic and the Saar as associate members in the same year. The Federal Republic became a full member in 1951. Austria joined the Council in 1956.

only in the form of recommendations. It could discuss nothing without the consent of the Ministers, who decided its agenda, and could not even meet for longer than a month at a time without the Ministers' permission. The admission of new members to the Council and the Council's budget were within the scope of the Ministerial body. To complete the emasculation of the Council the Statute expressly forbade any discussion of defence and instructed the Committee of Ministers, in deciding the Assembly's agenda, to have regard to the work of *other European inter-governmental organizations* (the wording is significant). The Council, in other words, was warned not to trespass on the territory of such bodies as the OEEC and the Brussels Treaty organization.[1]

Thus it was clear that when the Consultative Assembly met for its first session at Strasbourg in August 1949 it was, so to say, 'all dressed up and nowhere to go'. The Churchillian call 'Fiat Europa!' of 1946 had ended in a mere talking shop. For this Britain was widely held responsible. Bevin, it was noted, told a meeting of the Foreign Press Association in January, when the main lines of the Council's Statute became generally known, that the 'solid work of European unity' still rested on co-operation between the governments in economics and defence.[2]

But what Britain was doing was merely to state the obvious. In none of the countries which were taking part in the movement towards European unity had a clear mandate been given to the government to submerge the national identity in a definite federation. The question had never been put to the vote in Britain. The function of the Council, more particularly of the enthusiasts for union who sat in the Consultative Assembly, was therefore to help create the frame of mind in the public for the giving of this mandate. With this, however, they were not content, and instead they pressed forwards at once with the aim of converting the Council into a legislative body. Various proposals with this end in view were referred to its Committee on General Affairs by the Consultative Assembly at its first session but it soon became evident in the Committee's discussions that those who wished for a definite step towards federation to be taken, chiefly delegates from France, Italy and the Benelux countries, were in a minority. The majority of delegates, many taking their cue from Britain, preferred to move more cautiously through functional co-operation in specific fields until the habit of thinking and working within a European framework had become

[1] Treaty Series No. 51 (1949). Statute of the Council of Europe. Cmd. 7778.
[2] Quoted in *The Times*, January 29, 1949.

firmly established in the various countries. Hence the Committee's report, which was considered by the Consultative Assembly at its second session in August 1950, was cautious, and the Assembly's own recommendations, after discussion of the report, even more so. Apart from insisting on greater Parliamentary control over existing inter-governmental organizations and repeating the plea it had made the year before for more authority for itself, the Consultative Assembly confined itself to stating the general principle of 'limited functions but real powers' for the Council.

Even so the Committee of Ministers at its sessions in November 1950 and May 1951 made quite clear that there was no immediate future for any increase in the political authority of the Council. Britain was firmly opposed to the idea. The Under-Secretary of State for Foreign Affairs, Ernest Davies, told the House of Commons on November 13, 1950, that 'there cannot be any delegation of general powers to an outside body, to an outside authority which might not necessarily share the view of HM Government or with which compromise was impossible, and which might even deprive HM Government of powers without which they could not carry out the wishes of the electorate'.[1] There was certainly no support by Britain or the other anti-federalists on the Committee of Ministers for the recommendation in favour of giving executive and legislative authority to the Council which had been received from a special committee of seven appointed by the Consultative Assembly to consider a plan to that effect drawn up by the British Labour delegate and well-known federalist, R. W. G. Mackay. Kenneth Younger, the British Minister of State at the Foreign Office, said in a written answer in the Commons on January 24, 1951, that the proposal had such far-reaching political and constitutional implications that it could not even be taken as a basis for discussion without careful study.[2] At a meeting of the Committee of Ministers in Paris in March the British delegate disclosed that the careful study had resulted in the unsurprising negative. The only positive outcome of this struggle between the federal enthusiasts in the Consultative Assembly and the anti-federal group led by Britain in the Committee of Ministers was the agreement of the Committee to the amendment of Article 23 of the Council's Statute so as to give the Assembly authority to decide its own agenda.

The British position was strongly criticized in a debate held in Strasbourg in November 1951, when fourteen United States Con-

[1] 480 H.C. Deb. 5s. Col. 1402.
[2] 483 H.C. Deb. 5s. Written Answers Col. 29.

gressmen discussed the future of Europe with an equal number of members of the Consultative Assembly. The intention of the critics may have been to encourage the Conservatives in Britain, who won the general election held in October, though with an overall majority of only eighteen seats and on an actual minority of votes cast. During the Labour administration Conservative delegates to the Consultative Assembly, who included such leading figures as Churchill and his son-in-law, Duncan Sandys, Harold Macmillan, David Eccles and Robert Boothby, had always seemed more close in spirit to the continental federalists than Labour MPs, who, with some striking exceptions, followed the line of their Government. It was therefore not unnatural for federal enthusiasts to assume that under Conservative rule British policy would seriously move forwards. These hopes were, however, belied at the following session of the Consultative Assembly. On November 28th the chief British delegate, Sir David Maxwell Fyfe, the Home Secretary in the new administration, plainly said that it was unrealistic to expect Britain to join a European federation. The utmost she could do was to send a permanent delegation to the headquarters of the newly formed European Coal and Steel Community and consider a form of association with the proposed European Defence Community.[1] As if this was not enough to disillusion European federalists, the new Foreign Secretary, Eden, told a Press conference in Rome the same evening that Britain could not join the Defence Community, though there might be some association. This was after General Eisenhower, then the Supreme NATO commander in Europe, had told Eden that the United States understood and agreed with the British position.[2] The effect on European federalists was deadly. Spaak, the President of the Consultative Assembly, at once resigned in exasperation.

Personality played some part in the attitude of British Ministers on the European question. In the Labour Government Herbert Morrison, who took over the Foreign Office in March 1951 when Bevin was forced to resign on account of ill-health, was somewhat less hostile to the idea of European union than Bevin, though he did criticize the Council of Europe because of its cost.[3] Morrison joined the United States in a declaration issued in Washington on September 14, 1951, just before the Labour Government's fall, in which the two countries welcomed the Schuman plan for a coal and steel

---

[1] Council of Europe, Consultative Assembly, Third Session (Second Part), Official Report, Vol. III, pp. 512–14.
[2] *The Memoirs of Sir Anthony Eden. Full Circle*, London, 1960. pp. 32–3.
[3] Lord Morrison, *Herbert Morrison, an autobiography*, London, 1960, p. 279.

pool and the plan for a European army. Britain, so Morrison agreed in this declaration, desired 'to establish the closest possible association with the European continental community at all stages of its development'.[1] Eden, on the other hand, though seasoned in European diplomacy, had much of Bevin's mistrust of abstract federal schemes; his great emphasis, like Bevin's, was on the Atlantic community. He had accordingly always carefully dissociated himself from Churchill's championship of European union when the Conservatives were out of office. Nevertheless, Eden was under strong pressure to take more interest in the Council of Europe. Conservative leaders had been active at Strasbourg and the Rome speech was a shock to them. Moreover when Eden returned to the Foreign Office in October 1951 the inner ring of members of the Council, the Benelux countries, Federal Germany, France and Italy, were pressing ahead with their plans for closer integration in limited fields. By the time the Consultative Assembly met for its fourth session in May 1952 the Little Europe of the Six was forging ahead. The treaty for a European coal and steel pool had been signed and ratifications were almost complete. The Bonn agreements restoring West German sovereignty were signed on the day of the opening of the Strasbourg session, May 26th, and the treaty for a European army (EDC) on the following day. This movement among the Six was threatening to leave Britain and her friends in the Council of Europe far behind.

The British solution for this widening gap took the form of the so-called 'Eden proposals' (though the basic work was done by Eden's Under-Secretary of State, Anthony Nutting, and his Foreign Office staff). These were submitted to the Committee of Ministers by the Foreign Secretary on March 19th and adopted by the Committee at its tenth and eleventh sessions in March and May 1952. The purpose behind them, Eden said, was to save the Council of Europe from being stranded between the 'two streams' of the Atlantic community and the Six by linking the functional organs under construction by the Six with the Council. The Council's two main instruments, the Committee of Ministers and the Consultative Assembly, were to act in the same capacity for the coal and steel pool, the defence community and any other supranational enterprises of the Six, but in that event only representatives of the Six should have voting powers, while the other nine members of the Council would have only observer status, if they wished to share in these new activities of the Council at all.[2]

[1] Germany No. 10 (1952). Cmd. 8626, p. 3.
[2] For the text of the Eden proposals see Report of the Committee of Ministers,

K

The Eden proposals seemed to be acceptable to the Consultative Assembly when explained by Nutting and were adopted in principle in a resolution of the Assembly on May 30th. But it was clear that considerable suspicion existed among the Six that the proposals had only been put forward in order to give Britain a voice in the supranational communities of the Six, and perhaps enable her to put a brake on their development, without undertaking any of the obligations involved in membership. Spaak told Nutting at the Consultative Assembly in May that he and his friends 'had waited too long for Britain to get aboard the European bus . . . the Eden plan was a neat half-way house arrangement which might suit Great Britain, but half-way houses were not enough for Europe'.[1]

The result was that when the Assembly reconsidered the plan in September, on the basis of a report by its Committee of General Affairs, the British notion of the Council as the parent body of the new supranational communities was whittled down to that of 'organic links' of an innocuous character between the Council and the only supranational organ then in being, the coal and steel community. Even so the degree of integration actually achieved between the Council and the community was less than that contemplated in the Consultative Assembly's 'Opinion' on the matter.[2] The Six thus presented a clear choice to the Council between supranationalism and inter-governmental co-operation by securing in effect the rejection of the Eden proposals. They then went on to try to form the political community which they had failed to create through the Council of Europe. The drafting of a treaty to establish this community was entrusted to a so-called 'Ad Hoc Assembly' consisting of representatives of the Six together with observers from other members of the Council. This move was deprecated by British delegates to the Consultative Assembly as it would certainly consolidate the segregation of the Six from the rest of the Council. The problem had, however, been raised in a crucial form by the treaty between the Six for a European army, the original suggestion of which had come from a British delegate to the Consultative Assembly, Churchill himself. An army was inconceivable without a political executive to control it, and hence in Article 38 of the European army treaty

---

Documents, 1952, Doc. 11. For Eden's explanation see 498 H.C. Deb. 5s. Cols. 32–34 (March 24, 1952).

[1] Anthony Nutting, *Europe Will Not Wait*, London, 1960, pp. 44–5.

[2] Council of Europe, Consultative Assembly, Texts Adopted, September 1952; *European Yearbook*, Vol. I, p. 451; A. H. Robertson, *The Council of Europe*, London, 1956, pp. 100–1.

provision was made for a constituent assembly to draft the outline of a political community. Accordingly, with the collapse of the treaty for a European army in 1954, the political community fell with it. But the incident had served the purpose of showing the rising irritation of the Six with the persisting negativeness of Britain.

The Schuman plan

Considering that Britain had sided with the functionalists at the Council of Europe, that is, those favouring a piecemeal approach by co-operation in specific fields, as opposed to the all-out federalists, it might have been supposed that she would have warmly responded to the proposal made by the French Foreign Minister, Robert Schuman, in May 1950 for placing the French and German coal and steel industries, together with those of as many other countries as agreed to join, under a common higher authority. In his note of May 9th Schuman seemed to echo the familiar British argument that 'Europe,' to quote his words, 'will not be made all at once, or according to a single general plan'. France, taking the line so often heard from British speakers at Strasbourg, realized that Europe must be built 'through concrete achievements, which first create a *de facto* solidarity' and because she did so proposed to attack the problem at 'one limited but decisive point', namely the heavy industrial complex of north western Europe, which should be brought under supranational control. In fact the Labour Government's reaction, stripped of the formal tones of welcome, was cold, and when the treaty embodying the plan was signed by the Six in April 1951 Britain, the traditional leader, with Germany, in the heavy industries of Europe, was not among the signatories. An agreement was eventually signed in London on December 21, 1954, defining the relation between Britain and the coal and steel community, which had come into existence in July 1952, but this merely provided for a Standing Council of Association for consultative purposes only. The Council was to consist of four British representatives and four members of the High Authority of the community and was to concern itself more particularly with the co-ordination of policies in the event of restrictions being placed on the trade in coal and steel between Britain and the community. Otherwise Britain had no part in this most concrete step towards European union.[1]

Some attempt was made by the Conservative Opposition in the House of Commons to attribute this negative attitude to the socialist prejudices of Labour Ministers. Undoubtedly Labour delegates had

[1] A. H. Robertson, *European Institutions*, London, 1959, Appendix, pp. 286–92.

never been comfortable at the Consultative Assembly of the Council of Europe, where they were in a minority of one in four. The fact that the governments of the Six were predominantly Right-wing was no recommendation of the Schuman plan to Labour. A certain amount of evidence for the existence of these prejudices was provided by a pamphlet published by the Labour Party, entitled *European Unity*, which was completed shortly after the announcement of the Schuman plan and appeared on the same day, June 18th, on which Attlee gave the House of Commons the Government's provisional views on the plan. The pamphlet restated the Government's preference for inter-governmental co-operation since Britain's position in the Commonwealth and as the centre of the largest multilateral trading system in the world ruled out membership of a tight federation in Europe. It then made the curiously illogical statement that 'no Socialist Party with the prospect of forming a government could accept a system by which important fields of national policy were surrendered to a supranational European representative authority, since such an authority would have a permanent anti-Socialist majority and would arouse the hostility of European workers'. The Conservatives attacked this as reducing foreign policy to the level of party feuds.

Looked at in another light, however, the Labour pamphlet, in its insistence that only through planning of the national economy could full employment and high living standards be maintained, could serve to justify British entrance into the Schuman plan as well as to oppose it. The whole emphasis in the plan as presented by the French was on the expansion of production under the centralized direction of the higher authority. This, according to Schuman, would be charged with the task 'of securing in the shortest possible time the modernization of production and the improvement of its quality; the supply of coal and steel on identical terms to the French and German markets and those of other members countries; the development in common of export to other countries; and the equalization as well as improvement of living conditions of workers in these industries'. Though there was a hint of preference for the free market in these words, the spirit was clearly that of economic *dirigisme* such as was an article of faith with the Labour Party. This seemed to be conceded in the Labour pamphlet, which appeared to grasp the Schuman plan rather as a challenge to social democrats.

Until M. Schuman's historic proposal (it read) to pool the steel and coal resources of France, Germany and the Saar under a single authority appointed by the governments, the unwillingness of many governments to control their own basic industries made European planning of coal and steel impossible. The opportunity now exists to fill the greatest gap in European economic co-operation.

These words might still be taken as implying British detachment but an important role in the plan seemed to be assigned to Britain in the sentence which followed: 'It is the duty of all who have European unity at heart to see that the Schuman proposals are shaped in the interests of the peoples as a whole. The decisive part in co-ordinating Europe's basic industries must be played by the governments, as trustees for their peoples.'

It would hardly be true to say then that socialist prejudices were what caused the Government to hold back, though no doubt fear of socialist legislation in this country being disturbed by the Schuman plan won support for the Government's decision among its Parliamentary supporters. The reasons were more fundamental and would probably have operated with equal effect had the Conservatives been in power. First, there was the form in which the French proposed to announce the summoning of a conference on the plan. This obliged participating countries to declare before the conference that they had 'assigned to themselves as their immediate objective the pooling of coal and steel production and the institution of a new high authority whose decisions will bind'. This was asking Britain to buy a pig in a poke, or, in the more diplomatic language of the British reply to France of May 31st, to sign a communiqué which took decisions 'prior to, rather than as a result of, inter-governmental decisions'.[1] The Conservative position was that the communiqué could nevertheless have been signed and the conference attended in the hope of modifying the proposals in a sense more acceptable to Britain. They referred to the case of Holland, who took precisely this course at the Paris conference. But there are reasons why this scheme was not open to a British government. There was no real parallel, either in international standing generally or in the production of coal and steel, between Britain and Holland. For Britain to attend a conference on the basis of the acceptance of the principle of supranational control of basic industries, with which neither Labour nor the Conservatives agreed, would have been fraudulent.

[1] Miscellaneous No. 9 (1950). Anglo-French discussions regarding French proposals for the Western European Coal, Iron and Steel Industries, Cmd. 7970, p. 11.

There was no doubt whatever that the maximum which even the Conservatives would have been willing to accept by way of supranationalism was so much lower than what the French were demanding that a British attendance on such terms would have been understood on the continent as one more attempt to put a spoke in the wheel of the federalists.

The most important reason, however, for the failure of the Anglo-French exchanges on the Schuman proposals in May 1950 was that no British government was able to accept the principle of supranationalism by which the control of basic industries would have moved out of British hands. Supranationalism meant to the French, first, that the coal and steel pool was a step on the road to a federal Europe, as well as a means for making any future war between France and Germany 'not merely unthinkable', in Schuman's words, 'but materially impossible'. But the federal road was not one which either the Labour or the Conservative party was ready to follow. The reference to the Schuman plan by Attlee in the Commons on May 11th, which entirely omitted the federal aspect mentioned in the Schuman note and concentrated on the scheme as a means for speeding Germany's entry into the European comity of nations, might equally have been made by an Eden or Churchill.[1] But the Schuman proposal was supranational in a second and more immediately important sense. According to the original French note of May 9th the proposed high authority over coal and steel production was intended as a sovereign body, whose decisions would bind member governments, though the ownership of the industries themselves was not to be affected. The high authority's decisions would have 'executive force'; it would be 'independent of governments' and would constitute a 'partial fusion of sovereignty'.[2] It is true that when the coal and steel community treaty was signed by the Six in April 1951 these revolutionary undertakings were not quite fulfilled, showing that negotiation had, after all, diluted them, or that they had been originally stated in extreme form in order to face Britain with a clear choice. By the 1951 treaty the high authority, to consist of nine independent persons appointed by member governments for six years, was indeed to make its decisions by majority vote, which meant that its will could be imposed on minorities. But it was to be concerned, less with the day-to-day running of the industries, than with the removal of quantitative restrictions and discriminatory practices. The authority was buttressed by a Special Council of

[1] 475 H.C. Deb. 5s. Col. 587.
[2] Cmd. 7970, pp. 5, 11.

Ministers instructed to harmonize the action of the authority with that of governments 'which are responsible for the general economic policy of their countries'. It was answerable to a Common Assembly, to consist of seventy-eight members appointed every year by the Parliaments of member states from their own number, which could dismiss the authority by a vote of censure passed by a two-thirds majority. It was subject to a review of the exercise of its powers by a court of justice and although it was granted authority to tax coal and steel enterprises which is generally considered to be the right of governments, these levies could not exceed one per cent of the average value of production unless the Council of Ministers otherwise decided.[1] When all is said, nevertheless, the supranational element was distinctly there, and, what was much more important, might grow.

The Six were firmly insistent on this. The idea that they could be talked out of it by British delegates at the conference to draft the treaty sprang from the characteristic British illusion that, in the last resort, continental governments would abandon their wild schemes and come down to earth. How remote from the truth this assumption was became abundantly clear at the Consultative Assembly's session in August immediately following the announcement of the Schuman plan in May. There Harold Macmillan unfolded the kind of alternative to supranationalism which a Conservative government would no doubt have put forward had they been represented at the Paris conference. The essence of the proposal was that the veto should be retained on the committee of Ministers to supervise the coal and steel pool. Macmillan described this as retaining the principle of pooling the coal and steel industries. He was followed by Schuman himself who utterly rejected the Macmillan formula. 'He who agrees with me in principle,' the French Foreign Minister said, 'disagrees with me in fact.'[2]

During the Commons debate on the Schuman plan on June 26th and 27th there was no disagreement between Government and Opposition on the rejection of any European machinery which would take out of British hands control of the basic industries on which the export trade, full employment and the economic health of the country generally so vitally depended. The Government had no

[1] The text of the treaty is printed in *European Yearbook*, Vol. I, pp. 359–453· On the structure of the Coal and Steel Community generally see A. H. Robertson, *European Institutions*, Chapter 5.
[2] Council of Europe, Consultative Assembly, Second Session, Seventh Sitting, August 14, 1950, pp. 436–8.

mandate for such a step. The Opposition were unwilling to ask the electorate to give them one. The Leader of the Opposition, Churchill, seemed to be helplessly groping for some form of associate status which would halt at the brink. He did not say in so many words

> Mother, may I go out to swim?
> Yes, my darling daughter;
> Hang your clothes on a hickory limb
> And don't go near the water.

But his form of expression was to the same effect.

> We should in my opinion (he said) favour and help forward all developments on the Continent which arise naturally from a removal of barriers, from the process of reconciliation and blessed oblivion of the terrible past and also from our common dangers in the future and present. Although a hard-and-fast constitution for Europe is not within the scope of practical affairs, we should help, sponsor and aid in every possible way the movement towards European unity. We should seek steadfastly for means to become intimately associated with it.[1]

It was not surprising that the Conservatives should have placed European unity third among their foreign policy aims at the general election in October 1951, the first two being the defence of the Empire and Commonwealth and the maintenance of Imperial Preference respectively. Their manifesto did not raise the issue of the Schuman plan or of similar European supranational authorities.[2]

A European army?

Though the British rejection of the Schuman plan was in many ways a turning point in the relations between Britain and the Six, there were intelligible reasons why British opinion could not be wildly enthusiastic about the coal and steel pool. To join might well strengthen British relations with the Six and certainly help remove the now firm impression that Britain's chosen role in Europe was to hold others back. But it was far from clear in what way exactly membership of the pool would benefit British heavy industries, or why any such benefits could not be obtained by the ordinary forms of international co-operation without putting these industries under an authority whose policies were wholly unknown. But the case was different with the next supranational proposal to come from France,

[1] 476 H.C. Deb. 5s. Col. 2159 (June 27th).
[2] D. E. Butler, *The British General Election of 1951*, London, 1952, p. 45.

the suggestion made by the French Prime Minister, René Pleven, in October 1950 for a European Defence Community for the joint control of European military forces within the framework of Atlantic defence. In the first place the idea, if it had not originated with Churchill, had been publicly aired by him at the Consultative Assembly of the Council of Europe in August 1950, when he proposed a European army in which 'we would all bear a worthy and honourable part'. Churchill accepted an amendment to the proposal, which was then adopted by the Assembly, envisaging a European Minister of Defence with responsibility over the army. This may well have carried him further than he wished to go. Both the European army and the European Defence Ministry were rejected by the Labour Government as duplicating the NATO defence system, which covered the western part of Europe to which Churchill referred, and as proposing to hand over responsibility for defence to a non-governmental body, the Consultative Assembly of the Council of Europe.[1] Moreover, in the months following the outbreak of war in Korea in June 1950 it was feared in the West that Communist aggression might be repeated in Europe and since the United States was bearing far and away the greatest burden in Korea, it was evident that Europe must begin to look more seriously into its own resources for defence. If a Soviet attack in Europe were to come, it would have to be met as far to the east of the Rhine as possible. All this raised the vexed question of a German contribution to defence.

The three Western Foreign Ministers, Acheson, Bevin and Schuman, in a declaration issued in New York on September 19, 1950, agreed that the creation of a German national army was undesirable. But they went on record as being interested in the principle of German participation in an international force for the defence of Europe.[2] Grave doubts continued to exist in Britain about the wisdom of putting arms in any form into German hands, and also, though for somewhat different reasons, in France. The French solution to the dilemma of German rearmament, which they knew that, as European allies of the United States, they would eventually have to accept, was the Pleven plan for a European army to include German contingents. From the French point of view this had the treble advantage of avoiding the creation of an independent German force, of allowing for the incorporation of German units of the smallest

---

[1] Ernest Davies in the House of Commons, November 13, 1950; 480 H.C. Deb. 5s. Col. 1408.
[2] Royal Institute of International Affairs, *Documents on International Affairs, 1949–50*, London, 1953, p. 335.

size and thus insuring against the return of corporate military feelings in Germany, and of challenging Britain to enter the European army and thus help to control the Germans. Outside France, however, the Pleven proposal aroused suspicion. Washington inclined to regard it as threatening delay in the organization of Germany's defence contribution. In British official quarters the plan was seen to raise again the well-nigh insoluble problem of political control, while in Federal Germany fear was expressed that the scheme might prove to be a device for recruiting German manpower while Germany was still divided and denied the attributes of a sovereign state. But the French had their way. Their resistance to German rearmament in any other form was such that the United States agreed that no decision should be reached in the talks to be held in Bonn on a German contribution to defence between the three Western High Commissioners and the Adenauer government before the conference called by the French to consider the Pleven plan had arrived at conclusions. In the event the Bonn discussions failed and no alternative, for the time being, was left to the French plan.

The conference duly met in Paris on February 15, 1951, and was attended by representatives of Belgium, France, Italy, Luxemburg and West Germany. Britain was represented only by an observer, as were also Denmark, Holland, Norway and Portugal. The Canadian and United States Ambassadors in Paris were present as observers. According to an interim report issued by the conference on July 24th, the structure of the proposed defence community provided for a Defence Commissioner (or Commissioners), a Committee of Ministers, a parliamentary assembly and a court, thus following the lines of the Coal and Steel Community. The problem of control remained obscure, however, and, as we have already seen, Article 38 of the treaty as eventually signed envisaged the meeting of a constituent assembly to prepare a European political community, for it was clear that without some new type of fused sovereignty among the participating states the European army would remain leaderless. The other major problem was the delicate matter of the size of the national units. In the final report of the Paris conference, issued in November, it was planned to create an army of a million and a quarter men by 1953, to be composed of forty-three units of 30,000 men each (corresponding to a division of combat troops). France was to contribute fourteen units, Germany and Italy twelve each and the Benelux countries a total of five. Early in 1952 the EDC treaty was submitted to the NATO Council meeting in Lisbon for approval since the European army was to serve under the supreme NATO command in Europe. On the assumption that EDC provided a solution of the dilemma of German rearmament the Bonn agreements providing for the restoration of German sovereignty and the ending of the Occupation were signed on May 26, 1952. They were not to be effective, however, until the EDC was established. The EDC treaty itself was signed on May 27th.[1]

The French had come to regard British membership of the Defence Community as fundamentally essential to its success; without British membership the Community, France feared, would in all likelihood come under German domination, especially if French military strength was drained away in the struggle against nationalism in the oversea territories. Yet it was clear that Churchill's apparent offer of a British contribution to a European army would falter when the issue was put. If a British government could not permit the country's basic industries to be run by a supranational authority, it was even less likely that they would make an exception for the military forces, all the more so since British Ministers had always resisted with clenched teeth continental commitments which might interefere with the defence of Commonwealth and colonial interests. Hence Eden's rejection of EDC membership for Britain in Rome in November 1951, soon after the formation of the Conservative Government, and hence the statement by the Prime Minister, Churchill, in the House of Commons on December 6th, which was equally negative. The implication of both was the same: that Britain would remain a benevolent spectator of the progress of EDC. On the same day as Churchill's statement Paul Reynaud, in a speech at Trier, said that the British refusal meant the collapse of the whole scheme.[2] An attempt was made to offset the effect of these statements when the Prime Minister and Foreign Secretary visited Paris later in December and promised that Britain would keep the forces on the continent which she then had there. An encouraging reference was made to EDC, as 'one of the steps leading to unity in Europe', in the communiqué issued after the talks, but there was no mistaking the meaning of the words used by the British Ministers when they said that Britain 'would associate as far as possible with EDC at all stages of its political and military development'.[3] Eden privately believed that EDC was doomed, the only question for Britain being how to choose the timely moment for stepping in with an alternative.[4]

[1] The text of the treaty is printed in Miscellaneous No. 11 (1952). The European Defence Community Treaty, Cmd. 9217.
[2] *The Times*, December 7, 1951.
[3] *Ibid*, December 19, 1951. [4] The Eden Memoirs, *Full Circle*, pp. 33–4.

Towards the end of 1951 it was evident that the cold British attitude was having its effect in the marked decline of support for EDC
among the Six, especially in France, and once the decline set in it
increased at an accelerated rate. General de Gaulle and his party,
the Rally of the French People, ridiculed it, and the French Communists, with their hundred seats in the Chamber, and powerful
elements among the Socialists, for their own reasons, were against
it. Moreover, the more EDC was decried in France the weaker its
popularity in Federal Germany since much of the strongest opposition to EDC in France derived from the openly expressed fear that it
would be dominated by Germany and the Germans were not to be
trusted. It was therefore all the more vital for the two Powers outside
EDC, the United States and Britain, to go to the utmost in defining
their relationship to the Defence Community if it was not to find
itself without a friend in Europe. One solution, which in the event
had little influence on France, was to reaffirm the Anglo-American
agreement to maintain forces in Europe to assist the Defence Community in the protection of the Atlantic area. This was the burden
of a joint declaration by the British and United States Foreign
Ministers issued in London on February 19, 1952.[1] This was far from
satisfying French opinion since it seemed to underline the impression
that Germany was France's problem within EDC, while Britain stood
aloof and fancied herself on the same level of world power as the
United States. Nothing was beginning to irritate the French more
than the 'special relationship' which British governments claimed
with the United States.

France, supported by Holland, kept up the pressure on Britain
and in the result a further step was taken in London in April, when
Britain undertook to assist members of EDC if attacked in Europe,
using her right under Article 51 of the United Nations Charter, which
legalized individual and collective self-defence. This undertaking
was to last as long as Britain remained a member of NATO.[2] Eden
explained the commitment by saying that 'we have established a
formal and special relationship between the United Kingdom and
EDC. This clearly shows that, although we cannot join that community, we are linked with its future and stand at its side'.[3] In practice, however, the undertaking did little more than extend to West
Germany the commitment Britain had assumed towards her Euro-

[1] Royal Institute of International Affairs, *Documents on International Affairs,
1952*, London, 1955, p. 83.
[2] Miscellaneous No. 5 (1952), Cmd. 8512.
[3] 499 H.C. Deb. 5s. Col. 24 (April 21, 1952).

pean allies by the North Atlantic treaty to come to their defence
against armed attack. It was somewhat strengthened by being put in
the form of a treaty between Britain and EDC signed on May 27th,
the day following the signature of the Bonn agreements on Federal
German sovereignty.[1] Meanwhile the NATO Powers at a meeting of
their Council in Lisbon in February had agreed that any attack on
EDC should be regarded as an attack on the NATO countries generally.[2]

But these assurances did very little for France's comfort. The
French rightly pointed out that no real sanctions existed to prevent
the Anglo-Saxon Powers withdrawing from Europe if they wished.
Indeed one perverse consequence of EDC, if it ever succeeded, would
be to strengthen the arguments in Britain and the United States for
reducing their military commitments on the continent. But the chief
French complaint was that neither Britain nor the United States was
willing to do anything to guarantee France against a future withdrawal of Germany from EDC. The effect of such a withdrawal would
be that Germany, largely rearmed at the instance of Washington,
would again have an independent national army under her own
control.

By this time the situation was being complicated by two new
circumstances which served only to depress the prospects of EDC in
France and to drive a deeper gulf between that country and Britain.
The first was the decision of the United States Government to intensify the pressure on France to complete the ratification of the EDC
treaty since West German rearmament had already been held up
in deference to France and the undisguised arming of the East
Germans, later drawn into the 1955 Warsaw Pact, was increasing the
perils of the military vacuum west of the Elbe. Fearful, as always,
that America might return to her own fortress in disgust with Europe,
the British Government joined in this turning of the heat on France.
Eden and Dulles issued a joint statement in Washington in March
1953 plainly stating their hopes that the EDC treaty would be ratified
soon. This pressure reached a climax in December when, at a Press
conference in Paris, an angry Dulles spoke of an 'agonizing reappraisal' of United States policy should the EDC scheme collapse. This
was as much a warning to Britain as to France since a swing of
American opinion over to hemispheric defence would destroy all the
assumptions on which British foreign policy had been built since the

[1] Miscellaneous No. 9 (1952). Memorandum regarding Western support for
the European Defence Community, Cmd. 8562.
[2] Miscellaneous No. 4 (1952). German Defence Contribution and the European
Defence Community, Cmd. 8492.

end of the war. At the end of June in the following year a troubled
Churchill joined President Eisenhower in a final warning from
Washington against further delays in getting the European army into
being. Even Dr Adenauer, realizing that West German sovereignty
hinged upon EDC, added his voice, reminding France that the failure
of EDC would not, in the long run, deprive Germany of an army of
her own, and that German armed forces organized in EDC offered
a much safer prospect for France, and for democratic forces in
Germany too, than a purely national Wehrmacht. These various
urgings unfortunately coincided with the worsening situation in
former Indo-China, which was temporarily halted by an armistice,
but not until the summer of 1954. The Far Eastern crisis was a
reminder to France that, with her oversea commitments, she could
not hope to prevent a European army falling under German control.
To make matters worse for EDC, the French Prime Minister of the
day, the socialist Pierre Mendès-France, was an entirely different
politician from the French federalists of the immediate postwar
years. He personally had little faith in EDC and was not disturbed to
see opinion in France turn against it with each twist of the screw by
London and Washington.

The other notable event was the death of Stalin on March 5, 1953,
with its immense consequences in the form of the reconsideration of
policies and reassessment of the probable future by all states in all
continents. No movement taking place on the international stage
could continue as before after the passing of the Soviet leader and
the age of East-West relations symbolized by his name. The first
signs of a thaw in Russia after the long winter of Stalinism naturally
led the British Government, among others, to weigh the possibilities
of sounding the new men in Moscow on a better state of relations.
Churchill, though he had detected the nature of the Soviet military
threat at the end of the war more quickly than any other Western
statesman of note, had already chided the Labour Government in
February 1951 for reluctance to talk with Russia at the highest level
on the nuclear threat to civilization. With Stalin's death the prospect
seemed ripe again, especially as the outlook of his successor, Malen-
kov, was wholly unknown in the West. The result was Churchill's
speech in the House of Commons on May 11, 1953, which took the
world (and the Foreign Office) completely by surprise and proposed
an informal meeting at the heads of government level between a few
of the greatest Powers.

The idea of a 'summit' meeting with the new rulers of Russia,
however, not only opened up a new prospect in world affairs after

the seemingly endless Cold War. It also threatened to throw out of gear the building of the economic and defensive strength of the Western world which had begun as far back as 1947 and was proceeding at an intensive rate after the outbreak of the Korean war in 1950. For this reason Churchill's suggestion had a varied reception among Britain's allies. The United States Government, mindful of the aversion of Congress for the use of a 'summit' meeting as a means to delay German rearmament, were nervous and insisted on the most careful preparation of the ground if parleys with Russia were held. The official feeling in West Germany tended to be that the process of exploring the path to rapprochement with Russia might hinder the building of Federal Germany as a sovereign state and that if agreement with Russia were reached it might be at Germany's expense. In France, however, the 'summit' meeting proposal had a much warmer welcome. It held out possibilities of escape from joint imprisonment with menacing Germany in EDC. Despite Russia's crushing of a rising in East Germany in June 1953, the seeming improvement in East-West relations promised to reduce the pressure for German rearmament and thus give France more time to negotiate safeguards for herself in EDC. At the same time a rapprochement with Russia might have the effect of relieving the position in Indo-China. On the other hand, the French saw British interest in EDC shrinking even more as the grand vision of wrestling at the conference table with Russia seemed to grip Churchill. He had said, after all, in his May 11th speech, referring to the EDC Powers, 'we are with them, but not of them', and this with some asperity. Only after long argument was Nutting able to extract from the Prime Minister a letter to read to the Consultative Assembly of the Council of Europe in September stating that British relations with EDC would be closer than they were with the Coal and Steel Community.[1] Since the latter were tenuous in the extreme, this was not much of a reassurance to French supporters of EDC, who now had to fight a rising flood of enthusiasm about summitry.

Unfortunately at this time Eden was absent from the Foreign Office from June until October with a critical illness. His place was taken, first by Churchill himself, then, after the Premier himself stepped down with a temporary stroke, by Lord Salisbury. On instructions from Churchill Salisbury persuaded the Americans to accept a meeting with Russia at least at Foreign Minister level, though contrary to Churchill's wish Washington insisted on a strict limitation of the agenda to the questions of Germany and Austria,

[1] Nutting, *Europe Will Not Wait*, p. 53.

where progress was most doubtful. Salisbury himself was no 'summit' enthusiast, but his position hardly enabled him to do much to prevent the hopes of the Defence Community from continuing to fall. The French Government led by Laniel until its collapse on the Indo-China crisis on June 10, 1954, did succeed in winning two major concessions from France's allies to help with ratification, but these were not enough. In November 1953 Laniel obtained from France's EDC partners additional protocols giving her a privileged position in the Community. These permitted her to withdraw troops from the European army virtually as she wished without her voice in EDC affairs being affected. In the second place, after the failure of the Four-Power Foreign Ministers' meeting on Germany in Berlin in January 1954, Britain consented to sign a co-operation agreement with EDC which had in fact been worked out the previous summer but was kept in cold storage until the opponents of German rearmament in Britain and France had been convinced that there was no road to Four-Power agreement on Germany. The agreement, which, like all previous British offers, fell far short of French hopes, was signed on April 13th and provided for consultation with EDC in the event of a British decision to reduce British forces on the continent (four or five divisions) and for a British Minister to attend the EDC Council, but only when co-operation between Britain and EDC was actually under discussion. In an independent declaration issued at the same time as the agreement was signed the British Government stated that they proposed to maintain forces on the continent in such strength as was required and that they regarded the Atlantic Pact as being of indefinite duration.[1] The latter statement arose directly from the French complaint that the EDC had fifty years to run whereas the Atlantic Pact, by which Britain was linked to EDC, had no more than twenty.

Neither concession sufficed to win the necessary support for EDC in the French legislature. The writing became clear on the wall when the treaty was rejected by majorities in the Foreign Affairs and Defence Committees of the National Assembly since the pattern of party strength was the same in the Committees and in the Assembly. Undoubtedly one of the main reasons which had contributed to this result was the British refusal to undertake stronger commitments towards the Defence Community. Jules Moch, the socialist rapporteur of the Foreign Affairs Committee, let it be known that he and five other socialist opponents of the treaty would have voted the

[1] Miscellaneous No. 10 (1954). Memorandum regarding United Kingdom association with the European Defence Community, Cmd. 9126.

other way, which would have reversed the Committee's unfavourable decision on the treaty, had the British attitude been different.[1] But this is probably not the whole story. French foreign and colonial policy since the failure of EDC has not proved beyond reasonable doubt that the French were ever ready for complete political fusion with their partners in the Six at any time in the 1950s. Even after the conclusion of the Common Market treaty three years later, launched under entirely happier omens, the French continued to hesitate on the brink of federation. EDC had been embarked upon by France less as a premeditated step towards federal Europe than as a means for avoiding a German army; yet EDC, of all unity proposals since the war, demanded almost complete surrender of sovereignty, and almost at once.

It was Mendès-France's realization of the unreadiness of the French for complete loss of national indentity which led him to suggest withdrawal from the supranational aspect of EDC at an emergency conference of the Six at Brussels on August 19th. He proposed killing EDC in order to ensure its survival in the French Parliament. The idea was (it would have required the other five signatories to undo the ratifications they had already completed) to return to the principle of a veto for each signatory 'in matters relating to defence policy'. Supranationalism would be limited to technical questions and any one of the parties could 'suspend' a collective decision even on these questions if it 'affected its vital interests'. A further proposal by Mendès-France to the effect that in any case French forces outside Europe should not be integrated seemed to imply integration for everyone else but France.

The end of EDC and the British intervention

Isolated at Brussels, the French Prime Minister saw Churchill and Eden at Chertwell on August 23rd and told them he was quite definite that EDC would be defeated. The British Ministers replied that in that case Germany must receive political equality immediately and be included into some acceptable defence framework, preferrably NATO, shortly afterwards.[2] These last-minute threats were of no avail. The question was put to the vote a week later in the French National Assembly and wafted to defeat by a majority of 319 to 264. Among the thirty-four abstentions was the French Cabinet led by Mendès-France. All this had long been foreseen, but the practical effect was to leave the issue of German sovereignty sus-

[1] Nutting, p. 65.
[2] The Eden Memoirs, pp. 148-9.

L

pended in doubt since the Federal German Republic had been created as a sovereign state by the Bonn agreements of 1952 conditionally upon the entry into force of the Defence Community. A German defence contribution remained unavoidable in view of the increasing strain of the arms burden on the West. But, even in the United States, any such contribution was hard to accept without some means for bringing it under the common control of the Western Alliance. In Britain there was general agreement with the so-called 'Attlee conditions' for German rearmament, formulated in February 1951; one of these insisted that German military units must be integrated in Western defence in such a way as to rule out a recurrence of German militarism. According to a pamphlet issued by the Labour Party in 1954, entitled *In Defence of Europe*, these conditions had been largely met, with the failure of the effort for Four-Power agreement on Germany and the re-election of Dr Adenauer, the pledge of a democratic West Germany, the previous September. But the collapse of EDC opened up the most intractable 'Attlee condition' again, that of Germany's external control.

A possible solution was that Federal Germany should enter NATO as an ordinary member, there being no question of 'junior status' in a coalition of equals. This had never been acceptable to France, though the United States was no longer in a mood to listen to her. The chief objection was that in NATO there had never been (nor could there logically be) a system for limiting the maximum forces to be contributed by each ally. On the contrary, every NATO Power had an interest in the maximization of the forces of all the others. Alongside the NATO structure, however, was the older system, out of which NATO had grown, the Brussels Treaty organization, as a possible framework for a controlled German contribution to Western defence. It has the distinct advantage for France that Britain had been a member and had shared the same responsibilities as the other parties since the treaty was signed in March 1948. Moreover, it had none of the supranational features of the Defence Community which France had in the end found impossible to swallow. The Brussels Treaty alternative had occurred to Eden, by his own account, 'in the bath on Sunday morning'.[1] After completing his toilet, the Foreign Secretary, with his flair for the timely expedient, quickly inserted his alternative into the vacuum created by the French non-ratification of EDC. The Foreign Secretary of a Prime Minister who had suggested a European army in the first place thus made himself responsible for dealing with the effects of its failure.

[1] Eden, p. 151.

It required more than the choice of the alternative to make a success of the operation. Eden's diplomatic style, at once persistent and deft, was never displayed to better effect than in the autumn of 1954, when he first determined to raise the British military commitment to Europe and then managed his announcement of it in such a way as to dispel all doubt about the solution proposed. He began with a lightening tour of the west European capitals, Brussels, Bonn, Rome and Paris in that order, in September and, having secured the agreement of the first three to the Brussels Treaty organization as the framework of German rearmament, provided it was revised and strengthened, put the question to France. The Premier, Mendès-France, at first held out for a probationary period before Germany was admitted to NATO as part of the Brussels system. But he was now left with little bargaining power since the United States was prepared to rearm Germany with little in the way of safeguards. At length he agreed to the Eden plan, but continued to plead for the retention of British troops on the continent until the end of the century. Eden, bent on securing French acceptance of the main proposal, gave no definite answer.

The Foreign Secretary then summoned the six EDC Powers, together with the United States and Canada, to meet him in conference at Lancaster House, London, on September 28th in order to negotiate the revision of the Brussels Treaty and Germany's entry to NATO. Dulles reluctantly consented and opened the London meeting with a gloomy funeral oration on EDC, which included, however, a promise to ask President Eisenhower to renew the American pledge made to EDC if a satisfactory substitute for the Defence Community emerged from the conference. Eden then timed his own announcement to fall with masterly effect after the curtain had thus been raised. The pledge he gave was as far-reaching as that given by Austen Chamberlain at Locarno thirty years before.

> The United Kingdom (Eden said) will continue to maintain on the mainland of Europe, including Germany, the effective strength of the UK forces now assigned to the Supreme Allied Commander, Europe—four division and the Tactical Air Force—or whatever the Supreme Commander regards as equivalent fighting strength.

This was substantially the same assurance Britain had repeatedly given to the EDC Powers. Now it was backed by an undertaking which would have put the champions of EDC in France in an immensely stronger position, even if it had not carried them to victory.

The United Kingdom (Eden continued) undertakes not to withdraw those forces against the wishes of the majority of the Brussels
Treaty Powers, who should take their decision in the knowledge of
the Supreme Allied Commander's views. This undertaking would
be subject to the understanding that an acute overseas emergency
might oblige HM Government to omit this procedure. If the
maintenance of UK forces on the mainland throws too heavy a
strain on the external finances of the UK we would invite the North
Atlantic Council to review the financial conditions on which the
formations are maintained.[1]

This revolutionary pledge, principally levelled at French opinion,
did not commit Britain as much as membership of EDC would have
done, though, once Britain had gone as far as this, the extra obligations in EDC might have been justified in return for the political
advantages. Britain was in effect handing over to the other Brussels
Treaty Powers authority to demand the retention of the forces
named on the continent. But the two reservations Eden mentioned
were important. The 'acute overseas' emergency justifying a withdrawal or reduction of the forces would be judged by Britain alone,
who would have to decide whether or not she should seek her allies'
consent. As far as the reservation concerning the financial burden
was concerned, the final decision would not lie with Britain, but the
allies would have little alternative but to give their consent if Britain
insisted that she was unable to foot the bill. This was in fact the
position reached in April 1957, when Britain applied for and received
authority to reduce the force levels on financial grounds. Above all,
the Eden pledge, unlike EDC membership, extended supranationalism
to British forces only in so far as their minimum strength on the
mainland of Europe was concerned. There was certainly no implication that British forces as a whole, save with exceptions such as those
negotiated in the additional protocols by France, should come
under the control of a common European authority in which Britain
might be outvoted. The pledge, though revolutionary enough to take
the breath away when compared with previous British hesitations,
was in fact a step along the road from Locarno, rather than a step
towards British membership in European union. At Locarno Britain
had agreed to defend France against Germany and Germany against
France, should unprovoked aggression occur. Now she was pledged
to keep a specified fraction of her army (one far smaller than what

[1] Miscellaneous No. 28 (1954). Final Act of the Nine-Power Conference held in
London, Cmd. 9289, pp. 17–18.

she would put into the field if war came) permanently on the continent to help defend both against aggression.

The Final Act of the Nine-Power conference, signed on October 3rd, incorporated Eden's pledge, together with an undertaking by Britain and the United States to join France in dealing severely with any German failure to carry out a promise not to try to achieve reunification by force or to recover the lost territories annexed to Poland.[1] The essence of the London agreements, which were later embodied in the treaties signed in Paris on October 20th–23rd, was that the Federal German Republic should become a sovereign state, as already agreed at Bonn in 1952, and should simultaneously join NATO and a revised Brussels Treaty organization. The Allied High Commission in Germany and the Occupation Statute were both to disappear. German forces, which were not to exceed the twelve divisions fixed under the EDC treaty, were to be placed under the Supreme Allied Commander, Europe (SACEUR). No increase in German forces was ever to be sanctioned without the consent of the Council of the Brussels Treaty organization, now, with the addition as members of Germany and Italy, to be called West European Union (WEU). A parliamentary organ, on the lines of the abortive EDC assembly, was to be created and was to receive reports from the WEU Council. The most important new addition to the Brussels structure, however, was a special agency for the control of armaments. The function of this was to supervise the peacetime maxima of arms and arms stocks of the member states and to exercise surveillance over Germany's undertaking not to manufacture atomic, chemical or biological weapons or, at least during the early years, such armaments as guided missiles or large naval vessels. The new West European Union also provided a framework for the settlement of the vexed problem of the Saar, which had been detached from Germany in 1947 and included in the French military and economic system. Under the aegis of the 1954 treaties for West Europe a new statute for the Saar was agreed by Adenauer and Mendès-France, though this was rejected by the Saarlanders in October 1955.

After further hesitations on the part of France, only overcome after Churchill had firmly told Mendès-France that ratification of the agreements this time must come before any further talks with Russia, the London and Paris arrangements finally came into effect on May 6, 1955. Russia, whose sustained efforts to prevent West German rearmament by blandishments and threats had now failed, retorted by annulling the Anglo-Soviet treaty of 1942 and the Franco-

[1] Cmd. 9289.

Soviet treaty of 1944. This did not prevent the Soviet Government from attending a 'summit' conference with the three Western Powers in the summer of 1955.[1]

The ebbing tide

The movement for European unity, from the Marshall plan to the Paris agreements of 1954, thus represented a widening breach between Britain and her West European allies. WEU which might have served to lessen this breach, was not in fact subsequently exploited as much as Eden had hoped. Continental opinion concluded from this experience that the British principle of association with, rather than membership of, Europe was still intact and that only to preserve the Atlantic defence system could Britain be prodded into cautious steps forward. British Ministers continued to believe that they could influence world affairs more effectively by detachment from Europe, an assumption no doubt influenced by scepticism as to the capacity of continental Europeans to bring their visions out of the clouds. The idea of a special role for Britain was certainly not lacking in egotism, derived as it was from the tacit belief that the Western coalition could not be properly run without British experience and independent British initiatives. But it also had a plausible basis in fact. The Korean war and the Indo-China crisis of 1954, in both of which British restraint served to control the more reckless tendencies in the West, seemed to indicate that Britain still had an important part to play, not only in her own interest but in that of world peace as well.

There was also no doubt that the Commonwealth, and more particularly perhaps India, could do a great deal both as a bridge between the Western camp and the newly emerging countries and also to moderate the dangerous asperities of the Cold War. Commonwealth conferences repeatedly welcomed trends towards closer unity in Europe and appeared to raise no difficulty about British participation in these tendencies. But there is hardly any doubt that Britain could not have played quite the same role as she did in the Commonwealth had she been a mere unit in the process of federating Europe, and that the effect on Commonwealth unity would have been quite unpredictable. There was very little serious disagreement on this point amongst British politicians. Moreover, the Europe of the Six, as Schuman's reference to the development of Africa in the original outline of his plan showed, tended to regard the new world emerging from European colonialism rather as a prospect for European enterprise than as the birthplace of free and equal states. It is true that

[1] See Chapter VIII, below.

Britain, as a member of the community of the Six, might have been able to modify these tendencies from the inside and, for example, influence French policy in Algeria in accordance with her own practice of self-determination. Alternatively she might have found herself committed to the support of these policies. Such, at any rate, was the fear of liberal minded British people.

On the reverse side of the account the policy of patronizing detachment certainly had its cost, especially in that the gathering of forces towards unity among the Six after the failure of EDC left Britain stranded and increasingly cut off from one of the most notable forms of political change in the twentieth century.[1] Nor did this necessarily serve to consolidate the Anglo-American relationship on behalf of which British governments had sacrificed so much of their influence in Europe. The picture which more and more Americans tended to form of Britain in the second half of the 1950s was of an ageing, self-satisfied prima donna who insisted on holding the limelight though the glory and beauty of her youth were long passed, while her friends were forming successful business partnerships after their retirement from the political theatre. That little of this could be foreseen during the early years of the Council of Europe, and even as late as the death struggles of EDC, was evident from the similarity in attitude towards European union of Conservative and Labour politicians in Britain. The Right was certainly more sensitive to European opinion than the Left, but the lengths to which it was prepared to go when in office were not markedly different from those of Labour.

Perhaps the greatest weakness of British policy at this time was not so much the refusal to join the Six pilgrims on their golden road, but the apparent unwillingness even to work out and discuss publicly the gains and losses of various forms of membership or association. British Ministers, as we have seen, rightly felt that the electorate gave them no authority for the abandonment of national independence. But rarely if ever were the possible implications of the loss of independence set before the electorate for them to choose. This was partly due to the ingrained habit in British foreign policy of step-by-step decisions, of 'judging events on their merits', or 'never crossing a bridge until you come to it', without the need being felt to range ahead in thought or imagination. But it was also due to the assumption that if the electorate does not actually press for a change in policies which have worked reasonably well hitherto things can be safely left to go on as before. This assumption can be dangerous in a rapidly changing world society.

[1] See Chapter X below for developments in Europe after 1954.

CHAPTER SIX

The Anglo-American Partnership

After the Second World War British politicians had a habit of saying that Britain belonged to three overlapping circles, the Atlantic community, the dominant member of which was the United States, Europe and the Commonwealth. The three groups reflected the still widespread character of Britain's interests, even in the postwar world. So long as she was able to remain on intimate terms with all three, the chances were that her influence would extend over extensive areas, despite reduced military power and shrinking empire. The three groups had the advantage for Britain of being based on the minimum of contractual obligation and the maximum of real common interest; at the same time each was flexible enough to allow for development to suit almost any need which might arise. Structurally the most highly developed of these associations was the Atlantic community, with its NATO Council and agencies for the co-ordination of military and economic policies set up within the framework of the North Atlantic treaty of April 1949. Despite arguments for a stronger development of the NATO structure British Governments remained on the whole satisfied with its essentially consultative character. They did not welcome, for example, the proposal made by President de Gaulle in 1958 for a political triumvirate of Britain, France and the United States to give direction to the organization.

The other distinctive feature of the Atlantic community as a group which Britain sought to keep in a close relationship with herself was its recency compared with the other two. It is true, of course, that the British connection with the Western hemisphere goes back to the acquisition of Newfoundland in the fifteenth century. But it was not until the First World War that the strategic interdependence of Britain and the United States was really accepted by British politicians, and even so not until the collapse of Russia in 1917 showed that the survival of Britain and France was dependent upon American assistance. Not until the Anglo-French deadlock over German reparations which ended in the French occupation of the Ruhr in 1923 was the necessity for American financial help to European recovery understood in London. The history of Anglo-American relations since then could be written as a struggle of British and American public opinion against accepting and acting upon these facts.

The strategic interdependence of Britain and the United States passed, from the beginning of the nineteenth century until the middle of the twentieth, through two main phases and then began to hover on the brink of a third. The first was the period of the British Two-Power naval standard, when British dominance of the Atlantic provided a shelter behind which the United States could proclaim the Monroe Doctrine in 1823 and fight the Civil War of 1861–65 without interference from Europe. This phase ended with the acceptance by Britain of naval parity with the United States in 1921 in order to avoid a naval arms race with that country. Thereafter it was clear that no major British action could be brought against an enemy at sea without the benevolent neutrality of the United States. The assumption on which Britain went to war in 1939 was that the blockade of the Axis Powers would be sympathetically accepted by the American Government as being as much in America's interest as in Britain's, and that the Pacific could be written off for the time being as an effective theatre of British naval operations. In June 1940, when Germany overran Western Europe, New Zealand was confidentially told that in the event of war with Japan no British fleet could be sent to the Pacific and that New Zealand would have to look to the United States for its naval defence. In 1942, after America's entry into the war against Japan, Britain was unable to defend Singapore and lost some of her most powerful battleships in encounters with Japan. These events foreshadowed the Anzus pact of 1951, from which Britain was excluded and through which the United States assumed the chief responsibility for the naval defence of Australia and New Zealand.

Despite this dramatic change in status, however, British security continued to be vital to America's continental defence. Once Russia established herself as a military threat to Western Europe at the end of the war, little doubt was felt by responsible American leaders, Democrat and Republican, that the security of the United States could not be provided for without Britain, France, Italy and later Western Germany. The symbol of this was Marshall Aid and the Atlantic Pact. This phase, however, when Britain and other European allies, though definitely the junior partners, were as necessary to America as America was to them, began to be challenged by a third, marked by the development of missile weapons and the rivalry between America and the Soviet Union in the conquest of outer space which began with the launching of the first artificial space satellite by Russia in October 1957. These developments broadened the gap between American military capacity and that of Europe and raised questions in the United States as to whether the issue of war and peace, with its potentialities of utter destruction for America, should not be solely for her to decide on behalf of the non-Communist world as a whole.

The sharp decline after 1945 in the contribution which Britain was able to make to the defence of the Atlantic community was not accepted by British opinion without distaste amounting at times to positive disregard of the facts of the case by politicians out of office and sometimes even in office. The most outstanding example of this occurred as late as October 1956, when military action was initiated by Britain in company with France against Nasser's Egypt in the Suez Canal dispute, despite intense American disapproval. A feature of the psychology behind this action seemed to be the feeling of exasperation with a situation in which Britain, only a generation previously acknowledged as the greatest Power in the world, was now unable to enforce its rights upon a country of no military consequence without permission from Washington.[1] Similar exasperation was felt after the creation of NATO when an unduly large number of senior posts in the military structure of the organization seemed to be given to Americans, culminating in the announcement in February 1951 of the appointment of an American admiral to the Supreme Command of NATO forces in the North Atlantic. The only sop to British pride was the appointment of a British deputy to the American commander and of a British admiral to command the Eastern area of the Atlantic command.[2] The Labour Government, which agreed to these appointments, were roundly denounced by the Opposition in the House on April 19th; Churchill argued that the appointment of a Supreme Commander was unnecessary and that an American admiral would be able to switch naval forces from the Eastern to the Western Atlantic without the concern for the security of the Western approaches to the British Isles which actuated British seamen.[3] When the Conservatives returned to power in October 1951 they declared that they would secure a revision of the agreement. The subject was discussed during Churchill's first postwar visit to Washington as

[1] See the interesting analysis of this psychology by Geoffrey Crowther in 'The reconstruction of an alliance', *Foreign Affairs*, January 1957, pp. 174–83.
[2] 484 H.C. Deb. 5s. Col. 1459 (February 22nd); Col. 1755 (February 26th). Cmd. 8214 of 1951.
[3] 486 H.C. Deb. 5s. Cols. 2017–2036.

Prime Minister in January 1952, but he was unable to reverse the American decision.

The British nuclear programme

The reluctance of British Governments to accept the supremacy of the United States in Western defence, if this meant that in the last resort only Washington could decide the ultimate issue of peace or war, also accounted for the Labour Government's decision, which the Conservatives endorsed, to embark on a separate nuclear arms programme. This resulted in the test explosion of the first British atomic bomb on Montebello island, off the Australian coast, in October 1952 and of the first British hydrogen bomb in 1957. Behind the decision to create an independent nuclear deterrent was a feeling of resentment with the United States for attempting to monopolize a weapon which was to a large extent a joint wartime achievement of Britain, Canada and the United States. In October 1945, two months after the dropping of the first atomic bomb on Hiroshima, President Truman issued a statement declaring that the United States would preserve her monopoly of the manufacture of the bomb and the technical knowledge essential for its production. This was reflected in the MacMahon Act, which received the President's signature on August 1, 1946; it created a civilian body, the Atomic Energy Commission, to own and operate all atomic energy plants on behalf of the United States Government. At the same time it drastically curtailed, if it did not stop, the flow of information on the exploitation of atomic energy between British and American scientists.

Britain reacted to this measure by protesting that it infringed both the agreement signed by Franklin Roosevelt and Winston Churchill at Quebec on August 19, 1943, when they pledged themselves to 'full and effective interchange of information and ideas' in scientific research and development of atomic energy,[1] and the Agreed Declaration signed by President Truman, Clement Attlee and the Canadian Prime Minister, Mackenzie King, on November 16, 1945, which provided for 'full and effective co-operation in the field of atomic energy' between the three countries. This was the burden of a letter sent by Attlee to Truman on April 16th. Truman replied that the expression 'full and effective co-operation' applied only to basic scientific information and not to the construction and operation of atomic energy plants. This interpretation was denied in Attlee's rejoinder on June 7th, but the President delayed his reply until the MacMahon Act became law and rendered further exchanges point-

[1] Cmd. 9123 of 1954.

less.[1] The British Government had certain means to hand for modifying the complete closure of scientific information from America, namely an Anglo-American agreement of July 1946 for the division of uranium from the Belgian Congo. Since the American share was proving inadequate by the end of 1947 a new agreement, the so-called 'modus vivendi', was signed on January 7, 1948. Under this the United States was to give Britain information in nine specific fields of atomic energy production, none of which included the manufacture of atomic weapons, in return for Britain's agreement that all uranium produced in the Congo in 1948 and 1949 should go to America. Britain was pledged not to pass the information on to any other country with the exception of New Zealand.

A new agreement was worked out in the summer of 1949, but President Truman, who seemed to want a full partnership with Britain, provided all uranium coming into British hands was stored in America, found that strong mistrust of British security controls prevailed among Republican members of the joint Atomic Energy Commission of Congress and was obliged to instruct the American delegates at the talks for revising the agreement to confirm the exclusion of atomic weapons from the fields in which exchange of information might take place. The arrest of outstanding figures in British atomic establishments on charges of espionage, coupled with the rapid strides made in atomic development in the Soviet Union, served to entrench the MacMahon Act. In 1946 a leading British scientist, Dr Alan Nunn May, had been arrested in Canada as a Soviet spy. In February 1950 Dr Klaus Fuchs, a German-born scientist in British pay, was arrested on a similar charge. American nervousness as a result of these ruptures in the British security curtain was such that when the American scientist Dr Cyril Smith was sent to Britain at the end of July 1948 to convey information under the 'modus vivendi' of January a panic was caused among American senators when it was found that he had with him information on the basic metallurgy of plutonium, a prohibited item under the agreement. Frantic telephone calls to Dr Smith, who was touring in Scotland, ended when it appeared that he had not yet communicated the forbidden information.[2]

When British protests against the MacMahon Act produced little effect, the Attlee Cabinet secretly decided that the exploitation of atomic energy for military as well as peaceful uses must continue in this country if Britain was not to be left behind in research and

[1] Harry S. Truman, Years of Trial and Hope, 1946–53, London, 1956, pp. 15–17.
[2] The Forrestal Diaries, edited by Walter Millis, New York, 1951, pp. 470–1.

development techniques and if American legislation was to be encouraged to relax as the British nuclear effort grew. There was also the feeling that in the postwar world the atomic bomb was a symbol of international status and that, so long as Britain kept this weapon in her armoury, her voice would speak more loudly in the world's capitals. But perhaps the strongest reason impelling the Labour Government to make the bomb was the recognition that Britain might be forced to fight in self-defence when the United States was unwilling to do so, or, as in 1939, before American opinion had accepted the necessity of fighting. This was the justification of the decision to manufacture the bomb which Hugh Gaitskell, who became leader of the Opposition on Attlee's accession to the House of Lords in 1955, put forward in 1957, when criticism of the independent British nuclear deterrent was rising in the Labour Party. 'Our party decided to support the manufacture of the hydrogen bomb here,' he said in April 1957, 'and we decided that, quite frankly, because we did not think it right that this country should be so dependent . . . upon the USA.'[1] Behind this argument lay the assumption that Britain was able to wage a major war without American assistance, an assumption weakened if not destroyed by the steeply rising cost of delivery vehicles for atomic weapons. When the British Government decided in April 1960 to abandon plans for the British delivery vehicle 'Blue Streak', which was estimated to cost the taxpayer some £100 million, it was clear that a British atomic weapon relying upon American devices for launching it was hardly ever likely to be used except when the United States agreed.

None of this, however, altered the conviction of British politicians, whether Labour or Conservative, that only within the framework of the Atlantic community, based in the last resort on American military and economic strength, was it possible to provide for British and West European security. The real question was whether, since Britain and the United States were inevitably bound together in the postwar world, decisions might be taken in Washington which committed Britain to war before the possibilities of negotiation were exhausted or forced her into conflicts not central to her interests as she saw them. The greater the nuclear armament stockpiled by the United States the greater was this fear. It was intensified by the fact that Britain's pre-war appeasement policy suggested to many Americans (though their own hands were far from clean during that period) that she would shirk a Soviet challenge when it came, and hence that the United States should make up her own mind how to

[1] 568 H.C. Deb. 5s. Col. 71 (April 1st).

reply. American thought moreover, unlike British, tended to prefer the quick solution to the strategy of patiently living with a problem. As it happened, the threat to the democratic states in the postwar world was not that of direct military aggression as practised by Hitler. The form it took was tireless pressure against the soft places in the Western world, a pressure compared by George Kennan, the leading adviser to the State Department on Soviet affairs, to that exerted by water against a porous surface. This was precisely the kind of struggle for which the American mind was least prepared and in which it might be tempted to cut the Gordian knot in relief. 'The indecisiveness of the Cold War,' wrote John Foster Dulles, who became the American Secretary of State in 1953, 'is its most baffling aspect for the American temperament.' A considerable part of British diplomacy was therefore to be spent in urging restraint on the various American government departments which made their sometimes conflicting contributions to foreign policy. This advice was often taken but not without the irritating feeling that Britain was more active in applying brakes than in providing the motive power for the machine.

During the Berlin airlift in 1948, when President Truman's Cabinet agreed that the atom bomb must be used if war broke out with Russia, Britain accepted two groups of American B29 bombers, equipped to carry atomic weapons, and was willing to have them fly from British soil on missions to Russia.

Nevertheless the then British Foreign Secretary, Bevin, constantly urged Washington to continue negotiations and secured a postponement of the reference of the question to the United Nations until the latest possible moment since he feared that taking the issue to the Security Council would be read in Moscow as closing bilateral discussions.[1] A more critical instance of British restraint came in December 1950, when Attlee flew to Washington to caution President Truman against using the atomic bomb to repel Chinese forces which had come to the assistance of the North Korean communist army against United Nations forces under General MacArthur's command. In visiting Washington in person and immediately after Truman had given an ambiguous answer at a Press conference on November 30th on the use of the atomic bomb in Korea, Attlee sought to impress on the President the alarm felt by British opinion and expressed in the Commons on November 29th and 30th. In the conversations with the Prime Minister Truman maintained that it lay within the discretion of the United States Government what type

[1] *The Forrestal Diaries*, pp. 487–91.

of weapons they authorized American forces to use. In a communiqué issued on December 8th he was recorded as having expressed the hope that the atomic bomb would never have to be used and as being willing to inform Britain of circumstances which might change the situation.[1] Attlee's expression of British alarm at the possibility of war with China may have served to strengthen Truman's determination to repress General MacArthur, which he did by recalling him (and appointing Lieutenant-General Matthew Ridgeway in his place) in the following April.[2]

When Churchill visited Washington as Prime Minister in January 1952 he was not able to modify the American refusal to allow a foreign veto over the use of weapons by American forces. But it was agreed that consultation would always take place between the American President and the British Prime Minister of the day when American bombers took off with atomic bombs from bases in Britain and also that no order to release the bombs could be made effective without the British consent.[3] This arrangement was later extended to the firing of rockets with nuclear warheads from American bases on British soil. This being as far as British restraint on the actual use of atomic weapons by American forces could go, henceforward British policy concentrated on the effort to influence American foreign policy more generally towards negotiation with the Communist world.

Economic co-operation and conflict
The second important form of interdependence underlying the Anglo-American partnership was the economic. Here again the closeness of the association between the two countries tended to engender friction, while making such differences as arose all the more difficult to resolve. In the years immediately after the war the American market, owing to the high tariff traditional in that country and the greater industrial efficiency of American industry as compared with European, was not important to British exporters. During 1949–50, when British export trade was reviving after the war, only 4 per cent of British exports were marketed in the United States, as compared with 5 per cent in Canada alone and over 40 per cent in the rest of the Commonwealth. By 1956, however, as a result of the drive by British industry to penetrate dollar markets, the United

---

[1] Visit of the Prime Minister to the United States, Cmd. 8110, p. 5.
[2] See below, pp. 196–7.
[3] *The Times*, January 10, 1952.

States had become the biggest single export outlet for British goods.[1] Moreover, the American economy had grown in power to such an extent by 1945 that economic conditions in the rest of the world, outside agrarian countries living on a subsistence basis and the closed societies of the Communist bloc, moved in accordance with American economic life. This was strikingly shown at the end of the war when the sole prospect of the economic recovery of Britain and Western Europe lay in the grant of American dollars to tide over the period in which domestic industry was being started up again and international trade revived. The rapid exhaustion of the loan to Britain after eighteen months, largely owing to the rise in American prices, and the lack of balance between American surpluses and shortages elsewhere showed that without substantial subventions American allies could not hope to rise to their own feet and play their part. This sensitivity of the economy of the democratic world to the supply of American dollars was further shown both during slight recessions in the American economy, which had magnified effects outside, and during the period of intense rearmament in the West which followed the outbreak of the Korean war in June 1950.

The British rearmament programme, introduced at the end of 1950, contemplated an increase in defence spending of the order of £1,500 million a year, a figure which it was widely reported the United States had insisted upon, contrary to the original judgment of the British Labour Cabinet. The strain of rearmament of these dimensions and the world-wide demand for raw materials which accompanied it placed exceptional hardship on Britain, whose recovery from economic depression in the early 1930s had depended on low prices of primary raw materials. One effect was sharp dissension in the Labour Cabinet on the question whether a reduction in the outlay on social services was necessary in order to finance rearmament. When the budget embodying the new defence proposals was being prepared by Gaitskell, the Chancellor of the Exchequer, who intended to raise extra revenue by introducing charges for false teeth and spectacles provided by the National Health Service, Aneurin Bevan, a former Minister of Health and now Minister of Labour, resigned in April 1951 in protest. Harold Wilson, the President of the Board of Trade, also gave Attlee his resignation and so did John Freeman, then Parliamentary Secretary to the Ministry of Supply. Their argument was that the scale of rearmament envisaged was greater than the international situation and Britain's

[1] Andrew Schonfield, *British Economic Policy since the War*, Penguin Books Ltd., Middlesex, 1958, p. 82.

strength warranted and tended to divert attention from the real need, the alleviation of poverty in the underdeveloped areas of the world. Along with this went resentment that socialist Britain should have to take on a massive arms burden and lengthen conscription from eighteen months to two years, at the instance of the greatest capitalist nation in the world. Bevan, giving the reasons for his resignation in the House on April 23rd, said, 'we have allowed ourselves to be dragged too far behind the wheels of American diplomacy'.[1]

The formation of a distinct rebel group within the Labour Party under Bevan's leadership, which played an active role out of proportion to its actual support in Britain until Bevan and Gaitskell were reconciled in 1957, had adverse effects on Anglo-American relations. It provided a platform for Labour critics of the United States, and since many of the prophecies of Bevan on the economic effects of rearmament were proved right, the effect was to lower respect for America in Britain generally. On the other hand, the Bevanite movement underlined the fears of Americans who accepted the allegations of Senator Joseph McCarthy of Wisconsin that America's efforts to retain her freedom were being sabotaged by Communists in high places in the United States and her allies. One serious effect of the xenophobia to which McCarthy appealed was the passage by Congress over President Truman's veto of the McCarran Act in late 1952. This subjected British nationals, including seamen when they put in at American ports, to the indignity of security checks on entering the United States. On a more material level the rise in the price of primary commodities effected by rearmament jeopardized the gold and dollar reserve which British Chancellors of the Exchequer had husbanded with such care since the postwar years of stress. Between June and December 1951 Britain lost approximately £850 million in gold and dollar assets.[2] The resulting balance of payments crisis in the autumn of 1951, which seemed to confirm Bevan's warnings, unseated the Labour Government and left the Conservatives to deal with the problems of an overstrained economy in a world reflecting at every turn the movement of the steering wheel in Washington.

Given that the American economy was bound to be a dominant influence on economic conditions throughout the non-Communist world, it was vital that British and American economic policies should harmonize as far as possible. The difficulties of achieving this lay in the fact that American thinking tended to run in political and

[1] 487 H.C. Deb. 5s. Col. 38.
[2] F. W. Paish, 'The Sterling Area Crisis', *International Affairs*, July 1952.

M

moral grooves, whereas British thought, reflecting the greater British stake in world trade, was more influenced by economic considerations. This was despite the frequent American claims that 'business' principles were of prime importance and should prevail over political objects. When the reality of the Cold War with the Communist Powers was accepted in the United States, especially after the failure of the Foreign Ministers' meetings on Germany in 1947 and the formation of Cominform in the same year, United States Congressmen applied intense pressure for the cutting of foreign trade in materials useful for military purposes with the Communist states. With the creation of the Atlantic Pact an interallied committee (COCOM) was formed to regulate this trade. The most effective inducement resorted to by Congress, however, in order to line up America's allies behind the trade embargo was the Battle Act passed by the Senate and House of Representatives in August and signed by President Truman in October 1951. This threatened to stop American military and economic aid to countries exporting goods 'of primary strategic value' to the Communist bloc states. This blockade bore more hardly on Britain than on any other American ally, especially as the British percentage share of world trade was declining throughout the 1950s, and gave rise to the suspicion in Britain that the Battle Act was the doing of American business interests which competed with British exporters.

The disability Britain suffered through the trade embargoes was possibly even greater in the matter of trade with China, where the Communists had finally triumphed over the Kuomintang, or Nationalist, regime in 1949 and established the Chinese People's Republic. British afforded *de jure* recognition to Communist China in January 1950, while the United States held aloof and continued to regard the Nationalist leaders, under their President, Generalissimo Chiang Kai-shek, as the legitimate government of China, even though they were confined after the civil war to the island of Formosa and had less and less prospect as the years passed of returning to the mainland. If anything, American hostility was even greater towards the Chinese than towards the Soviet Communists. A great deal of American effort had gone into missionary and educational work in China and the triumph of Communism in that country left Americans with the feeling that China had not only embraced a wicked faith but had bitten the hand that fed it, especially as the foremost propaganda target of Communist China was American 'imperialism'. The United States therefore insisted upon a much harsher restriction of trade in strategic materials with China than with the Soviet

Union. The instrument of this control was CHINCOM, a consultative committee of NATO allies and Japan sitting in Paris and based on a UN General Assembly resolution of May 1951.

During the inter-war years it was the Left in Britain which tended to call for economic sanctions against disturbers of international peace and accused the National Government of subordinating respect for League Covenant obligations to profitable trade with the Axis. Now it was the Left wing of the British Labour Party, together of course with the unimportant Communist Party, which denounced the Battle Act, COCOM and CHINCOM as America's pursuit of a private anti-Communist vendetta at the cost of British trade and employment. On the American side, British complaints about the trade embargoes seemed, not only to McCarthyites, but to all those genuinely shocked by the price America was paying to defeat Communism in Korea, to be evidence of British 'softness' in the struggle, if not distinct sabotage by an ally. The issue was well suited for recriminations and counter-recriminations across the Atlantic; British anti-Americans accused Washington of tailoring the list of forbidden exports to suit American business interests, while anti-British Americans charged Britain with conniving with exporters to defeat the blockade. Yet for all the rancour they provoked, it is doubtful whether the embargoes really reduced Communist bloc military power, or if they did, whether other consequences did not outweigh these gains. In so far as the embargoes fell more heavily on China, they must have consolidated the Sino-Soviet treaty of alliance of February 1950, whereas the classic rule of diplomacy has always been to divide one's opponents. In fact, of course, it was always open to China to buy prohibited materials in the West through Russia. In so far as Russia herself was compelled by the embargoes to manufacture articles within the Communist bloc at a higher economic cost than that at which she might have purchased them in the West, the result may have been to increase the rigours of the Communist dictatorship which the Western Powers were seeking to relax and to reduce Russia's dependence on supplies from the outside world, which might have been a weakness for her in times of crisis.[1]

When the Korean armistice was signed in July 1953 the British Government pressed for the equalization of the strategic embargo as between China and the Soviet bloc. Prolonged discussions in the Consultative Group in Paris, however, produced no agreement be-

[1] Cf. Susan Strange, 'Strategic Embargoes', *The Yearbook of World Affairs, 1958*, London, 1958, p. 55.

tween the British and American points of view. When Americans asked Britain to appreciate the state of public feeling in their country in relation to Communist China, which had been responsible for the deaths in Korea of many young Americans, the British retorted that the same public opinion was insisting upon the rearmament of West Germany and Japan, countries which had taken a much greater toll of British lives during the war. It was clear that the deadlock could not be resolved and the British Government, largely as a result of pressure in Parliament, unilaterally decided to equalize the British strategic embargo between the Soviet bloc and China on May 30, 1957. According to a statement by the Foreign Secretary, Selwyn Lloyd, as from that day goods which were forbidden exports to China but not to Russia could be legally sent to China.[1]

While the strategic control of trade with the Communist bloc was a politically explosive issue without much real economic importance, differences of attitude between Britain and the United States on general commercial policy sprang from entrenched economic doctrines. For Britain the governing factor was her experience during the inter-war period, when the chief source of long-term unemployment was the failure of basic exporting trades to revive after the 1914–18 war. This led to the determination of the Labour Governments of 1945–51 to safeguard full employment and to refuse to allow British export trade to suffer the 'anarchy' of unrestricted international competition. In practice this meant three policies: adherence to a system of mutual Commonwealth preferences, which had provided the climate of British economic recovery in the 1930s; maintenance of the sterling area, in which a number of countries including the Commonwealth (but not Canada) agreed to hold their gold and dollar earnings from foreign trade in London and received liquid sterling assets in return; and a range of foreign trade and exchange controls the object of which was to adjust the foreign trade balance to the optimum level of activity within the country. These policies derived from an economic experience entirely different from that of the United States. They also ran counter to cherished American axioms of international trade. American opinion continued to revere classical theories of unrestricted multilateral trading, with their liberal political overtones, even though these theories had long been abandoned even in America. Relations between government and industry and agriculture in the United States no longer conformed to them. They were at variance with such American policies as Marshall Aid and the 'Point Four' programme of technical

[1] 571 H.C. Deb. 5s. Cols. 618–620 (May 30, 1957).

assistance to underdeveloped countries announced by President Truman in his inaugural address in January 1949, since these policies admitted that without positive government intervention American ideals of freedom in the world could not be realized. In the obligations assumed by members of the United Nations in 1945 and in such sections of the UN Charter as the Trusteeship Chapter the assumptions of 'free-for-all' economics were plainly set aside. None of this, however, prevented American spokesmen from demanding unrestricted free trade from the world outside.

As between British insistence on foreign trade controls and American pressures for a return to the multilateral system a head-on clash was inevitable. British opinion felt that there was something inconsistent in repeated American pleas that Britain should get to her feet economically and at the same time abandon supports such as Commonwealth preference which history had shown to be essential to her solvency. Apart from the American tariff, the massive American export surplus after the war, reflecting the higher efficiency of American industry, with its great internal market behind it, and the relatively minor after-effects of the war, resulted in a shortage of dollars in the outside world which unavoidably led to some control of the relations between the non-dollar and the dollar economies. The only alternative was that the American taxpayer should provide the missing dollars on the scale required. This was neither acceptable to him as a permanent policy nor was it consistent with the full independence of the recipients. But what tended to obscure these facts from American opinion was the imperialistic connotations of Commonwealth preference. So long as this 'relic of the British Empire' remained, American Governments felt bound to press for its liquidation.

On the British side, there was readiness to co-operate in international organizations which, it was wishfully hoped, would gradually steer the non-Communist world towards multilateralism, provided loopholes were left for second thoughts on the way. Britain took a leading part in the negotiations at Geneva from April to October 1947 from which sprang the General Agreement on Tariffs and Trade (GATT), the purpose of which was to negotiate tariff and and quota reductions.[1] She also took a prominent role in OEEC, originally set up for the distribution of Marshall Aid funds but subsequently used for negotiating tariff reductions in Europe. On the whole, however, Britain made few real concessions to American multilateralism and when she did, as in the negotiation of the

[1] Report on the Geneva Tariff Negotiations, Cmd. 7258 of 1947.

American loan in 1945, events showed that to do so in face of the facts was unwise. During the Labour Governments of 1945–51 economic recovery from the war seemed to require the kind of state controls which ruled out multilateralism. When the Conservatives returned to office after the General Election in October 1951, they found themselves in a balance of payments crisis for which multi-lateralism was to some extent responsible and for which it was certainly no cure. Since a strong gold and dollar reserve was thence-forward the symbol of successful government and quarterly figures of the size of the reserve were read as barometers of Ministerial popularity, there was little disposition to take risks by conforming to American trade doctrines. Moreover, by the middle 1950s Ameri-cans began to look apprehensively on the rate of growth in the Communist bloc and a world-wide competition in economic prowess between Russia and the United States developed. The encouragement of multilateral trading therefore began to take a lower place in American policy requirements. Nevertheless, it reflected the strains of the Anglo-American alliance. The older country, Britain, had given multilateralism to the world and then abandoned it as her competitive international strength in trade diminished. The new giant, the United States, began the postwar period convinced that economic freedom, in the Gladstonian sense, and political freedom were synonymous and later discovered that the world conflict of power with the Communist states demanded a world-wide economic strategy planned with almost the same central direction as a military operation.

Imperialism and post-colonial neutralism

In the light of this military and economic interdependence between Britain and the United States, it is now possible to review the points at which British and American policies met in the postwar world. Historically by far the greatest issue in Anglo-American relations was the conflict between British imperialism and American ideals of self-determination, though this issue played a less important role after 1945. At the end of the war it seemed as though the disestab-lishment of the British Empire was the first object of American policy. According to Lord Halifax, the British wartime Ambassador in Washington, almost the only positive proposal which Franklin Roosevelt ever made to him was that Hong Kong should be restored to China.[1] At the Yalta conference in February 1945 Roosevelt evoked some of Churchill's strongest indignation by his demand to

[1] *Fulness of Days*, London, 1957, pp. 249–50.

convert the Empire into international trusteeships. The British, Roosevelt told his Secretary of State, Edward Stettinius, 'would take land anywhere, even if it were only rock or a sandbar'.[1] It was largely on account of mistrust of British imperialism that American politicians did not warmly respond to Churchill's appeal in his Fulton, Missouri, speech in March 1946 for an Anglo-American partnership in the face of Russia's menacing attitude. The influential Senator, Claude Pepper of Florida, opposed America's 'ganging up' with British imperialism against Russia.[2] But, while suspicion remained, the ending of the Empire as an object of policy soon faded before two interrelated facts: Britain's decision to end the Empire herself and the dropping of British commitments, especially the commitment to assist Greece and Turkey, owing to financial stringency. The former, dramatically illustrated by the grant of independence to the Asian dominions in 1947, was widely applauded in the United States, though it provided an odd comment on the common American allegation that postwar Britain was too 'featherbedded' to stand up for her rights. The latter led straight to the Truman Doctrine which for the first time brought the United States into a peacetime relation with smaller countries not unlike that of a metropolitan Power with its colonies. After the Truman Doctrine the United States could no longer refer to the Philippines as a sample of how great Powers should treat their dependencies since the assumption that dependencies, once free, could protect themselves against the designs of other Powers was clearly untenable. The United States found that containing Communist expansion required it to support regimes many of which were alien to Western democracy in their internal policies and which occupied a client relationship towards America similar to that which many countries formerly had towards Britain.

The effect of these developments might have brought British and American attitudes towards imperialism so close to each other as to be practically identical. In certain instances this did happen, as for instance in the firm American support of British operations against Communist guerillas in Malaya. On the whole, however, British and American attitudes operated on different wavelengths. One reason for this was the unwillingness of many Americans to agree that the maintenance of British interests in the non-European world was necessarily helpful to the Western cause, and their suspicion that this cause was often weakened by a British tendency to hold on to posi-

[1] Stettinius, *Roosevelt and the Russians*, London, 1950, p. 212.
[2] *The Forrestal Diaries*, p. 154.

tions when local opposition forces were too strong. There was thus little American sympathy for British resistance to the Greek demand for the union of Cyprus with Greece, which took the form of open Greek Cypriot warfare against British forces in 1955. When the conflict threatened to embroil Greece and Turkey, which had joined NATO in 1952, American pressure was thrown on the side of an early British withdrawal from Cyprus. Another example was the British conflict with Egypt between 1951 and 1954 on the status of British forces in the Suez Canal zone and the future of the Sudan. When Churchill visited the United States as Prime Minister in January 1952 he appealed in an address to Congress for American forces to be sent to help British troops in the guerilla warfare in the Canal zone.[1] This appeal was wholly without effect, partly because, with the Korean war still continuing, America had no forces to spare, but also on account of resistance in Congress to the idea of shoring up Britain's tottering foreign estate. Again, as we have seen in an earlier chapter, American policy during the troubled last years of the British mandate in Palestine seemed to be moved by pro-Zionist considerations which derived much of their appeal from the always latent American belief in British territorial greed. Only at a late stage of discussion of the partition plan for Palestine was it realized that the withdrawal of Britain did not necessarily mean that the vacuum would be filled by forces favourable to American interests. How easily American distaste for British efforts in support of client states and dependencies could be aroused was also shown in the Buraimi oasis dispute when Britain, in the autumn of 1955, supported the occupation of the area by the forces of the Sultan of Muscat and the Sheikh of Abu Dhabi. The United States Government, who for their own reasons backed the opposing claims of King Saud of Saudi Arabia, privately told two countries friendly to Britain, Australia and the Netherlands, that they considered the British action 'an act of aggression'.[2]

But by far the largest influence tending to divide British and American attitudes towards countries either newly freed from Western imperialism or in process of being freed was the dominant place occupied by the world struggle against Communism in the American mind. The United States, especially after the accession to office of President Eisenhower in January 1953, when the State Department fell into the hands of the dedicated but unbending John Foster Dulles, tended increasingly to centre its policy on this conflict. To

[1] Cmd. 8468 of 1952, p. 7.
[2] Sir Anthony Eden, *Full Circle*, London, 1960, p. 334.

some extent this reflected a lack of confidence on the part of Americans in their own diplomatic skill; having less experience of diplomacy than an old Power like Britain, they seemed determined to make up for this by resolution to win the battle with Communism at whatever cost. It should also be remembered that Britain and America, during their periods of leadership of the democratic world, have not been in equally secure positions. During Britain's primacy there was always the consciousness that, at the eleventh hour, America might throw in its weight against Britain's enemies of the day. For America in the world after 1945 there has never been any such assurance. Hence Americans tended to feel that if they lost this struggle all was lost and no one remained to come to their aid.

The result was that when Britain resisted colonial nationalism American opinion tended to fear that allies were being created for the Communist side, and where Britain encouraged newly independent countries to follow their own policies, or placed no difficulties in the way of their doing so, Americans expressed irritation if these countries did not line themselves up in the anti-Communist front. The former was illustrated in differing British and American attitudes to Middle Eastern nationalism. British Governments, sensitive to the tendency of regimes in the Middle East to exploit signs of weakness among Western Powers, generally assumed firm attitudes in the face of nationalist challenges to Western rights, even though Parliamentary and public pressures in Britain had the effect of softening these attitudes. Critics of the policy of toughness, more often on the political Left than the Right, found themselves in a strange alliance with American Secretaries of State and diplomats, who accused Britain of driving anti-colonial nationalists into the arms of the Communists. Thus, in the Persian oil crisis of 1951–53 the American Government persistently urged restraint on London lest Dr Moussadig open the gates of Sovietism in Persia; moreover, according to Eden, the British Foreign Secretary of the time, the agreement finally signed in 1954, after Moussadig's fall, would have been impossible without America's good offices and quiet assistance to both sides.[1] Although on the whole Washington showed somewhat more sympathy during the British difficulties in Egypt in the early 1950s, much the same fears of nationalism taking on a Communist form were expressed. The United States appeared to support the unilateral Egyptian declaration of October 1951 placing the Sudan under the Egyptian crown and applied very strong pressure on Britain to come to terms with Egypt in March 1952.[2] The underlying

[1] Eden, *op. cit.*, p. 208. [2] *Ibid.*, pp. 231–3.

American anxieties behind these moves provided perhaps the strongest motive for Washington's firm dissociation of itself from the Anglo-French armed action in Egypt in 1956, even though the incident which had precipitated the Suez crisis, the withdrawal of the offer of a World Bank loan to finance the projected Aswan Dam, was in effect an Americal reprisal for Colonel Nasser's receipt of military assistance from Moscow. Two years later, in 1958, after a revolution in Iraq in July which swept away the pro-Western regime of King Feisal, it was now the United States which seized the initiative. American forces were landed in Lebanon, while a British airborne contingent was dropped on Jordan, both actions being defended on the ground that these countries were prospective victims of indirect aggression from Egypt, now combined with Syria in the United Arab Republic. Egypt, in the terminology of the Eisenhower Doctrine adopted as American policy in the previous year, was now in Washington's opinion little short of an agent for international Communism.

These shifts in the American attitude to anti-colonial nationalists, from protectiveness in order to keep them in the Western camp to hostility if they received aid and comfort from the Communist camp, reflected the dominance of the tension with Russia in American thought. British opinion, on the other hand, was apt to regard local nationalism within British overseas territory or along the routes of British communications as a separate issue to be dealt with on its merits. There was less fear in Britain that strong-arm tactics would produce new recruits for Communism and less suspicion that nationalist movements, if they showed interest in receiving help from Russia, would finish as pawns in the Communist game. At the same time, it was perhaps the changes in American attitudes to anti-colonial nationalism, rather than the attitudes in themselves, which caused irritation in Britain. It was vexing to find that the United States, having encouraged the formation of the Baghdad Pact, signed in 1955, thereupon stood aside from it, presumably not wishing to be branded as imperialist by Arab nationalists. This left Britain, which had joined, to bear the brunt of Arab hostility.

From these differences of approach to anti-colonial nationalism sprang an Anglo-American dispute about neutralism, especially as manifested in countries formerly belonging to the British Empire and now independent countries in the Commonwealth. If the ideological divide between Russia and the West was the most alarming feature of the postwar world, the feeling of detachment from this conflict on the part of states newly freed from European control was perhaps the most hopeful, since these countries provided a theatre of peaceful competition for the two main power groups, diverting their efforts from a purely military struggle. These newer states, consisting mainly of Arab countries in the Middle East and former colonies in South and South-east Asia, were too suspicious of Western capitalism and too resentful about the racial discrimination practised in many Western democracies to wish to join the containment belt formed by the United States around the Sino-Soviet heartland. Whatever their Governments may privately have thought, alignment with the West was too much like a return to the colonial nexus to make it a practical policy. Moreover, the intense demand in these countries for economic growth ruled out the massive rearmament required by membership of the Western bloc. On the other hand, there was not much more inducement for these countries to join the Soviet camp, which in any case Russia did not press them to do. The Sino-Soviet bloc was principally concerned to break up the ring of pacts and military bases which America had created. If the Communist bloc could dissuade the newer countries from aligning themselves with the United States, the first phase of their strategy would have been achieved. The result of the West's inability to attract and the East's encouragement to inactivity was the growth of a group of neutralist states. Their efforts to combine, as at the conference held at Bandoeng, Indonesia, in April 1955, generally produced only statements of innocuous principles, such as the Panch-Shila, or five principles of co-existence. Nevertheless, their resistance to American attempts to align them against the Communists was wholly successful.

Neutralism suggested to American politicians not only the blindness to facts from which they themselves had suffered in the 1930s, but indifference to great moral issues in terms of which Americans were apt to visualize all political conflict. Their reaction during the Korean war, when neutralists like the Indian Prime Minister, Mr Nehru, took an ambiguous stand and sought to confine United Nations action, for which America paid by far the highest price, to merely restoring the position to what it was when the North Korean attack occurred, was one of intense anger. It was as though conspicuous evil was being denied by Asians who otherwise sermonized so much on the need for morality in politics. When India and other Asian neutrals stood aside from the South-east Asia Collective Defence Treaty, signed at Manila in September 1954 on American initiative, neutralism became a word of contempt in the United States. For Mr Dulles, until the last few months of his life at least, the neutralist was more dangerous than the Communist because his function as a friend of Communism was veiled.

Britain could not share this view, even had the struggle with the Communists assumed for British people the intense aspect it had with Americans. The assumption in the Commonwealth was that, while members might complain about one another's policies in private, each country had a perfect right to pursue the policy of its choice. There was little doubt where the countries of the 'old Commonwealth', Australia, Canada, New Zealand and South Africa, stood in the East-West conflict. Canada was one of the pioneers of NATO and a partner with the United States in the defence of North America. Australia and New Zealand were, after 1951, linked with America through the Anzus pact and, after 1954, through the Southeast Asia Collective Defence Organization (SEATO). Both feared China's ambitions in Southern Asia equally with the United States. South Africa, though relatively isolated from world politics, could not be faulted on its anti-Communism by any American Russophobe. Pakistan, too, which stayed in the Commonwealth after independence in 1947, opted for the Western connection when she joined the Baghdad Pact in 1955 and received American military aid. This decision reflected in part Pakistan's fear of India in Kashmir and partly her suspicions of Soviet designs on Afghanistan. India and Ceylon, however, belonged decisively to the neutralist group.

For Britain the position of India was decisive. To attempt to bully India into a pro-Western alignment would have been to invite serious consequences for the Commonwealth.[1] It would have defeated Mr Nehru's efforts, which were otherwise successful, to show that Commonwealth membership left India entirely free to pursue her own foreign policy without being forced into an unwelcome military alliance. It would have discouraged those British colonies which were soon to attain their independence from following India's example and remaining in the Commonwealth. It might also, had it succeeded, have removed an element from the international stage which British opinion considered vital, namely a group of intermediaries, of which India was the natural leader, which offered some hope that the globe would not be ground to powder between the two armed camps. The British Government further believed that China's reluctance to offend India, so long as India remained neutral, provided the West with a means to influence Chinese policy.

For these reasons Britain refused to take the American view

[1] Hugh Gaitskell discusses this point in his article 'The Search for an Anglo-American Policy' published in *Foreign Affairs*, Vol. 32, No. 4, July 1954.

during the Korean war that holding aloof from the war was a form of disloyalty. She associated herself with Afro-Asian efforts to secure a hearing for Communist China, in so far as it was possible for an ally of the United States to do so. At least until the Suez crisis in 1956, Britain refused to believe that Asian neutralists were positive enemies if they found they could not be positive friends. This attitude was strongly criticized in the United States. Nevertheless, it appeared to have its reward when the Kennedy administration was formed in 1961 since the new regime seemed not merely to tolerate the neutrals, but to sympathize with their scruples.

America, Britain and Europe

A second area of discord in British and American policies was European union, to which reference has been made in the previous chapter.[1] Although American opinion generally favoured European union on the same federal basis as the United States and saw no reason why Britain should not be included, the strength of this opinion varied from time to time. In the early months of the Korean war, when bipartisanship in American foreign policy broke down and Republican leaders attacked President Truman's policy of alliances, a movement seemed to be gathering force for cutting adrift from Europe and retaining only the tie with Britain. The strength of the Communist parties in France and Italy, French resistance to the American pressure for German rearmament and the evident European interest in a settlement with the Communist bloc made their contribution to this feeling. In a notable broadcast on October 19, 1950, Herbert Hoover, the only living American ex-President at that time, said that only Britain and Japan could be relied upon. These anti-European sentiments were brought under control so long as Truman remained in office, thanks largely to the valiant defence of NATO before Congressional committees by the Secretary of State, Dean Acheson. But they revived with the return of a Republican administration under Eisenhower at the elections in November 1952. Continuing French hesitations over EDC and unmistakable signs of European hankering after 'summit' talks with Russia after Stalin's death in March 1953 led to the 'agonizing reappraisal' speech of Mr Dulles in December. In this Dulles seemed to threaten the abandonment of Europe and a return to the policy of selective allies recommended by Hoover in 1950. This time, however, the Federal German Republic seemed to be included among the allies.

But this tendency proved to be short-lived. With the renewed

[1] Chapter V, pp. 138–40.

movement towards European integration after the signature of the Rome Treaty for an economic community and common market in 1957, American policy reverted to its federalist position and Britain came under criticism for her reluctance to merge with the Six. Americans hoped that the British proposal for a European Free Trade Area, put forward in 1957, would prove acceptable to France. When this failed, their alarm at the political consequences of a divided Europe was increased by the remarkable change in the American balance of payments towards the close of the 1950s. The dollar shortage of the immediate postwar years now disappeared and American exporters met with stiffer competition in foreign markets. This gave the United States Government a new interest in European unity since the fracturing of Europe into competitive economic blocs was likely to increase the obstacles to American trade.

British Governments took note of American disapproval of their failure to enthuse over European union. When Ministers visited the United States they were expected to explain their position and they did so by arguing that the world-wide interests of the United Kingdom gave it a special place in the alliance which was profitable to America as well. Thus in January 1952 Eden, then Foreign Secretary in the newly formed Conservative Government, said in a speech at Columbia University that—

> The American and British peoples should each understand the strong points in the other's national character. If you drive a nation to adopt procedures which run counter to its instincts, you weaken and may destroy the motive force of its action. This is something you would not wish to do—or any of us would wish to do—to an ally on whose effective co-operation we depend. You will realize that I am speaking of the frequent suggestions that the United Kingdom should join a federation on the continent of Europe. . . . We know that if we were to attempt it we should relax the springs of our action in the Western democratic cause and in the Atlantic association which is the expression of that cause.[1]

The true framework of Western security, in British eyes, was the Atlantic community, whatever smaller unities might be formed within it. But one of the most effective links between the Atlantic community and the wider world of uncommitted countries surrounding the Communist bloc was the Commonwealth and this, it was argued, could not remain the same if Britain joined federal Europe.

[1] *New York Times*, January 12, 1952.

So long as France was in political turmoil and the problem of a German contribution to Western defence was unsolved, American Governments were bound to respect this argument. The picture of Anglo-American relations which prevailed during the first Conservative Government (1951–55) was thus one of a United States continuing to press a sluggish Britain into European affairs and of a Britain successfully resisting. Once the Economic Community created by the Rome Treaty in 1957 began to show signs of life, however, and promised to become the most rapidly expanding area in the non-Communist world, the position changed. France seemed to derive renewed strength from the return to power of General de Gaulle in June 1958 after the civil and military uprising in Algeria, while Dr Adenauer untiringly presided over an economic boom in West Germany which markedly contrasted with periodic alarms in the British economy. The apparent firmness of these two apostles of Franco-German rapprochement on the main issues in dispute with Russia also recommended them as allies to Washington. Moreover, the failure of the Four-Power 'summit' conference with Russia in Paris in May 1960, on which the British Premier, Mr Macmillan, had set his heart, seemed to mark a turning point in American attitudes towards Britain and Europe. After that event the British claim that they had a right to stand apart from Europe because they could in that way act more effectively as America's partner in dealing with Communism sounded less convincing. When President Kennedy visited Europe at the end of May 1961 his talks with de Gaulle seemed to carry more weight than those with Macmillan.

Asia in British and American eyes
In discussing the European issue with Americans British politicians had always to remember the attractive force which Asia and the Far East exerted on the American mind and how it threatened to separate the United States from a Europe which, through unity, might give the deceptive appearance of being able to stand on its own feet. American 'Asia-firsters' had in their make-up a strong element of isolationism and were known to critics in their own country as 'Asialationists'. British Governments considered that, without the restraint applied by an independent Britain, these elements might destroy the alliance between America and Europe which British policy had always sought to build.

During the 1930s Americans were more concerned about Japanese aggression against China than with Axis aggression in Europe. Even so forceful an opponent of appeasement as Winston Churchill agreed with the National Government that it would have been wrong to side with American appeals for a stand against the Japanese attack on Manchuria in 1931 so long as no promise was forthcoming of American assistance in Europe.[1] After the outbreak of war in 1939 not even the overrunning of Western Europe by Hitler prevented a Presidential contest being held between Roosevelt and the Republican Wendell Willkie in November 1940 in which both candidates promised 'to keep the boys off the transports'. It required a Japanese attack on the American fleet in Pearl Harbour in December 1941 to bring America into the war. In the course of the war Roosevelt constantly had to fight strong pressures for giving greater priority to the Pacific theatre and after the conflict, though the American Government intended to relieve itself of European commitments as soon as possible, they determined to continue in an active role in the Far East. The three elements in this policy were the retention of a monopoly of occupation in Japan; the encouragement of a strong coalition government in China with full control over Manchuria, which Russia occupied during her brief war against Japan after the Potsdam conference; and the taking over of the islands formerly under Japanese mandate in the Pacific in the form of American trusteeships under the United Nations.

This policy was largely frustrated through the unexpected success of the Chinese Communists in overthrowing the ruling Kuomintang regime in a civil war which broke out into the open after the Japanese surrender. The Communists received certain assistance from Russia whose forces handed over to them territory which they had overrun in Manchuria and placed difficulties in the way of the National Chinese Government landing troops at Manchurian ports in the struggle with the Communists. In providing this help Stalin himself appeared to have little expectation that the Communists would soon take over the entire country. Unlike their European counterparts, the Chinese Communists were not a minority party within the state but had in fact been administering a part of China, the province of Yenan, since the 1930s. They were a highly disciplined and united group, of impeccable personal integrity, and formed a sharp contrast with the inefficient, quarrelsome and corrupt Kuomintang leaders. They correctly realized that success lay in winning over the peasantry of the countryside, thus isolating the Nationalist Government's forces, which made the mistake of shutting themselves up in walled cities.

United States policy in the Chinese conflict, at first expressed

[1] Winston Churchill, *The Second World War*, Vol. 1, 1948, p. 68.

through the American Ambassador, Patrick Hurley, and subsequently through George Marshall, later Secretary of State, whom President Truman sent to China in December 1945, was to press for a ceasefire and the formation of a coalition government which would give recognition to Communist strength in the country. These efforts were without effect, much of the responsibility for this falling upon the Kuomintang, though it is extremely doubtful whether the Communists were ever likely to be content in a partnership with their bourgeois and landowning opponents. By the end of 1949 the Communists were in possession of all Chinese mainland territory and the Nationalist Government and army had retired to Formosa. The status of this rich island was uncertain. It had been wrested from China by Japan in 1895 and, in accordance with an inter-Allied declaration issued at Cairo in November 1943, should have been retroceded to China when the war ended. The civil war in China prevented this being done, with the result that Formosa (and the adjacent island group called the Pescadores) was in a state of legal suspension. As far as the new Chinese Communist regime on the mainland, now called the Chinese People's Republic, was concerned, Britain accorded de jure recognition in January 1950 consistently with the traditional British policy of accepting seemingly irreversible changes in the status quo however undesirable they may be. The United States, in keeping with the American practice of using recognition to express moral or political approval of new regimes, continued to accept the Nationalist Government under Chiang Kai-shek as the lawful authority in China, even though it was confined to territory which had not yet been formally retroceded to China.

In deference to American wishes Britain continued to recognize the representatives of the Formosan regime as Chinese delegates at the United Nations and repeatedly voted against consideration of the Communist claim to take China's seat in United Nations organs. This involved her in a double inconsistency. She was obliged to recognize one Chinese Government for general purposes and another for particular, or United Nations, purposes. At the same time she had agreed in 1945, and again mainly through American pressure, to giving China a permanent seat on the United Nations Security Council, even though this was as much a defiance of the facts of China's strength and unity as the American refusal to recognize the Chinese Communists after 1949 was a defiance of the fact of their effective occupation of the country. An entirely unrepresentative Chinese regime on Formosa thus came to have a veto on substantive questions before the Security Council to which China herself, by the

N

test of physical power, was not yet entitled. The absurdity of this was tempered by the fact that the Chinese delegate from Formosa at the Security Council was hardly like to vote except in accordance with American wishes, since without American support the Formosan regime itself would collapse.

The events in China drove the deepest wedges between Britain and the United States since the end of the war. The feeling in America of having been betrayed, either by the Chinese Nationalists, many of whom had received American weapons only to desert with them to the Communists, or by the Chinese peasant, now an ally of Russia, who had had so much American help in the past, created intense hostility towards all concerned: towards the Chinese People's Republic which, being planted in a region of ancient American hopes and fears, seemed far more dangerous than the Soviet system; towards the allies and especially towards Britain, who seemed to Americans to have joined hands with Communist China for the worst possible motives of improving her balance of trade; and towards people in high places in America itself, who were widely accused by Right-wing isolationists of having 'sold China down the river' through ineptitude or pro-Communist leanings. This mental atmosphere was fully exploited by Senator McCarthy who found, quite by accident, that insinuations against the loyalty of American policy-makers and America's allies gave him access to the inmost ear of a country shocked by the Communist triumph in China and desperately anxious for clear lines of battle, with Good on one side and Evil on the other, to be drawn. British legalism was apt to seem intolerable, especially, as we have seen, since Britain took a different view of the neutrals than was customary in America. The Asian neutrals, led by India, were less hostile in their attitude to the revolution in China than American opinion, at least until the Communist Chinese attack on the semi-independent state of Tibet in March 1959. Many of them seemed positively to sympathize with the leading propaganda theme of the Chinese Communists, namely the sins of American imperialism.

Such was the context of the attack by Communist-dominated North Korea on the pro-Western Republic of Korea, based on the southern half of the country on June 25, 1950. Korea was one of the territories liberated from Japan in 1945 after having formed a part of the Japanese Empire since 1910. Like Germany it represented the failure of East-West agreement on the nature of the regimes to be set up in areas overrun by Allied troops. A United Nations Commission created to supervise free elections throughout the country had been denied access to the Communist-held region north of the 38th parallel and Korea split into two. In the south the regime of the Republic of Korea was formed under the intemperate nationalist Syngman Rhee in August 1948, while a so-called Democratic People's Republic was created in the more industrialized north in September. Though the two regimes were equally bent upon the destruction of each other, observers from the United Nations Commission in fact reported that the attack on June 25th came from the north and this seems probable in view of the almost uninterrupted movement of northern forces to the south after fighting began. American spokesmen had to some extent invited the attack by repeated statements since 1947 that Korea was not an essential part of the United States containment belt in the Pacific, running from Japan to Formosa. Nevertheless, President Truman's response was prompt and decisive. On his initiative the United Nations Security Council met at once, called for a ceasefire and, when this was unheeded, asked United Nations members to assist South Korea on June 27th. On the previous day Truman instructed General MacArthur, in charge of American forces in Japan, to go to the aid of the Republic of Korea and thus was formed a United Nations Command in Korea under MacArthur. This was not an enforcement action by the Security Council, although, owing to the absence of Russia from the Council's meetings in protest against the non-recognition of Communist China, the Council's decisions were held to be valid. It was rather a form of general assistance by United Nations members to South Korea, an American general being placed at the head of a single command since the United States made by far the largest contribution.

The United Nations was firmly supported by Britain, but after a brilliant landing of United Nations forces at Inchon on the west coast which drove North Korean forces back across the 38th parallel dispute arose between London and Washington as to the wisdom of extending United Nations operations to the frontier with China in the north. Britain voted on October 7th for a United Nations General Assembly resolution which called for free elections throughout the country and this seemed to endorse the crossing of the parallel by South Korean forces the previous week and by American forces two days later. Strong warnings were received from Peking, however, that China would not 'stand idly by' if MacArthur's advance continued. The British Government were urged by Mr Nehru to heed these warnings, versions of which had reached him through his Ambassador in Peking. No sooner had this advice been transmitted to Washington than MacArthur's offensive of November 24th, designed to bring the rest of the country under United Nations control, ran into strong opposition and counter-offensives by Communist Chinese 'volunteers' were launched which drove MacArthur back to the 38th parallel. In the resulting military deadlock United Nations forces were superior to their opponents in air power and naval support, but were heavily outnumbered by Chinese forces on the ground.

This presented the United States with its most searching test in the postwar world. It was natural for Americans to express their feelings by securing a resolution in the United Nations General Assembly on February 1, 1951, condemning China for aggression. The British delegate, Sir Gladwyn Jebb, at first doubted whether this was a practical way of demonstrating that aggression did not pay; he said it would drive China into isolation and was therefore contrary to the opinion voiced at a Commonwealth Prime Ministers' conference in London on January 12th that 'we must do what we can to understand those who appear to differ from us'. In the end, after making the provision for sanctions in the resolution dependent on further efforts to come to an agreement with China, Jebb reluctantly voted for the resolution.[1] The more immediate question, however, was whether, as General MacArthur seemed to wish, all-out force, including perhaps the atomic bomb, was to be used to drive the Chinese Communists out of Korea. MacArthur argued that the force required merely to hold the 38th parallel was no less than that needed to drive the Chinese back into their own country, provided he was allowed to raid their bases in Manchuria. After having at first opposed the suggestion, he came out in favour of accepting Chiang Kai-shek's offer of 33,000 men and protested, more loudly that any British officer would consider proper for a serving soldier, that the scruples of allies should not be allowed to stand in the way of measures considered necessary by the commander in the field.

All this was deeply disturbing to Britain. MacArthur was not merely a politically inept general who stole the newspaper headlines owing to his services in the Pacific during the war, but a mouthpiece for powerful groups in America who wanted to turn a deaf ear to allies and do the right thing by their own consciences. In the event Mr Truman, who had been returned to office in November 1948 against all forecasts to the contrary, felt strong enough first to caution MacArthur about his expressions of dissent from government policy and then to recall him in April 1951 after one of his messages, advo-

[1] Korea No. 1 (1951), Cmd. 8159.

cating the bombing of Manchuria and the despatch of Chinese forces from Formosa to Korea, had been read out in Congress by Representative Martin. This courageous action was certainly not the result of British pressure, though the adoption of MacArthur's views would almost certainly have placed an unbearable strain on Anglo-American relations as well as on the Commonwealth. The fact was that MacArthur was widely recognized by the President's own advisers as likely to plunge America into what General Omar Bradley, chairman of the United States Chiefs of Staff, called 'the wrong war against the wrong enemy in the wrong place at the wrong time'. It was a further instance of the capacity of the United States to hover on the brink of war, and yet turn back to sanity at the eleventh hour. In this retirement from catastrophe Britain's influence undoubtedly played a part.[1]

American uneasiness at the indecisiveness of the Korean struggle, however, remained. It was not appeased by the long-drawn-out negotiations for an armistice which began at Kaesong in 1952 and and were then transfered to Panmunjom. There on July 27, 1953, an armistice was at last signed, after long and angry debates on the question whether prisoners-of-war should be repatriated against their will, as the Communists desired, or allowed to decide their future for themselves, as the Western representatives contended. The frustrated feelings aroused in America by the war in Korea continued to overhang relations with Britain and expressed themselves in the Presidential elections of November 1952. The victor in that contest, General Eisenhower, formerly the Supreme NATO Commander in Europe, was elected largely as a strong character who was believed to be able to hold his own with the Communist Powers, even though his political views were so imprecise that for some time he had seriously considered standing for the Democrats. With the return of the Republicans to power the more extreme 'go-it-alone' elements in the party which had rallied round General MacArthur and the isolationist leader Senator Knowland of California were brought under control. Nevertheless, the emotional aftermath of Korea and the armistice talks strengthened the inclination of the Eisenhower administration to recruit all available anti-Communist forces in the Far East, however dubious their liberal character, and increased their mistrust of neutralism. Under the Truman administration, peace had already been made with Japan in 1951 and full sovereignty was restored to that country in April 1952. The treaty was not signed by Russia since it clearly formed part of the American policy of rearm-

[1] Korea No. 2 (1951), Cmd. 8366.

ing Japan and converting it from a pacifist country, as originally conceived under the occupation, into a strong ally of America in the Pacific. Communist China had naturally not been invited to the San Francisco conference for completing the peace treaty and Mr Dulles, who was then acting for the Truman administration, extracted from the Japanese Prime Minister, Mr Yoshida, a letter promising to accept the Formosan regime as the legitimate government of China. After the signing of the Mutual Security Treaty between Japan and the United States at the same time as the signature of the peace treaty, the way was then open for the gradual building up of Japan's military strength on the basis of American financial support. Rearmament, however, proved to be a much slower process than the Americans had hoped and the curious situation arose in which American officials urged Japanese Ministers, some of whom had served terms of imprisonment as war criminals, to raise their military sights, while the latter gave the American-imposed consitution, with its renunciation of war, as a pretext for their unwillingness to increase taxation burdens in the country.

The British Government accepted the American decision to rearm Japan as the inevitable corollary of a fiercely anti-American China. But the return of Japan to an independent position in international relations was bound to arouse anxieties in London, all the more so since the American emphasis on the world conflict as a moral struggle compared strangely with the allies the United States was acquiring in the Far East, such as Chiang Kai-shek, Syngman Rhee and now the new converts to democracy in Japan. Australia and New Zealand, which had bitter memories of Japan from the war years, had little to fear from Japanese militarism so long as the Anzus pact continued. But the American injunction to Japan forbidding official relations with China meant that Japan's ninety million people might not always be content with their restricted position and might look elsewhere for opportunity and livelihood. Above all, the assumption by Japan of a favoured position in American esteem threatened to expose Britain to trade competition with that country which had proved so ruinous in the 1930s, especially as Japan's exports could no longer find their natural outlet in China. Hence, on the insistence of MPs representing British textile manufacturing constituencies, Britain continued to oppose Japan's entry into the General Agreement on Tariffs and Trade as a full member and the extension to her of Article 35 of the agreement, which extends most-favoured-nation treatment to all the parties.

The new order in China

It was, however, on the issue of the 'two Chinas' that British and American policies were most seriously divided, especially since certain members of the Eisenhower administration were reported as talking vaguely of the need to 'take the wraps off Chiang' and let him do his worst on the mainland, all presumably under the protection of the American Seventh Fleet, which had been sent to form a protective cordon round Formosa at the outbreak of the Korean war. British opinion was almost unanimous that giving encouragement to the Nationalists in the hope of unseating the Communists was the last word in reckless adventurism. Nor was it considered that the Nationalists would prove any more representative of the Chinese people or more capable of providing honest and capable government than they had in the past. Nevertheless, it was out of the question to press the case too strongly in Washington. In the first place, the Peking Government continued throughout the 1950s to threaten an invasion of Formosa. Reality seemed to be about to be given to this threat in 1955 and again in 1958 when shelling from the mainland was directed at the island of Quemoy and the Matsu group, just off the south China coast, which Nationalist forces had retained after the civil war. Had the threat to invade Formosa been carried out, Britain would have been bound to support American action in resisting it, since she did not admit that Formosa was part of the territory under the jurisdiction of the mainland government. A second factor in British restraint on the two Chinas issue was the fact that American public opinion and especially the Congressional groups which championed the Nationalists would clearly not allow the administration to abandon the Formosa authorities or accept the suggestions frequently made in Britain concerning a possible United Nations trusteeship for Formosa. Towards the end of his life, Dulles appeared to be feeling his way towards some such solution. On one occasion he said America might consider recognition of the Peking regime if it ended its aggressive policy. Shortly after this statement was made, however, the Chinese invasion of the priestly state of Tibet in March 1959 and the outbreak of Sino-Indian differences over their common frontier removed the prospect of an early change in American policy.

Britain's position as a junior partner with the United States in the Far East was therefore wholly anomalous, as was admitted by Eden when he gave the Government's view of the legal aspects of the Quemoy and Matsu crisis in answer to a Commons question on February 4, 1955.[1] In the Government's opinion, Eden said, the

[1] 536 H.C. Deb. 5s. Cols. 159–160 (Written answers).

islands were legally part of the territory of the People's Republic of China and hence, though the Foreign Secretary could hardly say so, their occupation by the Nationalists was a trespass against Chinese sovereignty. Eden then went on to say that any attempt of the People's Republic to assert its authority over the islands by force 'would give rise to a situation endangering peace and security, which is properly a matter of international concern'. Again, the unstated implication was clear, namely that the threat to peace would come from the American decision, lawful in the American view, unlawful in the British, to prevent the islands falling into Communist hands. Had war resulted from the offshore islands question, Britain would have been committed to a conflict for a cause which aroused little sympathy at home and which, in the Government's own view, was clearly illegal. Fortunately the situation was eased by restraint on both sides. The United States plainly intimated to Formosa that the offshore islands were to be regarded as part of the defence of Formosa, not a springboard for attacking the mainland. The Chinese Communists on their side, perhaps under pressure from Moscow, evidently decided that Formosa would fall to them in time as age and receding hopes destroyed the Nationalist regime and as the People's Republic grew in strength and became an object of pride in the eyes of all Chinese people.

Formosa was a matter of national prestige for the mainland Chinese and its recovery by them could be regarded as inevitable in the course of time. But Communist China's designs on south-east Asia, the ancient *Lebensraum* of Chinese rulers, were far more dangerous in that penetrations into the area would bring immense riches into Communist hands. For this reason Mao Tse-tung, the architect of the Communist revolution in China, saw great possibilities in the civil war intermittently going on in the three states of former French Indo-China, Cambodia, Laos and Vietnam, since the grant of independence within the French Union in 1947. By the nature of the terrain a difficult problem was presented to any external Power which sought to prevent Communist exploitation of this warfare. Pro-Communist guerrilla forces, especially in Laos and North Vietnam, could be quietly fed from south China cross the border without world opinion being alerted, while the Western Powers were unable to supply the other side without being accused of open intervention. Defences against Communist encroachment could only be provided in the last resort by armies recruited from the local peasant population, but these had little knowledge of the issues at stake or much desire to risk their lives in order to replace one set of rulers by another.

It was from every point of view a conflict to which the standard American policy of organizing a military front of democrats against Communist aggression was unsuited.

This was the argument urged by Eden on Dulles in the crisis in the spring of 1954, when French forces were beseiged in the fortress of Dien Bien Phu in North Vietnam. Dulles insisted on some form of Anglo-American action, possibly by bombing enemy forces at Dien Bien Phu, to relieve the French, while Eden replied that intervention would be repudiated by British opinion and by the Asian neutrals and would turn both Russia and China against a political solution while hope of such a solution still existed. France played an ambiguous role in the controversy, being anxious on behalf of her troops and yet afraid of a long and costly war which might weaken her political situation in Europe. But it was the Asian neutrals which occupied the criticial position. Eden was concerned to use India's influence in order to bring China to the conference table and urged Dulles to postpone the formation of a collective defence organization for south-east Asia since this would deter India from lending her assistance. Dulles for his part believed that only a strong military front would deter Communist advances and regarded the neutrals as doing a disservice to peace in so far as they blurred this fact. When the SEATO treaty was finally signed at Manila in September, however, only three Asian states joined, namely Pakistan, the Philippines and Thailand, and neither these nor the five other parties, Australia, Britain, France, New Zealand and the United States, were able to provide permanent forces in the area to make the treaty more than a symbol of solidarity.[1]

The quarrel between Eden and Dulles represented the differing psychological attitudes of Britain and America in all their relations, in particular the persisting search for accommodation on one side and the precise conception of good and evil in politics on the other. To which was added a personal element. Eden, though younger than Dulles, had had a long and distinguished diplomatic record going back to the early 1930s. In method and even appearance he suggested to many Americans the devious old-style diplomat seeking a form of words to accommodate conflicting positions and thus, to a person of strong religious faith like Dulles, obscuring the basic question of who is right and who is wrong. At the Geneva conference on Indo-China and Korea in 1954 Eden fought his way through many weeks' negotiation with the Russians and the Chinese from May 1st until July 21st until agreement was reached on armistices in the three

[1] Eden, *Full Circle*, Chapter V.

States, the division of Vietnam into a Communist North and non-Communist South, and a neutral status for Laos and Cambodia. Dulles, whose wish for a military intervention before the conference began had been outmanoeuvred by Eden, retired from the conference after a week and left the American case in the more pliable hands of Bedell Smith. The resulting sense in the Secretary of State's mind of having been frustrated by Eden may have contributed to his behaviour during the Suez crisis two years later, when roles were reversed and Dulles played the same accommodating part which Eden had filled in Indo-China in 1954. Another legacy of the Geneva conference was American pressure towards the establishment of a Right-wing regime in Laos after the failure of efforts to integrate the pro-Communist Pathet Lao forces with the Royal Laotian army, as provided for at Geneva, and to form a coalition government. In the autumn of 1960 Prince Souvanna Phouma gave up his attempts to form a neutralist administration and the capital, Vientiane, was seized by American-backed elements led by General Phoumi Nosavan. The neutralists then retired to join Pathet Lao in the north and their combined success against the Right led to a new crisis, with the United States and China openly supporting opposite sides. A second Geneva conference met in May 1961, but by this time the Western position in Laos had much deteriorated. American policy, which shared some responsibility for this, therefore concentrated on preventing the adjoining state of South Vietnam following the same course as the Communist north.

Cold War diplomacy: the two approaches
This pattern of Anglo-American differences, with the British emphasis on accommodation and the primary American concern with resistance to Communist encroachments, reproduced itself in East-West relations generally. While neutralism, in the sense of withdrawal from Western military pacts, was never acceptable to more than an unimportant fringe of British opinion, British Governments constantly looked for ways in which disagreements with the Communist bloc might be adjusted by negotiation. Americans, conscious of their major responsibility for the security of the West, regarded these British efforts with anxiety. Churchill's suggestion for a 'summit' meeting with Russia in May 1953 had a cold reception in America and British misgivings over the building up of West German military strength, lest Russia be provoked, were regarded as unrealistic. When the Geneva 'summit' conference finally met in July 1955 American officials looked with suspicion on the proposal put forward

by Eden, who had become Prime Minister in succession to Churchill in April, for a controlled *status quo* in respect of forces in central Europe, which had always won favour in the Foreign Office. A form of this proposal was taken by Eden's successor, Harold Macmillan, to Moscow in February 1959, when he sought to prepare the ground for an arrangement with the Soviet Premier, Nikita Khrushchev, after the latter had issued his demand the previous November that Berlin should be made a demilitarized Free City. At meetings of the four Foreign Ministers in Geneva in the summer of 1959 called to consider the Berlin problem, the British Foreign Secretary, Selwyn Lloyd, did his utmost to secure an interim arrangement for Berlin, pending German reunification, which would lessen the alleged 'provocativeness' of West Berlin to East Germany in return for a Communist reaffirmation of Western rights in the city. These efforts failed, but British advocacy of conciliation continued and it was largely through this that the four leaders, Presidents Eisenhower and de Gaulle, Khrushchev and Macmillan, assembled in Paris on May 15, 1960, to discuss Germany, Berlin and East-West relations generally.

The Paris conference never actually got down to business since the Soviet Prime Minister refused to talk with an American President who had, on his own admission, authorised a flight by an American espionage plane over Soviet territory which had been shot down on May 1st and who refused to apologize for the incident. It was uncertain whether this was the real reason for the Soviet change of attitude to the conference or whether the incident was seized upon to avoid talks which Kruschchev had already decided were likely to be either fruitless or unacceptable to Russia's allies. The effect was, however, to give pause to British pressure for explorations into the possibilities of agreement with Russia. After the Paris 'summit' failure Macmillan seemed to regret the initiative he had taken. During the sombre but sterile conversations between the new American President, Kennedy, and the Soviet Premier in Vienna in early June 1961 Macmillan seemed content to have the Western case stated by the young Western leader, provided the British were given a full account of the talks afterwards. While the rumours were denied that Kennedy told Macmillan, when the latter had gone to visit him in April 1961, that the West 'did not need further British efforts for conciliation with Russia', the President was clearly a much stronger figure than Eisenhower and intended to hold the leadership of the West which was America's due.

Policies of accommodation never came easy to the United States.

They jarred with the American desire for a clear moral pattern in affairs. They were hard to practise for a country which had to hold the allegiance of many allies, some of which, as Americans thought, might be tempted to flirt with the other side if it became known that Washington was prepared to bargain about their interests with Moscow. These considerations sometimes led American Governments into inconsistencies, when they acted contrary to their habitual insistence on the rule of law in world affairs and in conflict with their claim, often urged against Britain, that treating small countries with a big stick would drive them into the Communist fold. This was especially apt to occur in the Western hemisphere, where American fears were heightened by territorial insecurity. Thus United States action against the Left-wing regime in Guatemala in 1954, when a *coup* was engineered from outside so as to instal a more loyal ally, and the disastrous support given by the United States Central Intelligence Agency to an abortive landing in Cuba by exiles bent on unseating the anti-United States regime of Fidel Castro in April 1961 were widely criticized in Britain. Behind these actions was the American contention that in the struggle against Communism there was no room for shades of opinion. If Communist aggression threatened, then, as Dulles said in a famous speech in January 1954, there must be 'massive and instant retaliation'. If Communist imperialism overran free countries, as in Eastern Europe, the West should not accept the result as a *fait accompli* but should work for the day of liberation. If the struggle against Communism was recognized for what it was, an undeclared war, it mattered little whether Franco's Spain or Chiang Kai-shek's Formosa stood on one's side, so long as they fought the common enemy. Although American policy focused more on the economic front with the coming of East-West parity in nuclear arms, it never accepted the fundamental assumption of British thought that time and the advantages of good international relations would ultimately bring the Sino-Soviet bloc to terms.

Many of these Anglo-American differences appeared more at the level of public discussion than that of official contacts. The fact that both countries were democracies in which foreign policy was often a matter of intense debate tended to sharpen differences and sometimes forced the leaders on both sides into stronger expressions of their viewpoints than they wished. It could also be argued that the differences in themselves testified to the strength of the alliance in that only those who know that they cannot separate can afford open quarrels. All in all, the impressive thing about Anglo-American relations at this period was not so much policy differences but the fact that the transfer of primacy in the democratic world was effected so smoothly, despite its running against the grain of sentiment in both countries. By the 1960s British opinion readily accepted the dominant position of America, as was shown by its attitude to President Kennedy's visit to London in June 1961, though there was still a tendency to smile secretly at American reverses. On the American side, the feeling of discomfort with allies and the hankering to travel alone were being outgrown. However much Americans wrestled uncomfortably with the danger and uncertainty of being in the front line, the community with Britain remained firm.

CHAPTER SEVEN

Egypt and Arab Nationalism

Geography linked together the fates of Britain and Egypt. The security of Egypt, turning upon the massive military base which Britain had built up along the Suez Canal, was the linch-pin of British and Imperial security, the Suez Canal itself the nodal point of the British Commonwealth. Britain had defended Egypt against Napoleon. Egypt was the centre from which the campaigns against Turkey were fought in the First World War. Had Egypt been overrun by Field Marshal Rommel in 1941–42 Axis forces would have swept over the Arab States, breaking the link between Britain and the United States and their Soviet ally, and reaching out to join hands with Japan. After the war Soviet threats against Turkey and Iran and Soviet appeals to aggrieved Arabs to break with Western imperialism provided a new menace to the British position. Yet for Britain to maintain her connection with Egypt a relationship was required which would take account of rising Arab pride and Egypt's desire to be in full possession of her soil. This relationship necessarily had to move from master-client status to one of equality. There had to be a recognition of mutual interest in the connection on both sides. This was not soon attained. British Governments continued to regard Egypt as incapable of understanding her own security needs or of providing for them. Egyptian politicians, having the dual task of looking after their country's interests and bidding for the leadership of the Arab world, did not accept the British reading of the situation, which they regarded as a thinly disguised pretext for continued rule over Egypt.

The Anglo-Egyptian relationship at the end of the Second World War was expressed in the Treaty of Alliance signed by representatives of all the Egyptian parties in August 1936, when the situation in the Mediterranean was disturbed by Mussolini's conquest of Ethiopia and the outbreak of the civil war in Spain in July. For Egypt the treaty was a step forward from the Anglo-Egyptian agreement of 1922, which recognized Egyptian sovereignty but limited it in Britain's favour in four important respects. At the same time the 1936 treaty assured Egypt that in the probable event of war with the Axis Powers, Britain, the dominant naval Power in the Mediterranean, would be at her side. By 1945 the treaty, which could be renegotiated at the request of either signatory after twenty years, had become intolerable to Egyptian opinion. It committed Egypt to assist Britain in the event of war and in 1945 no war was in sight. It gave Britain authority to use Egyptian ports, aerodromes and means of communication and to call for martial law and censorship in Egypt, not merely in war, but in the event of an 'apprehended international emergency' (Article 7). Coupled with the right accorded to Britain to station forces in the Suez Canal zone 'as an essential means of communication between the different parts of the British Empire' (Article 8), this meant that the whole life of Egypt could be brought under British control, as it was during the Second World War, if an international conflict impended. Since in 1945 Britain was still a Great Power, with Great Powers as allies, and Egypt an insignificant Power, economically underdeveloped and overcrowded, the definition of the emergency in which these powers were assumed by Britain would in all likelihood be one designed to suit her interests rather than those of Egypt. Above all, the hinge on which the 1936 treaty turned was that the Egyptian army was unable 'to ensure by its own resources the liberty and entire security of navigation of the (Suez) Canal' (Article 8) and that until such time as Egypt was able to defend herself the special position of Britain should remain.[1] This was offensive to Egyptian national pride. Egyptian politicians saw no reason why, if India, Burma, Pakistan, Ceylon were deemed capable of governing themselves, Egypt should not be included. The British reply was that Egypt, being sovereign over the Canal, was in a special position and exposed to special dangers. Egypt admitted that the Canal was a peculiar responsibility but regarded this as increasing, rather than diminishing, her say in the future of the country. As for the special dangers, these were thought in Cairo to lie, not in potential aggression from another great Power, since for several years after the war the Soviet Union was almost indifferent towards the Arab States, but in the refusal of the traditional European Powers with interests in the Middle East, in particular Britain and France, to admit that they were no longer strong enough to retain what they had won by force and guile.

Although Britain was not obliged to enter into talks for the revision of the treaty until 1956, the Attlee Government agreed at the end of 1945 to negotiate, provided there was no prospect of British forces having to leave Egypt with nothing but the Egyptian

[1] Egypt No. 1 (1936), Cmd. 5270.

army to replace them. As Bevin said in the Commons on May 24, 1946—

> There must not be a vacuum. If the Egyptian Government try to force a situation in which there is a vacuum—meaning that we have gone and that there is nothing there for security instead, regional defence or other organization—to that I can never agree. But I have offered . . . a new basis of approach. Perhaps partnership is the wrong term, but it is a joint effort for mutual defence, not only in the interests in Great Britain and her Commonwealth, but in the interests ultimately of the contribution to what I hope will yet become a United Nations defence for the security of the world.[1]

The 'new approach' mentioned by Bevin was incorporated in a draft agreement the Foreign Secretary initialled with Sidky Pasha, the Egyptian Prime Minister, in October. Sidky Pasha had come to London with his Foreign Minister after talks during the summer between a strong all-party Egyptian delegation and a British delegation led by Lord Stansgate, the British Minister for Air, in Cairo. The essence of the agreement was that British forces would withdraw from Cairo, Alexandria and the Delta to the Canal zone by March 31, 1947, and from the zone itself by September 1, 1949. Egypt on her side promised to take action in the event of aggression against adjacent countries, to enter with Britain into a Joint Defence Board, intended to make recommendations to the two Governments about events threatening Middle East security, and to consult with Britain on the necessary measures to ward off a threat to the security of the area.[2] The draft agreement, although it committed Egypt neither to fight at Britain's side nor to provide bases for British forces in future conflicts, fell to the ground when King Farouk dissolved the Egyptian delegation to the talks on November 26th and forced Sidki himself to resign on December 9th.

The problem of the Sudan

A different outcome might have resulted from the Bevin-Sidki talks had they not been enmeshed with the future of the Sudan, since the Egyptian claim, partly on emotional, partly on economic grounds, that Egypt and the Sudan be united under Farouk gave the British Government a solid basis for refusing to sell the Sudan in return for Egyptian consent to a joint security pact. The Sudan was Egyptian

[1] 423 H.C. Deb. 5s. Col. 788.
[2] Egypt No. 2 (1947) Cmd. 7179.

territory when Kitchener conquered it in 1898 after the revolt of the Mahdi from the Khedive, who ruled Egypt on behalf of the Ottoman Sultan. The Condominium created in 1899 to govern the Sudan was ostensibly a joint Anglo-Egyptian arrangement; in fact the country was thenceforward to all intents a British protectorate. While the northern Sudanese were predominantly Arabs and Egypt's concern with the maintenance of the level of the Nile, on which her life literally hung, created an argument for unity, the southern part of the country was inhabited by more backward African peoples too unpolitical to decide whether they desired amalgamation with the more advanced state to the north. In the Anglo-Egyptian treaty of 1936 the question of sovereignty over the Sudan was left undecided, but 'new conventions in future' were envisaged to replace, if necessary, the 1899 arrangement. Britain wished to postpone the question again in 1946 and merely agreed that the Sudan should be considered as forming a 'dynastic union' with Egypt, but only so long as the British-appointed Governor-Generalship, created in 1899, and the arrangements for the defence of the Sudan continued in force. Since defence was mainly a British responsibility the 'dynastic union' could never be consummated without British consent, and the British Government made clear that they would not consent without having consulted Sudanese wishes.

Sidki Pasha, who seemed in London to have accepted the British argument that the Sudanese must decide their future for themselves, found himself under strong pressure on his return home to gratify public demands for bringing the Sudan under immediate Egyptian control. The slogan 'Unity of the Nile Valley' had become a shibboleth of Egyptian politics; behind it stood the fear that so long as Britain controlled the Sudan she could use the cultural division between north and south to prevent agreement on the question of unity with Egypt and hence be in a position to restrict the Nile waters in any future dispute with Egypt. The Egyptian people in fact had the same fears that Britain would use the Nile to advance her political ends against Egypt as Sir Anthony Eden had about Colonel Nasser and the Suez Canal ten years later. Sidki Pasha therefore issued a statement on his return to Cairo on October 26th stating that the protocol attached to the treaty which he had initialled with Bevin definitely united the Sudan with Egypt under the Egyptian crown. This was answered by a denial by Attlee in the House of Commons on October 28th, by the Governor-General in Khartoum on December 7th, after a visit to London, in which he said that the British Government were not deflected from their determination to prepare

o

the Sudanese for self-government and a statement issued in London which said that it was 'manifestly impossible for any British Government to acquiesce in an interpretation of a treaty with Egypt . . . which denies one of the fundamental rights of a free people—a right which Egypt has never ceased to claim for herself'.[1] Like all strongly held political positions, the British attitude was a mixture of self-interest and principle. No British Government could wish to increase the power of an Egypt whose inflammatory nationalism was considered highly dangerous, especially by extending Egyptian control in the direction of British colonial possessions in Africa whose future was still uncertain. At the same time, the traditional British concern for underdeveloped colonial or semi-colonial peoples forbade the handing over of the Sudan to Egyptian politicians whose own people could hardly be said to be self-governing in any true sense.

Since the two questions of the Canal base and the future of the Sudan remained tied together in the Egyptian mind no progress was registered during the following three years. Egypt took her case to the United Nations Security Council in July 1947 on the grounds, first, that British troops were 'an offence to Egypt's dignity, a hindrance to its normal development, as well as an infringement of fundamental principles of sovereign equality' and, secondly, that Britain had encouraged an artificial separatism in the Sudan in order to destroy the unity of the Nile Valley. Although the Egyptian delegation at the Security Council had the support of the Soviet Union on the first count, the Soviet delegate, Mr Gromyko, offered no solution of the Sudanese problem and the debate was at length adjourned without Egypt having established her contention that the 1936 treaty was no longer valid. A similar deadlock attended talks between Sir William Slim, the Chief of the Imperial General Staff, and Egyptian Ministers in March 1949 and again in June and July 1951; Egyptian Ministers continued to argue that British troops were intolerable not merely in peacetime, but even in times of imminent threat of war, and that Egypt and the Sudan were one country and should be ruled by one government. Detailed British proposals had been set before the Egyptians on April 11, 1951, at a time when British tempers were ruffled by the domestic financial position, which was not improved by Egyptian demands for release of Egypt's sterling balances in London, and by the Egyptian refusal to allow British tankers bound for Haifa, in Israel, to sail through the Suez Canal. The British suggested that their forces should leave

[1] 428 H.C. Deb. 5s. Cols. 295–6.

the Canal zone at the end of 1956, but that they should be allowed to return in an emergency; in the meantime the base would be kept in working order by British civilians, who entered as the troops left, and operated by a joint Anglo-Egyptian control board. These proposals were totally rejected by Egypt on April 24th, as were new British proposals on August 17th which involved a regional pact to guard the Canal zone. The United States, France and Turkey had already signified their willingness to join such a pact, Turkey having agreed to do so in return for her admission to the NATO pact along with Greece in September. When the proposal was set before Egypt by the three Western Powers and Turkey on October 13th in the revised form of an integrated Middle East Command it was pointed out that no British troops would remain in Egypt which were not under the new command, and that in any case Egypt would be able to forbid the movement of troops in her territory.[1] None of this, however, sufficed to remove Egyptian suspicions that the command was merely a new way of perpetuating the British occupation and the general Arab argument that the danger came not from Russia but from Israel, the alleged pawn of the Western Powers themselves. On October 15th, two days after the delivery of the Four-Power defence proposals, and of a British proposal for an international commission to watch over the constitutional development of the Sudan, the Egyptian Wafd Government under Nahas Pasha, who had signed the 1936 treaty, enacted two bills, one of which abrogated the treaty and the other purported to end the Condominium for the Sudan and to unite the Sudan with Egypt under the Egyptian crown.[2]

These enactments did nothing to change the situation, though they created bitter feelings in London against the United States Government, who, in their anxiety for stability in the Canal zone, endorsed by the Egyptian position on the Sudan, subject to ratification by the Sudanese. There was some American sympathy with the Egyptian charge that Britain was magnifying Sudanese party differences in order to retain her grip on the country, much as (so many Americans thought) she had written off proposals for partitioning Palestine in the same imperialistic spirit. What the Egyptian pronouncements did, however, was to add fuel to Egyptian nationalistic feeling against Britain to such an extent that it defeated Farouk's attempts to control it and set on foot a movement which led to his abdication. On October 16th, the day after the enactment of the bills, Egyptian students rioted against British camps at Ismailia and

[1] Egypt No. 2 (1951), Cmd. 8419, pp. 24–6, 43–5.
[2] Cmd. 8419, pp. 46–7.

Port Said and when the British commander, Sir George Erskine, imposed controls on traffic entering and leaving the Canal zone, Egyptian workers left the zone in large numbers. Attacks in December on British convoys going to and from water infiltration plants (without which water used in the zone was undrinkable) in the zone led to the construction of a new road by Erskine and when fifty houses in an Egyptian village were demolished to make room for it, the Egyptian Ambassador in London was recalled. By January 1952 British tanks were in action in the attempt to maintain order and security at Suez and battle raged at the end of the month at Ismailia, where British efforts to disarm the Egyptian auxiliary police resulted in the killing of forty-one Egyptians and three British. The fighting at Ismailia was the signal for 'Black Saturday' (January 26th) in Cairo where 500 auxiliary police mutinied and what seemed like organized gangs followed by hysterical mobs set fire to European buildings and the tourist quarter. Farouk, though he himself had left the calling out of Egyptian troops until the late afternoon, dismissed his Prime Minister, Nahas Pasha, for failing to maintain law and order. He then called on Ali Maher to form a government, thus ending the Wafd domination. Meanwhile, the officers who were called to put down the riot on January 26th set about preparing a *coup* which resulted in Farouk's abdication and the formation of the Revolutionary Command Council under Colonel Mohammed Neguib in July.

The officers' uprising provided an opportunity for a new start on settling the British deadlock with Egypt. The *coup* was welcomed in Britain as affording an end to the corrupt and unstable governments of the last few months of the Farouk era and since its architects were soldiers, they were thought better able to understand the security considerations which British Ministers were constantly urging on Cairo. Moreover, the United States took a favourable view of the reformist character of the Officers' regime, especially good relations being established between Neguib and the American Ambassador, Jefferson Caffery. Since American hopes of drawing Egypt into the projected containing belt against Russia in the Middle East thus revived, it could be expected that increased pressure from Washington would be felt in London to treat Egypt generously. But, while Neguib and his colleagues were not outwardly anti-Western, it soon became clear that they were no more willing than Farouk's Ministers to be hurried into a defence pact centred upon some new arrangement for the Canal base. Neguib's speeches were monotonously anti-British. Secret circulars distributed by the Free Officers' Organization soon after their seizure of power showed distinct neutralist leanings and the Minister of State for Propaganda (afterwards National Guidance) in the new Government, Fathi Ridwan, had been an advocate of a non-aggression pact with Russia. By the end of the year these tendencies were sufficiently in evidence for the Western idea of the Middle East Defence Organization to look distinctly a non-starter. In a dinner at the Officers' Club in Cairo given to the Syrian dictator, Colonel Shishakli, on December 14th, Neguib foreshadowed the basic principles of the foreign policy of his own successor, Nasser, when he said that 'in these difficult times, when the two great blocs are waging one of the greatest struggles that history has ever known, we wish to prove to the world that this part of the world belongs to its citizens and no longer accepts the tutelage of anyone'. At the end of the year, when British relations with the new regime were already embarrassed by the Conservative Government's refusal to supply heavy arms to Egypt except in return for Egyptian assurances on Middle East defence and compensation for the 'Black Saturday' riots, rumours spread that Britain was attempting to force the southern Sudan to secede and join Uganda. Neguib, himself partly Sudanese and educated at Gordon College, Khartoum, said that Egypt would fight to prevent the partition of the Sudan. At the same time he was active forming the five pro-Egyptian parties of northern Sudan into a coalition powerful enough to swing the impending Sudanese elections in Egypt's favour. Neither were negotiations on the Suez base in better shape. The British Minister for War, Anthony Head, who had admitted to an Egyptian journalist when in Cairo that Britain might, after all, leave the Suez base without the safeguards British Ministers had formerly required, was obliged to recant on his return to London in September and to reaffirm British interest in the base. Neguib described the revised statement as 'hateful and horrible'.

These inauspicious beginnings to British relations with the Revolutionary Command Council were belied in the following year, when the obstacle which had caused the difficulties since the war, the linking of the Sudan with the Suez base, was removed. The Neguib Government found it much easier than did the Wafd to separate the two issues. After the troubles in the Canal zone in January 1952 it was imperative to reach some agreement with Britain and it was worth Neguib's while to pay a high price to secure a final British evacuation from the Suez base in order to consolidate the new regime. The change of regime in Cairo also much improved the prospects of extending Egyptian influence over the Sudan as it approached self-government and independence. The passing of Farouk and, with him, the principle of the unity of Egypt and the Sudan under the monarchy opened the way to other forms of relationship more acceptable to the Sudanese than the rigid one of Egyptian sovereignty; Neguib's own popularity in the Sudan was obviously of considerable assistance here. Moreover, Eden told the House of Commons on October 22nd that the self-government statute would be put into effect in the Sudan and further obstinacy looked as if it might ruin Egypt's chances of influencing the new developments.[1] Neguib therefore devoted himself, not to opposing Sudanese self-determination until the principle of unity with Egypt was accepted, but to winning over the Sudanese parties to the Egyptian point of view in advance of the elections which had been promised for November 1952 under a draft constitution for self-government, which had been approved by the Legislative Assembly in Khartoum in April. Leaders of the main Sudanese parties were received in Cairo at the end of October, but it was notable that no representatives from the three Southern provinces were present. The Revolutionary Command Council, by fostering the amalgamation of the five pro-Egyptian parties into the National Unity Party, seemed to hope that this alliance would sweep the board at the elections provided they could be postponed for a year, during which time it might strengthen its position. In negotiations between Britain and Egypt on the latter's objections to the draft self-government statute which began in November Britain agreed to postpone the elections until November 1953.

The result of this change in Egypt's position in regard to the claim for compulsory unity under the Egyptian crown was the agreement on Sudanese self-government and self-determination finally signed on February 12, 1953. This provided for full exercise of self-determination at the end of three years, supreme constitutional authority in the meantime being exercised by the Governor-General with the aid of a commission consisting of two Sudanese, one British, one Egyptian and one Pakistani representative. An international commission of seven would prepare and supervise elections. British and Egyptian forces were to make arrangements to withdraw from the Sudan when the Sudanese Parliament, at the end of the three years, decided that the arrangements for self-determination should be put into effect. The latter would take the form of the election of a Constituent Assembly to 'decide the future of the Sudan as an integral whole', which would include the choice of uniting with Egypt or

[1] 505 H.C. Deb. 5s. Cols. 1014–5.

complete independence. During the transition period a special committee would effect the Sudanization of the administration, the police, the Sudan Defence Force and other services.[1]

The points at which the Egyptian Government were able to make themselves felt in the agreement were that, in the Self-Government Statute, the Governor-General was given special responsibility for fair and equitable treatment to 'all inhabitants of the various provinces of the Sudan', rather than to the south alone, as Britain had wished, and the creation of a Sudanization committee, although on British insistence the Governor-General, with the agreement of his commission, was given authority to withhold his assent to the committee's decisions. In the main, however, Neguib hoped to influence the Sudan from the inside and through the Sudanese parties. In this he seemed at first to be successful. With the help of anti-British propaganda from Cairo, which Eden alleged in the Commons on November 5th was a violation of the February agreement,[2] the pro-Egyptian NUP won fifty out of the ninety-seven seats in the Sudanese House of Representatives created by the Self-Government Statute and twenty-one out of the thirty contested seats for the Senate. Shortly afterwards, however, the coalition fell apart and the growth of a Sudanese nationalism, which the agreement of February stimulated, encouraged its members to drop their pro-Egyptian attitudes. The displacement of Neguib, with his Sudanese associations, by Nasser, whose writings showed pronounced imperialistic tendencies, played an important part in this result. This turn of events showed that Eden, who had threatened to resign if his self-determination proposals were not accepted by the Cabinet, had been right to seize the initiative from Egypt on the assumption that Sudanese nationalism would rebel against Egyptian attempts to bully the Sudan into unity.[3]

The Suez base agreement
The Sudan settlement opened the way for a solution of the far more difficult question of the Suez base. Some idea of the importance of the base may be gained from the fact that the installations, a tangled mass of workshops, railways and strongpoints in an area as big as Wales, were valued at between £500 million and £700 million. One of the factors making for a fresh approach in 1953 was the Government's belief that the base was of declining importance in an

---

[1] Egypt No. 2 (1953), Cmd. 8767.
[2] 520 H.C. Deb. 5s. Col. 320.
[3] Eden, *Full Circle*, p. 247.

age of atomic warfare, though the decision to move the joint head-quarters for the Middle East from the Suez base to Cyprus in December 1952 was criticized by the so-called 'Suez group' in the Conservative Party on the grounds that Cyprus, which in any case had no deep-water port, was equally exposed to hydrogen bombing. An even more important factor was the decision of Turkey to play a more active part in Middle East defence after her accession to NATO in September 1952. Turkey's move culminated in her defence pact with Pakistan in 1953 and her joining with Iraq to form the Baghdad pact in February 1955. Taken in conjunction with British adherence to the pact in April 1955, this meant that, from the British viewpoint, the defence line in the Middle East was now shifted away from the Suez Canal to the 'northern tier' of friendly Middle East countries with Turkey as the solid rim against Russia. A further consideration was that the 1936 treaty, the legal entitlement of Britain's use of the Suez base, would in any case come up for revision in 1956 and Egypt would be able to appeal to arbitration, which British circles feared might favour her viewpoint, on the issues in dispute. These developments, combined with financial reasons, which in any case demanded a reduction in the size of the British force in the base, now numbering some 75,000 men, and the abandonment of the plan for a Middle East defence organization, made a review of British defence strategy inevitable. The two questions remained, however, of the terms on which the base could be reactivated in emergencies if British forces were to leave and the manner in which a base too extensive for Egypt's own needs could be kept in a state of repair. Both questions involved Egypt's demand for full sovereignty over her territory and, over against this, the long-standing difference between British and Egyptian readings of the current world situation.

Ideally the British Government still preferred the evacuation from the base to be linked with the formation of a regional defence arrangement to include the base. This was also the American view. In talks with President Eisenhower and Secretary Dulles in Washington in March 1953 Eden gained their support for the idea of a phased British withdrawal on condition the base could be reactivated in the event of war and Egypt joined some regional defence scheme. The Americans were unwilling to press the point, however, when the Egyptian Government refused to allow the President's nominee, General Hull, to join the talks on the base, even though Egypt was in receipt of American economic aid which gave Washington abundant power to insist. Eden was in fact driven to make the strongest representations to Dulles when rumours reached London of an impending delivery of American arms to Cairo on the very eve of the talks.[1] Help was eventually to come to Britain not from Washington, but from the Indian and Pakistani Prime Ministers who conferred with Nasser on their way home from a Commonwealth Premiers' conference in London which had ended with the issue of a communiqué insisting that the base must be effectively maintained. Their influence was brought to bear on the Egyptian leader in the sense of the communiqué and a further initiative, this time by the Pakistani Chargé d'Affaires in Cairo, Tayeb Hussein, led to the resumption of informal talks by British and Egyptian teams at which progress was made with the two basic issues of the conditions of re-entry into the base and the status of British technicians who were to maintain the base after the evacuation.

After further difficulties and a postponement of the talks in the following year on account of the struggle for power between Neguib and Nasser, the Egyptian Government at length consented to the reactivation of the base in the event of an attack on the Arab League states or on Turkey, but not on Iran, thus providing a tenuous link between Egypt and the northern tier. Heads of agreement were finally signed in Cairo by the British Minister for War, Anthony Head, on July 27th and the treaty itself by the Minister of State at the Foreign Office, Anthony Nutting, in Cairo on October 19th. The agreement was to last for seven years and provided for the withdrawal of British forces from the Suez base within twenty months. The British Government undertook to maintain agreed installations at the base by means of British and Egyptian civilian technicians (thus, by denying them uniforms, avoiding injury to the Egyptian sense of sovereignty) while Egypt agreed that the base should be reactivated, that is, Britain should place it on a war footing again, in the event of an armed attack on either Egypt or any other member of the Arab League or Turkey. Egypt and Britain would consult together in the event of an attack or threat of attack on the above countries. The base agreement was accompanied by an Egyptian undertaking to continue to respect the Constantinople convention of 1888 on freedom of navigation through the Suez Canal and was sweetened by a financial arrangement by which Britain released £10 million in Egyptian sterling balances which she had previously blocked and Egypt freed sterling area imports from restrictions imposed during the troubles.[2] Although the agreement was sharply

[1] *Full Circle*, pp. 253–4.
[2] Egypt No. 2 (1954), Cmd. 9298.

criticized by Attlee, then leader of the Opposition in the Commons, on the ground that the Government had been compelled to take far worse terms for the evacuation than any they could have had since the war, and more bitterly by the Conservative 'Suez Group', twenty-seven of the members of which voted against their own Government, it was widely welcomed in Britain as ending a long and bitter struggle.

The Suez Canal: roots of conflict
Hence at the end of 1954 the two issues which had embittered Anglo-Egyptians relations since the war were both settled without either side having gained a decisive victory and yet with neither side, certainly not Egypt, having reason to feel that it had been the loser. In November an Egyptian agreement was concluded with the United States which seemed to represent Cairo's reward for partially accepting Western requirements on the Suez base: it involved a $40 million grant for development purposes, such as the improvement of communications and irrigation plants. Egypt, with her government finally stabilized under Colonel Nasser, who took the Premiership from Neguib in November, seemed set to become a firm friend of Britain and the West, if not an ally. Yet within a couple of years the two countries were to all intents at war over the Suez Canal. How did this remarkable change come about?

In the first place, there was a certain inevitability about the nationalization of the Suez Canal company which President Nasser announced in his speech at Alexandria on July 26, 1956.[1] A revolutionary nationalist regime is driven to appropriate any vestige of foreign control which exists in its territory; the campaign against foreign influence was in fact the essence of Nasser's revolution in Egypt in the same sense as the campaign against world capitalism was the essence of the Bolshevik revolution in Russia in 1917. The Suez Canal was the world's most striking example of foreign enterprise within the territory of a state passing through a nationalist revolution. In much the same way as the Versailles Treaty provided German nationalists with a programme of aims which they were inexorably driven to fulfil one after the other, Western rule left on Egyptian soil relics which the officers' revolution was bound to seek to eliminate. Of these the Suez Canal was the most dramatic, certainly the most vulnerable. Egypt had seen Moussadig nationalizing the Anglo-Iranian Oil Company with impunity in 1951 and the World Court declaring its lack of jurisdiction. Britain had refrained

---

[1] The Royal Institute of International Affairs, *Documents on International Affairs, 1956*, London, 1959, pp. 77–113.

from using force then, largely owing to American pressure, and if she challenged Nasser's action over the Canal in 1956 American restraints were likely to be even greater owing to the growing American desire to win over the uncommitted states and the occurrence of an American Presidential election in November 1956 in preparation for which the Republican incumbent, Mr Eisenhower, was being built up as a 'man of peace'. Moreover, while the nationalization of the Anglo-Iranian Oil Company involved Britain alone, most of the world maritime Powers would be affected by action over the Canal, and if one or two of these countries decided to come to terms with Nasser the commercial advantages to them would be very great. Nasser was too much of a realist not to understand the effect of economic need on countries who are proposing to stand together on a point of principle. True, Moussadig's action in 1951 had turned out unfavourably for Persia when a settlement was reached with Britain in 1954, since Persia had to be content with a smaller cut of the world oil market. But no such reverse could happen to Egypt since, barring the construction of a new canal through the Negeb, now in Israel, world trade must make use of this highway on an intensive scale. Thus, given the nationalist drive to acquire the Canal company, given the circumstances of the time which seemed to promise impunity when the first shock was over, nationalization probably figured on Nasser's programme long before the American and British decision to withdraw their promise of help for the projected High Dam at Aswan on July 19th and 20th respectively provided the pretext which ensured support at home and from countries not seriously inconvenienced by the nationalization.[1] Finally, since the lease of the Canal company was due to expire in 1968, Egypt, Nasser no doubt calculated, could not be utterly damned for anticipating what would be hers within a few years anyway. A successful seizure of the Canal in 1956 was likely to strike the Arab imagination better than waiting for the lease to end twelve years later, when Nasser and his colleagues might have passed from the scene.

Such were the factors which set the stage for the Anglo-Egyptian conflict precipitated by President Nasser's action of July 26th. At the same time more far-reaching forces were moving Egyptian policy, full account of which was not taken by British opinion during the crisis. We have seen in a previous chapter how Britain's adherence to the Turko-Iraqi pact in April 1955 caused division in the Arab world and threw Egypt into the leadership of the Arab faction which

[1] *Department of State Bulletin*, Washington, July 30, 1956; 557 H.C. Deb. 5s. Col. 252 (July 24, 1956).

opposed the pact.[1] For Nasser the Baghdad pact was a turning point. The fact that no other Arab state joined Iraq in the pact and that Nuri As-Said was left isolated as the solitary ally of the West among the Arab states gave Cairo a position of prominence in the eyes of Arab nationalists which the Suez nationalization consolidated. By 1955 the prospect of Arab leadership and the dream of realizing Arab unity lay at Nasser's feet. Ibn Saud had died in 1952 and Saudi Arabia began to loosen its ties with the West under his son and successor, King Saud. Syria, always restless, was ripe for the reformist brand of anti-western pan-Arabism which Nasser had made peculiarly his own. Although in Jordan the young King Hussein, who succeeded his brother in 1953 after the assassination of Abdullah in 1952, was later to become a considerable figure in his own right, he had to govern a state physically entangled with the Israeli enemy and with its politics wrenched by the inclusion of refugees from Palestine, now constituting two-thirds of Jordan's population. Amman was thus a natural object for Nasser's appetite; with the abrupt expulsion of Sir John Glubb and two other senior British officers from the Jordanian army, the Arab Legion, in March 1956, and the frantic efforts of Egypt, Syria and Saudi Arabia to supplant Britain as the source of financial help to Jordan, Hussein seemed on the brink of succumbing to Nasser's embrace. Moreover, during the middle 1950s a new world of independent Arab states was coming into existence, the so-called Maghrib in North Africa. Tunisia and Morocco received their independence in 1956 and in the intervening country between these two, Algeria, the struggle of the Moslems for freedom from France provided another Palestine the Arab cause in which any aspiring Arab leader must espouse, though to do so was to rule out the kind of Arab association with the West which Britain had been angling for in the form of a Middle East defence organization. Thus in 1956 Egypt, who in any case was marked out as the natural leader of the Arabs on account of her wealth and cultural attractions, found herself, not on the African fringe of the free Arab states, but in the centre, with the Fertile Crescent extending to the east and the Maghrib to the west. The Suez Canal had in fact become the midriff of the Arab world.

To this should be added the effects of the struggle with Israel. To almost every Arab without exception Israel was beyond all doubt the main source of danger and at the same time standing proof of the designs of Western imperialism. No Arab could admit that the Israeli victory in 1949 had been due to other reasons than the refusal

[1] See above, Chapter IV, pp. 127–8.

of the West to supply the Arabs with adequate arms and the means to acquire them; since weapons bought by the Jews on world markets with American money had, in the Arab view, won them Palestine, only weapons could revise the armistice lines of 1949, or, at best, drive the Jews into the sea. But the Arabs found it just as difficult to buy arms against Israel after the war as before. Under the Tripartite Declaration of 1950 Britain, the United States and France recognized that the Arab states and Israel needed armaments for internal security and legitimate self-defence and to permit them to play their part in the defence of the area as a whole, but opposed the development of an arms race. Moreover, Britain had made clear that while arms would be forthcoming for states who accepted her defence policy in the Middle East they would be denied to those who could not so commit themselves. Yet it appeared to Nasser that any danger from the Soviet Union would come, not in the form of a military attack, but in that of propaganda and subversion. To commit Egypt to a Western pact, he considered, would not only be to lose his freedom in foreign policy but to attract the very Communist subversion which Western policy sought to defend Egypt against.

The dilemma became crucial in February 1955 when Egyptian forces in the Gaza strip suffered a crushing defeat at the hands of Israel. Private Egyptian border raids had been going on in the Gaza strip since the end of the Palestine war, but the Egyptian army had never been involved. When the Israelis overran the frontier in force in February, Nasser's army was manhandled. Again the cry was heard that the West, having planted Israel in Arab territory, was starving the Arabs of the means to defend themselves against it. The logical corollary was the agreement concluded by Cairo with Czechoslovakia, which meant of course the Soviet Union, in September 1955. Between the two events lay Nasser's attendance at the Bandoeng conference in April and the signing of a friendship treaty with India. At one stroke Egypt found, or appeared to find, the arms which she could only get from the West at the cost of tying her defence policy to an East-West conflict which seemed increasingly irrelevant to the struggle with Israel. At the same time, the policy of positive neutrality which was growing in Nasser's hands, and which had received a fillip from Nuri As-Said's failure to win support in the Arab world for the Baghdad pact, promised at Bandoeng to give a new access to international importance to Egypt owing to the growing force of neutralism in Asia. This new company of the uncommitted in which Nasser moved during 1955 provided a sympathetic audience for the nationalization of the Canal. The sight of an uncommitted African country defying the West by obtaining arms from countries which expected no commitments in return, while taking over a profitable venture and using it to raise living standards which had been allegedly neglected under Western influence, was bound to raise Nasser's prestige, not only among the Arabs, but throughout the neutralist world.

The West's reaction to the Egyptian arms deal with the Soviet bloc, in the Arab eyes, seemed to demonstrate that the West was less interested in Arab independence than in its own struggle with the Communist states. At the end of 1955 Britain and the United States had agreed to supplement a World Bank loan to Nasser to finance the projected High Dam at Aswan. This project had been talked about in Egypt for at least twenty years;[1] the cost would be enormous and there was no immediate prospect of financing it either from Arab resources or from the Soviet bloc. It was the kind of undertaking which, if successfully launched, would give Egypt a secure predominance in the Arab world. For this reason Nasser was anxious to conciliate the West and during 1955 kept the anti-imperialist campaign under control. In fact during 1955, so long as there was a prospect that the finance for the Dam would come from the West, Egyptian policy was in a dilemma. The West had an interest in reducing Arab-Israeli tensions; with this end in view Eden made a speech at Guildhall on November 9, 1955, proposing in effect that Israel make territorial concessions in favour of the Arab states, and the government refused to arm Israel even after the Soviet bloc arms deal with Egypt.[2] Yet the conflict between Nasser and Nuri required Cairo to accentuate the struggle with Israel as a means of winning Arab opinion away from Iraq, which was accused of having betrayed the Arab cause and deserted the Arab Collective Security Pact of 1950. When the United States, followed by Britain suddenly withdrew the offer to help finance the Dam on July 19, 1956, the dilemma was suddenly resolved. The news was disclosed on Nasser's return from a conference with his fellow neutralists, Tito and Nehru, at Brioni in Yugoslavia. In his Alexandria speech on July 26th he boasted of these meetings as symbolizing Egypt's accession to the ranks of Powers which were shaping world history. To accept at this point a rebuff from the West which threatened both to destroy the dream of the Dam on which all Nasser's hopes were

---

[1] Colonel Nasser said the project had been in existence since 1924 (RIIA, *Documents on International Affairs 1956*, p. 95).

[2] *The Times*, November 10, 1955; 549 H.C. Deb. 5s. Cols. 2128–9 (Gaitskell, March 7, 1956).

pinned and to force Egypt into an international alignment contrary to the direction in which Nasser's foreign policy was moving might have shorn away the basis of his power. It was essential to make a move dramatic enough to rally Arab and uncommitted opinion and capable of putting the West in a position from which it could not effectively reply. Thus, although the nationalization of the Canal came under the general heading of the 'total expulsion of Western influence' to which the Egyptian revolution was dedicated, its timing necessarily coincided with the resolution of the dilemma of Egyptian foreign policy which the withdrawal of the Western offer to finance the Dam had forced on Egypt.

If an Egyptian nationalization of the Canal Company was predictable (though there is no evidence that the British Foreign Office predicted it, even after the denunciation of the 1936 treaty and the Sudan condominium agreement by Nahas Pasha in 1951), the British Government were equally bound to contest it. Britain was the largest single user of the Canal, accounting in 1955 for 28·3 per cent of an annually increasing tonnage passing through the Canal.[1] The Canal Company, though its shareholders were foreign, the British Government holding 44 per cent of the shares, was registered under Egyptian law and, at first sight, nothing in law prevented a Government nationalizing a foreign-owned concern operating on its own soil. On the other hand the Canal Company was part of an international agreement, the Suez Canal Convention of 1888 which was deemed to bind Egypt since it formed part of the obligations she had taken over from the Sultan of Turkey, who had signed the convention on Egypt's behalf; Egypt had reaffirmed the 1888 Convention when she signed the Suez base agreement in 1954. The legal position was thus not watertight from the British viewpoint, but there was little doubt that Nasser was not entitled to make off with a property which was part of international treaty when he was in no position to fulfil the undoubted legal obligation to pay compensation since he had implied in his speech on July 26th that he meant to use the Canal to finance the Aswan Dam. The alleged £35 million a year profit of the company, Nasser said, would be taken.[2] Above all, the unilateral and sudden seizure of the company threw doubt on Nasser's assurances, which he was careful to make and to try to uphold throughout the crisis, that freedom of navigation through the Canal would be respected in accordance with the 1888 Convention.

[1] 552 H.C. Deb. 5s. Col. 1969 (May 15, 1956, Mr Dodds-Parker, the Joint Under-Secretary of State for Foreign Affairs).
[2] RIIA, *Documents on International Affairs, 1956*, 1959, p. 11.

Countries such as the United States which had not been in conflict
with Egypt since the end of the war found it hard to see why these
assurances should not be accepted, seeing that, if Nasser really
intended to use the Canal to finance the Dam, he could hardly want
to turn away the ships which were his customers. There were three
good reasons why the British Government could not take the same
view, though in the event it proved to be the correct one. First,
Britain had been involved in bitter disputes with Egypt during the
previous ten years. Egyptian statesmen had used every resource to
strengthen their position in this conflict and, as we have seen, they
did their utmost to win over the Sudanese parties to their side and
thus frustrate the 1953 agreement on self-determination for the
Sudan. British Ministers could not doubt that while Nasser had the
power to interfere with British trade and oil supplies normally passing
in such vast quantities through this lifeline of the British Commonwealth he would do so whenever a conflict arose. An agreement with
Egypt on the Suez base had just been reached after long and hard
bargaining. Was it likely that if disputes arose in future about the
agreement Nasser would not make the kind of difficulties about
British ships using the Canal which would be too trivial taken singly
to justify forceful retaliation, but which together might force Britain
to acquiesce in the Egyptian viewpoint? Egypt had consistently
denied the Canal and the Straits of Tirana leading into the Red Sea
to Israeli trade since the end of the Palestine war, despite repeated
resolutions of the Security Council appealing to the 1888 principles.
British ships had suffered the same treatment, not only in trade with
Israel but even when taking arms to the Arab Legion in Jordan
through the port of Akaba at the head of the Red Sea.

Secondly, Britain had had a long and bitter experience of the one-
sided denunciation of international treaties which, if successful, only
whets the appetite for further violations. There was in the British
political consciousness the half-guilty memory of how the dictators
before the war had followed up their acts of force with assurances
which the good-natured democracies had accepted until they found
themselves in a position where there was no alternative but to fight
for survival. 'The pattern,' Eden said in a broadcast on August 8th,
'is familiar to many of us, my friends; we all know this is how
fascist governments behave and we all remember, only too well,
what the cost can be in giving in to fascism.'[1] This was a deep-seated
emotion affecting, by a curious perversion, the liberal-minded people
who otherwise were most averse to using force against Asian or

[1] *The Listener*, August 16, 1956.

Arab nationalism. Twenty years before Suez another dictator had sent his forces into the demilitarized Rhineland. Though British opinion was almost unanimously willing to condone this on the ground that the Rhineland was, after all, German territory, it was realized later that Hitler's action decisively turned the military balance of power in Europe to Germany's advantage. The Foreign Secretary then, Eden, was the Prime Minister in 1956. Only a year before he had succeeded the great architect of opposition to Axis defiance, Churchill, who, almost alone, had called attention to the lawlessness of the dictators in the 1930s. Eden tells in his memoirs how the old man, when he was told of the proposed military action against Nasser in October 1956, went home saying he would look up where Napoleon landed in Egypt.[1] Eden, who, when he resigned from the Government in 1938 rather than do further business with Mussolini, was called by Churchill 'one strong young figure standing up against long, dismal drawling tides of drift and surrender',[2] must have felt that his great predecessor would certainly approve.

But when it is asked how Eden and many other able and experienced politicians, such as the Leader of the Opposition, Hugh Gaitskell, could have confused Egypt with Germany, whatever the resemblances between Nasser and Hitler or Mussolini, the answer lies in the third factor which predisposed British opinion to react violently to the nationalization of the Canal. On balance, British public opinion accepted the decline of British power in the postwar world with tired resignation rather than truculence. The remarkable transformation of the British Empire effected by the grant of independence to India and Pakistan in 1947 was not only without precedent in its extent but also in the relative lack of dissension in Britain on the abandonment of the chief jewel in the imperial crown. One reason for this was that 'little Englandism' had always occupied a respected place in British Radical thought and when, after the war, Britain felt no longer in the mood to continue to bear the cares and cost of empire this tradition revived. Nevertheless, residues of resentment remained, often at an unconscious level. The feeling of having been pushed out of one place abroad after another was bound to produce an outburst, especially if the pushing was dramatic and seemingly without excuse. Along with this went latent resentment about American carping at British imperialism, mingled with some jealousy at the transfer of leadership of the democratic world to the United States. When American politicians seemed to be positively

[1] *Full Circle*, p. 534.
[2] Winston S. Churchill, *The Second World War*, Vol. I, London, 1948, p. 201.

P

egging on foreign nationalists against British rule and American diplomats privately comforted the Moussadigs and Neguibs with assurances that Washington did not entirely share the British view, the impulse to hit back was understandable. In the case of Egypt in 1956 these factors were brought to a focus by the general British lack of admiration for a country which had seemed to harass Britain for so long and was thought to be intriguing against Britain in the Middle East and Africa and denouncing British imperialism from its radio stations. Thus much of the support for Eden's apparent vendetta against Nasser came from ex-servicemen in Britain who had seen service in Egypt during the war and afterwards, and came home with uncomplimentary views of the 'Wogs'. Eden's championship of British rights against a restless dictator also echoed the rising resentment in Britain at the increasing strength of coloured peoples, not only in the world as a whole but in Britain as well. Eden's memoirs tell how his wife received a letter of sympathy from a London bus driver who observed, during the 'Law not War' demonstrations in the capital against the armed action in Egypt, that 'eighty per cent of the demonstrators were of foreign extraction and can be ignored'.[1] The fact that this element of blind dislike of the foreigner, who appeared to have kicked Britain off her old pinnacle, played a large part in the mood of the times is evident from the speed with which the Suez mood passed away in Britain. The incident dropped from sight, despite the fact that in 1956 it had aroused more controversy than any other international issue since Munich. People seemed conscious that they had given free rein to their ill temper and, having perhaps felt better for doing so, wanted to forget.

British policy and practical questions

There was no question therefore that the Egyptian seizure of the Canal should be met with the strongest protest and energetic efforts to secure redress. On this Parliamentary opinion was at one when the crisis was debated in the House of Commons on August 2nd; the same view was taken by the British Press. Eden took his stand on the two points, first, that Nasser's action was a breach of obligations and secondly that, as for the future, this vital international waterway should not be under the control of the politics of any one State.[2] The two claims had about them a surface plausibility, but difficulties inevitably arose when they were reduced to practical terms. The

[1] *Full Circle*, p. 546.
[2] 557 H.C. Deb. 5s. Col. 777 (Eden, July 27, 1956); *ibid.*, Cols. 1603–6 (Eden, August 2, 1956).

argument of the seizure as a breach of obligation (Eden's chapter in the memoirs on the first act of the Suez crisis is entitled 'Theft') was never put to the test of an international tribunal, such as the World Court, by the British Government. There was some reason for not doing so; it could be foreseen that by the time the case had been decided, Nasser would probably have consolidated his *fait accompli*, and in the meantime the upkeep of the Canal would either have deteriorated to the point where shipping was affected or, if he succeeded in running the Canal efficiently, world opinion would see no reason why he should not go on doing so, whatever the Court said. Nevertheless, British insistence that the nationalization was a breach of law, coupled with the refusal to put this to the test, undoubtedly weakened the legal argument in the ensuing controversy. Moreover, the fact of the Government having begun by basing itself on the sanctity of treaties meant that they were virtually under an obligation to keep within the law thereafter, or be accused of insufferable hypocrisy. The French, who tended to take the view that Nasser was a factor of general unrest in North Africa and should not be allowed to grow on that account alone, might have seemed more immoral, but at least they were consistently so. The Opposition in Britain were roused to fury because the Government, having ascribed to Nasser an illegal act, then proceeded to commit what the critics represented as another illegality in order to redress it. The argument of illegality, though it was a natural one for a British Government to make, also led to the contorted claim which the Government made on the eve of their withdrawal from the armed action in Suez, namely that they had to make war in Egypt in order to force the world's policeman, the United Nations, to take action.

The second argument, that the Canal could not be left to the unfettered will of any one state,[1] also had its weaknesses as a political argument in the world controversy which developed. For it seemed to imply that a non-European state was less capable than a European of administering an international amenity and less inclined to do so impartially. This argument might have had more force had the Egyptians failed to maintain efficient passage for ships through the Canal. But they did not. Since the reaction of world opinion to the nationalization would probably depend upon the success with which Egypt managed the Canal during the early days of nationalization, Nasser did his utmost to keep it going, despite British and French pressure on the Canal pilots to refuse to serve under the new Egyptian administration. After the initial angry statement in the

[1] 577 H.C. Deb. 5s. Col. 919 (July 30th).

speech of July 26th that he would 'use the Canal to finance the Dam' nothing more was heard of this threat and no complaints were registered that the Canal was less efficiently maintained than before the crisis. The more this seemed likely to be the case the more British doubts sounded like slurs on the capacity of non-Europeans. Taken along with the Arab allegation that they were not allowed to purchase arms from the West because they could not be trusted to use them responsibly, the effect could not but be to lower respect for Britain among the all-important Afro-Asian delegates at the United Nations. Two apparently fortuitous factors helped Nasser to win this victory in the matter of the management of the Canal during the early days of crisis. First, the mere fact that the British and French Governments advised their shippers to sail round the Cape rather than pay Canal dues to the Egyptian administration meant that traffic through the Canal was less during the first days of the crisis than it had been up to July 26th, thus allowing a breathing space for the transition of control to take place smoothly. Secondly, it soon became evident (and this was one of the many points during the crisis on which the British Government were poorly served by their experts) that pilotage through the Canal was much less difficult than had been assumed. The highly-paid Canal pilots naturally spoke of the impossibility of their being replaced by untrained Egyptians. But events showed that this problem had been overrated. Even the winter fogs in the Canal, which British newspapers at the time considered likely to upset the whole Nasserite plan and force Egypt to ask the Company to take over again, did not hinder the success of the operation. What the world saw, when Britain and France at length attacked Egypt on October 31st, was Egyptians sinking blockships in the Canal, which up to that time they had managed with tolerable efficiency, in order to prevent it falling into the hands of Governments who justified their armed action with the argument that they meant to keep the Canal open to international traffic.

But, apart from the political implications of the British argument that the Canal must not be left under the unfettered control of any one country, there was the question of how this was to be assured in practice. No one, not even Eden, denied that the Canal lay in territory under Egyptian sovereignty. This was affirmed with one voice by the Security Council when the issue was at length discussed by the Council on September 24th. The problem was what form of control of the Canal was to be exercised by the world trading community. The conclusion of the eighteen Powers which supported the British view at the conference at Lancaster House, London, which had been summoned for August 16th at British, American and French invitation, was that an international board representing the maritime Powers and Egypt should manage the Canal, thus replacing the nationalized Company.[1] The Australian Prime Minister, Robert Menzies, led a mission of five[2] to Egypt in early September to take this proposal to Nasser; Menzies described the proposed board as a 'tenant' which would enjoy the use of the waterway the ownership of which would remain with Egypt.[3] Although there might be some parallel to this in the international consortiums which exercised similar functions in non-European countries and in such international concerns exploiting a resource in another country as the Anglo-Iranian Oil Company, the board proposed by the eighteen Powers would be an inter-governmental organization, not a private body, and there was certainly no precedent for such an inter-state organ running an amenity as important as the Canal within the territory of a sovereign state. The only condition which would seem to justify such a derogation from Egyptian sovereignty was that Egypt was incapable of running the Canal with due efficiency. To admit such a suggestion was inconsistent with Egyptian pride and with Nasser's pretensions for Egypt as a leader of the Arabs.

The form of internationalization which Nasser proposed in return to the Menzies mission was a mere reaffirmation of the 1888 Convention on freedom of navigation through the Canal. It was in the conflict between these two conceptions of internationalization that the Security Council divided. The resolution unanimously adopted on September 24th, after the return of the Menzies mission on September 9th, held that, while the principle of Egyptian sovereignty should be affirmed, freedom of navigation must be the basic principle in the management of the Canal. On the other hand, the Anglo-French resolution calling for international management of the Canal was defeated by a Soviet veto which echoed the protest of India, and other neutralist states, that Egyptian sovereignty would be infringed if such a body were imposed. The reason why the British Government argued that the six principles which won the assent of all the members of the Council were inadequate was that experience had shown that Egypt would not uphold freedom of navigation but would use the Canal to serve her own political ends. That experience was the blockade of Israel. It was, however, abundantly clear that, although Britain had protested against Egypt's infringement of Security Coun-

---

[1] Egypt No. 1 (1956), Cmd. 9853, pp. 10–13.
[2] Representing Australia, Ethiopia, Persia, Sweden and the United States.
[3] Egypt No. 2 (1956), Cmd. 9856, p. 7.

cil resolutions deploring the denial of the Canal to ships bound for Israel, she had taken no further action. Indeed a serious incident in January 1955, when an Israeli ship, the *Bat Galim*, had been seized at Suez and the crew arrested, had been followed by British agreement with the United States to help finance the Aswan Dam, the effect of which assistance must surely have been to strengthen Egypt against Israel. If Britain was not content with a mere reaffirmation of the 1888 Convention, which was the utmost the Security Council would agree to, and beyond which it was perfectly clear that Nasser was unwilling to go, the inference seemed to be that she was not afraid on Israel's behalf but on her own. This led to the conclusion that 'Canal politics' could be played in London as well as in Cairo.

To press the British concept of internationalization in such unfavourable circumstances and against Nasser's stubborn resistance required a variety of expedients. The simple solution of sending a gunboat or two, which had settled countless quarrels between Britain and Middle Eastern States in the nineteenth century, was impossible in the age of the United Nations, even if Britain had the gunboats, or their equivalent, and if no other Power had been able to oppose their despatch. This did not mean that military preparations were not made from the outset of the crisis, though their co-ordination with the essential diplomatic moves was a problem of first-class importance and difficulty. To launch a sizeable military force from Britain and from British bases adjacent to Egypt required lengthy preparation, yet at the same time the unavoidable delay in giving the starting orders owing to unfinished diplomatic processes threatened not only the morale of the troops but the success of the whole operation. A second method, economic sanctions, was practically limited to the freezing of Egyptian balances in London. This was inconvenient to Nasser, but hardly more than that. Moreover, economic sanctions, in the form of the withdrawal of the offer to finance the Aswan Dam, had touched off the crisis. Inflicting economic hardships would probably strengthen Egypt's determination to make friends elsewhere rather than bring her to heel. Concerted diplomatic measures were therefore essential and necessarily this meant obtaining United States support for the British viewpoint. Eden, himself a strong protagonist of the NATO alliance, lost no time in attempting this and Washington, bearing in mind the economic value to the alliance of the Suez Canal, had an obvious interest in lending support. This, however, was not forthcoming, despite the risk that Nasser's *coup*, if permitted to succeed, might stimulate Panama, whose territory the

United States had leased to build the canal there, to follow his example.

Eden had good reason for anger at the lukewarm support from Washington during the crisis, which culminated in the United States joining with the Soviet Union to call for an end to the Anglo-French intervention in the Egypt-Israeli war following the ultimatum of the two Powers. The refusal of the United States to support Britain forced the British Government to use its first veto on the Security Council on October 31st, precipitated the calling of an emergency session of the General Assembly of the United Nations on November 1st, at which the British and French intervention was overwhelmingly condemned by delegates under combined Soviet-American and Afro-Asian leadership, and at length provided the strongest factor in Britain's decision to withdraw her forces from Egypt. What irked Eden was not so much the frank difference of American views on Nasser's seizure of the Canal from his own, as the way in which Secretary of State Dulles appeared to go along with the Prime Minister, himself suggesting expedients for dealing with the crisis peacefully while securing the principal British desiderata, and, when once the Anglo-American front was firm, promptly made statements which Nasser was bound to read as confessions that Western resistance was merely token. The United States was bound to see the nationalization differently from Britain, though Dulles's apparent sympathy for the British case at the outset somewhat obscured this. The background to the American attitude was sneaking sympathy for Arab resistance to British control, all the stronger after Farouk and his licentious court had disappeared, coupled with American desire not to offend the Arab states which were sought as allies in the struggle with Russia. It could be argued in reply that Washington had not hesitated to withdraw the offer to assist the Aswan Dam, informing but not consulting Britain when doing so, in retaliation against Egypt's arms deal with Czechoslovakia in September 1955. But an influence equally important in that decision was the revision of the American view as to Egypt's capacity to service foreign loans for the Dam, especially after her cotton crop had been pledged to pay for the Soviet bloc arms. After all, the arms deal was in September 1955; the withdrawal of the offer of finance for the Dam was not effected until July 10th, when the financial implications of Nasser's arms policy were becoming clearer. Besides, 1956 was election year in America and nothing was more capable of destroying the image of the Republicans as the 'peace party' than to be seen helping Britain and France to impose their will on a Middle Eastern state.

All this was understandable, but Dulles certainly appeared to lead Eden into believing that the United States would remain at least benevolently neutral if force had to be used. The French never really believed this. At the decisive meeting between the British and French Prime Ministers and their Foreign Secretaries in Paris on October 16th, when the ultimatum and the intervention were prepared, it was the British belief in American neutrality which apparently carried the day. This belief had already suffered more than one shock. Dulles told Eden when he came to London for a Three-Power meeting at Foreign Minister level on August 1st that Egypt must be forced to 'disgorge' the Canal. Yet he seemed to be in no hurry to attend a meeting of the maritime Powers and, despite British warnings of the dangers of delay, the conference was put off until August 16th. At this conference Dulles insisted that the main stand should be on the 1888 Convention; with the Panama parallel in mind, he did not care to press the general principle of internationalization, to which British policy was dedicated. After the failure of the Menzies mission and with the apparent object of postponing resort to more drastic measures, he came out with the outline of a Canal Users' Association (SCUA). Eden had no alternative but to accept this and another conference was called to design the new body. This represented the eighteen Powers of the August Conference and met in London from September 19th to 21st. The principle was that as many maritime nations as possible should be induced to club together for the purpose of employing pilots, collecting dues from members, part of which would be kept to defray the expenses of the Association and the rest passed on to Egypt, and co-ordinating traffic through the Canal. The Association could only be a makeshift and even so its success would be largely dependent upon two conditions, which Eden assumed would have American approval. The first was that member-states would bring pressure to bear on ships sailing under their flags to pay their Canal dues to the Association and act under its directives, using legal compulsion if possible. The second was that if the Association was to serve its primary purpose of demonstrating to Nasser the determination of the maritime Powers not to submit to his *coup* it must in the last resort have the backing of force. Eden made these two conditions clear in a speech describing the purpose and functions of the Association in the House of Commons on September 12th.[1]

Dulles not merely negatived these two conditions, thus removing the basis of SCUA, but did so in circumstances almost suggesting

[1] 558 H.C. Deb. 5s. Cols. 10–15.

collusion with Nasser in defeating British purposes. The United States Government failed to compel American shippers to act through SCUA and though ships sailing under the United States flag formed a small proportion of the total number of vessels using the Canal, this failure reflected upon American seriousness in regard to an organization they themselves had suggested. Far more damaging to the prospects of SCUA was a statement made by Dulles at a Press conference on September 13th, immediately after Eden's speech in the Commons on the Association. In this he professed ignorance of the actual words used in the House of Commons by Eden, in itself an alarming statement in regard to a diplomat as precise as the Prime Minister, and then said that Eden surely could not mean that force would be used to impose SCUA on Nasser. The Association, Dulles said, never had any 'teeth' in it and there was no suggestion of fitting 'teeth' now.[1] Such a declaration on the eve of the second approach to Nasser, this time to negotiate the establishment of SCUA, was an intimation to the Egyptian President that if he held his ground no harm would come to him. Eden thereupon determined that no further good could come from working with the United States. The most he thought he could hope for was that Washington would stand quietly by while Britain went into action. Even this hope was disappointed.

Dulles's behaviour may be explained to some extent by personal factors, which played a more important part in the shaping of American foreign policy at this time than if the Secretary of State had not exercised the domination over that policy which he did. Dulles's diplomatic style ran to the grand gesture, often only summarily discussed with senior colleagues in the State Department before being given to the world, to be speedily followed by qualifications which robbed it of all meaning, the whole enterprise leaving friends more daunted than enemies. This had been the case with the doctrine of 'massive retaliation', launched in 1954, which was no sooner uttered than it required to be sub-edited until few understood it as a precise maxim for practical policy. The same was true for the Middle East defence organization, which Dulles encouraged, allowed Britain to join, then held back himself when Arab opposition mounted against it. The idea of an 'agonizing reappraisal' of American policy towards Europe, formulated during the last days of EDC, fell into the same category. SCUA belonged to this family of abortive ideas sprung from Dulles's fertile brain, much of the resulting inconvenience of which fell upon other countries. Moreover, considerable

[1] RIIA, *Documents on International Affairs, 1956*, 1959, pp. 210–19.

personal rivalry existed between Eden and Dulles. They had been at cross purposes over the war in Indo-China in 1954; Eden had snatched victory from the defeat of EDC in the same year, when Dulles was washing his hands of Europe; Dulles had been far less willing to work with Eden in the negotiations leading up to the Suez base agreement in 1954 than either President Eisenhower or Dulles's Assistant Secretary, Bedell Smith. It is thus not surprising that Dulles should have been slow to help Eden out of his difficulties in 1956. Dulles could not get Eden, as he failed to get most European statesmen, to recognize what was to him the primary importance of the conflict with Soviet Communism. To Dulles, the Suez crisis was an unfortunate diversion from the main battle front in the war against atheistic Communism. To Eden, it was a challenge to Europe, and to British influence, in the whole non-European world. For Dulles, armed action against Egypt was an incitement to the Arab States to call in the Russians as their allies. To Eden, it symbolized those acts of restraint which, had they been applied in time in the 1930s, would have prevented a war which, apart from being a tragedy in itself, had brought Britain to a state of powerlessness where she could not defend her most vital interests without American permission.

The military phase

In the absence of Washington's support but on the assumption of its neutrality the Cabinet determined, when the two London conferences had failed and the Security Council debate had not wrested the Canal from Nasser's hands, to work with France. This decision moved the controversy with Egypt to a new plane. Previously the emphasis had been on the inability of the maritime community to allow a highway on which it depended for its trade and supplies to be held at the discretion of a doubtfully law-abiding State. Now the attack broadened out against Nasser as a general factor of disturbance in the Arab world. This was satisfactory to France for she had every interest in stopping Nasser's support, though this was more verbal than material, for the Algerian rebels against which increasing detachments of her army had to be pitted. But it had the effect of weakening support for the anti-Nasser front among the other maritime Powers, since countries like Norway and Sweden had no concern with the Anglo-French political conflict with Nasser. It also tended to strengthen suspicions in the Asian Commonwealth countries that Eden was more interested in dethroning an Arab nationalist than in the principle of international freedom to use the

Canal; and it made Britain the enemy of all the Arab States, whereas the Baghdad Pact had made her the enemy of all but one, Iraq. The more was this so in that the plan decided by the British and French Ministers at their Paris meeting on October 16th contemplated one-sided assistance to Israel, the common enemy of the Arabs, when the impending invasion of Egypt by the Israeli army took place. To invade an Arab country in order to displace its leader was sufficient to destroy the prestige of any Western country which attempted it; to do so as a scarcely-veiled ally of Israel was to make it unlikely that that prestige would ever revive.

The full story of the Paris meeting on October 16th has not yet been disclosed. But there is enough evidence to show that Eden had prior knowledge of the Israeli attack on Egypt and that, by his own account, he brought pressure to bear on France to make sure that if and when Israel did make her attack it would be on Egypt rather than on any other Arab State. If Israel attacked Jordan (though there was only the remotest prospect that she would) Britain would have to go to Jordan's assistance under the treaty of alliance and friendship concluded in 1948. Eden therefore urged that if there were to be a break-out Israel should be encouraged 'to break out against Egypt'.[1] He may not have known, nor did he desire to know, the full extent of French collaboration with Israel in the attack on Egypt which was unleashed on October 25th. But the statement in the *Memoirs* that Egypt provoked the attack and that 'the marked victim of the garrotte' (that is Israel) 'is not to be condemned if he strikes out before the noose is round his throat'[2] cannot be sustained in view of the total and instantaneous success of the Israeli attack. If Eden considered that this success was attained without French assistance in the form of Mystère fighters and naval support in the Levant to protect Israel against Egyptian retaliation, his intelligence sources must have been more than usually at fault. Moreover, even if the Israeli invasion was not expected or planned by the British and French Ministers, the Anglo-French ultimatum delivered to the warring sides on October 30th could only have been written by allies of Israel who were as much interested in her success as in their reported purpose of defending the Canal.

The ultimatum called upon the belligerents to retire to beyond ten miles east and west respectively of the Canal. If the ultimatum was not complied with within twelve hours Britain and France undertook to 'intervene in whatever strength may be necessary to

[1] *Full Circle*, p. 513.
[2] *Full Circle*, p. 523.

secure compliance' (using for the purpose the forces which had been mustered since the beginning of the crisis in July).[1] Israel agreed, since she was asked to withdraw to Egyptian territory a hundred miles from her own frontiers, thus leaving the whole of the Sinai peninsula in Israel's possession. Egypt, who would have had to disengage her forces and draw them back ten miles west of the Canal, refused and the Anglo-French intervention began. It is difficult to resist the conclusion that the Israeli attack was somewhat more than a happy accident which gave Britain and France the pretext to occupy the Canal. It seemed rather part of a general compact between the two Western Powers and Israel—though Eden may be excused from the charge that he was privy to the arrangements with Israel—to set on foot a train of developments which would result in the expulsion of Nasser from Egypt. An admirer of Eden, Randolph Churchill, an intimate of many of the leading British politicians of the day, describes the evidence of collusion as 'massive and conclusive' in his biography of the Prime Minister.[2]

An enterprise launched in such suspicious circumstances was almost bound to fail. In fact no sooner had troops landed, six days after an intensive Anglo-French air bombardment of Port Said, than they were given orders to stop when, in their advance along the 100-mile length of the Canal, they were within sixty miles of its southern extremity, Suez. Forces were operating in London to put an end to the adventure, though the French would have willingly continued. No doubt if Britain had been better prepared to launch an amphibious exercise (and one of the effects of the Suez affair was to show how unprepared she was) the whole Canal could have been seized before these forces had time to work themselves out. The French were fully prepared to continue the operation when Britain gave the ceasefire order on November 6th. So were the British General Staff, who advised Eden that Suez could be reached within forty-eight hours and that it was dangerous to leave the Anglo-French force strung along the Canal highway on an exposed open road. Eden mistrusted this estimate of the time it would take to reach Suez, possibly angered by the inaccurate expert advice he had already received from various quarters during the crisis. But the most powerful factor in the ceasefire was the forces which made the enterprise as a whole practically and morally impossible.

The least of these forces was the Soviet threat, addressed in a letter to Eden by Marshal Bulganin, the then Soviet Prime Minister,

[1] 558 H.C. Deb. 5s. Cols. 1274–5 (Eden, October 30, 1956).
[2] *The Rise and Fall of Sir Anthony Eden*, London, 1959, p. 265.

on November 5th that Russian rockets would fall on Britain if the armed action was not called off.[1] This bore every appearance of being largely intended to demonstrate Soviet fraternity with the victims of colonialism. The Soviet Union had no commitment to come to Egypt's defence; the Anglo-French action could hardly develop into a threat to Soviet security. So far from the Soviet threat being a disincentive to Britain and France, they might well have wished the threat was real, since only if it were was the United States likely to come to their aid. The manifest and almost unanimous opposition of the United Nations to the Suez enterprise, as shown in the General Assmbly resolution condemning it on November 2nd, was certainly much more important, particularly on account of its effects on British public opinion. The more isolationist wings of that opinion, represented by such newspapers as the *Daily Express*, argued with some plausibility that the unrepresentativeness of the General Assembly and the far greater relish with which the Assembly condemned the Anglo-French action, as compared with its condemnation of the simultaneous crushing of a nationalist uprising in Hungary by Soviet armed forces, implied that its voice need not be taken too seriously when vital British interests were at stake. This view perhaps coincided with that of the man-in-the-street, who, it later appeared, applauded Eden's resort to force in much the same way as the British public throughout history has risen to the challenge offered by foreign dictators. In this respect the impression given by the more politically conscious people in the British capital, who took United Nations reprimands more seriously, was incorrect for the people as a whole.

Nevertheless, United Nations censure, coupled with the fact that in that body most of the Commonwealth was arrayed against Britain, was deeply shocking not merely to the Parliamentary Opposition, but to many supporters of the Government as well. Though there were only two resignations from the Cabinet, the Under-Secretary of State at the Foreign Office, Anthony Nutting, and the Parliamentary Secretary to the Treasury, Sir Edward Boyle, the indications were that only the strong tradition of cohesion in the Conservative Party prevented an open split on the issue of defiance of the United Nations and of a considerable proportion of the Commonwealth. The Government's majority in the House fell to forty on one occasion, the figure required to defeat the Chamberlain Government in 1940, and the Minister who was in effect deputy leader of the party, R. A. Butler, is reported to have asked an acquaintance when the crisis

[1] *Soviet News*, November 6, 1956.

was over whether he thought he should have resigned.[1] The outburst of world opinion against Britain, as compared with the more quali-fied outcry against Russia over the Hungarian affair and the rela-tively minor attacks on France, was at once flattering and melancholy. The world seemed to look to Britain not to stoop so low as to con-spire with other Powers to attack a weak African State and then resort to all manner of subterfuge in her effort to make the attack respectable.

This sense of shame affected Eden himself who resigned owing to illness in January 1957, his long and distinguished career tarnished by an ill-considered enterprise in which his judgment must have been continuously undermined by the ill-health which forced him to resign. Eden's role had always been that of the practical negotiator, unburdened by lofty political visions but seeking above all things to arrive at solutions to tide over awkward problems. Since the work of such a man is the making of international agreements, it is wholly dependent upon the assumption that such agreements, once made, will be kept. If they are broken, he may hope that the international community will force the defaulter to respect his bond. But if the consensus is not forthcoming, or if it is too weak to compel the guilty, no alternative is left but force. Force, as Clemenceau said, is too serious to be left to the generals. But nor can it be left to the diplomat. The wide-ranging considerations which arise where force is contemplated, especially for a power of shrinking status, like Britain in the 1950s, are not necessarily within the diplomat's scope. Moreover, the diplomat, essentially a man of peace and order, may lack the stomach and ruthlessness for the fight. A President Truman may, after struggles with his conscience, decide to order the atomic bombing of Japan and then give no further thought to the question. An Eden, on momentous issues of peace and war, is apt to decide and then undecide, order and then insist that the order be carried out in such a way that the unavoidable consequences of putting the order into effect be avoided. This happened in the Suez operation. The heavy bombardment for six day of military targets in the Port Said area was designed to avoid inflicting injury on the civilian popula-tion (as though the distinction is a tenable one in the international use of force) and hence held up the landing of the troops. The cease-fire order on November 6th was given partly because the whole idea of fighting was too terrible to contemplate. The name 'armed action' or 'police action' was bestowed on the operation, not solely for external propaganda purposes, but in order to avoid the dreadful

[1] Churchill, *op. cit.*, pp. 306–7.

admission to oneself that one was actually at war. True, Eden had served as a leading Minister in the wartime British Government which had carried on military operations of the most drastic character, but in the last resort the moral burden lay on another's shoulders. He was himself too good a man to wage war effectively, and yet also too good to keep the peace in so far as breaches of the law were intolerable to him. He could not refrain from seeking to redress them even when to do so was not within his or Britain's power.

This leads to the decisive factor in the calling off of the Suez operations, the failure of Eden's assumption that the United States would remain passive. Fearing that the conflict would embroil the NATO Powers with Russia, or that in any case the laborious Western effort to conciliate the Arab States would be utterly foiled if further damage was done in Egypt, Washington went beyond voting against Britain, France and Israel at the United Nations and threatened economic sanctions if the action were not called off. The precise form in which this threat was levelled has not yet been disclosed, but on Eden's own account the serious loss of British reserves reported by the Chancellor of the Exchequer, Harold Macmillan, in the midst of the operation forced the action in Egypt to a halt. $279 million was lost in November, about fifteen per cent of the total gold and dollar reserves. It is almost certain that the American Government were responsible for this; in any case it was easily within Washington's power to tide Britain over the crisis had the will been there. America's refusal to assist and the implied, if not explicit, threat to force Britain to desist was the most dramatic demonstration that the postwar world had seen that no British armed action on any considerable scale could be launched without the approval of the United States. Eden's greatest failure was his omission to be abundantly clear that this approval was forthcoming before the order to intervene was given. On his side it could be said that the strength of American opposition could not be foreseen and might well not have been witnessed had American foreign policy been in the hands of a less powerful personal enemy of Eden's than Dulles. The fact that American policy towards Nasser almost immediately changed after Eden's resignation, when Egypt came to be regarded in Washington as a hotbed of Communism and when, with the fall of the Nuri As-Said regime in Iraq in July 1958, the United States herself landed forces in Lebanon, ostensibly to defend this country against Nasserism, showed that there was some force in this argument. The 'Eisenhower Doctrine', promulgated in January 1957, which pledged the United States to assist countries threatened by international

Communism at their own request, on which the American action in Lebanon was based, seemed to take almost the same view of Nasser as a source of unrest in 1958 as had inspired Britain and France. Nevertheless, the Dulles of 1956, not 1957 and 1958, represented the United States with which Eden had to deal, and whose benevolent neutrality in the Suez operation he believed that he had.   '

Aftermath

The Anglo-French intervention in Egypt is therefore hard to conceive as other than a serious miscalculation, apart from the deficiencies in British military preparations which it showed and the issue of its moral character. Its cost, in loss of Commonwealth and American sympathy and in the blow inflicted to the already shaking British prestige in the Middle East, was grave. It violently disrupted the long tradition of mutual consultation in the Commonwealth. In being based upon the assumption that the Canal would be less efficiently or honestly run under Egyptian than under the Canal Company's management it was mistaken, as well as deeply wounding to Arab, Asian and African pride. It achieved none of its ostensible objects and few of its secret ones. The Canal was not brought under international management or insulated from the politics of Egypt. Indeed the intervention, if anything, consolidated Nasser's grip. The Anglo-French action, it is true, led to the ending of the Israeli invasion of Egypt and scored a triumph in securing the creation of a United Nations emergency force to patrol the Gaza Strip as the belligerents withdrew. The force is still there (1961), though its financial support had always been under threat, and it has, apart from providing a model for similar forces elsewhere, provided a cushion between Israel and Egypt which has helped to keep the peace between these apparently irreconcilable antagonists. But, as we have seen, the Arab-Israeli war which began on October 25, 1956, so far from being a fortuitous event which precipitated and justified the Anglo-French action was, on any account, an integral part of the developments and preparations which led up to that intervention.

The United Nations was indeed forced to take action and send the force. To that extent, the Anglo-French intervention helped in the pacification of the area. But this was an almost wholly accidental result and the argument was resorted to only at a late stage in the Anglo-French action. As the Opposition in the Commons pointed out, it was somewhat like the plea of a thief who argues that one satisfactory result of his attempted theft was the appearance of the police on the scene of the crime.

Yet the unpredictability of international affairs is such that although the intervention may be criticized in the circumstances of the times, none of its after-effects was as serious as was feared and prophesied by the critics. The Commonwealth survived the shock. The Anglo-American partnership was not irremediably shattered. Thanks to the careful nursing of the alliance by Eden's successor in the Premiership, Macmillan, and the revulsion of feeling in the United States against the anti-British sentiments of 1956, the alliance was not seriously affected. Hardly a trace of Suez was left when a heads of government meeting of NATO Powers assembled in Paris in December 1957 to discuss the British principle of 'interdependence' in the alliance and the siting of American medium-range missiles in Europe.

Q

CHAPTER EIGHT

The Great Divide

The world situation facing Britain after 1945 was dominated by the tension between Russia and the West which overshadowed every international problem. British Ministers commonly ascribed this tension to Soviet expansion, backed by a revolutionary faith, which showed itself in the imposition of Communist regimes in Eastern Europe and the crushing of attempts in East Germany in June 1953 and in Hungary in October 1956 to break free. 'The plain fact is,' said the Prime Minister, Harold Macmillan, in the Commons on November 5, 1957, 'that Communist doctrine, which has never been repudiated and often acted upon, calls for the eventual overthrow of everything that we understand by freedom and democracy. . . . 1 believe that never has the threat of Russia and Soviet Communism been so great or the need for countries to organize themselves against it so urgent.'[1] Once Russia had added the atomic bomb in 1949, and the hydrogen bomb in 1953 to her land army of some 200 divisions, and then shown her ability to deliver these weapons accurately to the most distant continent by launching the first artificial earth satellite in October 1957, it was natural to single out her policy as the chief cause of the schism menacing peace.

As in all quarrels, however, there were two sides to the story. The Bolshevik Revolution which created Soviet Russia in November 1917 met with little but the frankest hostility from Western states, extending from the efforts of the Allies during the civil war, which followed Lenin's seizure of power, to crush the new regime to the scarcely veiled preference shown by many British and French Ministers for the Fascist governments in Germany and Italy in the 1930s. When Stalin met Churchill during the Second World War he discussed postwar collaboration with a man who had spent much of his life opposing the Soviet system and who justified his welcome to Russia's entrance into the war by saying that he would welcome the devil himself in the fight against Hitler. These recollections, inevitably in a one-sided form, provided the historical introduction to the famous 'Khrushchev note' of November 27, 1958, which made the Berlin

[1] 577 H.C. Deb. 5s. Cols. 35–9.

issue the central question at the opening of the 1960s.[1] When to this experience was added the dogmatic Marxist belief that the West was fated, regardless of its own wishes, to attempt the military destruction of Communism, the basis of Soviet hostility towards the West was laid. The precautions taken by the Soviet Union against the partly imagined, partly real, threat from the West engendered Western defensive reactions which in their turn strengthened Soviet suspicions. The resulting vicious spiral might have been broken had it been possible for statesmen on both sides to form the continuous and informal contacts which British Prime Ministers, notably Churchill, Eden and Macmillan, persistently sought. In Stalin's time the personal seclusion of the old Communist made little progress possible, though Stalin, unlike his successors, seemed to have the power to enforce his will at home if a settlement with the West could be reached. Although with his death in March 1953 East-West relations at once improved, especially since it coincided with the arrival of the nuclear stalemate which made war all but impossible, the real forces behind Soviet policy became even harder to fathom. The exact position of Nikita Khrushchev, who assumed the Premiership from his former partner, Bulganin, in April 1958, after having defeated a coalition of his enemies, the so-called 'anti-party' group in the Central Committee of the Soviet Communist Party, in the previous year, was never entirely clear. Considerable doubt existed, for instance, at the meeting of the Heads of Government of the Four Powers in Paris in May 1960, whether Khrushchev's refusal to hold the conference was due to the influence of the military, expressed through the Minister of Defence, Marshal Malinovsky, who accompanied Khrushchev in Paris wherever he went; or to the rising influence of Communist China, whose leaders were known to disagree with Khrushchev's policy of 'peaceful co-existence' and his attack on Stalinist theory and practice at the Twentieth Congress of the Soviet Communist Party in 1956; or whether Khrushchev himself had abandoned hope of a settlement with the West.

Whoever directed Soviet policy and whatever the philosophy behind it, relations between the West and Russia could never be easy or devoid of unpleasant surprises. The mere extent of Russia's land mass, her interminable frontiers and many neighbours, encouraged a suspiciousness towards the world outside which the messianic Communist ideology only hardened. Russia's long history of invasion from Europe, extending back to the Vikings, gave her the kind of interest in East Europe which the United States under the Monroe

[1] See below, p. 263 ff.

Doctrine had in the whole of the Western Hemisphere, which France had in the Rhine and North Africa, and which Britain had in the Low Countries or the Persian Gulf. The fact that Soviet politicians did not share the Western belief that Parliamentary democracy and individual freedom ensure a peaceful foreign policy, and that in any case the states of East Europe had never made a brilliant success of Parliamentary democracy, did not lead them to welcome democratic regimes on the Western pattern in those countries at the end of the war. France in 1919 would have imposed any regime on Germany which promised to keep that country powerless. Russia's attitude towards Germany and East Europe after 1945 was the same, except that, unlike France, she had the power to carry out her object, at least as far as the Elbe in Germany. Above all, Russia had suffered a devastating German invasion during the Second World War which no Soviet citizen, from the Prime Minister downwards, could forget. Twenty million Soviet people had died, the equivalent of five million British. Cities, notably Stalingrad, in which the struggle against Germany had been fought hand to hand and house by house, had become legends.[1] All this united the Soviet Government with their own people in their attitude towards Germany and the West (of which Hitler Germany, to them, had always formed a part) and created perhaps the strongest bond between the Soviets and the people of East Europe, such as the Poles and Czechs, whose experience of Germany had been almost as terrible.

The policy of German reunification
Although British Ministers repeatedly asserted their understanding of these facts, they joined with their American and French colleagues in urging solutions of the German problem, the central issue of East-West relations, which any Government in Moscow, Communist or other, could hardly have regarded as a basis for serious negotiations. The most persistent of these proposals was the reunification of Germany by means of free and internationally supervised elections and with freedom afforded to Germany to join any alliance she chose. No attempt was ever made to disguise the assumption behind this proposal that a Germany so united would join the NATO alliance. Selwyn Lloyd, then Minister of State at the Foreign Office, told the Commons in July 1955 that 'these arrangements were drawn up to meet what everybody admitted to be the probable contingency. It really was not worth wasting time on the others, because it was

[1] The name of Stalingrad was changed to Volgograd in November 1961 as part of the de-Stalinization policy.

confidently thought that this was the choice a free Germany would make'.[1] The plan for Germany submitted by Eden on behalf of the three Western Powers at the Four-Power Foreign Ministers' conference in Berlin on January 29, 1954, envisaged five stages in German reunification: (1) free elections throughout Germany; (2) the convocation of a National Assembly resulting from those elections; (3) the drafting of a Constitution and the preparation of peace treaty negotiations; (4) the adoption of the Constitution and the formation of an all-German Government responsible for the negotiation of the peace treaty; (5) the signature and entry into force of the peace treaty.[2] This plan was again submitted to Russia at the Four-Power Heads of Government meeting in Geneva from July 18 to 21, 1955. At the same time the question of German territory under Polish administration beyond the Oder-Neisse line was left open. At the Nine-Power conference in Paris in October 1954 which brought Western Germany into the NATO pact the three Western Powers, Britain, France and the United States, had declared that the final determination of Germany's boundaries must await a freely negotiated settlement between Germany and her former enemies.[3] Obviously, a united Germany in the NATO pact would be in an immensely strong position to demand the return of these lost territories. Equally clearly, Poland, who had surrendered large portions of her eastern territories to Russia in 1945 in return for the Oder-Neisse line, would be unable to survive if this German claim was made good.

Russia would have needed to be in a parlous condition to accept the principles of such a settlement. She already had reason to fear that the Paris agreements of October 1954, which came into effect on May 6, 1955, would lead to a remilitarized West Germany (which controlled three-quarters of the population of 1939 Germany and most of its industrial wealth) and that NATO policy, however defensive in character before Germany's admission, would be dominated by the same irredentism which had characterized German policy since 1918. Under the Western plan East Germany, with its seventeen million people, would almost certainly slip from Russia's grasp and go to swell the military resources of the West, with consequences for Russia's hold on the rest of Eastern Europe which could not be foreseen. A new Germany would come into existence, armed with nuclear

---

[1]. 557 H.C. Deb. 5s. Col. 248 (July 24th).
[2] Miscellaneous No. 5 (1954), Berlin Conference, Cmd. 9080, Annex A, pp. 120–2. See Also Eden's report on the Conference, 524 H.C. Deb. 5s. Cols. 401–16 (February 24, 1954).
[3] Miscellaneous No. 32 (1954), Paris Conference, Cmd. 9304, p. 56.

weapons which, it was commonly said, might have made the difference between victory and defeat for Hitler in 1945. Russia was
told that if she accepted this proposal she would help lessen the
tension between herself and the West; Eden said at the Geneva
'summit' conference in July 1955 that 'until the unity of Germany is
restored there can be neither confidence nor security on this continent'.[1] This might have been the case, but only through turning the
balance of power wholly against Russia, and even so only on the
assumption that Germany when united would remain peaceful.
This Russia doubted.

It is true that Russia was offered compensation for her losses
under the 'Eden plan' in the form of security assurances, but these
were in themselves somewhat insubstantial and were not tendered
until the Geneva 'summit' conference in July 1955, that is, after the
Federal German Republic had been well and truly incorporated into
the Western camp. The assurances were to be embodied in a security
treaty between the Four Powers and a reunited Germany and would
operate in nine stages, but it was clearly laid down that none of
them were to be effective until a reunited Germany decided to enter
NATO and West European Union. The first two stages were merely
declaratory, involving renunciation by the parties of the use of force
'in any manner inconsistent with the purposes of the United Nations',
and an undertaking not to assist an aggressor and to 'seek such
measures as are necessary to maintain and restore international peace
and security' if aggression occurred. The third stage comprised a
limitation of forces and armaments in a region between united
Germany and the East European states along the following lines:

> In a zone comprising areas of comparable size and depth and
> importance on both sides of a line of demarcation between a reuni-
> fied Germany and the East European countries, levels for armed
> forces would be specified so as to establish a military balance
> which would contribute to European security and help to relieve
> the burden of armaments. There would be appropriate provisions
> for the maintenance of this balance. In parts of the zone which lie
> closest to the line of demarcation, there might be special measures
> relating to the disposition of military forces and installations.

This arrangement was to be supervised, at the fourth stage, by
'progressive measures of mutual inspection', which would also warn
against any preparation on either side for a surprise attack. Then
would follow the establishment of a system of radar warning on

[1] Miscellaneous No. 14 (1955), Geneva Conference, Cmd. 9543, p. 16.

either side of the demarcation line, the western system being operated by Russia and the Warsaw pact countries and the eastern radar system by NATO forces. The two following stages introduced the principle of consultation to implement the treaty and reasserted the right of individual and collective self-defence, on which the NATO and Warsaw pacts were based, and the right of any country to forbid the use of its territory to foreign troops. The eighth stage, however, was the most crucial, involving the most concrete of the under-takings by the Western Powers to meet the contingency of a German military revival, of which the Soviet authorities represented them-selves as being most afraid. Instead, however, of a pledge to come to the assistance of a victim of aggression, it was merely proposed that:

> Each party would agree that armed attack in Europe by any party, which is also a NATO member, against any party which is not a NATO member or vice-versa, would endanger the peace and security which is the object of this treaty and that all the parties would then take appropriate action to meet that common danger.

During the ninth and final stage the whole treaty, to which the Four Powers and Germany would be signatory, would come into effect 'by stages as later agreed'. This meant that not even the first stage could come into force until the treaty as a whole was operative, that is, after Germany had entered NATO and WEU; that the time intervals between the stages was still subject to negotiation; and that the critical eighth stage, in itself no strong assurance of help to Russia in the event of further hostilities with united Germany, might be almost indefinitely postponed.[1]

Since the proposed security treaty, which the French delegation presented on behalf of the three Western Powers at the Four-Power Foreign Ministers' meeting at Geneva on October 28, 1955, could not be operative unless and until Germany was an ally in NATO of the three Western Powers, perhaps armed with nuclear weapons by the United States, the chances of the three Powers siding with Russia in any future quarrel with Germany were slight, especially as united Germany would probably inherit all the close ties with France which the Bonn Republic was contracting in the 'Little Europe' of the Six. Moreover, by the NATO alliance signatories were pledged to assist each other against 'armed attack'; it is not legally essential that they be victims of 'aggression', which is not mentioned in the treaty, to qualify for that assistance. The three Western

[1] Miscellaneous No. 21 (1955), Geneva Conference, Cmd. 9633, Annex I, pp. 99–101.

Powers, under the treaty of assurance proposed to Russia, would thus be pledged both to assist Germany, as a NATO member, against 'armed attack' and also to 'take appropriate action' in the event of an armed attack by Germany against Russia, which in itself must provoke an armed attack on Germany by Russia. It is not hard to see which of these conflicting obligations they were likely to prefer, except perhaps in the most flagrant case of German aggression towards the east.

Disengagement: British initiatives and the allies

A second compensation tentatively held out to Russia in return for her agreement on German reunification along Western lines was the proposal for a 'demilitarized area between East and West' which Eden raised at the Geneva 'summit' conference in 1955.[1] This conception continued to interest the British Foreign Office throughout the 1950s and became the inspiration of many schemes for 'disengaging' the armed forces of East and West from the line in Central Europe where they confronted each other. The British view was that disengagement offered hope of relieving Russia's grip on East Germany, Poland, Czechoslovakia and Hungary, that it might provide for mutual inspection on a limited scale which could be developed more generally in a larger disarmament agreement, and that the creation of a 'no-man's land' between the opposing forces in Europe would lessen the risk of collision. The demilitarization proposal of 1955, however, ran into the strongest opposition on the Western side and seems to have dropped from view after the Geneva conference. It evoked alarm in Federal Germany, where it was feared that at worst it might develop into the neutralization of Central Europe and the retirement of American forces from their protective role in Germany, or, at best, consolidate the division of Germany. British ideas on disengagement found little more support amongst NATO commanders. General Norstad, who became Supreme Commander, Allied Powers in Europe, in November 1956, regarded almost any form of disengagement as hampering Western defence, while leaving Russia free to deploy her massive land forces, no doubt further back than the existing western boundary of Soviet Germany, but still within easy reach of Western Europe if the signal to move were given.

British ideas on disengagement therefore had to be watered down in deference to the allies. On one occasion, Selwyn Lloyd, who became Foreign Secretary in succession to Macmillan in 1955, denied

[1] Cmd. 9543, p. 18.

that the Eden demilitarization plan amounted to anything more than a proposal for mutual inspection, thus implying that it had been submerged in the Western security plan already referred to, with its provision for the limitation of forces and armaments in a zone between a reunited Germany and Eastern Europe. Nevertheless, official British interest in disengagement continued. A qualified welcome was given by British Ministers to the proposal of the Polish Minister, Adam Rapacki, for the creation of a zone in central Europe from which all nuclear weapons and missiles for launching them would be removed, which the Minister explained at the United Nations General Assembly on November 7, 1957. While Rapacki assured Western newspaper correspondents that the plan was a Polish one and represented a genuine Polish initiative, it could hardly have been put forward without Soviet agreement. The Soviet Prime Minister, Bulganin, in fact supported the plan in a letter to Macmillan on December 11, 1957.[2] Naturally he did so because the plan had the advantage for Russia of denying nuclear arms to Germany while allowing Russia herself to retain her heavy superiority in conventional forces.

Since the Rapacki plan was thus plainly weighted in Russia's favour the general reception accorded to it in the West was unfavourable. This was particularly the case in West Germany, where, after 1955, the demand was increasingly voiced that German troops under NATO command should not be denied any weapon available to other NATO forces. The British Government, however, were determined to see whether the Polish plan could not be moulded into a more acceptable shape. The Prime Minister replied to Bulganin on January 16, 1958, that it was under close study;[3] a month later the Minister of State at the Foreign Office, Ormsby-Gore, gave some of the Government's impressions in a Commons debate. He was far from rejecting it out of hand.[4] The British objections were formulated in a note to Poland on May 17th and focused on the continuing Communist preponderance in conventional arms under the plan, its lack of clarity in the matter of control and inspection, and the absence of any reference to German reunification. Revised proposals were therefore announced by the Polish Foreign Minister on November 4, 1958, which envisaged two stages: first, there was to be no production of nuclear weapons in Czechoslovakia, Germany or Poland

[1] 570 H.C. Deb. 5s. Cols. 19–21 (May 13, 1957).
[2] Soviet Union No. 2 (1958), Cmd. 381, p. 7.
[3] *Ibid.*, p. 26.
[4] 582 H.C. Deb. 5s. Col. 1339 (February 19, 1958).

and armies in those countries which did not possess nuclear arms were not to have them; in the second stage the reduction of conventional arms was to be carried out 'simultaneously with the removal of nuclear weapons'. Both stages, Rapacki said, would be subject to adequate measures of control.

It was clear, however, by now that the whole principle of denying atomic weapons to German forces was inconsistent with the terms of West German membership of NATO; although discrimination against Germany was necessarily involved in that membership, in so far as nuclear weapons entrusted to German forces would remain American property and under American custody, no German Government could ask their forces to prepare for an emergency in which other armies, allied and enemy, would have up-to-date weapons while they would not. In addition, the fact that British policy, as a result of the Defence White Paper of 1957, had come to rely upon nuclear arms as the first line of defence against even a conventional attack made British enthusiasm for the Rapacki plan look like an aspect of British anti-Germanism. Hence, when Selwyn Lloyd gave the Government's considered position on the revised Rapacki plan on December 4, 1958, he said that, while there was no difficulty about forbidding the production of nuclear weapons in Germany, since this was already provided for under the Paris agreements, a freeze on atomic forces in Germany would impair the defence capabilities of NATO and 'involve discrimination against the troops of particular countries'.[1] Beyond this, British interest in the Polish proposal could not go.

A reflection of this interest, however, reappeared in February 1959 when Macmillan paid a twelve-day visit to the Soviet Union the object of which, as he described it, was not to negotiate but to make a 'reconnaissance' of the Soviet position and attitude.[2] At the end of the visit, on which the Prime Minister was accompanied by the Foreign Secretary, Selwyn Lloyd, a communiqué was issued in which it was stated that the British and Soviet leaders:

agreed that further study could usefully be made of the possibilities of increasing security by some method of limitation of forces and weapons, both conventional and nuclear, in an agreed area of Europe, coupled with an appropriate system of inspection.[3]

The reaction in Federal Germany to this British initiative, when the

[1] 596 H.C. Deb. 5s. Col. 1376.
[2] 599 *Ibid.*, Col. 579 (February 5, 1959).
[3] Soviet Union No. 1 (1959), Cmd. 689, pp. 2–3.

Rapacki plan seemed dead and buried, was one of intense anger, the
Macmillan journey to Moscow leading to perhaps the worst period
in postwar Anglo-German relations. During the general election in
Britain in October 1959, when the Conservative Government were
returned with the increased majority of 108 seats over Labour, Dr
Adenauer, the Federal German Chancellor, accused Macmillan of
promising a British acceptance of the Rapacki plan in order to win
votes. This was not true, but the fact that Macmillan's principal rival
at the election, Hugh Gaitskell, the leader of the Labour Party, had
approved as far back in 1956 a disengagement plan based upon the
withdrawal of Warsaw pact forces from East Germany, Poland,
Czechoslovakia and Hungary and of NATO forces from Germany,
forced the Conservatives to keep an open mind on disengagement,
on which in any case they had always looked with sympathy.[1]

In discussing disengagement British Ministers had to bear in mind
the dangers of widening the breach with Federal Germany, whose
position was supported (except on the Oder-Neisse Line) by France,
especially at a time of difficult and delicate negotiations on the British
proposal for a Free Trade Area in Western Europe.[2] Moreover, they
feared that Opposition pressure might force them into the acceptance
of a particular disengagement plan (and there was no dearth of such
plans in 1957–59) and hence into cutting themselves off from their
allies. This danger was stressed by the Prime Minister, Macmillan,
in a Commons debate in February 1958, when he repeated that the
crucial factor in the consideration of any disengagement plan was
not its attractiveness in British eyes but the likely judgment of the
allies. This was another way of saying that no plan could become
practical politics unless it offered substantial advantages to the
United States and Federal Germany. The former, bearing the heaviest
share of responsibility for Western defence and having the strongest
interest in the liberation of East Europe from Communism, could
only consider disengagement in Europe in exchange for significant
reductions in the capacity of the Communist war machine, to which
Soviet acceptance of mutual aerial inspection on the lines of the
'Open Skies' plan presented by President Eisenhower at the Geneva
'summit' conference in 1955 would make a contribution, and in
return for the restoration of freedom to Eastern Europe. Discussion
of alternative schemes of aerial inspection continued between East
and West during 1957, but foundered on the normal dilemma of

[1] For the Gaitskell plan see *Labour's Foreign Policy*, published by the Labour
Party, 1958, p. 4.
[2] See below, Chapter X, pp. 315–20.

such proposals, namely that neither side can be wholly satisfied that what it learns about the military preparations of the other is equivalent to, or if possible more than, what it must disclose itself.[1] As for the prospects of a withdrawal of the 'iron curtain' to the old Soviet frontier, there seemed some hope in 1956 that Russia might consent to this in exchange for reliable assurances about Germany's military revival. What with the troubles in Poland and Hungary in that year, British advocates of disengagement considered that she might be tempted to abandon the East European security belt she acquired in 1945 if the price were high enough, especially since its military value was declining with Russia's advance towards nuclear parity with the United States.[2] How slender this hope eventually proved to be was shown by an article published in the Americal journal *Foreign Affairs* by Khrushchev in October 1959, coinciding with a visit to the United States. In this the Soviet leader's main theme was that peaceful co-existence between East and West must be securely based upon recognition of the spheres of interest of both sides, or, in the jargon of the ideological conflict, there could be 'no roll back of Socialism from the People's Democracies'. The effect of this was to rule out any policy of disengagement for Germany and East Europe and at the same time to shrink almost to nothing any concession which even the most hopeful British advocates of disengagement could consider on the Western side.

The West German objection to disengagement was different, stemming as it did from German preoccupation with unity, which every German understood could only be won without loss of democratic freedom through a sympathetic NATO alliance. Dr Adenauer, leader of the Christian Democratic Union, who was returned as Chancellor with massive majorities in 1953 and 1957, though he lost his overall majority in September 1961, feared that any agreement to limit forces on either side of the facing lines in Europe could only harden the division of Germany and seriously handicap the defence of Federal Germany if war came. Indeed it was clearly in order to secure these results that Russia held out the bait of disengagement to the West, and it was in the half-conscious hope that German unity would be relegated to the distant future that disengagement found such support among Western liberals and socialists. Although the British Government repeatedly claimed that German reunification was essential to European security, very few in Britain really

---

[1] For an account of the disarmament negotiations since the war see Chapter IX.
[2] See Denis Healey, *A Neutral Belt in Europe?*, published by the Fabian Society, London, 1958.

believed it, certainly in the Labour Party, whose annual conference approved the principle of German rearmament in 1954 only with the greatest misgiving. This lack of sympathy for German aims in Britain, an influential NATO country, was a matter of concern to Dr Adenauer and strengthened his suspicion of the motives behind disengagement proposals.

Britain and Federal Germany

It is a remarkable fact that although after the First World War Britain was the most anxious of all the Allies to conciliate Germany in the accepted British tradition towards a beaten opponent, she was after 1945 perhaps the most unrelenting of all countries towards Germany, with the exception of the Communist states. The Germanophile and Germanophobe roles played by Britain and France respectively after 1918 seemed reversed after 1945. The mere fact that easy-going British assumptions about Germany were proved cruelly wrong in 1939, and that many British people grew ashamed of themselves for having been duped by German politicians in the 1930s, together with experience of German bombing during the war and revulsion against the unspeakable horrors of the Nazi regime, made many British people even more mistrustful towards Germany than they had been during the conflict. The result was that British Ministers tended to speak of German reunification as the key to stability in Europe somewhat with tongues in their cheeks; they listened sympathetically to Opposition spokesmen who did not regard it as a drawback of disengagement that it might postpone the unity of Germany. Unlike the Opposition, however, they had to work within an alliance in which Federal Germany was becoming an increasingly important factor. This meant, when combined with Russia's patent refusal to offer hope of any liberation of East Europe, that when disengagement was at length officially adopted by the West in a declaration issued by the three Western Powers and Federal Germany in Berlin on July 29, 1957, it was made, like the 'Eden plan' of 1955, firmly conditional on the reunification of Germany by free elections.

Moreover, it was to apply only to the part of Germany then under Soviet control, that is, the territory of the 'German Democratic Republic', which would naturally be swept away. The declaration stated that the Western Powers, as part of a mutually acceptable security arrangement, were prepared 'to give assurance that, in the event of a reunified Germany choosing to join NATO, they would not take military advantage as a result of the withdrawal of Soviet forces'.[1] This offer, which Selwyn Lloyd told the House in February 1958 had originated with Dr Adenauer,[2] and which therefore probably represented the rejection of a more negotiable proposal, was in a sense even more disadvantageous to Russia than that of 1955. No inspection or other guarantee of execution was included in it. It was in fact not an offer of a treaty, which the British Government had always sought as the instrument of disengagement, but merely of a Western declaration the fulfilment of which Russia could presumably only verify through espionage. What was more, if it were true, as the Western Powers contended in all the controversy about disengagement, that a 'vacuum' could not safely be created between the two sides in Europe, pressure would certainly be felt to re-occupy Eastern Germany if ever Russia consented to this scheme. But it was as certain as anything could be that she would not.

It is at first sight not easy to see why the British Government accepted German reunification on Western terms as the condition of any European settlement, or why they agreed in the Berlin declaration of July 1957 that even disarmament talks must be dependent upon progress being made in political settlements, especially German reunification. It should be remembered, however, that notwithstanding British mistrust of Germany, the aim of German unity was in line with much in the tradition of British foreign policy. While Britain had never been a champion of the strict theory of national self-determination, there was a widespread idea mong British politicians that governments genuinely based on popular consent could hardly become threats to peace. Many of these politicians considered that the best means of keeping democracy alive in Germany was to rivet that country in the Western camp, while avoiding the kind of frustrations which weakened the Weimar regime in Germany in the 1920s. Moreover, British Governments had generally upheld the maxim of the integrity of the great established Powers, whose interests should not be too restricted on behalf of smaller and weaker nations. This principle inspired British attitudes towards Germany at the Peace Conference in 1919 and made it possible for a British Government to contemplate truncating Czechoslovakia in 1938 in order to satisfy the 'legitimate interests' of a powerful member of the international establishment. When British Ministers argued in the 1950s that the struggle for German unity would agitate European affairs until it was settled, they recalled Germany's refusal to forget the loss of the

---

[1] For the text of the Declaration see *Department of State Bulletin*, v. 37 (August 19, 1957), pp. 304–6.
[2] 582 H.C. Deb. 5s. Col. 1341 (February 20th).

'Polish Corridor' and Danzig after 1919, just as their predecessors in the 1920s had recalled France's refusal to forget the loss of Alsace-Lorraine after 1871. Besides, if ever the Western Powers abandoned German claims to unity there was always the possibility that Russia, who alone could make Germany's dream of unification true, would do so and hence pull Western Germany into her own camp.

Behind this fear lurked the nightmare of another Rapallo, where in 1922 the two pariah nations, Germany and Soviet Russia, made their accord behind the backs of the Allies, and perhaps of another Nazi-Soviet pact of 1939. To be sure, at those earlier periods of Russo-German alliance Germany was the more highly industrialized and wealthier partner and could therefore make her own terms, whereas now the roles were reversed. Nevertheless, Russia held most tempting cards in her hands should ever German opinion be alienated from the West. By abandoning East Germany she could gratify Germany's predominant aspiration; by abandoning Poland she could satisfy German irredentism. She could return Königsberg, the old Prussian city which she had taken in 1945; she could make Britain, France and the United States look like opponents of German unity by proposing to abolish the occupation status of Berlin and making it the capital of a reunited Germany. West Germany, admittedly, would first have to be driven to the extreme of desperation to accept any terms remotely agreeable to Russia in return for all this. But the Western Powers wished to ensure that German thoughts should never even stray in that direction.

German unity was therefore imposed as an aim of Western and hence of British policy by the after-effects of Federal Germany's creation as an independent state. The Western Powers were also legally committed to it after the signing of the Paris agreements in 1954 which brought Federal Germany into NATO and West European Union. By those agreements Britain, France and the United States declared that they considered the Government of the Federal Republic 'as the only German government freely and legitimately constituted and therefore entitled to speak for Germany as the representative of the German people in international affairs'; they also stated that the 'achievement through peaceful means of a fully free and unified Germany remains a fundamental goal of their policy'.[1] These statements were in effect the price paid by the three Western Powers to West Germany for placing her territory and resources in the forefront of NATO defence in Europe, although it remained possible that she would have done so in the interests of her security

[1] Cmd. 9304, p. 56.

even without this inducement. Without these German facilities it was hard to see how NATO as a military shield could exist at all.

France in her troubled political state was a doubtful quantity and after the outbreak of fighting in Algeria in 1954 the bulk of her army was no longer available for NATO purposes in Europe. Britain decided to minimize her contribution to NATO land forces in Europe and base herself squarely upon the nuclear deterrent. The smaller NATO countries would probably be swept aside in any massive Communist attack in Western Europe. Accordingly, opinion in the United States saw little reason why vast American armies should be stationed in Europe merely because the British had qualms about the reliability of Germany. All this pointed to West Germany as the contributor of at least twelve of the thirty divisions which the NATO command required as the minimum force to take the first shock of a Soviet offensive until the NATO Powers had time to put themselves on a war footing, unless, that is, full-scale nuclear resistance was to be launched before it was clear whether an 'incident' was intended to develop into wholesale Soviet aggression. British opinion, Americans noted, expressed horror at this possibility and yet hesitated to authorize the Germans to provide the conventional forces to avoid it. But if West Germany, by a perverse fate, had come to hold the key to the defence of the Western democracies it was assumed that she would not be willing to use it unless German unity was the general aim of Western policy.

Dr Adenauer did not argue against that assumption. In September 1956, a year after the opening of diplomatic relations between Bonn and Moscow and when opinion in Britain was resentful because a settlement with Russia on European security and disarmament was allegedly being held up by the West German claim to unity, he wrote to the British Government reminding them that:

The linking of the problem of disarmament with that of reunification is inevitable. It would be rendering a disservice indeed to the cause of disarmament to detach it from all political prerequisites and to argue, so to speak, in a vacuum. Viewed from a realistic standpoint, general disarmament can be brought about only if the necessary political conditions exist. No state—as experience has amply shown—will be prepared to carry out disarmament in earnest as long as there are smouldering conflicts which may burst into violent flame. . . . The Federal Government, however, have repeatedly emphasized that they think it entirely possible to solve the problem of disarmament hand in hand with that of reunification.[1]

As though to hint at the alternative, Dr Adenauer included in the letter a copy of his reply to Bulganin's invitation, addressed to the Chancellor on September 13, 1955, 'to help mutual understanding and co-operation between the USSR and the Federal German Republic'.

Hence, as the British Prime Minister, Macmillan, continued to insist in 1958 when faced with Opposition criticism of the sterile character of German reunification as a political object, unless the critics could show some alternative to reliance upon German forces that object could not be avoided. Official foreign relations are, however, too polite for the point to be put in that form. The West, Macmillan said, was distinguished from the Communist bloc in being a coalition of separate states, which could not dictate to each other. Intervening in an angry debate on the German question in the Commons in February, during which the Foreign Secretary, Selwyn Lloyd, had expressed veiled sympathy with disengagement, Macmillian said: '(the allies) are all concerned, but perhaps the Federal Government of West Germany is one of the most concerned. We must discuss (disengagement plans) also with the rest of the NATO allies and with the United States, for nothing could be more terrible than if the result of some plan lightly entered into was the dissolution of NATO, the loss of Germany and possibly the driving of America back into isolation.'[2]

Soviet counter-proposals

Soviet reactions to the West's German policy were as grimly logical and hence, in the circumstances, as unhelpful to East-West agreement as that policy itself. In the early stages, while the long debate continued in France on EDC and British opinion was vocally hostile to German rearmament, Russia sought to prise Federal Germany out of the Western bloc and Western Europe away from the United States. These were the manifest aims of the proposals on Germany submitted by the Soviet Foreign Minister, Molotov, to the Four-Power Foreign Ministers' conference in Berlin on February 1, 1954, and of his 'additional proposals' on European security of February 10th. The idea was that the two Germanies should be left alone by the four Powers to try to form an all-German provisional govern-

[1] Germany No. 4 (1956), Cmd. 29, p. 7.
[2] 582 H.C. Deb. 5s. Col. 1520 (February 20th).

R

ment, to be formed from the Parliaments of the two German states. This would draft an all-German electoral law clearly designed to favour the Communists. Foreign Powers were not to 'interfere' in these elections, although by the peace treaty which was to be concurrently negotiated with Germany 'the existence of organizations hostile to democracy and the preservation of peace' was not to be allowed on German soil. The electoral law was to provide for the 'participation of all democratic organs' and 'eliminate the possibility of any pressure by powerful monopolies on the voters', while the provisional government would ensure the 'banning of the existence of Fascist, militarist or other organizations hostile to democracy and to the preservation of peace'. The peace treaty, which provided for the withdrawal of occupation forces from Germany, would apparently be proceeded with whether or not the two Germanies agreed on a provisional all-German government, since they were to be allowed to take part in the drafting of the treaty. In order to break all links between Germany and NATO, the peace treaty was to prohibit German membership of any 'coalition or military alliance directed against any Power whose armed forces took part in the war against Germany' and East and West Germany were to cancel all military or political obligations resulting from previous treaties and agreements. Before the peace treaty was actually signed or Germany reunited, the four Powers would undertake to withdraw their forces from Germany within six months of the proposal being agreed, except that 'limited contingents' might remain for 'guard duties arising from the control responsibilities of the four Powers' and forces might be recalled 'if a threat to security in either part of Germany arose'. The agreement on Germany, Russia said, should be complemented by a 'general European Treaty on Collective Security in Europe', the repetition of the word 'Europe' making quite clear its aim of excluding the United States. Interested European states, including Germany (or the two German states if unity had not been attained), would assume mutual obligations somewhat similar to those of NATO, but the parties would release themselves from 'any coalition or alliance . . . the objectives of which are contrary to the treaty'. Western Europe would thus be severed from the United States, who was expected to join with Communist China in 'observing' the treaty.[1]

This scheme, which was as little likely to receive serious consideration from the West as the opposing plan was to receive such

[1] Cmd. 9080 Annex B, pp. 123–4; Annex C, p. 125; Annex D, pp. 125–6; Annex F, pp. 127–8.

attention from Russia, found some encouragement in the French rejection of EDC in August, but Soviet appeals on July 24th and November 13th for a general European conference to draft a collective security treaty on the lines of Molotov's February proposals fell to the ground. The Western replies of September 10th and November 29th argued that the Soviet proposals made no contribution to German reunification in freedom and alleged that they were 'openly and explicitly' aimed at delaying the ratification of the Paris agreements for the admission of Federal Germany into NATO. The note of November 29th indicated that in the Western view the steps essential to a successful conference on Germany were: the signing of the Austrian state treaty, the Soviet version of the disputed articles of the draft of which the West was ready to sign; the 'clarification of Soviet views on free elections in Germany'; the examination through the usual diplomatic channels of questions which might be examined by a later high-level meeting on Germany; and a Four-Power Foreign Ministers' meeting to consider the German problem afresh, but only 'when there is a prospect of agreement and after the ratification of the Paris agreements'.[1] The conference on European security which the Soviet Government convened in Moscow on November 29th, the day on which the latter note was sent, was therefore attended only by the seven Communist states of the Soviet bloc and Communist China. The declaration issued by the conference on December 2, 1954, followed standard Communist lines.

Since Russia had threatened that dire results would follow from the absorption of Federal Germany into NATO, many British Opposition spokesmen feared that the ratification of the Paris agreements would remove all prospect of agreement with Russia and intensify the tension. So far was this from happening that the coming into force of the agreements on May 6, 1955, seemed to open up a milder period of East-West affairs than any that had been seen since the war. On May 10th the Soviet delegate at the Sub-committee of the United Nations Disarmament Commission embarrassed Western representatives by tabling a disarmament scheme which accepted many of the features of the Anglo-French plan of 1954, especially in regard to inspection and control.[2] Two days later the Austrian state treaty was finally signed in Vienna as a result of a Soviet reversal of an obstructive stand maintained for many years. Five days later the

[1] *Department of State Bulletin*, September 20, 1954, pp. 397–8; *ibid.*, December 13, pp. 901–2.
[2] See below, Chapter IX, p. 288.

Soviet Government accepted a Western invitation to a Heads of Government meeting intended as 'a new effort to resolve the great problems which confront us'. At the 'summit' meeting at Geneva in July the Soviet position had changed hardly at all, the only modifications in the security proposals of the previous year being a provision for the NATO and Warsaw pacts to remain in being during a first phase, in which forces stationed in the territory of other countries were to be stabilized, and acceptance of the United States as a party to the collective security treaty.[1] The four leaders were able to agree only on directives relating to European security, the unification of Germany by free elections and with due regard to the interests of Germany and her neighbours, and increased contacts between East and West. These constituted the agenda for a continuance of the debate at Foreign Minister level in the Swiss capital in the autumn. Here again, East and West remained separated by the inevitable conflict between German reunification and European security. The West's acceptance of the principle of assurances to Russia in return for her agreement to German unity was paralleled by Soviet acquiescence in NATO, between which pact and the Warsaw alliance the Soviet Foreign Minister proposed a non-aggression pact 'until replaced by another treaty for the establishment of a system of Collective Security in Europe'.[2] But these movements towards a middle ground were too slight to enable the remaining distance between the two sides to be bridged.

Nevertheless, the 'Geneva spirit' mellowed the tone of East-West exchanges. In September diplomatic relations were established between Russia and the Federal German Republic and Dr Adenauer was invited to Moscow, where he was asked to consider the neutralization of Austria in May as a model for Germany. He was not impressed. In April of the following year the Soviet pair, Khrushchev and Bulganin, after a tour of south-east Asia at the end of 1955 in which they had denounced British imperialism to all and sundry, were given a cordial welcome in Britain, accepting an invitation extended by Eden at Geneva in July. Amicable talks were held with British Ministers, stormy ones with Opposition leaders at a dinner given by the Labour Party, and a long list of proposed Soviet purchases in Britain (a half of which, probably by design, included goods prohibited to the Communist bloc under the strategic embargo) was handed over. The effect of the trade agreement which they desired,

[1] Cmd. 9543, pp. 21–3.
[2] Cmd. 9633, Annexes II and III, pp. 104–7; Annex IV, pp. 107–8; Annex VI, pp. 108–9.

the Soviet leaders said, was that Russian imports from Britain would increase in the five years 1956–60 by from nine to eleven billion roubles, or £800–£1,000 million. A statement issued at the end of the visit recorded that Britain and Russia both 'attached particular importance to maintaining security in Europe' but regretted that 'an understanding on the means to achieve that end was not reached'.[1] After the visit Eden, the then Prime Minister, said that the danger of global war had receded and that forces were at work in Russia which could assist the relaxation of tension, among which he spoke of recent increases in living standards in that country, the new status of technicians, with their interest in construction rather than military adventures, Khrushchev's policy of de-Stalinization and new legal reforms which tended towards the independence of the courts as understood in the West. 'I believe,' so Eden summarized the position, 'that there has been an essential change in the international outlook in the last two years, between the Berlin Conference (in 1954) and now. That change has been between rigidity and flexibility. All was rigid then. Much seems flexible now.'[2]

Although the Suez affair and the Hungarian tragedy dragged Anglo-Soviet relations back into the depths in the autumn of that year and the correspondence between Bulganin and Eden's successor, Macmillan, which began hopefully in the spring of 1957, degenerated into the bald statement of positions on either side early in 1958, it was clear that the Soviet leaders wished to come to another 'summit' meeting as soon as possible. The British Government were unwilling to write off this desire as merely one more propaganda exercise. West Germany's entrance into NATO in 1955 seemed therefore not to close the door on further negotiation with the Communist bloc, as had been feared, but rather to intensify Soviet anxiety for further talks. The conclusion which could reasonably be drawn was that 'toughness' did not necessarily provoke similar reactions from Russia, and that fear of outraging Russia and readiness to sympathize with her viewpoint tended only to make the Soviet Government more difficult to deal with, no doubt because they hoped by these reactions to weaken the opposition against them.

Berlin crisis: Soviet moves and motivations
This inference might have been correct had Russia no effective means to hand of replying to the Paris agreements. When at the end of the Paris conference on October 23, 1954, the Soviet authorities

[1] Soviet Union No. 1 (1956), Cmd. 9753, p. 3.
[2] 557 H.C. Deb. 5s. Col. 47 (July 23rd).

addressed a note to the Western Powers stating that 'if (the Paris) decisions are implemented, it would make it impossible for West Germany to be considered a peaceloving state, which would make the unity of Germany impossible for a long time to come',[1] this was regarded as an empty threat since it was thought that the accession of West Germany to NATO would improve the West's bargaining strength in the matter of German unity. But it soon became clear that, whatever her previous attitude to German unity, Russia would in no circumstances entertain it after May 1955. In Bulganin's words at the Geneva 'summit' meeting on July 23, 1955:

> The Soviet Government . . . has drawn attention even before the ratification of the Paris agreements to the fact that the coming into force of these agreements would create difficulties for talks on the German problem and makes pointless any discussion on the reunification of Germany. The Soviet Government believes that it is necessary to take the facts into consideration. War in Europe ended ten years ago. . . . Since that time two Germanies have appeared—the German Democratic Republic and the German Federal Republic—each with its own economic and social structure.[2]

Nor could Russia have taken any alternative position without decisively turning the European balance of power against herself. Since therefore German unity on Western terms was impossible for Russia and unity on Communist terms impossible for the West (and for exactly the same balance of power reasons), almost the only course left to Moscow was to abandon the cause of German unity, which it had espoused only so long as there was a chance of alienating West German opinion against the NATO Powers, and to come out in favour of 'drawing a line under World War Two'. This meant abandoning the Potsdam understanding to reshape a united Germany.

Russia, it should be remembered, had no legal commitment to the Germans to pursue German unity, since Germany had unconditionally surrendered in 1945. The case was, however, different with the Western Powers. In their public statements, in the Paris agreements and in their declaration in Berlin of July 29, 1957, they had saddled themselves with an undertaking which in the last resort only Russia could fulfil, yet which it was now clear she would indefinitely refuse to fulfil so long as the basic aims of Western policy in Germany remained the same. By making German unity on Western terms

[1] *Soviet News*, October 26, 1954.
[2] Cmd. 9543, p. 29.

virtually non-negotiable, Britain, France and the United States threw away an important card which they might have dealt effectively when Russia at length made her reply in 1958.

That reply was a threat to denounce the occupation regime in Berlin, where troops of all four Powers remained despite the failure of Four-Power administration of the city, and in doing so to bring the two and a quarter million inhabitants of the Western sectors under Communist control. This threat was contained in a long note circulated to the Western Powers by the Soviet Union on November 27, 1958, which began by denouncing the remilitarization of West Germany and then proposed within six months to hand over to the East German authorities Russia's occupation rights in Berlin, if by that time an agreement had not been reached between the Four Powers for making West Berlin a demilitarized 'free town', which would mean of course the departure of Western troops. The Four Powers, the note went on, could undertake 'obligations to respect the status of West Berlin as a free city as was done, for instance, by the Four Powers in respect of the neutral status which the Austrian Republic has assumed', and the Soviet Government would not object 'if in the observance of the status of West Berlin as a free city the United Nations Organization also took part in some form'. Any such guarantees, however, would clearly have to recognize the fact that the East Germans, as sovereigns over the hundred miles of territory between West Berlin and the Federal Republic, would become responsible, under the Soviet proposal, for access between the city and the West.[1] This initial statement of Soviet policy on Berlin was revised and revised again, with varying shades of flexibility and menace, during the following three years. The most important supplement, however, was provided by Khrushchev at a Soviet-East German friendship meeting in Moscow on June 19, 1958, when he said that if within a limited period, namely eighteen months, agreement was not reached by an all-German committee representing East and West Germany on the methods of German unity, Russia would sign a peace treaty with East Germany and 'all vestiges of Western rights would disappear'.[2] At no time, however, did the Soviet authorities make clear whether they would take action to implement a new legal position which, in their opinion, would then exist.

The implications of the note for the West were serious. There was no question that the 'free city' notion was a sham, all the more so as the same status was not proposed in the Soviet note for East Berlin.

[1] Germany No. 1 (1959), Cmd. 634, pp. 7–21.
[2] Selwyn Lloyd in the Commons, July 9, 1959; 608 H.C. Deb. 5s. Col. 1377.

The mediaeval Free Cities, Augsburg, Nuremburg, the Hansa towns of the Baltic, had all been swept away with the coming of modern nationalism and the best known modern example, Danzig, created in 1919 as a compromise between German nationalism and the new Poland's demand for access to the sea, had been a continuous source of conflict and tension in the inter-war period, ending in the violent collapse of the experiment in 1939. Possibly the only condition on which a 'free city' can remain independent is where it is protected by a substantial hinterland of friendly territory. This, however, was the very circumstance lacking in the case of West Berlin, an isolated Western outpost in a Communist ocean. Moreover, both Russia and the Communist regime in East Germany hardly troubled to hide their intention to interpret the epithet 'free' in their own way. The severance of the link with West Germany, on which the prosperity of West Berlin was based, and the repeated Communist charge that West Berlin (in the words of the November note) was a centre of 'subversive activity against the German Democratic Republic, the Soviet Union and other members of the Warsaw pact' indicated that the western sectors of the city would be forced to conform to Communist ideas of 'democratic centralism' the moment that Western forces left. In the November note it was plainly stated that unrestricted communication between West Berlin and the outside world would depend upon the West Berlin authorities undertaking 'not to permit on (their) territory any hostile or subversive activity directed against the German Democratic Republic'.

On the other hand, if Western occupation forces were to remain it was difficult to see how they could avoid coming to terms with the East German authorities since, if a Soviet-East German peace treaty were signed, these authorities would take over from Soviet officials at the road, rail and canal checkpoints for access to West Berlin from Federal Germany, and at the air safety centres controlling the air corridors. This meant that some form of *de facto* recognition of those authorities would have to be granted, even though the three Western Powers were committed to regard the Federal Republic as the 'only legitimate government' for Germany and the basic assumption of West German politics was that the East German regime was a Soviet puppet with no title to respect. It is true that for some time East German officials had been responsible for checking the papers of West German travellers who crossed East German territory to reach West Berlin. But Soviet officials maintained dealings with Western occupation forces in Berlin and the Soviet Government determined policy on access to Berlin generally. At the end of

November Dulles, for the United States, admitted at a Press conference that the East Germans might be accepted as 'agents' acting
on behalf of Russia at the checkpoints, the ultimate responsibility
remaining in Moscow. Selwyn Lloyd, for Britain, agreed, provided
the agents were limited to 'minor technical functions on our lines
of communication to Berlin'.[1] But if Russia really washed her hands
of her obligations and withdrew, the power to cause incidents which
might contain the makings of war or peace would lie with the puppet
rather than the master. Khrushchev himself seemed well aware of
this, to judge from his scarcely concealed mistrust of the Ulbricht
regime in East Germany and his determination to seek an understanding with the West which would achieve his main purposes.

Despite Khrushchev's verbosity, however, it was not clear just what
these purposes were. The phraseology of his declarations on Berlin,
with the continuous reference to the 'Hitler generals' of West Germany, seemed designed less to reveal his thought than to curry favour
with opinion in Britain and France which remained suspicious of the
Germans. Khrushchev could hardly seriously believe that West
Berlin, with its 10,000 Western troops, was an advance guard for an
aggressive attack towards the East when Russia alone was said to
have 350,000 troops in East Germany, although the debate on the
siting of American medium-range missiles in Europe at the NATO
'summit' meeting in Paris in December 1947 suggested that not even
West Berlin could be entirely ruled out as a missile base. It was also
possible that pressure in favour of a move on Berlin had been applied
by the East German leaders during their visit to Moscow in August
1958 and that this resulted in Khrushchev's reluctant conversion to
the 'free city' proposal. Russia's first presentation of the idea to the
world had an appearance of haste about it which possibly reflected
the sudden recognition that if the Ulbricht regime was to be spared
another uprising in East Germany like that of June 1953 it would
have to be reinforced by giving it control over both parts of the
former German capital. This interpretation was strengthened by the
serious economic position of East Germany, the shabbiest of all
Communist enterprises in East Europe. So long as a free West Berlin
existed, with its well-advertised attractions of western life, so long as
East Germans could escape from the Ulbricht regime through West
Berlin, the consolidation of Communism in East Germany remained
in doubt. The sheer loss of manpower through the escape hatch of
West Berlin provided the mounting note of urgency behind Khrushchev's demands, especially in 1961, for a liquidation of the 'anoma-
[1] 596 H.C. Deb. 5s. Col. 88 (written answers, December 1, 1958).

lous' situation in Berlin. During the ten years' life of the East German regime ending in 1961 the authorities in Bonn estimated that four million East Germans had made their way to the West via West Berlin, almost a quarter of the total population. These refugees, who, as Lenin said of the Russian army in 1917, had 'voted for freedom with their feet', were to a large extent young and well qualified persons, including large numbers of doctors and technicians. When at length the East German Communists brutally and illegally put an end to this drain on August 13, 1961, by building a wall to cut off West Berlin from the eastern sector and created a 'dead zone' extending over the whole 860 miles between East and West Germany, they no doubt calculated that this loss of the Ulbricht regime's lifeblood had gone as far as it safely could.

That Khrushchev's aim was to stabilize East Germany by making Berlin its capital, yet to do so without serious risk of war, seemed evident from his repeated postponement of the threat to make peace with East Germany. In November 1958 six months were allowed for the negotiation of a solution to the German problem. This was extended to a year at the Four-Power Foreign Ministers' meeting at Geneva in June 1959 and, before the conference recessed, to eighteen months.[1] During the next two years the time limit receded into the background. Then, when Khrushchev met President Kennedy in Vienna in June 1961, to take stock of the position after the change from a Republican to a Democratic administration in the United States, he reaffirmed his intention to sign the peace treaty. This was made more specific in subsequent statements in Russia and it was expected that the date of the conclusion of the treaty would be announced at the Twenty-second Congress of the Soviet Communist Party which opened in Moscow on October 18th. Instead, Khrushchev told the Congress that the treaty would not be signed before the year's end if the Western Powers were businesslike about negotiations. It is hardly conceivable that Khrushchev genuinely feared that the mere handing over of East Berlin to East Germany in a peace treaty would be forcibly resisted by the West, since the West was no more in a position to make war about the signature of a peace treaty than they were when Russia concluded an agreement to recognize the East German Government on September 20, 1955. So long as no interference was offered to Western rights of access to Berlin and the freedom of West Berlin was not attacked, the West, it was clear, would probably refrain from force. The fact that force was threat-

[1] Miscellaneous No. 11 (1959), Conference of Foreign Ministers at Geneva, Cmd. 797, pp. 22, 40.

ened from the West if either of these vital conditions was not met seemed to show that Khrushchev's hesitation were part of a tactic of waiting for the time and circumstances in which he could encompass the two objects of closing access to West Berlin and ending its freedom without risk of war. War, Khrushchev knew, was equally suicidal for Russia as for the West, despite his repeated boasts that Communism would survive nuclear conflict.

This interpretation seemed borne out by Khrushchev's efforts to divide the West on the Berlin issue, in order to avert a united resistance from the West when direct Communist pressure on West Berlin began, and to demonstrate Russia's increasing military might in the crudest form. The former tactic was expressed in direct appeals to Britain, France and Italy not to incur nuclear destruction merely to serve the interests of German 'revanchists and revenge-seekers' and in the wholly misleading representation of the crisis as having arisen from Russia's decision to make peace with East Germany. The idea that the military precautions taken by the West with the mounting tension in Berlin after the closing of the sector boundary in August 1961 were the prelude to an attack on the Communist bloc if Russia made peace with East Germany was indeed absurd, but no doubt it was hoped that, by describing the situation in this way, Russia could erode support for the Western position among the European NATO countries so that it would not be available when the real issue arose of a Communist attack on West Berlin. At the same time it may have been hoped that Western determination not to be edged out of Berlin would be undermined by a war of nerves in which the main theme was Russia's hideous nuclear destructive power. Russia's decision to break off the nuclear test suspension conference in Geneva in August 1961 in order to hold a series of nuclear tests in September and October in plain defiance of world opinion, after three years in which no country except France had tested nuclear weapons, and Khrushchev's announcement at the Twenty-second Party Congress in October that Russia had 100-megaton bombs and would test a 50-megaton weapon before the month was out, all seemed to have a political rather than military significance, namely to frighten the West out of its position in Berlin. Evidently it was hoped that a prolonged alternation of threats with offers to negotiate would bring the West to accept Russia's proposals for Berlin for the sake of peace and quiet.

The principal meaning of Berlin for Russia however (except in so far as the issue was not part of the general trial of strength between her and the United States for supremacy) seemed to be that it might

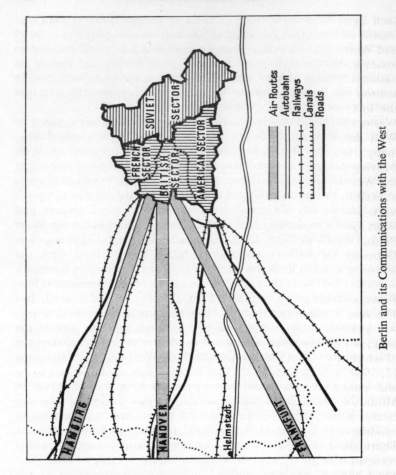

force the West to accept the division of Germany and abandon the cause of Germany unity, possibly with serious effects on the unity of the West itself. This had been a theme of Soviet policy since 1955 and increasingly since 1957.[1] Acceptance of the 'free city' idea for West Berlin would clearly have that implication. So would Western acceptance of the East German regime, even if only on a *de facto* basis, as part of a bargain for strengthening Western rights in Berlin. Even if no agreement were reached with the West (and almost any

[1] See Bulganin's letter to the NATO Powers and Switzerland, January 8, 1958, Soviet Union No. 2 (1958), Cmd. 381, pp. 16–24.

such agreement must embody Western concessions to the Communist viewpoint) continuous conflicts between East German officials and Western forces in Berlin might one day drive the West to cut its losses and withdraw, which would again consolidate the German national division. Whichever way things worked out (provided the tension did not lead to war) the result must almost certainly strain the links between West Germany and other NATO Powers. Any Western agreement with Russia designed to secure the freedom of West Berlin would probably involve some sacrifice of West Germany's larger ambitions; on the other hand, the frictions accompanying the lack of agreement might cause more and more people in the West to hold Federal Germany responsible for the tension. If, as a result of the Berlin crisis, strains between West Germany and other NATO States grew, Russia herself might step in with some offer to West German opinion. Having a decisive voice in the future of Berlin, she might not be regarded with such contempt in West Germany as she was when the three Western Powers could still seriously pursue German unity.

Western reactions

The Western position in reply to this Soviet policy was as clear as it was awkward to protect. Western occupation rights in Berlin went back, not to the Potsdam agreement of 1945, the precise legal force of which in 1958 was in doubt, but to the agreements of September 12, 1944, and May 1, 1945, which divided Berlin into four sectors and established the inter-Allied Kommandatura, or Council of Military Governors, in the city. These agreements in effect permitted forces of the three Western Powers to enter Berlin in return for handing over to Soviet armies large parts of Mecklenburg, Saxony, Thuringia and Anhalt, which were then absorbed into the Soviet occupation zone.[1] Russia was of course a party to these agreements, which had been signed before the German Democratic Republic was conceived, and also to the Four-Power Agreement of June 20, 1949, which ended the Berlin blockade and reaffirmed Soviet obligations to ensure the normal functioning of transport and communications between Berlin and the western zones of Germany.[2] On more than one occasion Khrushchev admitted the validity of these agreements, although his repeated argument that, after so many years, wartime agreements should be allowed to lapse seemed at times to persuade

[1] Germany No. 2 (1948), Cmd. 7534, p. 5; Germany No. 1 (1945), Cmd. 6648, p. 7. See above, Chapter IV, p. 66.
[2] Miscellaneous No. 11 (1949), Cmd. 7729, p. 18.

him that Russia was free to ignore them. Throughout the crisis, however, he returned to the point that Western rights were valid and he was evidently anxious to have them re-written in a form which would allow for their liquidation at a later date.

At the same time, legal rights formed a relatively small part of the Western case on Berlin. West Berlin depended upon Western protection, without which it could not exist as a free community. No Western statesman could contemplate another Munich in which such people were abandoned in favour of a respite which could not last long. The British reply to Khrushchev's note on Berlin, sent on December 31, 1958, neatly reversed the charge that Munich showed the pro-Hitler leanings of Britain in the 'thirties by saying:

> On this point HM's Government would only observe that whatever views may now be held on the motives and actions of the British Government at that time, HM's present Government are resolved to profit from the historical lessons which were then learnt. In fact they are determined not to pursue a policy of appeasement or to be deterred by threats, from faithfully adhering to their international engagements.[1]

Without doubt far-reaching moral and political consequences would result from an enforced Western retirement from Berlin. Throughout the world a struggle was continuing between East and West to win and hold the loyalties of men. Any sign that the West would sacrifice those who had entered under its protection, if it was necessary to do so to save its own skin, would clearly have momentous effects on this struggle, especially in West Germany.

There was thus no difference of view between the Western Powers that a Communist attack on West Berlin would be resisted by Western occupation troops, which would inevitably draw the Western Powers themselves into the conflict. The same would apply to any attempt to sever access between West Berlin and the West. That had been the position during the Berlin crisis in 1948.[2] There were, however, important differences between the position in 1948 and the situation ten years later. At the earlier crisis Russia had no nuclear weapons, while in 1958 she was able to deliver hydrogen weapons of the greatest magnitude to the most distant countries, possibly with more accuracy than her rivals. Perhaps because of her nuclear inferiority in 1948, she had left open the air entrances into West Berlin, thus providing the West with a pretext for not attempting to

[1] Cmd. 634, p. 23.
[2] See above, Chapter IV, p. 89.

force a passage into the city. There was some doubt in the late 1950s whether Russia would do the same again if indeed she meant to isolate West Berlin, or whether the air corridors could be successfully used again if she did. By 1958 aircraft passing between West Berlin and West Germany were dependent upon radar and landing systems which necessitated the co-operation of authorities in East German territory. Moreover, although supplies in West Berlin were in much better state than in 1948 (it was thought likely in November 1958 that the western sectors could keep going for six months on accumulated stocks), larger imports would be needed from the outside world in 1958 to sustain the standards to which West Berlin had become adjusted. On the other hand, if armed conflict did result from the crisis it might not take a form which would allow the West to appear to be acting on the defensive, as was essential in order to win over opinion at home and at the United Nations. Measures applied by the Communists against West Berlin would probably not come as a military attack, but as repeated interferences with access from East Berlin or West Germany or with the various services used by the city, none of which would be easy to represent as justifying universal nuclear destruction. After the closing of the sector boundary on August 13, 1961, Communist efforts seemed to focus on creating inconveniences for the West Berliners and the occupation forces, rather than on preparing a military *coup*. This meant that if the West decided to use force to prevent the erosion of their rights and those of the West Berliners, it might be they who would have to fire the first shot. This would be the case for example if, after taking over supervision of access to West Berlin under a peace treaty with Russia, the East German authorities began introducing cumbrous traffic regulations, without actually forbidding entrance or exit to any vehicle. It was precisely this danger which made Russia, on her side, anxious to postpone making a peace treaty with East Germany, and the United States, on her side, anxious if at all possible to incorporate some provision governing West Berlin in the proposed Soviet-East German treaty.

In any event force, with its hideous consequences, could not be contemplated unless after serious efforts to negotiate a peaceful solution. Throughout the crisis that fact was fully appreciated on both sides. From the Western viewpoint, however, there were serious difficulties about negotiation. In the first place, it was vital not to create the impression that the Soviet Union had only to create a crisis in order to bring the West to the conference table with proposals for solving it. Among the reasons which prompted the Soviet move on November 27, 1958, seemed to be impatience with Western reluctance to come to a 'summit' meeting and insistence on discussing the wrong issues (from the Soviet viewpoint) if a 'summit' were held. Berlin clearly had its uses as a means of forcing the West into a more accommodating mood over the whole range of international issues.

Throughout 1957 and 1958 the Soviet Government pressed for a 'summit' meeting, although it was all too obvious that the basic positions of East and West had not materially altered since the Geneva meeting of 1955.[1] The Western reply, which was in part a compromise between Britain, who favoured such meetings, and her three allies, who suspected them, was that 'summit' conferences required careful preparation if they were to stand any chance of success and that a hastily prepared meeting which failed might make the atmosphere even worse than before.[2] This had not in fact happened in 1955; nevertheless there was a case for trying a new formula. In 1955 the 'ice-breaking' type of Heads of Government meeting had been attempted, the object being to create an atmosphere of trust favourable to the solution of detailed problems at a lower level later on. In 1958 the Western view was that the process should begin at the other end, with preparatory work by Ambassadors and Foreign Ministers which would, as Macmillan put it, 'choose agenda calculated to achieve concrete results on specific issues' and 'disentangle points of disagreement and reveal the most promising areas of agreement'.[3] This approach was normal in Western diplomacy, but took little account of the concentration of authority at the top in Russia, which Khrushchev's own dominating and restless personality only served to entrench. Soviet diplomats and Foreign Ministers were notoriously governed by rigid instruction from above; Khrushchev once said of his Foreign Secretary, Gromyko, that he would 'sit naked on a block of ice' if he were told. Moreover, the Soviet Government did not seem to consider 'summit' meetings as serving the same purpose as the West had in view, namely to sound out the position of the other side and bargain and barter until an acceptable compromise is reached. Since Soviet leaders believed that Western society must in good time collapse through its own 'internal contradictions', 'summit' meetings, while holding off a Western attack on

---

[1] See Bulganin's letter to the NATO Powers, January 8, 1958 (Cmd. 381, pp. 16–24) and Western proposals for 'summit' conference agenda: Soviet Union No. 4 (1958), Cmd. 469, p. 21.

[2] Macmillan to Bulganin, February 8, 1958, Cmd. 381, pp. 26-8.

[3] 582 H.C. Deb. 5s. Col. 1221 (February 19, 1958).

Russia, helped to provide a footing from which differences in the Western group and between that group and the rest of the non-Communist world could be exploited.

Western diplomacy had never been equipped for this kind of struggle. Nor could the Western leaders of 1958, President Eisenhower, Macmillan, the enigmatic de Gaulle, compare (except perhaps for the first) with Khrushchev in the 'summit' art of debate-cum-mass entertainment before world audiences. They therefore raised difficulties, at length agreeing to a 'summit' only after the revolution in Iraq which removed King Faisal and Nuri As-Said in July 1958, provided it was held at the United Nations Security Council and limited to the Middle East. After a period in which Khrushchev's agreement to this seemed likely, he drew back, possibly owing to the influence of the Chinese Communists, who had no place within the United Nations, and proposed instead an extraordinary session of the General Assembly.[1] On this Western reluctance about East-West talks the Khrushchev note on Berlin certainly had an impact, as was no doubt intended. Replying to the note on December 31, 1958, the British Government, along with the allies, said they were ready to negotiate on Berlin, though only 'in the wider framework of negotiations for a solution of the German problem as well as that of European security'.[2] More important, some of the most vital positions of the West, which had been held until the receipt of the Soviet note, at once began to relax. Dulles spoke of 'other means' of uniting Germany than by free elections. Selwyn Lloyd said in April 1959 'what we have to consider is whether some phasing is possible so that the free elections (in Germany) can take place at a time acceptable to all parties and yet not be postponed indefinitely'.[1] Prominent Americans, notably Senator Fulbright, Chairman of the Senate Foreign Relations Committee, and Senator Mansfield, a leading member of the Committee, came out in support of disengagement in central Europe, formerly almost too delicate a subject to mention in America. Since it was evidently one of the aims of the Khrushchev note on Berlin to compel some such relaxation of the Western position, there were good grounds for thinking that readiness to negotiate did not necessarily produce a frame of mind in Russia conducive to successful negotiation.

This was the position taken up with increasing insistence by President de Gaulle, who showed much the same obstructiveness in his relations with his allies as he had done as an exiled leader of Free

[1] Soviet Union No. 5 (1958), Cmd. 516, pp. 6–7, 7–8, 14–16.
[2] 604 H.C. Deb. 5s. Col. 907 (April 27th).

S

France during the war. Since West Germany was a close ally of France in the community of the Six, de Gaulle was almost bound to support the German argument that negotiation must not be allowed to involve sacrifices by Germany, and it was hard to think of effective negotiation unless the West Germans abandoned some of the illusions which they had cherished so long. But it was entirely in keeping with de Gaulle's conception of diplomacy that he should announce that so long as the West stood firm and paid no attention to Russia's bluster, no harm would come to them. This attitude also seemed to be held by the United States until the accession of the Kennedy administration in January 1961. Kennedy's position was a weak one from which to force a change in the American position, in that he had won the elections in the previous November with the narrowest margin in American history. Yet he realized that the passage of time without settlement with Russia being reached did nothing to improve the West's bargaining position, but merely increased the risk of war through one side or the other being forced into a position from which it could not retreat. Kennedy's phrase used in his inaugural address in Washington in January 1961, 'we shall not fear to negotiate but shall never negotiate through fear', also summarized the British position, though France was not convinced.

The deadlock remains

Assuming, however, that negotiations were attempted, the fact remained that the West had placed itself in a position, or been placed by events, in which it had few inducements to hand to cause Russia to accept the situation in West Berlin until Germany was reunited. Ideally, what would have suited the West, assuming that German unity on the basis of a modified Eden plan of 1954 was not possible, was a new statute for Berlin which committed Russia even more unambiguously to respect the freedom of West Berlin and access to it. It was in order to agree upon such a statute that the Foreign Ministers of Russia and the three Western Powers laboured at Geneva from May 11 to June 10, 1959, and from July 13th to August 5th without success. British aims at the conference, according to the Foreign Secretary were:

First, some progress towards the reunification of Germany on acceptable terms; secondly, reaffirmation of the right of the people of West Berlin to choose their own system of society and also acceptance of the need for satisfactory arrangements for the free access to West Berlin upon which their freedom depends; and thirdly a reduction in tension and an improvement of stability in Europe.[1]

Discussion of the first of these items yielded as little result as previous exchanges, even though the West agreed to a committee of East and West Germans, whose vote could not overrule the former, to expand contact between the two parts of Germany and draft a law for free elections. The West also conceded that free elections need not be held until two and a half years after the signature of the agreement.[2] With the failure of discussion on the wider German question Western security proposals, based upon a zone of stabilized forces and special measures for military forces and installations on the frontiers of a reunited Germany, fell to the ground.[3] Agreement seemed within an ace of being reached, however, on an interim statute for Berlin, in which Western rights and freedom of access would be reaffirmed in return for measures to prevent West Berlin from being a provocation to the Eastern bloc. But difficulties arose on the question of the position at the end of the interim period, during which efforts at German reunification would be continued, supposing that these efforts had failed. The Soviet paper issued in the night between June 19th, when the Ministers agreed to recess, and June 20th, when they formally recessed, appeared to concede that in this event the Geneva conference would 'resume the consideration of the West Berlin question'.[4] It soon appeared, however, when the conference met after the recess on July 13th that by signing the interim statute the West would in effect be placing their rights on a provisional basis.

If Russia was to consent to the kind of permanent statute which would have suited the West, after repeated Soviet allegations that occupation troops in Berlin were 'anomalous' so many years after the war, she would clearly require some solid *quid pro quo* in return. This was even more likely if her aim was not to prevent West Berlin from being a source of disturbance to the eastern parts of Germany, but to draw West Berlin into the Communist camp. Yet it was hard to see what the West could offer in any negotiation. It was committed not to accept any solution of the German problem which did not envisage free elections, and hence the linking of all Germany with NATO, at some stage. Since it was precisely this Western position

[1] 604 H.C. Deb. 5s. Col. 904 (April 27, 1959).
[2] Miscellaneous No. 11 (1959), Conference of Foreign Ministers at Geneva, Cmd. 797, pp. 5–7.
[3] *Ibid.*, pp. 7–9.
[4] *Ibid.*, p. 42.

which had prompted Russia to create the crisis over Berlin, the deadlock remained. The Geneva Foreign Ministers' conference in the summer of 1959 seemed to relieve the tension, though no agreement was reached, and a similar contribution was made by talks between President Eisenhower and Khrushchev at Camp David, Maryland, in September. As a result of these discussions the President at length reversed his stand that more preparation was needed before a 'summit' could be held and this enabled Macmillan to reveal to the Commons in a Debate on the Address in October that Britain had been strongly pressing for such a conference.

> We would like a summit meeting (the Prime Minister said) at the earliest practicable date, in order to keep up the momentum. The general situation has improved; we do not want it to slip back again. Tension has been lowered; we do not want it to increase again. . . . So we shall continue to work for a date for the 'summit' meeting as early as practicable. I hope that we shall succeed. It will not be for want of trying.[1]

This was less definite than his statement on September 30th, during the general election campaign, that 'within a few days the actual date of the "summit" talks will be fixed', but it showed the way in which British influence had been used in Washington, now bereft of the trenchant Dulles, who died in May. When the four leaders at length met in Paris in May 1960, however, these efforts came to nothing when Khrushchev refused to begin the talks for reasons not yet fully known. One explanation is that at the Camp David talks with Eisenhower he had been led to think the Western position was about to crumble, whereas it was clear by the time the gathering assembled in Paris that in all basic respects that position was unchanged. The Soviet leader seems then to have used the pretext of a flight by an American espionage plane over Russia on May 1st to break up the conference and return home, there to await the coming of a new American administration. Criticism of Khrushchev's 'coexistence' policy by his Chinese allies, who had not taken kindly to Khruschchev's visit to America and Vice-President Nixon's Soviet tour in the summer of 1959, and by unrepentant Stalinists in the Soviet Communist Party may have worked in the same direction.

When President Kennedy assumed office in the following January official Soviet reactions seemed to be cordial owing perhaps to the favourable associations of a Democratic administration created by Franklin Roosevelt during the war. Nevertheless when the two

[1] 612 H.C. Deb. 5s. Col. 78 (October 27th).

leaders, Kennedy and Khrushchev, met for two days in Vienna at the beginning of June the exchanges seemed grim and fruitless, although it soon became apparent that a new wind was moving in Washington. The idea that East Germany must be accepted as a real, if disagreeable, fact was gaining acceptance and with it, the possibility that nuclear weapons might not, after all, be handed over to West German troops. Both eventualities were hinted at in President Kennedy's first address to the United Nations General Assembly in September. Meanwhile, talks in New York during the Assembly's meetings between Dean Rusk, Kennedy's Secretary of State, and the Soviet Foreign Minister, Gromyko, which were joined by the British Foreign Secretary, Lord Home, seemed to make progress, reflected in Khrushchev's speech at the Twenty-second Party Congress in Moscow on October 18th, in which he said he would not after all make peace with East Germany before the end of the year. With the series of Soviet nuclear tests during September and October, however, culminating in the explosion of a 57-megaton weapon on October 30th, and with Soviet and American tanks lined up against each other at the sector boundaries in Berlin, the situation remained tense in the extreme.

CHAPTER NINE

The Problem of Arms Control

Between the two wars Britain played a leading part in the efforts to secure multilateral disarmament. She was one of the sponsors of the Washington and London naval treaties signed in 1922 and 1930 respectively, the only really effective arms agreements of the period, and was prominent in the world disarmament conference which met at Geneva in February 1932 and petered out two years later. Her position as one of the leading Powers of the day naturally gave her this prominence and the strong unofficial bodies in Britain which were active in the cause of disarmament, such as the League of Nations Union, encouraged British Governments to give a lead to the movement. Moreover, Britain, along with her allies of the 1914–18 war, began the twenty years' peace with certain commitments, if not to disarm, at least to try to do so. The Versailles Treaty of 1919 between the Allies and Germany laid down that the enforced disarmament of the latter was intended 'to render possible the initiation of a general limitation of armaments of all nations'.[1] Many British politicians considered that this phrase constituted a legal obligation on the Allies to disarm and that German disarmament would no longer be valid if the obligation was evaded. Britain was also a permanent member of the Council of the League of Nations, which was charged by Article 8 of the League Covenant to formulate plans for the reduction of armaments 'to the lowest point consistent with national safety and the enforcement by common action of international obligations'.

There were fewer such incentives leading Britain to take the initiative in disarmament negotiations after 1945.[2] So far from being a Power of the first rank, without whom a world arms agreement was inconceivable, she was largely dependent for her military protection on the United States and, after 1949, on the North Atlantic

[1] Preamble to Part V of the Treaty.
[2] A useful short account of the disarmament negotiations since 1945 is given in *Disarmament: an outline of negotiations*, by Anthony Nutting, London, 1959. Bernard G. Bechhoefer gives a more detailed survey in *Postwar Negotiations for Arms Control*, Washington, DC, 1961.

Alliance generally. This meant that any arms agreement to which Britain was a party must in the last resort have NATO approval, if she was to continue within that organization, and that disarmament must not have the effect of increasing even more the distance between her own strength and that of the two giant Powers of the day. Thus the British Government, like the French, rejected the Soviet call at the end of the war for an immediate one-third cut in armed force levels on the ground that, as in progressive taxation, the 'have' states should give up proportionately more than the 'have-nots'. Public opinion still deplored the waste of money on arms, the burden of which became greater as from 1951 than ever before, but fewer people now believed that arms were a prime cause of war and could be scaled down without political tensions being first resolved. Even in the Labour Party, which had been an active partisan on behalf of multilateral disarmament between the wars, many prominent figures were sceptical about disarmament as a road to peace. The Labour MP, R. T. Paget, echoed this strand in postwar British thinking when he said:

> The instability which has caused war has been far more often in history the result of too few arms than too many. That happened after the last war (i.e. in 1945). We had a very insecure situation because we demobilized too quickly and the Russians did not. We have a vastly better security today (1954) and a vastly more stable world than when war broke out in Korea. That is because we have armed, because we have corrected that unbalance and because we have given frontiers the look of security.[1]

The Labour Party, it should be remembered, was in Government immediately after the war, took Britain into the North Atlantic pact in 1949 and initiated the great rearmament drive of 1951. This meant that pressure towards disarmament from Labour, the traditional champion of disarmament, did not really begin until the Conservatives returned to office in November 1951 and did not acquire strong force until an American thermo-nuclear weapon was exploded in the Pacific on March 1, 1954.

Britain moreover had fewer commitments to promote disarmament after 1945 than after 1918. The Atlantic Charter, signed by Roosevelt and Churchill in August 1941, merely bound them 'to aid and encourage . . . practicable measures which will lighten for peace-loving peoples the crushing burden of armaments'. The United Nations Charter, which Britain signed in June 1945, was even less

[1] 531 H.C. Deb. 5s. Col. 894 (July 30th).

specific; it merely assigned discussion of the 'principles governing disarmament and the regulation of armaments' to the General Assembly of the new organization. On the other hand, only four years after the war Britain pledged herself by the Atlantic pact to afford military assistance to eleven other countries if they should fall victim to attack, and to 'maintain and develop (her) individual . . . capacity to resist armed attack' in order to render that assistance more effective.[1]

In addition, the international situation in 1945 did not favour strong British initiatives towards disarmament negotiations, except in one respect. In 1919, once Germany had been disarmed by the peace treaty, Britain's disarmament efforts were chiefly directed towards allies, especially the United States and Japan, as far as naval armaments were concerned, and France and her East European allies, as far as land armaments were concerned. These she wished gradually to reduce to Germany's level. In 1945, on the other hand, one of Britain's two principal allies, Russia, at once made clear her acquisitive policy in East Europe and maintained a massive land army as a threat to West and South-East Europe and to the Middle East. Her other principal ally, the United States, demobilized her armies as soon as the war ended and relied for her continental defence on her monopoly of atomic weapons, thus causing British Ministers to fear that friendly forces would not be available if Soviet power extended to West Europe. Strategically speaking therefore, Britain was engaged from the moment of Germany's collapse in a struggle on two fronts: one against Soviety military and ideological pressure, the other against the American inclination to retire from Europe when the war ended. In neither of its aspects was this struggle conducive to an active British disarmament policy.

The one respect in which disarmament retained its urgent character was that the atomic bomb, used by American forces against Japan in August 1945, posed a new problem for mankind, though of a nature which made it uncertain whether multilateral disarmament was the right solution. The atomic bomb drastically shortened the time allowed to man to learn other methods than force for settling his differences. Since it was doubtful whether he could change his habits so quickly, the case for eliminating the bomb from the world's armaments was strong. Yet the atomic bomb at once immensely magnified the difficulties of providing for the enforcement of an arms limitation agreement and made the risk of failure to

[1] Articles 5 and 3 respectively of the North Atlantic Treaty signed on April 4, 1949.

secure complete enforcement so great that to some it seemed safer not even to try to achieve it. A system of inspection to ensure that fissionable material, the source of atomic energy, was not being secretly diverted to military uses would clearly have to be so thorough that none but the actual rulers of the country concerned could practise it. But this was as nothing compared with the difficulty of preventing hidden stores of nuclear weapons being accumulated before the treaty came into effect. Selwyn Lloyd, the British Minister of Supply, said in December 1954 that, in view of the existing nuclear stockpiles of the three nuclear Powers, it was impossible to have an inspection system more than 95 per cent efficient. adding 'I think we shall do well to get that'.[1] But a margin of error as small as 5 per cent could be fatal. At the Four-Power meeting of Foreign Ministers at Geneva in November 1955 Macmillan, then Foreign Secretary, said that 'in the case of conventional weapons one could reconcile oneself to a certain margin of error or deception in any control system. This would not be disastrous. But the thermonuclear weapons are now so deadly that the slightest margin of error or deception could be decisive for the fate of nations.'[2] Macmillan's conclusion ('the risks involved are quite unacceptable') could not be more fatal to the hopes of nuclear disarmament under existing inspection systems.

Alongside these problems posed by nuclear arms for traditional disarmament methods was another factor: the effect of the achievement of substantial nuclear parity on both sides by the mid-1950s, which held statesmen back from embracing disarmament as the answer to all their fears. It seemed that the nuclear stalemate, by ruling out war as too terrible to contemplate, might succeed, given caution and patience on the part of the leading Powers, in keeping the world at peace. In that event, as Churchill said, 'we shall by a process of sublime irony have reached a stage where safety will be the sturdy child of terror and survival the twin brother of annihilation'.[3] By the 1960s this hope seemed much slimmer, but its effect was to rob disarmament proposals of the desperate urgency they seemed to have between the wars. Disarmament advocates argued that the failure of the 1932 disarmament conference had inevitably led to war in 1939. Yet there was an equal logic in the argument that success in disarmament might lead to war in the future if it abolished the 'balance of nuclear terror' which kept the Powers from fighting.

[1] 535 H.C. Deb. 5s. Col. 633 (December 6th).
[2] Quoted in *The Disarmament Question, 1945–1956*, HMSO, 1957, p. 21.
[3] 537 *ibid.*, Col. 1899 (March 1, 1955).

The international control of atomic energy

The revolutionary implications of nuclear weapons for all existing international relations were strikingly shown by the plan for atomic energy control presented to the United Nations on behalf of the United States, with the support of Britain and Canada, by Bernard M. Baruch in June 1946. The origin of the plan was a declaration by these three Powers in November 1945 that they would share their knowledge concerning the industrial application of nuclear energy, given safeguards against its diversion to military ends, and that they proposed the creation of a United Nations Commission to prevent the abuse of atomic energy for destructive purposes and to promote its widest exploitation for industrial and humanitarian objects.[1] The safeguards referred to in this declaration were elaborated by a Board of Consultants to a United States Committee on Atomic Energy which the Secretary of State appointed in January 1946. The Board reported in March that nothing short of a world development authority would suffice, with power to own all fissionable material, control directly all nuclear activities dangerous to world security and licence less dangerous activities. The authority (IADA) would have full powers of inspection in all countries, but the essence of the plan was that it would be far more than an inspectorate. By endorsing the Acheson-Lilienthal plan (named after the chairmen of the Committee and the Board respectively) Britain and the United States agreed in principle to place their nuclear enterprises under the authority, but on two conditions: first, that no state would be allowed to carry on nuclear activities outside the new authority's scope and, secondly, that no state would be able to infringe the agreement, for instance by manufacturing nuclear energy for war purposes, while protecting itself through the exercise of a veto over the application of penalties against it.[2]

The 'Baruch proposals', based on the Board of Consultants' report, was eventually accepted in part by a majority of the United Nations General Assembly in November 1948 and hence became known as the United Nations plan. It was, however, strongly opposed by the Soviet Union, with the support of her Communist allies. Russia urged in preference to this revolutionary plan a mere general undertaking to renounce nuclear weapons, to destroy existing stocks and to establish subsequently a control organ the precise

[1] US Department of State, *The International Control of Atomic Energy*, 1946, pp. 118–20.
[2] *A Report on the International Control of Atomic Energy*, US Government Printing Office and HMSO, London, 1946.

character of which was to form the subject of later negotiations. The control organ, it transpired, would be able to report an infraction of the agreement by majority vote of its members, but the United Nations Security Council would decide what to do with the report on the basis of unanimity. This meant that the veto of the great Powers would remain. In view of the Soviet attitude the United Nations Atomic Energy Commission, which the General Assembly had created in January 1946, had little useful work to do and at the end of 1951 it was merged with the Commission on Conventional Armaments to form the Disarmament Commission for dealing with both kinds of arms.

Soviet hostility to the Baruch scheme was generally thought to stem from fear that Russia's own nuclear development would be handicapped by a world authority in which she and her allies would be in a minority.[1] In any case her own atomic bomb was under construction (the first Soviet bomb was tested in September 1949) and, like all states engaged on rearming, she probably considered that her influence in these discussions would be increased once she had become a nuclear Power. This decision, leading to the defeat of the plan, was later deplored by the British Foreign Secretary in 1956, Selwyn Lloyd, as a 'tragedy'.[2] But it is questionable whether the purport of Baruch's claim that 'there must be no veto to protect those who violate their solemn agreements not to develop or use atomic energy for destructive purposes' was well understood by the British and American Governments which supported it or, if it was, whether they thought a real prospect existed of its being accepted. To endow such an authority as that contemplated in the plan with power to decide the whole future development of atomic energy and to create a supranational force to impose the agreement, even, if necessary, against the greatest military Powers, required a radical amendment of the entire basis of the United Nations Charter. It is doubtful whether American public opinion would have endorsed such a massive surrender of sovereignty. It is hard to imagine British opinion doing so, considering that only four years later the British Government and Opposition refused to surrender control of the coal and steel industries to a West European supranational body. The American Board of Consultants were no doubt right to report that, after examination of the problem, no other proposals seemed adequate to the task. But this merely underlined the nuclear dilemma:

[1] See Gromyko's speech at the United Nations Security Council, March 5, 1947; United Nations Security Council, Second Year, OR No. 22, p. 453.
[2] 557 H.C. Deb. 5s. Col. 259 (July 24, 1956).

either world government (or something closely akin to it) would have to be created to take over this new source of power or no country could rely upon traditional techniques of international control to insure itself against secret hoarding of nuclear supplies by a rival State.

The inspection problem

With the failure of the Baruch plan East-West disarmament negotiations tended to take the form of efforts by either side to weaken the other in that type of defence (or offence, depending upon the side from which the struggle was looked at) in which the other was for the time being superior. The Western Powers, unwilling to surrender their nuclear shield except in return for an international authority as strong as that proposed in the Baruch plan, sought to reduce Russia's massive superiority in continental forces. On her side Russia tirelessly insisted on the verbal renunciation of nuclear weapons and proposed a one-third cut in force levels which would have increased her relative lead in continental forces. This struggle was fought out in the Commission for Conventional Armaments, created by the Security Council in February 1947, which took the same road towards deadlock as the Atomic Energy Commission. The main issues were Russia's refusal to agree to international verification of the force levels from which the agreed reductions were to take effect and the problem of ensuring by inspection that the reductions were carried out, both issues being intensified by the differences between Soviet and Western society. The closed society of Communist states was perhaps immoral by Western standards, but it existed and was an element in the military strength of those states which they were unwilling to abandon without some adequate return, although Soviet science, high as its achievements were later shown to be, undoubtedly suffered from its meagre intercourse with the outside world. The effect of the resistance maintained by Soviet delegates at the arms talks to thorough inspection and verification was that Western public opinion tended to assume that it was itself ready for any measure of inspection which was necessary to ensure that agreements were kept. But this was never put to the test, at least until the Soviet Government appeared to consent to far-reaching controls in 1955. Western reluctance to press Soviet delegates further at that time may well have been due to the sudden recognition that the West might have to throw open its own secret places to foreign eyes.

With the coming of the Korean war in 1950 and the intense rearmament drive in the West, followed by the testing of the first

Soviet thermo-nuclear weapon in August 1953, a change in Western disarmament policy appeared. These new factors in the situation also affected Soviet arms policy, though the gap between the two sides remained as wide as before, despite a gradual improvement in the tone of the exchanges. On the one hand, the West proposed at the end of 1951 to substitute for the United Nations Atomic Energy Commission and the Commission for Conventional Armaments a single new body, the United Nations Disarmament Commission, consisting of all eleven members of the Security Council and Canada, when her representative was not a member of the Council. The creation of the Commission in January 1952 was a concession to Russia's demand to set the West's nuclear armaments against her own conventional forces, and with the increase in the West's conventional strength as a result of the Korean war and Russia's acquisition of thermo-nuclear weapons the West had no reason for objecting further to the amalgamation of the two sets of discussions.[1] On her side, Russia now conceded that the convention to enforce her call for the renunciation of nuclear weapons should operate 'simultaneously' with the renunciation and not later.

None of this however affected the gap between the Soviet conception of inspection systems as having to be placed 'on a continuing basis' and the Western contention that the control organ must be created and ready to work before any agreement on a particular weapon could operate.[2] The difference was well illustrated by Selwyn Lloyd's criticism of the Soviet conception of 'simultaneity' at the eighth session of the United Nations General Assembly in 1953.

How do you declare the establishment of a system of control? (Lloyd asked). You have all the complexities of establishing a control organ, of deciding its terms of reference, of recruiting its staff, and of establishing its offices and its communications and its various other organs. How do you produce all that by a declaration? . . . I do not think that it is any use concealing the facts. The facts are these. Our fear is that we and our friends would abide by the prohibition and that the Soviet Union would not. . . . I do not think that we are dissuaded from that view by any regard that the Soviet Union has had for international morality since 1945.[3]

[1] Selwyn Lloyd at the United Nations General Assembly, December 11, 1951; United Nations No. 1 (1952), Cmd. 8547, p. 51.
[2] First Report of the Disarmament Commission, Cmd. 8589, pp. 9–10, 15–20.
[3] United Nations General Assembly, 8th Session, Official Records, First Committee, 665th meeting, pp. 215–6.

But on this issue Russia was beginning to have second thoughts, with the result that the comprehensive Anglo-French arms plan submitted in the following year came to have its attractions for Moscow.

The Disarmament Commission languished after its creation in 1952 and met only once during 1953. In order to facilitate progress Britain proposed the calling of a sub-committee of the Commission, to consist only of the four major Powers and Canada, and this more intimate group met for the first time at Lancaster House, London, on April 23, 1954, and received the Anglo-French proposals for disarmament by stages on June 11th. The essence of the plan was that, consistently with Western fears of Soviet preponderance in conventional arms, a beginning should be made with the reduction of armed forces to agreed levels first, the abolition of nuclear weapons forming a later stage. In effect, 50 per cent of the reductions needed to bring the armed forces of the United States, the Soviet Union and China down to one and a half million men each (with appropriate ceilings for the smaller Powers) would have to be achieved and confirmed by inspection before a beginning was made with the 'cut off' in nuclear weapons production and the elimination of nuclear stockpiles. Before this second stage was reached, the parties would have to be satisfied that the control organ was 'positioned' and effectively operating.[1] In all material respects Soviet reactions seemed unchanged. Soviet delegates repeated their call for a declaration by the major Powers of their unconditional renunciation of nuclear weapons as a preliminary to their total abolition, a one-third cut in the armed forces of the five permanent members of the Security Council and the 'simultaneous' establishment of controls. The leader of the British delegation, Selwyn Lloyd, pressed the Western objections to these principles during the five weeks before the Sub-Committee recessed on June 22nd, at length proposing that the Russians submit a specific list of those weapons which were to be prohibited and reduced and which could be definitely controlled by existing techniques. The Soviet reply was that it would be a waste of time to get down to details about weapons until the Powers had shown their will for disarmament by agreeing to an immediate ban on nuclear armaments.[2]

By the autumn, however, the outlook had distinctly improved. On September 30th, at the ninth session of the United Nations General Assembly, Vyshinsky coupled a general attack on Western

[1] Report on the Proceedings of the Sub-Committee, 1954, Cmd. 9204, Annex 9, pp. 31–2; Cmd. 9205, pp. 225 ff.
[2] Cmd. 9205.

politics with the reading of a Soviet resolution which omitted the call for an unsupervised ban on nuclear weapons and even proposed that the Anglo-French plan be taken as a basis for discussion. When talks were resumed in the Sub-Committee in London in February 1955, Soviet proposals still hesitated to authorize the control organ to do more than inspect and make recommendations, whereas the British delegation pressed for the inspectorate to have powers to order the cessation of activities in any country which infringed the treaty. Nevertheless, the Soviet plan was a step towards Western ideas in that the first stage, intended to cover a six-month period, provided for a 50 per cent reduction in conventional arms, armed forces and budget appropriations as from 1953 levels, though the reduction was merely to be reported to a temporary control commission, which would have authority only to request information from states on the enforcement of the reduction and to observe such enforcement. The second stage of the Soviet plan covered the remaining 50 per cent reduction in conventional arms to the agreed levels and the prohibition of nuclear weapons and their elimination from the armaments of States not later than the second stage of conventional arms reductions. The establishment of a permanent international control organ with rights of inspection 'to the extent necessary to ensure the enforcement of these measures' did not come until the end of the Soviet plan.[1] Selwyn Lloyd, giving British reactions to the proposals, doubted whether, as Vyshinsky claimed, they were really based on the Anglo-French plan. There was sufficient likeness, however, between the proposals of the two sides to show that the Soviets' policy had acquired a fluidity never before seen since the war.

By this time some of the implications of inspection and control, which had been central features of Western plans from the outset, were becoming somewhat clearer. During the Sub-Committee's meetings in June 1954 Selwyn Lloyd had come to the conclusion that effective inspection must involve something in the nature of 'parallel managements' in all arms factories, especially in plants for the production of nuclear energy, the 'international managers' not actually running affairs but knowing everything that was going on.[2] Later he explained in the House of Commons that:

in each place dealing with atomic production there should be in parallel with the actual management a unit or cell provided by the

[1] DC/SC.1/PV 23; United Nations No. 1 (1956), Cmd. 9648, pp. 29–33.
[2] Verbatim records of meetings of the Sub-Committee, Cmd. 9205 of 1954, p. 281.

international organization. Although they would not actually take the decision, they would know exactly what decision was taken.[1]

Selwyn Lloyd admitted that this implied a 'totally different conception of national sovereignty', but it remains doubtful whether the new conception had been fully considered either by the British Government or their allies. A vast inspectorate would clearly be needed, staffed by men and women both highly skilled and utterly impartial, yet having to do work no more constructive than that of checking the work of others. Powers of a quite unprecedented order would have to be given to them, if, as Western delegates contended at the General Assembly discussions in the autumn, they were not merely to oversee local factory managements but to give enforceable instructions within the plant. Above all, the vital question of the force to be used to coerce states which broke the arms agreement was not even squarely posed, much less answered. British delegates criticized Soviet proposals for leaving enforcement in the last resort to the Security Council with its veto. But they had no alternative to suggest. No great Power, Communist or non-Communist, was yet willing to stand aside and allow force to be used against itself or its ally without using force in return, a result which would have nullified the whole object of the arms agreement.

1955: the Soviet change of front

The consequence was that when the Soviet Union at length partially accepted effective control none of the Western Powers were ready for it. The change in Soviet policy was unexpected, despite signs of a milder attitude in Russia towards the West after Stalin's death in March 1953. In the spring of 1955 Gromyko reverted to the demand for a one-third cut in force levels without reference to verification of the levels at which the cut applied, which all Western countries had opposed since 1948. He further offended by giving an interview to the Soviet news agency Tass in London on March 24th, thus violating the agreement on secrecy in the Sub-Committee until the session was ended, on which Britain had been especially insistent. All this did not discourage Britain and France from modifying their proposals of the previous year so as to bring nuclear disarmament into the plan at an earlier stage, as Russia wished, provided there were really drastic reductions in the force levels and conventional arms of the five major Powers and an effective control system.[2] This move led

[1] 531 H.C. Deb. 5s. Col. 899 (July 30, 1954).
[2] DC/SC.1/24; United Nations No. 2 (1955), Cmd. 9636, pp. 30–1.

the way to a sharp reversal of the Soviet stand on May 10th when new Soviet proposals were tabled which appeared to adopt many of the key ideas favoured by the West. The force levels suggested in the revised Anglo-French plan, that is, one to one and a half million men each for the United States, the Soviet Union and China and 650,000 men each for Britain and France, with proportionate limits for armaments and military budgets, were accepted. Russia agreed with the proposal conditionally suggested by Nutting, for Britain, and Moch, for France, on April 19th that nuclear weapons should not be prohibited until 75 per cent of the agreed conventional reductions had taken place. She also agreed to the stationing of observers at large ports, railway junctions, highways and aerodromes as safeguards against surprise attack and, in the second stage, to a single control organ with expanding powers, to operate throughout the disarmament programme and with unimpeded access to all 'objects of control', which were not, however, clearly defined until a year later. Many of Russia's proposals for the peaceful uses of atomic energy also reflected the Western viewpoint. Above all, the new Soviet plan was coupled with a proposed Declaration on outstanding political issues of the Cold War, the solution of which, it was said, would 'promote the creation of the necessary confidence between States and will thereby facilitate the carrying into effect of a broad disarmament programme'.[1] This was in tune with what now had become an agreed Western attitude.

Western reactions to the change of Soviet front were at first favourable and none more so than the British. Nutting, now the chief British representative on the Sub-Committee, told the House of Commons in June that several 'obscurities' remained in the Soviet proposals, especially the question whether the powers suggested for the control organ were enough to guarantee faithful excution of the agreement. But the proposals were, he said, 'an important step forward . . . an encouragement to the Western policy of patient and resolute negotiations'.[2] The new Soviet attitude, after so many years of refusal to budge from unacceptable positions, seemed the product of a general Soviet relaxation following Stalin's death and the evident anxiety of the new Soviet leaders to create the most favourable atmosphere possible for the Geneva 'summit' meeting in July of the same year. There were also the effects of Soviet nuclear armaments which were influencing defence and disarmament policy in much the same way as Western nuclear weapons had affected Western policy.

[1] United Nations Document DC/71, Annex 15, pp. 17–25.
[2] 542 H.C. Deb. 5s. Cols. 270–2 (June 13th).

T

These armaments seemed to make large standing armies less necessary, thus enabling Russia to accept Western proposals for conventional force levels. On May 14, 1956, the Soviet announced reductions in the armed forces by 1,300,000 men by May 1, 1957, equivalent to the abandonment of sixty-three divisions. The British Minister of Defence, however, still estimated Soviet forces after the reductions at 300 divisions, as compared with the 100 divisions available to NATO countries.[1] At the same time, Russia's acquisition of nuclear weapons and her discovery of their destructiveness may have given her the same interest in the possibilities of eliminating these weapons as the West. But possibly the strongest factor in Russia's change of policy, as reflected in the proposals of May 10th, was her realization, like that of the West, that existing nuclear stockpiles could not be brought under the 100 per cent efficient control which alone would be safe. This fact was frankly recognized in the Soviet plan which admitted that 'there are possibilities beyond the reach of international control for evading this control and for organizing the clandestine manufacture of atomic and hydrogen weapons, even if there is a formal agreement on international control'. Any Soviet official who read reports of the Commons debate on disarmament on July 30, 1954, must have concluded that this was now the British view, since a leading Opposition spokesman, Denis Healey, could say without contradiction by Ministers that 'it is almost impossible to conceive of any effective international control organ which could be quite certain that none of the parties to the agreement had salted away some of their nuclear fuel and atomic bombs before the control organization had been introduced'.[2] If Russia therefore wished to force the West to abandon its prepared positions, with resulting loss of face, she had merely to walk over to those positions without much risk to herself.

If this was Russia's hope it was fulfilled. The next development in Western policy was to suspend the search for comprehensive disarmament and to press instead for partial measures. Illustrative of the latter were the 'Eden proposals' in favour of a zone in central Europe in which the forces on either side might be supervised by inspecting teams appointed by the military commands of both sides (if Germany was not united) or limited within a defined zone part of which would be demilitarized (if agreement on German unity was reached).[3] An American partial proposal was put forward by

---

[1] 552 H.C. Deb. 5s. Col. 199 (written answers, May 17, 1956).   [2] 531 *ibid.*, Col. 883.
[3] Miscellaneous No. 14 (1955), Cmd. 9543, p. 18; Department of State Publication 6046, Washington, p. 59.

President Eisenhower in the form of a suggestion for safeguarding against surprise attack by an exchange of blueprints of all military establishments of the United States and the Soviet Union and the reciprocal grant of facilities for taking aerial photographs as an insurance against aggression.[1] Both sets of proposals were submitted to the Geneva 'summit' conference in July 1955 and were later developed at the Sub-Committee and at the Foreign Ministers' conference in Geneva in October and November. It was clear, however, that for the time being further progress was not to be attempted on the basis of the revised Anglo-French plan or the Soviet counter-proposals of May 10th. When the Sub-Committee resumed its discussions at the end of August the United States delegation announced a reservation on their pre-Geneva substantive positions pending the outcome of joint and separate study of inspection methods, and the talks were forced to mark time.[2] American influence in Western disarmament policy thus began to make itself felt, whereas hitherto the running had been left mainly to Britain and France. Undoubtedly the strongest American interest lay in warding off attack as sudden as, but far more devastating than, the blow American forces had suffered at the hands of the Japanese at Pearl Harbour in December 1941. With Russia's construction of missiles capable of delivering nuclear warheads to American cities practically without opposition, American demands to penetrate the secrecy surrounding Soviet military preparations took precedence over almost everything else.

British Ministers justified the decision to abandon the search for a comprehensive arms agreement in terms of the vagueness of Soviet ideas on control. 'The Soviet Government,' Macmillan said in November, on returning from the Foreign Ministers' meeting in Geneva, 'have never accepted control and never made any direct and straightforward proposals in favour of control.'[3] On March 27, 1956, the expression 'objects of control' in the Soviet plan of May 1955 was further defined as a result of these criticisms; they were now stated to be 'military units; stores of military equipment and ammunition; land, naval and air bases; factories manufacturing conventional armaments and ammunition'. In addition the Soviet Union referred for the first time to aerial inspection; 'at a specified stage in the execution of the general disarmament programme,' the statement ran, 'when confidence among States has been strengthened, the countries concerned shall consider the possibility of using aerial

---

[1] United Nations No. 2 (1955), Cmd. 9363, pp. 48–50.
[2] United Nations No. 4 (1956), Cmd. 9651, p. 746.
[3] 546 H.C. Deb. 5s. Col. 2301 (November 30th).

photography as one of the methods of control'.[1] Selwyn Lloyd described these advances as still implying only 'strictly limited control, really amounting to limited observation'; the Soviet Government, he went on, 'will not accept any control which constitutes a real interference with their sovereignty'.[2] Nevertheless, it was evident that not even the West could find any formula for the technically necessary control measures short of the creation of a virtual world state in which existing national independence would disappear.

The impact of the German problem

Another consideration, however, was by this time operating on both sides, namely the commitment to German unity which the Western Powers had undertaken by the Paris agreements of October 1954 and which they sought to fulfil at the Geneva talks in 1955. As we have seen in the previous chapter, Russia firmly opposed Western plans for German unity since they were clearly intended to pull both parts of Germany into the Western orbit. But if Russia was genuinely anxious for disarmament (and some considered that her plan of May 10th showed that she was) there was no reason why she should not be pressed to accept Western plans for German unity in return for an acceptable arms agreement. Yet, once West Germany had been drawn into NATO no arms plan was acceptable to Russia unless it served to limit West Germany's contribution to Western defence. This was the object of Bulganin's proposal at the Geneva 'summit' meeting on July 18th that forces other than those of the five great Powers should be limited to 150,000–200,000 men, which Gromyko repeated at the Disarmament Commission in July 1956.[3] It was also one of the purposes behind Soviet endorsement of the Rapacki plan of 1957, which would have denied nuclear weapons to and the siting of nuclear arms in Germany. Such ideas could hardly be agreeable to the West, since Federal Germany had been drawn into NATO partly on the assumption that she would represent a net addition to Western defensive strength. The consequence of the Paris agreements therefore was that the West must now make the settlement of all but insoluble political questions the condition of a comprehensive arms agreement which British Ministers, among others, in any case no longer admitted to be technically feasible. The effect of this on existing Soviet mistrust of the West is easily imagined.

Until 1954 British Ministers denied that political settlements were

[1] Disarmament Commission, Official Records, DC/83 Annex 5.
[2] 557 H.C. Deb. 5s. Col. 260 (July 24, 1956).
[3] Cmd. 9543, p. 21.

a pre-condition of disarmament. In February 1952, Selwyn Lloyd said it was not futile to try to reduce armaments while causes of friction still existed; the two tasks of political conciliation and disarmament, he said, must proceed concurrently.[1] This position changed with plans to incorporate West Germany into Western defence. At the first meeting of the disarmament Sub-Committee on May 13, 1954, Lloyd said it was 'true that substantial disarmament cannot come about unless there is a real relaxation of world tension, including a settlement of the major international differences dividing the world today'. A further prerequisite was added by Anthony Nutting, then Minister of State, in January 1956, when he said that the scientific problem of controlling an arms agreement must also be settled first. 'A comprehensive disarmament scheme,' Nutting said, 'was not possible in present political and scientific circumstances.'[2] It was the political difficulty, however, which was repeated again and again to Russia. Macmillan told Bulganin on June 14, 1957, in the course of his long correspondence with the Soviet Premier, that he could not agree even to the reduction of force levels as a partial disarmament measure, as Russia proposed, without the assurance of 'parallel settlements in the political field'.[3]

The Soviet arms plan of May 10, 1955, admitted the importance of political settlements in general terms, but when the Western Foreign Ministers made clear at the Geneva meetings in the autumn of 1955 that they were referring to Germany, Russia seemed to retract from this concession, as shown by her proposals to the Sub-Committee in London of March 27th of the following year. Nevertheless the West continued to press the German problem. Eden, as Prime Minister, wrote to Bulganin on July 9th that German reunification was one of the urgent political questions which had to be 'taken into account' by comprehensive disarmament arrangements.

Towards the end of July Selwyn Lloyd, then Foreign Secretary, said that the Opposition in the Commons were 'completely divorced from reality' if they supposed that a comprehensive disarmament agreement could be carried out 'with matters like the reunification of Germany and other problems throughout the rest of the world still to be settled'.[4] A further revision of the Anglo-French comprehensive proposals for disarmament by stages which was submitted to the Sub-

[1] 495 H.C. Col. 930 (February 5th).
[2] 548 H.C. Deb. 5s. Col. 601 (January 30th).
[3] Soviet Union No. 1 (1958), Cmd. 380, p. 11.
[4] 557 H.C. Deb. 5s. Col. 263 (July 24th).

Committee in London on March 19th, however, did not define the political conditions attached to the second and third stages of the plan.[1] When Soviet delegates asked for definitions to be given at the discussions which began in London on March 18th of the following year they were told that 'it would be unwise to lay down in advance the exact nature of the political settlements required'; all the West proposed at the moment was that 'the necessity for political settlements should be recognized in principle'.[2] This seemed to leave Western delegates free to object to any disarmament proposal unless it was accompanied by a political settlement which the West could always bring up for discussion at the last moment.

The search for partial agreements

Comprehensive disarmament being thus deferred for the time being on both political and scientific ground, each side submitted numerous partial proposals the evident object of which was to hamper the defence preparations of the other side while leaving its own relatively untouched. The Soviet arms plan of March 27, 1956, dealt only with conventional weapons and forces, Russia having apparently come to the same pessimistic conclusion as the West on the problem of control of nuclear weapons. The revised Anglo-French plan of March 19th made no reference to the abolition of nuclear stockpiles. During talks in the Sub-Committee in London from March to August 1957 partial agreements were the utmost sought by either side.[3] The West developed the 'Open Skies' proposal, bringing forward maps of suggested coverage of territory in East and West, which Russia, after resisting the principle of aerial inspection during most of 1956, countered with maps more favourable to herself. The Soviet Union canvassed the Rapacki plan, returned to the old proposal for a ban on nuclear weapons and suggested various schemes for disengagement in Europe, though without provision for German unity. The basic obstacle, even to proposals which preserved the balance of military strength, remained the same: inspection and control. The vaguer were Soviet statements on the subject of control the more Western Governments suspected that Russia was trying to trick them into mere promises to disarm which public opinion in the West would insist upon being kept, whereas there was little likelihood of similar pressures being felt by the authorities in the East. On their side, the more Soviet delegates heard Western Ministers talk about

[1] Disarmament Commission, Official Records, Doc. DC/83, Annex 2.
[2] Miscellaneous No. 17 (1957), Cmd. 228, p. 6.
[3] *Ibid.*, p. 7.

inspection the more convinced they were that the main Western object was to pry into their military secrets.

A new factor now began to appear on the Soviet side, namely dissatisfaction with a position in which Russia was generally in a minority in disarmament discussions. So far the Western Powers had been able to obtain majority backing in the United Nations General Assembly for their disarmament proposals. This support they actively recruited, even though it was clear that majority votes in the Assembly could not compel the Soviet Union to accept disarmament proposals which she felt to be inconsistent with her security. Thus, when the General Assembly resolved on December 18, 1955, by fifty-six votes against the seven votes of the Soviet bloc that a control system was the 'keystone of any disarmament agreement' the West counted this as a victory for its own principles. As from 1955, however, many new countries, many of them non-aligned politically, were admitted into the United Nations and Russia began to bid for their support herself. At first she was unsuccessful, but her skill in winning sympathy grew. These efforts began at the twelfth session of the General Assembly in November 1957, when the Soviet delegation urged the dissolution of the Disarmament Commission and its replacement by a new body representing all members of the United Nations, then eighty-two in number. The fact that it was proposed that the proceedings of this organ should be held in public showed that propaganda now loomed more largely in the Soviet mind than serious negotiation. The Soviet proposal was not accepted by the Assembly, which adopted a suggestion supported by the West for enlarging the Disarmament Commission from the eleven members of the Security Council (or twelve when Canada was not represented on the Council) to twenty-five. The chief Soviet delegate, Kuznetzov, was prepared to accept the compromise figure of thirty-two proposed by Albania, but only if there was equal representation as between Communist and non-Communist states.

This failed to gain the necessary majority but the hollowness of the West's victory was shown during the next two years, when the Soviet Union refused to work with the new Commission. The result was that when, at the Four-Power Foreign Ministers' meeting in Geneva in the summer of 1959, Gromyko proposed a new ten-nation body for arms talks, five representatives to come from the East and five from the West, the three Western Powers had no alternative but to agree if they wished to resume discussions. The new ten-nation committee duly met at Geneva in March 1960, but in June Valerian

Zorin, the leader of the Soviet team, left the conference, followed by his allies from East Europe, before hearing the United States presentation of Western proposals.

It was clear that for the Communist states disarmament had become an instrument for winning general diplomatic support, rather than a subject for detailed negotiation with a view to ultimate agreement. For this their disappointment with the results of the concessions they had made in 1955–56 may have been partially responsible. 'Winning friends and influencing people' certainly seemed the purpose behind Khrushchev's appeal at the fourteenth session of the General Assembly on September 18, 1959, for 'general and complete disarmament', to which a time-limit of four years was later set. The question of control, on which East-West discussions had foundered for so many years, was dismissed by the argument that control should be proportionate to disarmament, or, in the Soviet Premier's words, general and complete disarmament would 'clear the way for the establishment of comprehensive and complete control'. This was contrary to the West's contention that the control machinery should be worked out and in operation before disarmament actually began. Although Khrushchev coupled his appeal with a plea, pending complete disarmament, for progress to be made with the more limited problem of controlling the testing of nuclear weapons, it was clear that his highly simplified statement of the issues was mainly intended for the ears of the new United Nations members. The same tactic of using large-scale disarmament proposals to win the widest support seemed to inspire President Kennedy's appeal for all-round disarmament in his address to the General Assembly on September 25, 1961. The President, however, was more insistent upon effective control, which he called 'creating world-wide law and law enforcement as we outlaw world-wide war and weapons'.

Meanwhile, the long debate on the details of disarmament was beginning again at a lower level. During the summer of 1961 an American team under the President's chief disarmament representative, John McCloy, held talks with Soviet officials in the Russian and American capitals. Despite a political situation which could not be more discouraging, a surprising measure of agreement on principles was reached as a basis for the next round of debate. But it was significant that disagreement was recorded on the issue of the verification of the levels of armed forces from which reductions would take place, the same point on which the Commission on Conventional Armaments had met defeat in the early postwar years.

Geneva conferences on surprise attack and nuclear tests

Disarmament negotiations thus continued as a permanent accompaniment of the East-West conflict. East side made proposals intended to shift the balance of power in its own favour at a lower level of arms all round, hoping thus to insure itself against the risk that an arms agreement might be violated by the opposing side. The vast majority of people in all countries were shocked by the waste of resources on war preparations and could not really accept the optimistic view that the arms race maintained the peace by making war too ruinous to contemplate. Objectively considered, neither side's case was wholly unreasonable. There was some sense in the Soviet view that nothing less than complete disarmament sufficed, since in a period of swift technical progress partial disarmament must favour one side or the other. Yet there was also reason in the viewpoint advanced by Britain at the Sub-Committee in July 1957, namely that what was needed was study by technical working parties to discover the minimum interference with national sovereignty which would allow for the implementation of a dependable arms plan.[1] Two such expert studies initiated in 1958, however, showed that even when the problem of arms control was deliberately limited, all the basic difficulties of disarmament still faced the negotiators.

On November 11, 1958, a ten-nation meeting, with five representatives from East and five from West, assembled in Geneva to study 'possible measures which might be helpful in preventing surprise attack'. The meeting had sprung from East-West exchanges concerning President Eisenhower's 'Open Skies' proposals and the Bulganin plan for ground inspection as a measure against surprise attack. The aim was supposedly technical: to identify the objects to be controlled; to discover the techniques required to produce evidence of a surprise attack; and to assess the results which adoption of these techniques might produce.[2] Nevertheless, the chief Soviet delegate, Kuznetzov, who, as deputy Foreign Minister, was a political figure rather than an expert, plunged at once into a tirade against the Western policy of 'positions of strength'. Effective measures to end the danger of surprise attack, he argued, were conditional upon the total banning of nuclear weapons and their elimination from national armaments, the abolition of foreign bases and substantial reductions of conventional forces and arms.[3] Western delegates, who supposed they had come to Geneva for technical discussions, found themselves

[1] United Nations No. 2 (1957), Cmd. 333, p. 15.
[2] *The Times*, November 7, 1958.
[3] *Manchester Guardian*, November 11, 1958.

in a general debate about disarmament. The conference therefore disbanded in December without result.

A second expert study, this time on the controlled suspension of nuclear weapon tests, seemed destined for more success. During 1957 the Soviet Union had pressed for the immediate discontinuance of tests as a separate measure from disarmament. The Western reply was that a test suspension was not in itself disarmament and that in any case no agreement to stop testing could be satisfactory without technical knowledge on the means to control such an agreement. At the disarmament Sub-Committee on May 6th, Britain proposed, as measures which could be carried out at once, the advance registration of tests with the United Nations and the setting up of an expert group to consider possible methods of limitation and control of tests. The British delegation insisted, however, that there could be no cessation of tests before the production of fissionable material for war purposes was prohibited as part of a general disarmament agreement.[1] Soviet delegates answered on June 14th with a proposal for a two- or three-year moratorium on tests under the supervision of an international commission responsible to the Security Council, but the West maintained its position in a Four-Power statement on July 2nd which confirmed that any supervision of tests must form part of a 'cut-off' in production of nuclear material. Towards the end of 1957, however, it became increasingly difficult to resist test suspension as a separate measure.[2] With the testing of weapons by all three nuclear Powers fears as to the largely unknown effects on the health of present and succeeding generations grew. Strong pressure to end tests was exerted by the uncommitted countries and by Japan at the United Nations. There were also fears among the great Powers themselves concerning the spread of nuclear weapons to states which might not exercise the same restraint as they did. Although an agreement to suspend tests would not in itself prevent the promiscuous spread of nuclear arms, since it would be valid only between Britain, Russia and the United States, these states would be in a strong position to discourage other countries from acquiring and testing nuclear weapons once they had agreed to end their own tests. When the Soviet Union, after an intense spate of nuclear testing, suspended further tests on March 31, 1958, for a trial period of six months, reserving the right to resume tests if the other nuclear Powers continued theirs, it was no longer morally possible for Britain and the United States to resist talks on a separate test agreement.

[1] Cmd. 333, p. 50.   [2] United Nations Document DC/112, Annex 11.

An expert committee representing East and West met in Geneva in July 1958 and reported at the end of August that the detection of violations of a possible agreement on the suspension of nuclear tests was technically feasible. The machinery required was some 180 stations distributed throughout the world and equipped with instruments capable of distinguishing between nuclear explosions and natural events such as earthquakes. Soviet participation in the expert committee seemed to imply acceptance of the principle of control from within Soviet territory, a concession which matched the British and American agreement with the isolation of a test agreement from disarmament proper. When a diplomatic conference met in Geneva on October 31st to agree on the requisite political conditions, however, it was evident that in disarmament the technically feasible is often widely separated from the politically possible. For some time it was doubtful whether the talks could begin at all in view of Russia's demand for a declaration of intention to suspend tests in advance of discussion and agreement on methods of control. When the Soviet chief delegate, Semyon Tsarapkin, finally abandoned this position the Western Powers acquired a new interest in the talks since for the first time Russia was co-operating in working out details of effective control. The British Government, in particular, considered that if agreement could be reached on controlling a test ban treaty (where the inroads made by inspection into national sovereignty are relatively small) vital lessons would be learned on the general problem of arms control, which had frustrated all disarmament hitherto. They were therefore active in devising expedients when the Geneva talks ran into disagreement on the circumstances in which mobile teams could be despatched from the control stations to investigate events the nature of which could not be determined by the stations themselves. The British solution to this problem, in the form of quota of 'on-site' inspections which any party to the agreement could demand in a given year, was taken to Moscow by Macmillan in February 1959 and seemed to obtain the Soviet Premier's approval.[1] Questions remained as to the size of the annual quota and the conditions in which an 'on-site' inspection could be demanded. The Soviet side at Geneva argued that the quota must be small and should be determined by political criteria, while the two Western Powers wanted a larger quota and one fixed by scientific inquiry. On this, however, a compromise seemed possible.

More serious difficulties emerged after the discovery by American

[1] For Selwyn Lloyd's account of the proposal see 604 H.C. Deb. 5s. Col. 900 (April 27, 1959).

scientists that deep underground tests could not be detected by existing methods and that more research into seismic techniques was needed before the treaty could be proceeded with. From this sprang various proposals for excluding underground tests below a certain magnitude from the treaty pending further investigation by experts. Here was a fertile field for hair splitting, especially since Soviet suspicions were now aroused as to American good faith. The Soviet attitude was that underground tests were too expensive to be practically useful and that atmospheric tests, which were easily verified, were the real danger to health. This dispute, again, might have yielded to a compromise formula had not a sharp change in Soviet policy showed itself in the attitude of Soviet delegates at Geneva as from March 1961. They now insisted that the treaty should be administered by a three-man council, representing East, West and the neutrals separately, on which decisions would be unanimous. This was a retreat from previous Soviet agreement to a single administrator and clearly threatened the efficiency of the control system. The demand formed part of the now general Soviet claim that the secretariat of all international organizations to which Russia belonged should be placed on a three-part basis, with East, West and neutral secretarial chiefs each having a right of veto over collective decisions. It was notable, however, that Russia withdrew this demand in order to allow U Thant of Burma to be appointed acting Secretary-General of the United Nations on November 3, 1961, after the former chief of secretariat, Dag Hammarskjoeld, had met with a fatal air accident in the Congo six weeks before. Had Russia's demand for a tripartite Secretary-Generalship been continued, it is possible that the Soviet bloc, which alone supported the proposal, would have been definitely isolated from the rest of the United Nations. An influential position in the United Nations, however, was still useful to the Soviet Union, whereas it was now clear that she had lost all interest in the nuclear test ban negotiations. This impression became inescapable when Russia resumed nuclear tests on a scale never before attempted at the end of August. In November, Britain and the United States appealed to Moscow to resume the talks and, though they were encouraged by a General Assembly resolution supporting this course, Russia continued to argue that the test ban talks must be merged with general disarmament discussions. Britain and the United States had themselves taken this position in 1957; they now replied that to return to it would mean re-negotiating the treaty afresh, after almost three years' patient work, and with wholly different parties.

One objection raised by the Soviet Union to the continuance of the Geneva talks was that France, who by 1961 had tested four of her own nuclear devices in the Sahara, could still hold tests on behalf of her NATO allies even after they had signed the treaty. This had not formerly prevented Soviet participation in the talks, however, although President de Gaulle had maintained from the outset of the negotiations that he would not adhere to a test ban agreement unless nuclear weapons and missiles were abolished. Some importance was attached by observers to criticism of Khrushchev's co-existence policy within Russia and from foreign Communist parties as the real cause of Russia's withdrawal. Strong disagreement was voiced by the critics with the attack on Stalinism which went with that policy. When American delegates at Geneva raised doubts about the detection of underground tests and the West refused to give way in the Berlin crisis, advocates of a 'tough' line in the Communist camp may have compelled the Soviet withdrawal from the negotiations. The very fact that the test ban treaty was almost completed, and that Russia must soon open her territory to international inspection, may also have played its part. Once she admitted foreign inspectors to supervise this agreement it would have been difficult to continue refusing to do so for more far-reaching arms agreements. The whole principle of the closed society, without which the Communist dictatorship might have been difficult to maintain, was thus in jeopardy.

The arms race and Britain

The failure of the test ban negotiations seemed decisive for all arms control agreements in the prevailing international tension. If a treaty could not be concluded in this limited field because of the basic mistrust on each side which surrounded all arms negotiations, it was hard to see how it could be reached elsewhere. Sixteen years' debate on disarmament had led to the same basic dilemma. Total disarmament, which all states professed as their aim, had to begin somewhere; yet once a point of departure was proposed one side or the other objected that it weakened itself more than its rivals. Apart from this, at the back of statesmen's minds was fear that, dangerous as the arms race was, the wholly unknown world of complete disarmament might be even more so. 'It is extremely difficult,' said the chief American delegate to the United Nations, Adlai Stevenson, in November 1961, 'for the mind to grasp a clear vision of a world without arms, for it is a condition totally foreign to human experience.'[1] To few countries was this discovery as bitter as it was to Britain, who had little to gain and almost everything to lose from an arms race.

[1] *The Guardian*, November 16, 1961.

British policy, according to the Defence White Paper of 1957, assumed that 'the only existing safeguard against major aggression is the power to threaten retaliation with nuclear weapons'.[1] In the 1958 White Paper it was laid down that even if Russia used only conventional weapons to launch a major attack the West would have to reply with strategic nuclear weapons.[2] Yet it was frankly admitted that there was 'at present no means of providing adequate protection for the people of this country against the consequences of an attack with nuclear weapons'.[3] Moreover, with the abandonment of the British 'Blue Streak' missile in April 1960 Britain was forced to retire from active participation in the arms race as an independent nuclear Power. It was thus a melancholy paradox that the country had come to rely for its safety on a weapon to which it was possibly more vulnerable than any other state and the upkeep of which it could no longer afford. Yet it was no less of a paradox that a genuine arms agreement with the Communist states, which might have made the burden of maintaining the most up-to-date weapons tolerable for Britain, might also have increased the general insecurity, if the assumptions of the Defence White Papers were true.

[1] Defence: an outline of future policy, Cmd. 124, p. 3.
[2] Report on Defence, Cmd. 363, p. 2.
[3] Cmd. 124, p. 2.

CHAPTER TEN

Commonwealth
and Common Market

By the 1960s the idea in terms of which British politicians had conceived the country's international position since the war was plainly in need of revision. The three circles of Commonwealth, Atlantic Community and Europe no longer overlapped with Britain as the common element uniting them. Two of these circles, the Commonwealth and the Atlantic Community (by which British Ministers really meant the United States), had ceased to hinge so largely on Britain, while Europe was moving in paths which threatened to leave her far behind. The task of British policy in the sixties was therefore that of redefining these three relationships. Primarily this meant coming to terms with the new Europe. But it also meant closing one volume of British foreign policy and opening another.

The Commonwealth, representing the evolution of the old Empire into a pattern of independent states, was in little danger of breaking up. The burdens it placed on member-countries were too slight for that, except perhaps to certain hypersensitive Africans and Asians. True, Burma had seceded on attaining independence in 1947, but at that time the formula for republics to remain in the Commonwealth, with the Crown merely as a symbol of the free association of independent member nations, had not yet been discovered.[1] At the Commonwealth Prime Ministers' conference in London in April 1949 this form of words, signifying the Crown's new status as Head of the Commonwealth, was invented to permit the continuing membership of India and later of other republics.[2] The Irish Republic dropped out of the Commonwealth in 1948, with the repeal of the External Relations Act of 1936, which made southern Ireland an 'external associate' of the Commonwealth. But Eire had never really formed a part of the Commonwealth since the treaty of Irish independence in 1921. As compared with the unexacting conditions of

[1] Treaty between the Government of the UK and the Provisional Government of Burma, Cmd. 7360 of 1947.
[2] *Documents and Speeches on British Commonwealth Affairs, 1931–1952*, ed. Nicholas Mansergh, Vol. II, London, 1953, pp. 846–7.

Commonwealth membership, the benefits were still considerable. Economically, Commonwealth countries enjoyed the trading preferences in each other's markets which originated with the Ottawa agreements of 1932. The impact of these in the 1960s was less than it used to be, partly because, some said, British Governments had done little to strengthen Commonwealth trade. Nevertheless, for such products as Canadian wheat and manufactures, New Zealand lamb and butter, Australian wool and Ghanaian cocoa a privileged position in the British market was valuable. The chief use of the Commonwealth to its members, however, was diplomatic; it provided at practically no cost a group of sympathetic ears into which grievances and claims could be poured. The Commonwealth was far from being a political bloc; United Nations debates often sharply divided it. But the fact that one or other member of a widely scattered group of nations might one day use its influence in one's own cause had practical importance.

The mere growth in size and diversity of the Commonwealth brought centrifugal forces with it. Most former British possessions admitted as independent countries after 1945 were underdeveloped countries bent on economic growth, which to them was the real certificate of sovereignty. There was no disguising the fact that the greater part of investment funds for these countries (and also for the older Commonwealth states) must come from outside the sacred circle. Three-fifths of this capital was already so derived in the 1960s. Much of it came from the United States and to a less extent the Soviet Union, two giants engaged in competition as rival suppliers of capital to underdeveloped areas. The West European 'Little Six' would soon be entering the field. In time these new sources of Commonwealth capital must have the effect of opening Commonwealth members increasingly to other influences than that of Britain.

Strategically, too, the Commonwealth was less of a unit than it ever had been. Australia, New Zealand, Canada and, in somewhat less degree, Pakistan were now dependent upon defence arrangements in which the United States played a leading role. After the Anglo-French intervention in Egypt in 1956 it was clear that Britain was no longer able to execute a sizeable military operation in defence of her own interests, even with the co-operation of another Power, much less in support of Commonwealth countries all of which were distant from Britain. If global war came Britain would be hard put to survive herself and could give them little help. The more did this seem likely as the economic strains felt by Britain in the early 1960s raised doubts whether the various overseas military garrisons were really worth maintaining.

Above all, the now closer fusion of the Commonwealth with world politics meant sharp divisions of opinion on the political and ideological issues of the day. In pre-war days the British Commonwealth (as it was then significantly known) tended to identify itself with Britain on the principal issue of totalitarianism versus democracy, with some hesitation on the part of South Africa. Now the main issues were less clear. Soviet Communism was without doubt totalitarian; yet for former British territories in Africa and Asia this seemed less shocking than it did to democratic peoples in Europe and North America with generations of self-government behind them. Communism purported to telescope the painful process of economic growth; it sided with racial equality. These ideals had a strong emotional appeal in capitals like Delhi, Lagos and Accra. The impact was felt at the Commonwealth Prime Ministers' conference in London in May 1960, held in the shadow of the Sharpeville and Langa riots in South Africa in March, when native blood had been shed by Nationalist forces upholding the racial segregation policy known as 'apartheid'. The conference came near to endorsing racial equality as the basic rule of the Commonwealth with the issue of a communiqué in which the Ministers 'emphasized that the Commonwealth itself is a multi-racial association and expressed the need to ensure good relations between all member states and peoples'. When the Prime Ministers met again in London in March 1961, this time to consider South Africa's application to remain in the Commonwealth after having decided by referendum to become a republic, Dr Verwoerd, the South African Premier, made the momentous decision to leave the Commonwealth after strong condemnation of Nationalist racial policy by Ministers representing the non-European countries.

This was the first instance in Commonwealth history in which a country's internal policy had strained relations with other members to the point of secession. In general British public opinion considered that race relations could no longer be an internal affair in an association most of whose 650,000,000 people were of non-European descent. The question was, however, whether policies formally internal, however wide their implications, would continue to be regarded as tests of fitness for Commonwealth membership. If so the credentials of Ghana, one of the chief critics of South Africa, were in doubt. Since independence in 1957 the Ghanaian President, Dr Nkrumah, had increasingly practised a form of one-party dictator-

U

ship accompanied by all the trappings of totalitarianism, including imprisonment without trial of opponents, suppression of newspapers and measures against foreign journalists, especially British. Some distinction could be drawn between Ghana and South Africa, in that the latter was an old and settled country deliberately pursuing a policy abhorrent to the millions of coloured peoples of the Commonwealth, while Ghana's abandonment of democracy was not unusual in newer countries faced with problems of tribal and religious diversity and strains of independence. None the less, these bitter open quarrels between Commonwealth countries sharply interrupted a tradition of silence on matters of internal policy.

The Commonwealth's usefulness was still assured, though the changing pattern of world affairs and political ideals brought strains. Much the same was true of Britain's relations with the United States, which formed the second of the contexts of postwar British foreign policy. We have seen in an earlier chapter how British governments after 1945, while acknowledging the primacy of Washington in the Western alliance, took for granted that Britain occupied a special place in American eyes and was able to enjoy the influence attached to that position.[1] This assumption was partly the legacy of Britain's wartime role as one of the three major allied Powers, partly the effect of Britain's extensive foreign commitments, which brought her into contact with American policies in areas of the world from which other European countries had retired. It also reflected a natural reluctance to quit a privileged status earned by centuries of leadership in international affairs. Americans could hardly share these feelings but the skill shown by British diplomacy in the immediate postwar years still won their respect. Events, however, served to weaken this respect and British errors of judgment made their own contribution. Thus, British scepticism on the subject of West European union, an old American dream, seemed warranted when EDC was defeated by the French Parliament in August 1954. But when the six West European states of the European Coal and Steel Community (ECSC) went on to create two new bodies in 1957, the European Economic Community (EEC) and the Atomic Energy Community (EURATOM), and these looked viable, British disdain began to seem misplaced. Moreover, British insistence upon high-level negotiations with Russia culminated in the fiasco of the Paris 'summit' encounter in May 1960. The subsequent intensification of Soviet pressure against West Berlin and Russia's extreme belligerency throughout 1961 appeared to vindicate the former American policy of firmness,

[1] See Chapter VI.

which had been relaxed at the end of President Eisenhower's term, partly at Britain's suggestion.

Although the new American President, John Kennedy, almost at once showed his readiness to hold talks with Russia, thus setting his face against extreme American Russophobes who opposed any sign of concession to the Communist bloc, he did not consider that he had been converted by Britain. On the contrary, Kennedy symbolized a break in the tradition of Anglo-American intimacy at the highest level. Unlike Franklin Roosevelt or Dwight Eisenhower, he had few close connections with British politicians. A book he had written twenty years before, *Why England Slept*, was not an eulogy on British politics. As alert as any British Minister to the total destructiveness of modern war, he differed in his approach to Communism from British politicians. British distaste for Communism was never in doubt, but British thinking half-consciously assumed that in the last resort Communist statesmen (as distinct from unofficial Communists) would subordinate their ideology to profitable deals on behalf of their countries. Lloyd George talked in this way about Lenin in 1922; Macmillan pressed for 'summit' talks on much the same assumption in 1959. President Kennedy seemed unimpressed. His early speeches as President suggested a conception of world Communism as being almost the same kind of implacably hostile force which Soviet leaders professed to see in the capitalist West. This premise did not turn the President against all negotiations with Russia, but he saw their scope and purpose differently from British politicians. Negotiations seemed to him primarily a means for avoiding war, in which no state could survive. Again like Soviet leaders, he tended to mistrust hopes of increasing mutual confidence, stemming from continued East-West talks, which inspired British diplomacy. One effect of this attitude was that when Macmillan went to Washington in April 1961 to meet Kennedy for the second time as President, and spoke of the 'special relation' between Britain and the United States, the President is reported to have asked what he was referring to. The story may be apocryphal but the new atmosphere it symbolized was real.

The reality of British sovereignty

One condition of Britain's special position within the Commonwealth and Anglo-American circles in the years after the war was her continuing independence, if no longer as a state of the first rank, at least as a factor to be reckoned with and one which made its own decisions. To a large extent no doubt sovereign independence is mythical for every country in a world tightly packed with states, each thickly enmeshed with its neighbours in cultural, economic and strategic matters. The decisions of even the greatest Powers are hedged about with restrictions arising from limitations of means and the need to take into account the wider implications of various choices. So long, however, as a feeling of free choice remains and is not bluntly contradicted by daily experience, a country will tend not to question the reality of its sovereignty. Americans and the Soviet people still felt free to make meaningful national choices. So did China; so perhaps did the non-aligned countries. But the reality of sovereign independence had long ceased to count with West European peoples and was becoming less convincing even in Britain.

Differences of viewpoint on the reality of national independence in the mid-twentieth century had divided Britain from Europe in the early postwar years. Britain, unlike most of western Europe, had never lost her independence during the war. Moreover, she had undergone a mild social revolution at the hands of a Labour Government at the end of the war. This led British people to suppose that the sovereign state, so far from being obsolete, was capable of quite considerable reform and rejuvenation. The failure of EDC confirmed British indifference towards European union. But what was not understood in Britain was the ensuing bitterness of feeling among continental federalists. British Conservatives had applauded the federalists, had proposed a European army, stating that Britain, in Churchill's words, would play 'an honourable part'. Disillusion came in 1951, when the Conservatives returned to office only to explain that they had been misunderstood and that in all essential respects their adherence to British sovereign independence was as strong as Labour's. Paul-Henri Spaak, the Belgian Foreign Minister, described European reactions in the words: 'we went ahead on our own. We decided that it was better to go somewhere without Britain than to go nowhere with Britain.'

British Ministers not only stood aside; they frankly doubted whether schemes of European integration would ever come down to earth. When, as from 1957, the idea of creating a single trading bloc in Western Europe, as a step towards political union, not only materialized, but matured at a faster rate than many of the federalists themselves thought possible, The European sense of triumph over British discouragement was unbounded. These feelings were strongest in France, both before and after the accession of General de Gaulle to the French Presidency in June 1958. Britain and France had been allies for half a century, but their relations were rarely as cordial as the Entente implied. After the First World War British opinion sympathized with German discontent with the peace treaty, to France's shame and disgust. Britain and France were at daggers drawn in the Middle East and rarely worked as allies in any part of the world. The rise of Nazi Germany brought the two countries together, though when France fell in 1940 the Vichy regime wrote off the Entente and the exiled France of de Gaulle was never friendly to Britain. After the war the Entente lost its purpose as soon as the Bonn Republic entered the western camp in 1954. The Schuman plan for pooling coal and steel in West Europe, intended to make war between France and Germany impossible, led to an interfusing of Franco-German policies as revolutionary as it was destructive to the Entente. The mutual rapprochement across the Rhine which Britain had striven for after 1918 thus came about despite her discouragement. No longer dependent upon Britain for security against Germany, France determined that the British should not now force her way into Europe in order to set the clock back.

While the Anglo-French schism grew, momentarily bridged by joint action against Egypt in 1956 only to widen afterwards, British confidence in the reality of national independence faded. Ever since the beginning of the Korean war in 1950 the main lines of British policy lay within the NATO framework, the scope for genuinely independent initiatives being small. Where British influence could be usefully exerted was in helping to check the more intransigent trends in American policy and in urging negotiated solutions of Cold War issues. With the arrival of the nuclear stalemate, however, it was no longer clear that the United States required advice of this kind. President Kennedy certainly seemed to need few lessons in diplomatic caution from London. The difficulties in the western alliance appeared rather to come from France and West Gemrany, whose objections to negotiate with the Soviet Union on the Berlin question effectively deferred talks throughout 1961. Britain clearly had little influence on French and German policies as an outsider in Western Europe. It was at least conceivable that she would wield more authority in the alliance by taking an active part in the politico-economic grouping which these countries were now forming with Italy and the Benelux states. The more was this so as hopes faded of negotiated agreements with Russia leading to the kind of settled relations which had always been an aim of British policy. The apparently unshakeable Soviet suspicion and hostility towards the West, the uncertain balance of political forces within the Soviet Union, the unknown portent of Communist China, where fatalistic

Marxism was preserved in virgin form, all seemed to imply an infinitely prolonged period of armed co-existence between East and West, in which tenacity and strong nerves, rather than signed agreements, would be the main characteristics. If this was so, the solidarity of the Western bloc and the political and economic health of its members would count for more than the kind of diplomatic initiatives which Britain had clung to her independence so as to be able to promote.

At the same time somewhat cruder facts were undermining British belief in the reality of sovereignty in the 1960s. On the strategic level the rising cost of delivery vehicles threw into doubt the independent nuclear deterrent. After the abandonment of the British missile 'Blue Streak' in April 1960 it was impossible to foresee British nuclear weapons ever being delivered, other than by bombers, except in American rockets. This made the assumption behind the British nuclear force, namely that Britain might one day fight with nuclear arms while America was neutral, so unreal that for practical purposes it could be ignored. Even the use of British conventional forces on any scale without United States approval was hard to conceive after the Suez affair in 1956. Perhaps the greatest blow to the British nuclear deterrent, however, was the decision of General de Gaulle, after his return to power in France in 1958, not only to manufacture a few nuclear bombs as a national status-symbol, but to equip France with the means of delivering them to any part of the globe. This policy was widely deplored in Britain, yet practically all the reasons in favour of the British deterrent were valid for France. British nuclear policy, when mirrored in the actions of another country, thus began to seem unnecessary and uneconomical. Especially was this so when the question of nuclear arms for West Germany arose. By the Paris agreements in 1954 Federal Germany was prohibited from manufacturing or possessing nuclear weapons. Since Dr Adenauer insisted that German forces in NATO should be protected by the same armaments as those available to other NATO troops an arrangement was reached for stationing American nuclear weapons in West Germany, to be operated by German forces but not without American consent. Yet the element of discrimination even in this procedure was bound to provoke discussion in Germany of revision of the 1954 prohibition and, on the analogy of the British, and now French, independent nuclear deterrent, it would be hard to make out a case on the other side. Yet the disturbing prospect of German armies having their own nuclear weapons was enough to make many British politicians wonder whether the British deterrent should not be merged in some larger Western nuclear force or whether European NATO states should not confine themselves to conventional forces. Whatever the solution, the British deterrent, together with the assumption that as a sovereign state she was in certain circumstances free to use it, was now seriously in doubt.

Economic factors also weakened confidence in independent statehood. British economic experience since the war, despite the severities of the late 1940s, provided a favourable contrast with the position after 1918. Full employment, notwithstanding trade unionists' fears, was maintained and working-class people were raised to an affluence inconceivable in pre-war times. Yet the British economy as a whole remained sluggish as compared with that of other countries of similar size and wealth. The rate of growth of national product was lower than rates in Western Europe; chronic tendency towards inflation had to be checked by 'credit squeezes' and 'pay pauses'; established markets for British exports abroad were steadily encroached upon by German, Japanese and Italian competitors, providing a curious comment on the result of the Second World War. Along with these tendencies went continuous tension in industry, bad labour relations and a crop of strikes in important export trades over which official trade union leaders often had little control.[1] A basic factor of weakness, economists generally agreed, was the failure to attain an adequate rate of new investment for modernizing old industrial structures and striking out along new lines of production essential for maintaining a foothold in world markets. Yet the vicious circle was such that new investment was deterred by high interest rates intended to correct balance of payments difficulties caused by export weaknesses, and also by a heavy home demand, swallowing up all that industry currently produced, behind which was working-class discontent with the failure of living standards to expand. This situation might have continued by stops and starts, as it had done during the 1950s. What made radical change imperative was the creation by the six West European countries of a powerful and efficient economic complex which threatened to isolate Britain more and more from continental trade. With a shrinking rate of expansion in inter-Commonwealth trade, with increasing resistance to foreign imports in the United States, a market which British firms had successfully penetrated, and with mounting competition in world markets generally, the European Common Market was evi-

---

[1] Some of the factors in Britain's economic position are reviewed in Andrew Schonfield, *British Economic Policy since the War*, Harmondsworth, Middlesex, 1948, and Michael Shanks, *The Stagnant Society*, London, 1961.

dently a threat to Britain's economic position which it might repay a considerable sacrifice of national independence to ward off. National sovereignty seemed unreal in an age of nuclear weapons. It was positively absurd without a firm economic basis.

The Rome Treaty

The six members of the European Coal and Steel Community (Belgium, Federal Germany, France, Italy, Luxembourg and the Netherlands) had agreed at a Foreign Ministers' meeting at Messina, Sicily, in June 1955 to submit proposals by the three Benelux countries for a common market covering all commodities and for an atomic energy pool to an inter-governmental committee under the chairmanship of Paul-Henri Spaak, the Belgian Foreign Minister. This committee, after working through expert groups at Brussels from July 1955 until April 1956, produced a report which was discussed at Venice by the Foreign Ministers of the Six at the end of May 1956.[1] At the Venice meeting the Spaak report was adopted 'as a basis for negotiations intended to work out a treaty setting up a general common market and a treaty to create a European organization for atomic energy (EURATOM)'. These negotiations began in Brussels on June 26th, again under Spaak's chairmanship, but ran into difficulties when France claimed that social policies among the Six must be harmonized along with the proposed co-ordination of commercial and tariff policies and that overseas territories having relations with member-states should be associated with the common market. These issues were dealt with at a further meeting of Foreign Ministers in Paris in October and during talks between Dr Adenauer and the French Prime Minister, Guy Mollet, in the French capital in November. The two treaties creating respectively the Common Market and EURATOM were then signed in Rome on March 25, 1957. After remarkably swift ratification proceedings the treaties came into effect on January 1, 1958.

Although the undertakings to create a common tariff for the Six and progressively to abolish customs and quotas between them were what principally concerned Britain, and the Rome Treaties were often referred to together in Britain as the 'Common Market Treaty', the aim of the Six, as Article 1 of the Treaty makes clear, was 'to establish among themselves a European Economic Community'.[2]

---

[1] A translated summary of the Spaak Report is given in Planning No. 405, published by Political and Economic Planning, London, December 1957.
[2] The principal clauses of the Rome (Common Market) Treaty are printed in *The Common Market* by Stuart de la Mahotière, London, 1961, pp. 148–92.

This, according to the preamble, was intended as a step towards political unification. The Common Market was in fact merely one of two means for promoting within the territory of the customs union a 'harmonious development of economic activities, a continuous and balanced expansion, an increased stability, an accelerated raising of the standard of living and closer relations between its Member States'. The other means, in the words of the treaty, was the 'progressive approximation of economic policies of Members'. This was to take the form, over a transitional period of twelve to fifteen years, of the gradual abolition of obstacles to the free moment of persons, services and capital within the Community, the inauguration of common policies for agriculture and transport, the adoption of procedures to co-ordinate economic policies and prevent disequilibria in the balance of payments, and the control of competition so as to prevent 'distortions'. In order to facilitate the smooth working of the Community a Social Fund was to be established to finance the resettlement of workers and such retraining as might be needed on account of changes in the economic pattern of the Community. A European Investment Bank was to be created for granting loans on a non-profit basis to finance new activities and the modernizing of old ones and to assist the less developed areas within the Community. Moreover, territories outside Europe which were associated with the Community were to be assisted from an Overseas Development Fund into which the Six were committed to pay the equivalent of $581,000,000 within the first five years.

The Economic Community could not be understood except as one more attempt to 're-launch' European union, the movement towards which had ebbed and flowed since the war. The Council of Europe had remained high and dry after the British refusal to grant the limited but real powers asked for by the federalists. The Coal and Steel Community was a new start, creating its own common market for goods and labour in the coal, steel and scrap industries. Then came the failure of EDC, whose demise the proposed Political Community shared. But the movement gathered strength again with the Spaak report, showing how profoundly the concept of national sovereignty failed to satisfy leaders of West European thought, who drew their inspiration from Jean Monnet, of France, the architect of supranationalism. That the Rome Treaty was a product of this movement (and not merely a tariff device) was made clear at the first

---

For an analysis of the Treaty see J. F. Deniau, *The Common Market*, London, 1960.

session of the Parliamentary Assembly of the new Community at Strasbourg in March 1958, when Professor Hallstein, the President of the Commission of the Community, denied that it involved discrimination against outsiders, as the British alleged. The EEC, Hallstein said, was in process of becoming a single political entity which would deal with the outside world as a unit, like any other state. Countries wishing to join the Community were not merely entering a customs union. They were asking to merge themselves in a new entity on the political map. The EEC, Hallstein explained,

> does not mean only the abolition of customs barriers and of innumerable restrictions on trade between the six Member States; nor is it only a customs union with a uniform external tariff. It is the harmonization, co-ordination, even unification of major aspects of economic policy and profoundly modifies the economic policy of the six States. . . . Thus there can only be discrimination, in other words, an unwarranted differentiation in the treatment of other European states, if the Six deny to other European states the treatment which they accord one another, that is, if they refuse admission to a State which is willing to pay the same price as the Six for the advantages of membership of the customs union. Obviously that has not happend.[1]

Negotiations for a European free trade area
The meaning of the Rome Treaty for Britain was momentous, though this was not fully admitted for some time. 'We must all agree,' said the Prime Minister, Macmillan, in August 1961, 'that the problems involved in the future of our relations with Europe are among the most difficult and the most important that the nation has ever had to face.'[2] During the Spaak Committee talks in 1955 it was still too early for British Ministers to contemplate revision of their attitude towards supranationalism; the mere fact that a common tariff, if Britain joined the Community, would convert Commonwealth preference into discrimination against the Commonwealth was enough to damn it. A British representative who attended the Spaak committee therefore withdrew at the end of 1955, when discussion turned from the question of the *how* of the Economic Community to the question of *whether*. Since, however, there was no prospect of ignoring the new development for a country which did

[1] European Economic Community, Statement by Dr Hallstein to the European Parliamentary Assembly, March 20, 1959, p. 24.
[2] 645 H.C. Deb. 5s. Col. 1480 (August 2nd).

at least one-sixth of its trade with intending members of the Community, the British Government proposed at the Ministerial meeting of the Organization for European Economic Co-operation (OEEC) in July that possible forms of association between the Six and the other eleven OEEC members should be examined by a study group, and that particular regard should be paid to the possibility of a free trade area, which might include the Six as one of its members. This procedure was adopted by the Council in preference to a proposal for all-round tariff cuts put forward by its low-tariff members. When three working parties created by the Council to inquire into the detailed problems involved had ended their labours, however, the French asked for consideration of the working party reports to the deferred, pending ratification of the Rome Treaties. Hence it was not until October 1957, less than three months before the Rome Treaties came into effect, that the Council decided

> to secure the establishment of a European Free Trade Area which would comprise all Member Countries of the Organization; which would associate on a multilateral basis the European Economic Community with other Member Countries and which, taking fully into consideration the objectives of the European Economic Community, would in practice take effect parallel with the Treaty of Rome.[1]

At the same time the Council appointed an inter-governmental Ministerial committee to carry on detailed negotiations on the free trade area proposal.[2] The chairman of this committee, Reginald Maudling, the British Paymaster General, had been appointed special co-ordinator on free trade area questions by the Cabinet.

A British outline for a free trade area had been launched as early as February 1957 with the encouragement of a technical report by an OEEC committee which confirmed the feasibility of operating such an area in Europe so as to include the customs union of the Messina Powers. The essence of the British scheme was an undertaking by members to eliminate in respect of each other's products all protective duties and other commercial restrictions, including quantitative controls. Each member, however, would be entirely free to determine its tariff on imports from outside the area, subject to any international engagements by which it was bound. Meanwhile the EEC would be evolving a single uniform external tariff on imports from outside the free trade area; this would ultimately represent an

---

[1] Negotiations for a European Free Trade Area, Cmd. 641 of 1959, pp. 48–9.
[2] *Ibid.*, pp. 49–50.

arithmetic average of the tariffs of the four customs areas making up the Community (the three Benelux countries forming one union) and could not be changed except by common consent. The British free trade area would therefore have left Commonwealth preference unaffected. The British Government also rejected for the free trade area the far-reaching proposals for economic integration favoured by the Six. While in the British scheme economic co-operation would develop within the area 'over a period of years', no advance commitments were provided for. A further difference between the British proposal and the aims of the Six was that, whereas the latter meant to include all goods and services within their Community, the free trade area was limited to industrial products; in fact its title, Britain suggested, should be 'European Industrial Free Trade Area'. The British Government were resolved to oppose the free entry of agricultural, and especially horticultural products, so as to safeguard British farmers and Commonwealth growers. Although the Six seemed to have the same difficulty about agriculture before the drafting of the Rome Treaty, Article 40 of that agreement in fact provided for a common agricultural policy, with common prices, before the end of the transitional period in which the Community would come fully into effect. During the transitional period, however, members of the Community were permitted to apply minimum prices to certain farm products under specified conditions and to suspend imports from within the Community if prices fell below these levels. Moreover, Britain modified her exclusion of agriculture when negotiations began in the Maudling committee in January 1958; she then proposed common rules on the use of farm subsidies and import and export restrictions, together with a 'complaints procedure' to mitigate injury to other free trade area members. In no case, however, did these concessions alter the essentially industrial character of the area in the British scheme.

Finally, the British proposals firmly opposed the supranational features of the EEC as a model for the free trade area. According to the British paper the area was definitely to be established within the OEEC, in which national sovereignty was strictly respected. Departures from the rule of unanimity in making collective decisions were allowed only in 'certain carefully defined matters', as for instance when a member sought release from its original obligations to the area, or when an inquiry was held into whether a country had failed to discharge its obligations or into the measures to be adopted if a failure was established.[1]

[1] A European Free Trade Area. United Kingdom Memorandum, Cmd. 72 of 1957.

In the Rome Treaty, on the other hand, supranationalism was clearly indicated at the end of the road, though the road itself was studded with concessions to national sovereignty; there were even exits by which signatories could leave the highway if they felt, in the event, that supranationalism was not for them. Ultimate authority still rested with a Council consisting of government delegates. Unlike the ECSC Council, which merely mediated between the Community and governments, the EEC Council determined basic policy, gave precision to the general provisions of the treaty and had authority to modify it. In general, most Council decisions had to be unanimous during the first phase, lasting four years; thereafter qualified majorities became the rule, so that at the end of the transitional period a member could in theory be overruled on matters of economic, financial or commercial policy. Twelve votes out of seventeen were required for a qualified majority, but although France, Germany and Italy had four votes each, they required the support of at least one of the Benelux countries to gain a majority, except in matters affecting the Development Fund. France and Germany, having contributed most to the Fund, were given a bigger voice in its affairs.

Moreover, although the Council, that is, the Ministerial element, was the policy-making body, the power to make proposals normally lay with a Commission of nine, which acted as the executive or administrative organ. The Commission was to be independent of governments, although each member government had a veto on the appointment of its members. In addition, governments could compulsorily refer disputes concerning the interpretation or application of the treaty to a Court of Justice, which was to be the same as that used by the ECSC and EURATOM. The legislative element was provided by a Parliamentary Assembly consisting of delegates appointed by the Parliaments of member states according to their size and importance; this again was to be the same as the Assembly of the coal and steel pool and EURATOM. The Assembly could dismiss the Commission by a two-thirds majority, but had no powers similar to those it exercised in the other two communities, whereby it could control the Council. By Article 138 of the Rome Treaty the Assembly was charged to draw up proposals for election by direct suffrage, though this was clearly envisaged as a somewhat remote eventuality. In this structure the supranational element was thus carefully controlled by checks and balances, though with the lapse of the transitional period the power remaining with member governments dwindled. But whether at beginning or end, the implied loss of sovereignty was greater than Britain, the Scandinavian states or the European neutrals were ready for.

Discussions in the Maudling committee during 1958 brought out fundamental differences between the free trade area and Common Market philosophies. The most intractable problem arose from the fears of the Rome Treaty states that diversions of trade from high to low tariff countries within the area would disturb the balanced economy they were trying to build within the Community. The British solution for this problem was that goods should be regarded as originating externally, and hence denied the advantages of free trade within the area, if less than 50 per cent of their value was created in countries within the area. The Six objected that this would be administratively impractical. A formula suggested by the Foreign Trade Minister of Italy, a country strongly interested in keeping the talks going, would have imposed compensatory taxes on imports from outside, when these were sold within the area, if the tariffs of the country importing them in the first place exceeded a specified margin on either side of an agreed norm.[1] A system on these lines would have been relatively easy to administer, but had the drawback of imposing taxes even on goods originating within the area if the country of origin happened to have tariffs outside the agreed norms (though it provided an incentive towards tariff harmonization).

No more success was achieved with the 'sector approach', in which the different commodities in regard to which a particular country feared difficulties were to be treated separately. When all the various interests drew up claims for exceptional treatment (the French pulp and paper industry, for example, feared competition with Scandinavian products) it was apparent that any agreement would have to be so loaded with reservations as to defy the best efforts of administrators. Commonwealth preferences moreover still remained a stumbling block; the EEC countries argued that the privileged markets these created for Britain might cause 'disequilibrium in the conditions of competition' and serious deflections of investment.[2] Difficulties also abounded on the issue of the harmonization of social policies, on which the British could make no concession to the Six, and the latter continued to insist that tariff changes, even if the principle of differential duties were agreed, should only be by collective consent, whereas British delegates refused to go further than agreeing to a 'code of good conduct' under which members would

[1] Cmd. 641, p. 64.
[2] Cmd 641, p.69.

bind themselves to take into account the impact on other member countries of changes in their tariff policy. These differences were such that by the end of the year, when Maudling drew up his report, the work of the committee had come to a standstill, despite the considerable concession Britain had made in agreeing to abandon her high tariff policy when she entered the free trade area.

Apart from the clash of supranationalist and inter-governmental approaches to European integration, Anglo-French tension permeated the talks, reflecting British suspicion that France meant to use her new friends in the Six to force Britain to her knees and French fears that Britain had concocted the free trade area scheme merely in order to wreck the Community. Political instability in France also played its part. When the Maudling committee first met in January 1958 the Fourth Republic was passing through its death throes and finally expired in the officers' rising in Algeria in May. General de Gaulle, who left retirement to become French President on June 1st, was thenceforward too preoccupied with turning France into a Presidential autocracy and too out of touch with the details of European economic integration to take any part in effecting compromises with Britain, despite the evident anxiety of other members of the Six for a solution. Moreover, de Gaulle was in no position to oppose French industrial interests, which stood to lose if the West German market were open to all OEEC countries instead of merely to Community members, especially before popular endorsement of his constitutional reforms. The result was the issue of an announcement by the Gaullist Minister of Information, Jacques Sustelle, at the end of a fruitless two-day session of the Maudling committee on November 13th to 14th, which repudiated the OEEC Council decision to negotiate the free trade area. The French Cabinet, the statement said, had concluded that it was not possible 'to create the Free Trade Area as wished by the British, that is, with free trade between the Common Market and the rest of the OEEC but without a single external tariff round the seventeen countries, and without harmonization in the economic and social spheres'. Two days later Maudling postponed *sine die* any further meeting of the committee and although a conciliatory statement was issued after talks between Dr Adenauer and de Gaulle at Bad Kreuznach on November 26th, this restated the Six's intention to carry out the first 10 per cent reduction in the internal tariffs of the Community on January 1st despite the incomplete state of the free trade area discussions.

When the OEEC Council met on December 15th to take stock of the position, Anglo-French relations were in a worse state than at any time since the war; veiled warnings issued from London that economic, political and military co-operation in Western Europe might cease if France remained obstructive. The Bad Kreuznach communiqué had referred to Franco-German anxiety for a formula associating the Six with other OEEC countries, but no advance could be made in the Council with a British suggestion, presented by the President of the Board of Trade, Sir David Eccles, that the proposed increases of import quotas by the EEC should be placed on an OEEC-wide basis, so that all OEEC members could compete for them. The schism between the Six and the rest remained, though France's partners in the Community were uneasy. The EEC Commission issued a report in February denying the feasibility of a free trade area and proposing negotiations for improving relations and expanding trade with the OEEC countries on a provisional basis.[1] The report was not accepted by the Ministerial Council, in which, however, differences of view prevented any positive decision being taken.

During the Maudling committee negotiations the Scandinavian, Swiss and Austrian representatives generally sided with Britain against the Six. When the negotiations failed the possibility of forming a free trade area among this 'outer' group was mooted. With strong encouragement from Sweden, officials of the six countries (Austria, Britain, Denmark, Norway, Sweden and Switzerland) met to consider further co-operation at Oslo in December 1958 and, with a free trade area definitely in view, at Stockholm on March 18th and on June 1st. Ministers of the Six, now joined by Portugal, then met at Stockholm on July 20th and 21st and approved the plan for a European Free Trade Association (EFTA) which the officials had drawn up. The Stockholm convention creating the Association was signed on January 4, 1960, and come into effect on May 3rd Although EFTA was valuable on its own account, its chief aim was to keep the seven countries together during further negotiations with the Six and generally to improve their bargaining position. 'The primary purpose of founding it,' said a British Minister, 'was to enable us to reach agreement with the other countries.'[2]

With this end in view the Stockholm convention was kept as simple as possible. The abolition of obstacles to internal trade, which was to begin in July 1960 and continue along with the development of the Common Market until free trade was attained in 1970, was limited to tariffs and quotas, with provision for a 'complaints

[1] EEC, First memorandum from the Commission of the EEC to the Council of Ministers, Brussels, February 26, 1959.
[2] Edward Heath, 640 H.C. Deb. 5s. Col. 1669 (May 18, 1961).

procedure', as in the original British plan presented to the OEEC, to ensure some slight co-ordination of economic policies. The convention was reticent, however, about freedom of movement for other factors than goods, and even more so about the co-ordination of social and financial policies; the intergovernmental principles of association favoured by Britain were strictly preserved.[1] Moreover, even as a bargaining tool EFTA was weak. The member of the Six the Association sought most to influence, France, did little trade with the Seven, Britain excepted. EFTA's trade with EEC was more valuable than the trade between its members.[2] On the other hand, EFTA would be of limited value to Britain if it was to become permanent. Most of the trade done by Britain with other EFTA countries was already either duty-free or subject to low duties and the Association's economic effect would therefore be small. Nor did powerful industries exist among the other six capable of giving a competitive thrust to British industry. The somewhat hasty formation of EFTA thus left the problem much as it was, if it did not harden the division of Europe into two trading blocs.

Common Market developments and British reactions
What made the Six less enthusiastic about renewed negotiations on the free trade area was the early and striking success of their own experiment. Contrary to British expectations, the reduction of internal tariffs proved less difficult than had been expected, with the result that the programme was speeded up. By the end of 1960, that is, after three years, tariff cuts amounted to 30 per cent, the figure originally supposed to be reached after four years; cuts at the end of 1961 were expected to total between 40 and 50 per cent, as compared with the 30 per cent of the plan. Internal trade among the Six rose 30 per cent in 1960 as compared with a rise of 16 per cent in EFTA's internal trade in the same year. The strength of the Community began to attract funds from the United States which had previously gone to Britain. According to the Lord Privy Seal over a half of American investment in Europe formerly came to Britain, but in 1960 only 41 per cent did so, while over 50 per cent was expected to go to the Six.[3] Part of the economic success of EEC (which was not shared by all its members, Belgium being less affected) was due to extraneous causes, such as the devaluation of the French franc and

[1] Treaty Series No. 30 (1060), Cmd. 1026.
[2] PEP. *The European Free Trade Association. A Preliminary Appraisal*, by Miriam Camps, London, September 1959, Table I, p. 36.
[3] 640 H.C. Deb. 5s. Col. 1388 (May 17, 1961).

X

the influx of refugees into West Germany from the East. Neverthe-less, this growing giant of 169,000,000 people, with its evident appeal to American opinion, threatened to by-pass Britain and throw her into the background.

The more enterprising organs of opinion in Britain were gradually influenced by these facts. The *Guardian, Observer* and *News Chronicle* (so long as it existed) were early converts to the cause of joining the Six. They were followed by the *Daily Herald* (with qualifications), the *Daily Mirror* and *Daily Mail*, while *The Times* remained hesitant and a strong campaign against the Common Market was started by the Beaverbrook Press. The British newspaper reader was thus pre-sented with an increasingly favourable view of the Six. Industry was not hostile, though its general mood seemed to be that of waiting for a lead from the Government. Although high-cost firms working in lines competitive with the Six would clearly lose if Britain joined the Community, the attractions of a free market larger than that of either Russia or the United States were strong. Farm interests, on the other hand, especially in horticulture, were apprehensive. Three-quarters of the farmer's net income came from 'deficiency payments' by the Exchequer; these would disappear if British agriculture was financed by the same method as continental.

Since any movement to remove trade protection generally pro-vokes more alarm from those expecting to suffer than support from those likely to benefit, the political parties (except for the Liberals) and Parliament remained cold to the idea of reversing the British stand. The two main parties made little reference to Europe during the general election campaign in October 1959. The new Conserva-tive Government resulting from the election seemed at first bent on mending its links with 'Little Europe', but little was made public. A visit by the Prime Minister to Bonn in August 1960 was without much subsequent effect in Paris and for the following year no major discussion on Europe was held in the Commons. During a two-day debate on foreign affairs on May 17th and 18th the Lord Privy Seal indicated that the Cabinet were contemplating an approach to the Six, but the unexpected manner in which this subject was introduced suggested that Ministers doubted whether Parliament would approve a decisive change of policy. Both Government and Opposition parties were divided on the Common Market, the right wing of the Conservatives forming a curious alliance in opposition to entry with the left of Labour. The Conservative Right, maintaining the imperial traditions of the party, deplored any loss of British independence and the implied damage to the Commonwealth, while their Labour allies believed that entry into the Common Market would inhibit a future Labour Government in pursuing a socialist policy and would commit Britain to support the allegedly reactionary policies of the ruling Catholic groups in Western Europe; the EEC Treaty was sometimes darkly referred to by religious non-conformists in the Labour Party as the 'Act of Rome'. These Labour critics tended to suppose that British social services were in all respects superior to those of the Six, whereas German pensions schemes and French family allowances were more generous than those in Britain. Labour fears as to possible loss of the power so socialize British industries seemed equally misplaced, since there was nothing in the Rome Treaty to prevent nationalization, although difficulties might arise if a Labour Government sought to control capital movements or protect the British currency within the Common Market. Labour opposition to the EEC also derived, like Conservative, from anxiety about the effects of entry on the Commonwealth. This was at first sight puzzling, considering Labour's old hostility towards the Empire from which the Commonwealth had evolved. The Commonwealth appealed to Labour, however, mainly because it seemed to offer an alternative to the apparent powerlessness of Britain within the Atlantic community. The Commonwealth, according to Jennie Lee, MP, was 'an area of relative coolness between the hot total capitalist attitude which comes from business pressures on both sides of the Atlantic and the equally dedicated Communist pressures which come from the other side of the Iron Curtain'.

Leaders of both parties seemed impressed with the consequences of remaining outside EEC but were conscious of the deep isolationism of their rank-and-file. On the whole, the Conservatives, being the party in office, had less difficulty in accepting the case for British membership in EEC if terms satisfactory to the Commonwealth, agriculture and other EFTA countries could be negotiated. At the annual conference of the Conservative Party in October 1961 the Lord Privy Seal, two days after making a statement before EEC Ministers in Paris on Britain's application to join, emphasized that the time for making up one's mind was short; if the moment was not seized, he said, it might be many years before another chance came and meanwhile Britain would be left outside one of the greatest forward movements of the age. The Secretary of State for Commonwealth Relations, Duncan Sandys, denied that it was a matter of choosing between Commonwealth and Common Market; while the Commonwealth could not provide the huge internal market of the Six and a Commonwealth customs union found very little support,

Britain, he said, would be an even more effective Commonwealth country by joining the EEC since her economy would be sounder. Despite strong opposition from Sir Derek Walker-Smith and Lord Hinchingbrooke, who lamented the price to be paid by the Commonwealth, a resolution supporting the Government's decision to apply conditionally for membership was adopted with few dissentients.[1] The hostility shown towards the EEC at the Labour Party conference a week before was a strong contrast. Although a resolution unconditionally opposing entry was rejected, the successful composite resolution on Europe was framed in the markedly negative sense of disapproving entry except on stringent terms, which included the retention of 'freedom to use public ownership and planning as means to social progress in Britain'. Most speakers evidenced sharp mistrust of mixing British affairs with continental, deplored any exchange of Commonwealth for European friends and feared the loss of Britain's freedom to shape her own affairs. The Parliamentary party's deputy leader, George Brown, though unable to offer a clear judgment since the terms of entry were still undecided, was disposed to favour entry and seemed to regret the Labour Government's decision in 1950 not to support the Schuman plan, which first set Britain apart from the Six. The balance of the economic argument, he concluded, was probably in favour of going in, while the political objections were possibly not quite as strong as had been said.[2]

The Government, reviewing the position early in 1961, assumed the balance of advantage to lie with entry into the Economic Community, which implied entry into ECSC and EURATOM as well. 'We now see opposite to us on the mainland of Europe,' said Heath, 'a large group comparable in size only to the United States and the Soviet Union, and as its economic power increases, so will its political influence.'[3] Britain's entry, especially if followed by other Outer Seven countries, would heal the economic breach in Europe with such consequences for Britain as bringing back the market of West Germany on which higher tariffs would be otherwise imposed by the Common Market, and would forestall the risk of political disunity in the West as well. Though the partial surrender of sovereignty involved was hard to swallow, the approach towards supranationalism in the Rome Treaty was gradual. None of the Six was yet ready for federation, President de Gaulle for instance preferring a confederal pattern, to which he applied the name 'Europe des

[1] *The Times*, October 13, 1961.
[2] *Ibid.*, October 6, 1961.
[3] 640 H.C. Deb. 5s. Col. 1388 (May 17, 1961).

patries'. Maudling, then President of the Board of Trade, told the Commons that 'neither by the terms of the Treaty itself nor by the expressed views of the Governments concerned in the Community would our membership commit ourselves in any way to ultimate political federation'.[1] The extent to which Britain could be out-voted on major issues during the early transitional stages would depend upon revisions effected in the voting procedures when and if British membership was completed, but France and Germany had preserved to a considerable degree the sovereign right to say 'no', at least during the first stages, and Britain as a member would be able to influence the pace of supranationalism. The same applied to fears that Britain in the Community would be dragged in the train of French Algerian policy or German irredentism. The Rome Treaty had little to do with general foreign policy and even if the latter was discussed in the Community's organs it was pessimistic to assume that Britain would always get the worst of the argument. If by remaining outside Britain could impress the world with her inde-pendent influence the case for staying unfettered was strong. Unfor-tunately the likelihood was that other Powers would come to think of her as shut off from the main current of affairs, like an elderly and impoverished aristocrat trying to keep up the pretence of respect-ability. 'In a changing world,' the Premier said in August, 'if we are not to be left behind and thrust out of the main stream of the world's life we must be prepared to change and adapt our methods.'[2]

Economically, entry into the Common Market was bound to hit the less efficient British industries and even some of the more efficient firms would feel the strains of readjustment. But the former could be spared if Britain hoped to keep her competitive position in the world, as she must. Losses suffered by the latter might well be offset by access to a free market of vast extent, in which the normal benefits of specialization and economies of scale would probably be reaped. The most favourably placed industries in this respect were motor vehicles, motor-car components, chemicals, electrical engin-eering, agricultural machinery, wool textiles, rubber, hosiery and clothing.[3] Some of these gains were admittedly speculative; the existing British market of 50,000,000 people seemed already big enough for the greatest economies of scale to be realized. But the psychological results of thrusting a British economy which had lost much of its resilience into this new and adventurous *milieu* were

[1] 640 H.C. Deb. 5s. Col. 1598 (August 3rd).
[2] *Ibid.*, Col. 1494 (August 2nd).
[3] See the special article in *The Times*, 'Industrialists look for a lead', July 13, 1961.

likely to be good. Furthermore, competition within the Common Market might have the effect of reducing the wasteful reduplication of such resources as steel works and port facilities in Britain, while the challenge to throw off old habits was vital to a country which had to earn its keep by enterprise and skill. In particular, the restrictionist mentality prevalent on both 'sides' of British industry would come up for healthy revision. Free movement of labour within the Common Market might raise certain difficulties for a country in which resentment against foreign and even Commonwealth immigration since the war was already strong; but there was a substantial movement of workers from the Community as things were and this was not likely to create a problem unless heavy unemployment overtook the Six. Over and above this balance sheet of prospective gain and loss, however, was the growing sense among many observers of British life that the country was indeed falling behind the times and required new stimuli.

Implications of the decision to apply for membership
Given that, on balance, becoming part of the Common Market was more profitable than continued abstention, associate membership, as provided for in Article 238 of the Rome Treaty, raised all the problems of the Commonwealth's position while conferring none of the advantages of full membership. The wording of Article 238 also seemed to leave it to the Six to invite outsiders to accept associate status. By Article 237, however, countries desirous of full membership had first to file an application with the Community, after which the necessary amendments (in the French text, *adaptations*) in the Treaty would have to be negotiated. An announcement was therefore made in the Commons by the Prime Minister on July 31, 1961, that a British application for membership of the EEC was to be made, though the ultimate decision whether or not to join would depend upon whether the negotiations on the *adaptations* had proved satisfactory.[1] The conditions which Britain sought, and which she proposed should be stipulated in protocols attached to the Treaty, were outlined by the Lord Privy Seal when he made the application at an EEC Ministerial meeting in Paris on October 10th.[2] Two of these conditions, that the interests of British agriculture and of the Commonwealth must be adequately safeguarded, were inherited from the Maudling committee negotiations. The third, suitable provision for the other EFTA countries, had arisen as a result of the failure of the

[1] 646 H.C. Deb. 5s. Cols. 928–31.
[2] Miscellaneous No. 14 (1961), Cmd. 1565.

Maudling talks. It was this, however, which was likely to prove the easiest of the three to dispose of.

Many of the reasons which inclined Britain to seek EEC membership had equal force with other EFTA members. Denmark and Norway would probably seek full membership concurrently with Britain. Austria and Portugal might be eligible, for different reasons, as associated members despite the assumption generally made during the drafting of the Rome Treaty that this status was not for European countries. Switzerland and Sweden, however, as permanent neutrals would have difficulty in joining EEC (in effect a sub-group of NATO) without some provision to exclude them from its political implications. The case of Finland, to whose associate membership of EFTA her powerful Soviet neighbour had not objected, was also a hard one. She was committed to afford most-favoured-nation treatment in respect of imports from Russia and no one had yet explained how this was compatible with Common Market membership. During November 1961 moreover, Russia began to warn Finland (and indirectly Sweden too) against any wavering in her neutrality. The necessary reassurances from Helsinki were forthcoming and, with them, hope faded that Finland could safely consort with Western Europe.

Of the other two problems, agriculture raised hardly more difficulty than British obligations to EFTA. Agricultural policy was still being worked out among the Six and there was every likelihood, despite liberalizing tendencies to the contrary in the Commission, that the intention would be to keep farm prices higher than world levels. British farming was on balance as efficient as continental and, at least by the standard of food prices during 1959–60, British farmers would probably get higher prices for cereals and possibly also for meat, though the reverse might obtain for eggs and milk.[1] It was true that the annual price review, at which the Government decided its scale of support for British farming, promised somewhat more financial security than the continental method under which it was the consumer who paid for artificially maintained price levels. But if the general tone of the British economy was improved through membership of the Common Market agriculture could be expected to profit from the resulting consumer demand. Horticulture, however, was a different matter, since it was likely to suffer from the higher efficiency and better marketing systems of Dutch and Italian growers. Britain relied upon the tariff as the main support for this branch of farming and therefore, as Heath said in his statement to Ministers of the Six

[1] *The Times*, July 12, 1961, 'The Farmer's Price'.

on October 10th, arrangements would have to be devised for the different horticultural products if the Government were to fulfil their obligations to British growers.

The most delicate problem remained that of the Commonwealth. During visits by the Commonwealth Relations Minister to Australia, Canada and New Zealand in the summer of 1961 acute anxiety about the British decision was conveyed to him. The communiqué issued after the talks in Ottawa, for instance, stated that the Canadian Government 'expressed grave concern about the implications of possible negotiations between Britain and the EEC and about the political and economic effects which British membership in the EEC would have on Canada and the Commonwealth as a whole'. The position would have been different had full or associate membership been open to Commonwealth countries; but this would have destroyed the essentially European character of the Community and was acceptable neither to the Six nor to most Commonwealth States. The problem was therefore twofold: that of the optimum terms which Britain could obtain from the Six for protecting her trading relations with the rest of the Commonwealth, and that of the process by which Britain should decide whether these terms were acceptable. The second of these issues could not be adequately disposed of by the traditional formula 'consultation', in view of the strong concern of certain Commonwealth Governments about the British proposal and the powerful interests and emotions engaged. The Government undertook in a Commons resolution which they sponsored on August 3, 1961, not to enter into any agreement with the Six until it had been approved by the House 'after full consultation with other Commonwealth countries, by whatever procedure they may generally agree'.[1] This phrase left the door open if necessary for a special Commonwealth Prime Ministers' conference on the subject (which the Opposition asked for), though the Cabinet seemed unwilling to commit themselves to this. It was also stated by Maudling that the Government had

> given the same undertaking to our Commonwealth partners and to the other EFTA countries, namely that will not join the EEC unless special arrangements have been worked out in negotiations to protect their essential interests.[2]

Nevertheless, the ultimate decision would rest with Britain and the question remained whether the more directly concerned Common-

[1] 645 H.C. Deb. 5s. Cols. 1785–6.
[2] *Ibid.*, Col. 1602 (August 3rd).

wealth Governments would not conclude that consultation was likely to be little more than a formality once Britain had decided that the terms offered by the Six were acceptable.

The substantive issue, however, was the effect of a common Europe tariff (even with all the qualifications which Britain could introduce through negotiation) on British trade with the rest of the Commonwealth, including dependent territories. Though this trade was declining in comparison with that of other great trading groups, Britain still derived 36 per cent of her imports from that source either duty-free or with preferential margins. The importance of this trade to the various Commonwealth countries was far from uniform. Among the dependent or newly independent countries, Mauritius sold 82 per cent of her exports to Britain, Sierra Leone 70 per cent, Nigeria 51 per cent. Of the older Commonwealth countries New Zealand marketed 56 per cent of her exports in Britain, including almost all of her exports of basic foodstuffs, mutton, lamb, butter and cheese. Australia, India and Ceylon sent almost one-third of their exports to Britain. Clearly the problems of such a diverse trade would have to be dealt with separately. For some dependent territories associate status within the Community could be applied for, similar to that which France had obtained for her own dependencies. For independent countries, however, such as India and Ceylon, whose tea exports to Britain were in question, and Ghana, whose staple export, cocoa, was involved, associate membership might not be available. The Government therefore proposed either allowing free entry for such products into Britain while fixing the Common Market tariff for the rest of the Community at a level appropriate to the interests of all concerned, or setting the Common Market tariff on all such imports at zero. The second major problem, raw materials, raised less difficulty since the common tariff was already zero, but special arrangements would have to be made in regard to aluminium, wood pulp, newsprint, lead and zinc, which were of special importance to Commonwealth countries and where the common tariff was substantial. Manufactures from old Commonwealth countries, especially Australia, Canada and New Zealand, and low-cost manufactured imports from Asia and Hong Kong were also a special problem; these would have to be dealt with either by compromises struck on a commodity-by-commodity basis or, in the case of Asian imports, by some form of associate status. Perhaps the greatest difficulty, however, was that of temperate food imports into Britain from the developed Commonwealth countries, especially the dairy produce and meat of New Zealand. Much would depend upon

Y

how agricultural policy developed in the Economic Community; there were also certain British contractual obligations with the Commonwealth, providing a basis of stable prices for food exports, which had to be taken into account. The Government believed that solutions to all these questions could be found by the utilization of a wide range of expedients, but it was clear that negotiation would be long and technical and certain not inconsiderable interests were bound to suffer.[1]

Return to Europe?

It was still doubtful when British negotiations with the Six opened at the end of 1961 how far the latter were prepared to dilute the Community still further in return for the undoubted advantages of British membership. It was clear that the expected loss to Commonwealth trade would have to be an appreciable one if it was to deter the Government now that the decision had been made to approach the Community, whose Commission was appropriately sited in the Avenue de la Joyeuse Entrée, Brussels. At the same time Macmillan gave a veiled warning in the Commons at the end of July that the consequences might be serious for everybody if the Six, by asking too high a price, forced Britain into an impossible choice.

If we cannot succeed in bringing this negotiation to a satisfactory conclusion (he said), we of course will not abandon the obligations that we have both internally and externally, but if it fails then I think we ought to be quite clear ourselves, and perhaps the countries with which we are to negotiate ought to be quite clear, that quite a lot of things will happen and quite major changes may have to be made in the foreign policy and the commitments of Great Britain.[2]

Perhaps the greatest effect on the Commonwealth of Britain's joining the Six, however, was likely in the long run to be political rather than economic. Adjustments could be made to economic changes. The old Commonwealth countries, with their developing industries, were very different from the primary producers wholly dependent upon the British market which they were in the 1930s. The newer Commonwealth countries were looking to other centres besides London for capital for their economic growth. The prosperity of the new, enlarged Economic Community, if the progress of 1958–60 was maintained, would be shared by Commonwealth coun-

[1] Cmd. 1565, p. 12.
[2] 645 H.C. Deb. 5s. Cols. 937–8 (July 31, 1961).

tries, either in the form of increased European demand for their goods or higher capital investments from European sources. Nor would British independence be so drastically reduced that she could no longer play her part in the political community of the Commonwealth. But when all was said, the temper of Commonwealth relations would hardly remain the same. The Empire, reaching its greatest extent after the wars against Napoleon, had detached Britain from Europe and given her the oceanic vision of Canning, Disraeli, Salisbury. Now the dependencies of the Empire had grown up and gone out into the world. Their progenitor was entering another family of old nations whose imperial past, like hers, was over. How long could the children continue to believe in the family? How long would she have the unity of the family in the forefront of her mind, now that more and more of her decisions would be swayed by European considerations? The British people no doubt, if the optimists proved right, would become more prosperous and enterprising. Their politics, as always, would be bound up with the world. But mental perspectives would change. Britain would return to Europe, of which she had geographically once formed a part and from which, in the past at least, had come much sorrow and little joy.

Bibliography

Note: Parliamentary Command Papers and other British and foreign State papers are not listed here. They will be found in footnotes to the text.

GENERAL

Max Beloff, *New Dimensions in Foreign Policy*, London, 1961.

Matthew A. Fitzsimons, *The Foreign Policy of the British Labour Government, 1945–51*, Indiana, 1953.

Sir Oliver S. Franks, *Britain and the Tide of World Affairs*, London, 1955.

The Royal Institute of International Affairs, *British Foreign Policy. Some relevant documents, January 1950–April 1955*, London and New York, 1955.

Lord Strang, *The Foreign Office*, London, 1955; *Home and Abroad*, London, 1956; *Britain in World Affairs*, London, 1961.

C. M. Woodhouse, *British Foreign Policy since the Second World War*, London, 1961.

A. J. Youngson, *The British Economy, 1920–1957*, London, 1960.

CHAPTER I

Winston S. Churchill, *The Second World War*, Vol. VI, *Triumph and Tragedy*, London, 1954.

Herbert Feis, *Churchill, Roosevelt, Stalin*, Princeton, New Jersey, 1957; *Between War and Peace. The Potsdam Conference*, Princeton, New Jersey, 1960.

W. H. McNeill, *America, Britain and Russia. Their Co-operation and Conflict, 1941–46*, London, 1953.

William L. Neumann, *Making the Peace, 1941–45*, Washington, DC, 1950.

Edward R. Stettinius, *Roosevelt and the Russians*, London, 1950.

Harry S. Truman, *Year of Decisions, 1945*, London, 1955.

Chester Wilmot, *The Struggle for Europe*, London, 1952.

Sir Llewellyn Woodward, *British Foreign Policy in the Second World War*, HMSO, London, 1962.

CHAPTER II

T. Balogh, *The Dollar Crisis*, Oxford, 1949.

H. S. Booker, *The Problem of Britain's Overseas Trade*, London, 1948.

A. J. Brown, *The Great Inflation, 1939–51*, London, 1955.

James F. Byrnes, *Speaking Frankly*, London, 1947.

Robert A. Fearey, *The Occupation of Japan: Second Phase, 1948–50*, New York, 1950.

W. K. Hancock and M. M. Gowing, *British War Economy*, HMSO, London, 1949.

W. H. McNeill, *The Greek Dilemma*, London, 1947.

Redvers Opie and others, *The Search for Peace Settlements*, Washington, DC, 1952.

Harry Bayward Price, *The Marshall Plan and its Meaning*, Ithaca, New York, 1955.

The Royal Institute of International Affairs, *Documents on European Recovery and Defence, March 1947–April 1949*, London, 1949.

H. Seton-Watson, *Neither War nor Peace*, London, 1960.

Harry S. Truman, *Years of Trial and Hope, 1946–53*, London, 1956.

CHAPTER III

Lucius D. Clay, *Decision in Germany*, London, 1950.

James Forrestal, *The Forrestal Diaries*, ed. by Walter Millis, New York, 1951.

Alfred Grosser, *Western Germany. From Defeat to Rearmament*, London, 1955.

The Royal Institute of International Affairs, *Documents on Germany under Occupation, 1945–54*, Selected and edited by Beate Ruhm von Oppen, London, 1955.

J. P. Nettl, *The Eastern Zone and Soviet Policy in Germany, 1945–50*, London, 1951.

Walter Bedell Smith, *My Three Years in Moscow*, Philadelphia and New York, 1950.

Hans Speier and W. Phillips Davison (eds.), *West German Leadership and Foreign Policy*, Evanston, Ill., 1957.

James P. Warburg, *Germany: Key to Peace*, Cambridge, Mass., 1953.

CHAPTER IV

Sir Reader Bullard, *Britain and the Middle East*, London, 1952.

R. H. S. Crossman, *Palestine Mission: a Personal Record*, London, 1947.

Sidney N. Fisher, *The Middle East*, London, 1960.

Ben Halpern, *The Idea of the Jewish State*, London, 1961.

J. C. Hurewitz, *The Struggle for Palestine*, New York, 1950.

George Lenczowski, *The Middle East in World Affairs*, Ithaca, New York, 1951.

John Marlowe, *The Seat of Pilate: an Account of the Palestine Mandate*, London, 1959.

The Royal Institute of International Affairs, *British Interests in the Mediterranean and Middle East*, London, 1958.

Harry Sacher, *Israel. The Establishment of a State*, London, 1952.

M. V. Seton-Williams, *Britain and the Arab States*, London, 1948.

Benjamin Shwadran, *The Middle East, Oil and the Great Powers*, London, 1956.

CHAPTER V

William Diebold, *The Schuman Plan*, New York, 1959.

E. B. Haas, *The Uniting of Europe*, London, 1958.

James Joll (ed.), *Britain and Europe*, London, 1950.

Louis Lister, *Europe's Coal and Steel Community*, New York, 1960.

Anthony Nutting, *Europe Will Not Wait*, London, 1960.

A. H. Robertson, *European Institutions*, London, 1959; *The Council of Europe*, 2nd edition, London, 1961.

The Royal Institute of International Affairs, *Britain in Western Europe*, London, 1956.

CHAPTER VI

H. C. Allen, *Great Britain and the United States*, London, 1954; *The Anglo-American Predicament*, London, 1960.

J. B. Conant, *Anglo-American Relations in the Atomic Age*, London, 1952.

Leon D. Epstein, *Britain—Uneasy Ally*, Chicago, 1954.

John King Fairbank, *The United States and China*, Cambridge, Mass., 1958.

Herbert Feis, *The China Tangle*, Princeton, New Jersey, 1953.

Peter B. Kenen, *British Monetary Policy and the Balance of Payments, 1951–57*, Cambridge, Mass., 1960.

George F. Kennan, *American Diplomacy, 1900–50*, Chicago, 1951.

William C. Mallalieu, *British Reconstruction and American Policy, 1945–55*, New York, 1956.

Reinhold Niebuhr, *The Irony of American History*, London, 1952.

Henry C. Roberts and Paul A. Wilson, *Britain and the United States: Problems in Co-operation*, London, 1953.

Harold M. Vinacke, *The United States and the Far East, 1945–51*, Stanford, California, and London, 1952.

CHAPTER VII

Merry and Serge Bromberger, *Secrets of Suez*, tr. by James Cameron, London, 1957.

Randolph Churchill, *The Rise and Fall of Sir Anthony Eden*, London, 1959.

The Memoirs of the Rt Hon Sir Anthony Eden. Full Circle, London, 1960.

Sir John Glubb, *Britain and the Arabs*, London, 1959.

P. M. Holt, *A Modern History of the Sudan*, London, 1961.

Walter Z. Laqueur (ed.), *The Middle East in Transition*, London, 1958.

John Marlowe, *Anglo-Egyptian Relations, 1800–1953*, London, 1954.

The Royal Institute of International Affairs, *Britain and Egypt, 1914–51*, London and New York, 1952.

D. C. Watt (ed.), *Documents on the Suez Crisis*, London, 1957.

CHAPTER VIII

Zbigniew K. Brzezinski, *The Soviet Bloc*, Cambridge, Mass., 1960.

R. V. Burks, *The Dynamics of Communism in Eastern Europe*, Princeton, New Jersey, 1961.

Hugh Gaitskell, *The Challenge of Co-existence*, London, 1957.

Eugène Hinterhoff, *Disengagement*, London, 1959.

George F. Kennan, *Russia and the West under Lenin and Stalin*, London, 1961.

Wladyslaw W. Kulski, *Peaceful Co-existence. An Analysis of Soviet Foreign Policy*, Chicago, 1959.

Wolfgang Stolper, *The Structure of the East German Economy*, Cambridge, Mass., 1960.

CHAPTER IX

Bernhard G. Bechhoefer, *Postwar Negotiations for Arms Control*, Washington, DC, 1961.

Hedley Bull, *The Control of the Arms Race*, London, 1961.

Denis Healey, 'Britain and NATO' in *NATO and American Security*, ed. by Klaus Knorr, Princeton, New Jersey, 1959.

John H. Herz, *International Politics in the Atomic Age*, New York, 1959.

Henry A. Kissinger, *Nuclear Weapons and Foreign Policy*, New York, 1957.

Seymour Melman (ed.), *Inspection for Disarmament*, London, 1958.
Jules Moch, *Human Folly: to Disarm or Perish?* London, 1959.
Philip Noel-Baker, *The Arms Race*, London, 1958.
Anthony Nutting, *Disarmament: an Outline of the Negotiations*, London, 1959.
The Royal Institute of International Affairs, *Britain and the United Nations*, Report of Study Group by Geoffrey Goodwin, London, 1957.

CHAPTER X
Emile Benoit, *Europe at Sixes and Sevens*, New York, 1961.
J. F. Deniau, *The Common Market*, 1960
The 'Economist' Intelligence Unit, *Britain and Europe*, 1957.
Isaiah Frank, *The European Common Market*, London, 1961.
Sir Ralph Hawtrey, *The Pound at Home and Abroad*, London, 1961.
F. V. Meyer, *The Seven*, London, 1960.
J. D. B. Miller, *The Commonwealth in the World*, London, 1960.
John Pinder, *Britain and the Common Market*, London, 1961.
The Royal Institute of International Affairs, *Documents and Speeches on British Commonwealth Affairs, 1931–52*, Vol. II, ed. by Nicholas Mansergh, London, 1953.
G. D. N. Worswick (ed.), *The Free Trade Proposals*, Oxford, 1960.

Index

338   BRITISH FOREIGN POLICY